WAITING FOR
BETTER TIMES
IN BULGARIA

OR

Marilyn Monroe was Our Mother

Conor Ciaran

In print for 2008 at 3 Muses
Waste Heat
Coyote Remasked
Tropomorphoses
Musings
Night Wolves

Soon to be out in 2009 from 3 Muses
Lucifer Dreaming
Two Diaries
Coyote Rebooted
Eutopian Dreams
Domiture: Convergence of Culture & Nature
Redesigning the Planet

WAITING FOR
BETTER TIMES

In Bulgaria

OR

Marilyn Monroe was Our Mother

Conor Ciaran

Mozart & Reason Wolf Ltd.
Sarasota
2009

Acknowledgments

The following parts had been published before:
  "Ecological Thought Experiments," Alan Wittbecker *Sofia Echo*
  "Spoofs," Boris Badenuf *Rakia Times*

Photographs: Novo Celo 1920 (Page 7), Old Church Novo Celo (8), Traditional Dance, Novo Celo (9), Vasil Levski School, Dupnitsa (15), Ilievi Living Room (23), Sunday Pazaar, Aprilci (25), Dumpster, Vasil Levski Street, Novo Celo (29), Apartment Entrance, Pazardjik (32), Volunteer B10 Graduation (43), Stara Planina Fire Area (44), Maragadhik Mountain (62), Wolf Survey 4 NPCB (65), Chavdar Bus in the snow, Aprilci (74), Vegetable Stand, Vasil Levski Street, Aprilci (81), Traditional Bulgarian Wedding Hall, Sofia (98), Aprlci Tourist Bureau (105), Religious Wedding US Embassy House, Sofia (113), The Great Horse Race, Vidima (121), Horse Cart, Novo Celo (124), Agrotel Meat market (154), The New Magazine, Novo Celo (159), Advanced English Class (169), Public Library, Novo Celo (172), Party No. 91 (174), Two rangers at Mandrata Chakalo (187), Wolf crossing river, Balkani Wildlife Society (189), Crafts Meeting No. 9 in Tourist Office, Novo Celo (198), Craftsman knives (202), Mandrata stream (220), Mill Harvest (222), Rangers' Horo (228), Wolf mating dance area (237), Wolf track (241), Bag Tur Poster (244), Wolf scat (249), Simeon II and Panagakos (272), Aprilci Telecenter Grand Opening (281), Kebabche girls in Novo Celo (290), View of Aprilci from Mt. Botev area (294), Beautiful dawn near Chakalo (298), Boiling wolf traps in Sadovik (311), Black Mountain (306), Dead wolf on firewood (331), Setting a trap near Paramunska (323), Bus Station, Sofia (352), Conor Ciran, Alaska (353), Ban saw at the Mill, Aprilci (354)

ISBN 0-911385-37-1 978-0-911385-37-3

Mozart & Reason Wolf, Ltd.,
Post Office Box 1551, Tallevast, Florida 34270
Mozart@ReasonWolf.com, Design@RianGarciaCalusa.com
Editor@3musesbooks.com, www.3musesbooks.com

Contents

Novo Celo 1920

Dedications

To the Bulgarian Team: Doncho, Pesho, Petar, Petko, Elena, Mariya, Desislava, Valentina, Valya, Yordan, Violetta, Dimetor, Pavel, Dimitar, Nikolai (4), Lalyo, Damian, Denitsa, Kamen, Atila, Kostaden, Cedar, Klementine, Xristo, Micho, Pepa, Kaloti, Plamina, Krusthew, Gencho, Nela, Raicho, Anton, and everyone.

To the National and Regional Parks of Bulgaria

To the Wolf Family: Calpurnia, Alta, Christine, and Pan, who never sang at the Closing Ceremony

The Old Church in Novo Celo

Learning to Dance

None of this seems real. Probably because it is not real. None of this happened. I am confined to a wheelchair and a keyboard. This is an adventure, but the adventure is imaginary, like all of my adventures. This adventure, however, is not drawn from a dream, like most of mine, but from the ardent desire to see distant places. It is an adventure of ideas, of different cultures and different ways of looking at things, and of different species and different landscapes. It is an adventure of words, which are based on the actions, deeds and ideas of others. And, I learned to speak Bulgarian, in a way.

I am grateful to my friends, some of whom were Peace Corps Volunteers, and to pen pals, most of whom are Bulgarian, for their generosity with their stories and experiences. Of course, I have incorporated some of them in this work, to make a tattery story for which I, the shady bricolateur, alone must accept the blame. At the time I was making up titles, I was watching *Rocky and Bullwinkle* reruns — please forgive me for the alternate titles. I am also grateful to my Bulgarian contacts, who sent me dolls, knives, photographs, videos, and bread from that unique country situated on the crossroads of Africa, Asia, and Europe. And I learned to dance, in a way.

Folk Dancers in Novo Celo

Entering Bulgaria Or Cultural Shock Therapy

My name is Andrew Panagakos. I volunteered for the Peace
Corps after a bizarre series of events cost me my home, land, car,
retirement, savings—everything in fact—and after another series of
events left me without any grants for restoration or wolf projects. In
fact, volunteering was a joke first suggested by a colleague who had
a grant. He was studying Amur tigers in Siberia. I was proposing
to study tiger-wolf interactions in the Bochinsky Reserve, but alas,
wolves were not perceived to be as charismatic as tigers and did not
attract the same level of funding. He suggested that if I could find
support for my own expenses, room and board, through the Peace
Corps perhaps, then the project could go on as planned. We had
already met with the Russians, as well as with numerous granting
agencies in Seattle and Portland. A bonus was that I would have
noncompetitive eligibility for government jobs as a biologist when I
returned to the states.

So, I volunteered to serve in Siberia. The Peace Corps
had a Parks program that allowed research. But, after months
of paperwork, Russia was closed to new volunteers and the last
two volunteers were shipped home, due to the dangers from the
Russian Mafia and Chinese bandits in the area (and from a third,
unspoken danger, American loggers, desperate to cut old-growth
trees in Siberia). The only other country available, with wolves, was
Bulgaria, so I was allowed to switch requests.

I left my cabin in Oregon, where I was staying, and visited
my parents in Florida for a few weeks, before leaving with an
old suitcase of old clothes and an old briefcase with a new laptop
computer. At the Chicago airport I wandered around looking for
idealistic volunteers. The first volunteer I met, Cliff Noble, was
dressed like a banker; he said he was a business consultant. After
an awkward moment, similar to two different species sniffing each
other's rears, we took an airbus to the Radisson Schaumberg hotel to
continue paperwork.

At dinner at TGI Fridays, I met my roommate for the night,
Joe Rehman, a nice guy from Kansas or somewhere. We apologized
in advance if either of us should snore. At the introductory meeting,
the moderator asked if anyone had been in the Peace Corps before.
One couple had. Then he asked if anyone had to wait more than a

year for their paperwork. I raised my hand and mentioned that I had applied in 1967 but they had lost my paperwork when we were staging in Tucson; and by the time they found it, I was teaching zoology at the University of Arizona.

The next day after still more paperwork, introductions, and explanations, we all raced to a Kinko's to get new passport photos. On an impulse, I bought a digital camera with my last $220.53. Joe did not snore, fortunately.

Finally, the following day, we left by gigantic plane. I sat with Barbara Tainter, a cute girl, from Oregon also, and we compared cities and lives; she had worked on river restoration so we had fun talking ecostuff. I introduced myself as "And" (not Andy or Drew or Andrew; the word "and" was a universal connector and a better label for me, who studied connections). After lifetimes of stale air, we switched planes in Frankfurt Germany. I used my forty-year-old German to order lunch, thus impressing myself and perhaps countless others, although I think the Stewardess was looking at where my finger was pointing on the menu, during my spiel. The food was excellent.

Uneventfully — the best way to travel if your goal is not the travel — we arrived in Sofia, Bulgaria, a breadbasket of the former Soviet Empire. Walking off the plane, down rickety metal stairs, we marched towards a large, decrepit, concrete barn of a building. The sign, in Cyrillic, was falling off the face of the building. Inside we waited for our luggage and went through customs, which was quite relaxed for some reason. Perhaps no one was worried that we were bringing in large amounts of cash or cameras.

We were met by the exiting volunteers, who gave us wads of toilet paper and bottles of spring water or hand cleaner. I did not understand the gifts, so I did not take any, a decision I would regret quite soon.

Night at a Luxury Resort, Communist Style

Outside was a large, faded bus. But first we loaded our baggage into old Soviet-style jeeps. After leaving the city, with its gigantic concrete blocks, and threading down an old highway, the bus wound its way through small villages and then up narrow mountain roads to Panichishte, a former Soviet-style hotel in mountains, once reserved as a reward to party functionaries for loyal service to the state.

We were each assigned new roommates; mine was Dan Partana, a retired Nebraska State Trooper. The room was very plain with two small beds pushed together. We looked at each other and started pushing them apart, the very first thing before introducing ourselves; we found them glued together by an old, yellowed,

11

obviously-used condom. I threw it away, although carbon-dating
it might have proved interesting. The room was musty and moldy,
apparently not used either since 1989. Dan opened the window for
air conditioning. There was a separate bathroom: toilet in the corner,
sink in the middle and a shower head against the wall; the drain was
in the floor for the shower; the water was finicky and cold.   There
was no toilet paper. Throughout the evening the water and electricity
went off regularly.

    We were called downstairs to meet our hosts, who were very
proud that we would start our service in comfort in this resort. It
actually was luxurious to me, after living in a cabin without water
or electricity, but to the younger volunteers I suspect it was the first
of their trials. We had a short language lesson, saying the alphabet,
while food was brought to the tables. Finally, we ate dinner by 10
p.m. Good dinners, mostly chicken or pork, which I could not eat as
an official vegetarian (yes, and I was a liberal democrat, also). Music
started; the band had a sheepskin bagpipe, flute, and portable organ.

    During dinner, several of the hosts started dancing traditional
Bulgarian dances, somewhat like a line dance in Oregon territory.
The band was quite good with traditional instruments, the bagpipe-
thing and accordion. The dancing got faster as evening moved on.
Then the music became very wild, revealing its Greek and Turkish
influences. Then all the hosts started dancing, a long line-dance, and
pulled all of us into the line. It was a most enjoyable introduction,
although I had to stop after twenty minutes of spinning and kicking
(without really knowing what to do or how to do it). It was quite
enjoyable actually, although I was huffing like the old blowhard I
had become.

    After a few days of lectures, language lessons, nature walks,
and exotic foods, we were prepared to go to our host city, Dupnitsa,
and meet out host families. Each person was to be farmed out to a
Bulgarian family, who would introduce us in depth to their culture.
They would also be responsible for our food, bed, supplemental
education, health, and happiness. So, we got back on the bus, which
looked even older and more faded now, and drove back down the
mountain on the narrow, pot-holed roads.

First Impressions Or Searching for a Family
From a distance, Dupnitsa resembled another concrete Soviet utopia.
But, the giant blocks of concrete were interspersed with traditional
houses with red tile roofs. Everything had a poor, decayed look, as if
there had been no repairs for twenty years. Imagine America with no
infrastructure repairs for twenty years (although come to think of it,
many of our bridges and highways haven't been repaired in at least

that long). Then, imagine no trash pick-up for a year. Then imagine what—oh, never mind.

The bus rattled up beside a concrete apartment block, close to a concrete school with many broken windows, As we got off, we passed closely, very closely, to a barrel of rotting fish and parts of a sheep, including the hide, ribs and feet. Since then I always looked in trash barrels and dumpsters for signs of human eating habits. Humans are almost as interesting to study as wolves—if only humans could tell me why they do what they do.

We walked to the playground at the school, where we were given halved paper cutouts with family information; each family had the other half of the cutout, with volunteer information. Then at the stroke of six thirty, we had to match up with the correct family. I had them matched visually before we walked across the courtyard, an older retired couple, Rumiana and Ilian Iliev. They waved as I walked towards them. I greeted them in Russian, which resulted in quizzical looks. They helped me pick up my suitcase and then drove me to their home in an older Lada (a Russian Fiat, which I learned later was used only on special occasions once a month).

We drove over housed hills and over a rotten concrete bridge. As soon as we got home, a three-story stucco concrete box, they introduced me to their son Luboslav, daughter in law, Inga and grandson, Henrim. Then I realized that I would be living with them, since Rumiana and Ilian lived upstairs in the attic. We sat in a parlor room for an hour and tried to base all communication on my six words of Bulgarian. Finally, I pulled out my photos and showed them everyone, using a Bulgarian dictionary to say father, mother, wolf, cabin, vegetarian, biologist, and so on.

My room was a small delightful room with a balcony; obviously, it had been their living room, converted for a guest. The balcony overlooked a courtyard shared with another apartment building; it had ten clotheslines stretched across it. The room was small but had an oriental carpet, day bed, with a hammock-like set of springs, a desk, table, two chairs, two hassocks, a cedar chest, and a massive armoire that rose to the ceiling.

After an hour, they left to let me put away my clothes, which I did. I then walked upstairs with my dictionary to try to be courteous. I asked them about food, not having eaten for ten hours, and they described foods. I asked them when they ate and they described Bulgarian customs about time. I finally said I was hungry and tired. They asked me what I liked. I said tomatoes, potatoes and bread. So they deep-fried some of each with three little pieces of pork. I ate some of it, and it was quite good, actually. I told them I was a vegetarian, however, and they seemed to understand.

I took a shower. The water system was much like Norway

(the inexpensive hotels and homes, where I had lived while studying their few remaining wolves) in that it was very difficult to get the hot and cold water balanced for more than three seconds. The bed was too uncomfortable, and bent my back, so I took off the mattress and put it on the floor, like a thin futon but at least it was straight. I slept in my running shorts, since it was very hot; all windows were always kept locked against evil spirits, even in the heat.

One Word at a Time

The next day, Saturday, Ilian came in at Nine to ask if I was hungry. So, awake anyway, I went upstairs and had some bread with kashkaval cheese. We spent the rest of the morning doing dictionary exercises. Then I asked, with dictionary words, if we could go for a walk. Ilian was only slightly older than I was, so it seemed strange to be dependent on him. We went to a park above the house, a nice large hilly park with many trees, mostly familiar European beeches and pines, and a hotel at the top. Some young men were playfully washing a car. We walked back down hill and then had lunch, tomatoes, potatoes and pork. I tried to explain that I was a vegetarian, so they brought chicken for me.

After lunch, we went back to the dictionary, then I asked for time to write a letters to friends and family. I took a nap, wrote a few letters, and then it was 7:30, time for dinner. All of the food was on serving dishes in the middle of the table, so I was able to avoid the chicken, and just have salads and bread.

After dinner we talked and watched a blank television for a few minutes; then a cartoon came on and finally the soccer game came on at Nine. I went to bed at 10:30, putting the mattress back on the floor again — putting it back on the bed in the morning became a daily routine, so they would not think I was rude or unhappy.

On Sunday June 18, I slept until Ten, but they were kind enough to feed me some bread and fruit juice then; they had eaten at Six as they did every day. We then continued our dictionary translation marathon until lunch, which was soup (cold cucumber) and bread with yogurt for dessert. Fortunately they did not ever offer rich chocolate desserts, so I started losing a pound a day. After lunch, more language work. Then about Five their son and his family (Luboslav, Inga, and Henrim) asked me if I would like to walk in the park. We went to a different park, this one called Gratska Gravina, which had a restaurant and several cafes. We sat and named things while Henrim rode his bike around us. We got back after Nine, and I went up and had dinner with Ilian and Rumiana. I repeated that I was a vegetarian, so they offered me chicken soup with the potatoes. Then we worked on a few sentences. I went to bed at Ten.

Monday I had breakfast with Rumiana and Ilian at 7:15. We made a schedule so that they would know when I was at school, when I was on field trips, or when I was exploring. Ilian walked me to school. Ilian was 65, only six years older than me; my beard and hair were whiter than his. I still felt 6 years old, especially since it was an elementary school and the real kids were attending their last few days before summer. He waved from the sidewalk as I went in through doors framed by broken windows.

The School   Levski School 2000

We had a general meeting to introduce us to the staff, then a general assembly in the gymnasium to describe our requirements for medical shots. And, then we started classes.

The first class was a language class with Hassan, a young dynamic social worker who also taught English for the Peace Corps. I asked that he speak only Bulgarian (*samo Bulgarski*) and he thought that was a good idea. Since I had studied Russian in 1958 and 1999, when I worked in Siberia last, I thought it would be easy to learn Bulgarian, from which Russian was derived. Ten minutes later I started to reconsider that request, since it was difficult to understand what in the hell he was asking us to do.

We would have three languages classes per day for five and a half hours. We would have one technical session per day for an hour and a half, then one medical, social or history session for an hour and a half.

Every morning I had toast or fruit, with tea, orange juice, and boiled whole milk for breakfast. For lunch I drink a sugary lemon soda. For dinner I had the regular Bulgarian dinner of cold cucumber soup, rakia (plum brandy), wine, fried vegetable matter—honest, that was the translation in the book although I thought it was plantain—or chicken sometimes, a plate of tomatoes, a plate of salami, and kashkaval cheese. Desserts had been yogurt (with honey and peanuts), goat's milk curds, cherries, plums, and some sort of other edible fruit-like thing. Bread was served with every dinner; as it got older it became toasted, then fried, then dog food.

Difference Engines Or *Cursing the Calculus of Culture*

Highlights Number 6: On Tuesday I learned the alphabet. On Wednesday I ordered sodas for Daring Deborah and me, asked for the check and paid it, in Bulgarian. On Thursday, I won the contest for the most correct answers on word endings — our group was the most advanced language class (of ten).

I borrowed some books from Pentcho, the environmental manager. Pentcho said that next week a scientist from The Balkan Reserve would be coming to see me — must be from the resumes I mailed two months ago, I thought.

Every day after class I walked for a few hours, as far as I could in that time before dinner — partly to avoid going home and speaking so much. Despite the appearance of the town as mostly tall, square, unimaginative and decaying apartment blocks, there were thirty small quaint houses for every block. Each of these two-to-three story houses was completely surrounded by grape arbors that shaded the entire yard. People spend much of their time sitting underneath them and visiting, while the children played around them.

The traffic was unimaginably loud and reckless. One evening as I was walking home, coming towards me on the narrow winding street was a motorcycle doing 50 mph or so. Suddenly the car behind him passed him honking, as if the cycle was going too slow (the streets were built for 25 mph). The police paid no attention to any speeding in town. However, on the roads outside town, they set up elaborate speed traps for people going over 40 kph.

I started making notes on differences between American life and Bulgarian life. For instance, farming: There were no big farms, but a lot of truck farms and small-scale fields; there was some mixed agriculture, e.g., corn planted under apple trees. Even wheat was planted in 1-5 acre plots alternating with corn and grapes.

Vegetation: Much of the vegetation was similar to Oregon. We must be the same latitude. I needed to look that up, but books were rare here. Beech trees abounded. Scots Pine and Douglas-fir I'd seen, and willows, poplar, and birch. A lot of the plants that were weeds in Oregon were native here.

People: Bulgarian people were shorter and darker for the most part. They recognized me as being from another country. I was balding (tonsured I suppose); very few of them were bald, if any. All women and most men walked in couples, holding hands or arms. The only people who wore hats were old people. I didn't see any hats the first twelve days. I wore a beret. People were curious about me, but rarely spoke first. However, they would answer me immediately if I said good morning or good evening in Bulgarian (or whatever I was actually saying).

The clothes they favored seemed like things I had seen in Goodwill Stores in Oregon. Too bright and too polyester; too many primary colors and too many bad fits. Of course, the girls wore skintight clothes. In Sofia, the capitol, I saw many well-dressed women, but most of the money seemed concentrated there, as well as one-seventh of the population. My father need not worry about his Dupont pension— Polyester was the state fabric.

There were no leash laws. There were few veterinary clinics. People liked dogs, and thought it was cruel to have them fixed, so there were many of them and many packs on the streets. This meant piles of dog manure on the streets and sidewalks, and some danger from the packs. Very few cats were in evidence, perhaps due to the regional vampire tradition.

Horses were everywhere. The Roma (gypsies) seemed to all have horses drawing wagons. A few people used horses and wagons to deliver firewood. The horses were all small workhorses, broken to the halter and fatalistic about their lot.

The Motley Fools Or Jewels of the German River

As a way to learn each other's names. We introduced ourselves with nicknames and had to learn all of them by introducing the entire circle of volunteers. My nickname was "And Pan." Daring Deborah was next to me, and she was indeed very pretty with red hair, but she was young and full of her self, which made her dull and uninteresting at the same time. One of the more interesting people was "Boss Jo," the second oldest person ever to join the PC at 78; she had previously worked in Bulgaria for five years as a Television producer. She had already tried to enlist me as one of her male trophy slaves.

There were some other "elders." "Dapper Dan" was a retired Nebraska State Trooper (I thought he was 60 and second oldest). I was the third oldest. "GI Joe" Kaye was a retired army officer, but only 43, with three tours in Germany, Korea and the Philippines; he spoke German, Korean, and Tagalog. "Caesar's Calpurnia" was an engineer with Dupont in Wilmington. "Gem Amber" Booker had worked in China after going to school in Kentucky. Most others had just graduated from college. The average age was 24. Most would be fated to teach English at small villages throughout Bulgaria.

One day, we all went on a day trip to the big city. We took two buses to Sofia to buy supplies (books for me, of course) and to see the historical monuments—we had just had two lectures on Bulgarian history. I had not realized that the Bulgarian empire had once covered the whole of the Balkans and had defeated Constantinople and the Eastern Empire. We went to three churches; the first was in

17

the courtyard of government offices, where the president presided. It was built about 650 AD, making it one of the oldest buildings in Europe. Many of the churches had been built below ground, due to the Turkish rule that a Christian church could not be higher than a Turk on horseback; only now were they being excavated and restored. The folk museum was okay, mostly costumes; the building was just as interesting, having been a palace and later a military barracks (only the ornate ceilings were left). I walked with Georgeva, who was educated in LA. She pointed out many places that we had no time to see at all.

Sofia was much like Oslo, and most European cities — for a while I forgot I was in the PC and could have been just a tourist (a poor hurried one at that). Many old buildings, many dramatic vistas, many big things, big cars — all at a hurried tourist pace.

We ate at a garden cafe off a street that had a bazaar of books and small businesses (hundreds of flea market tables; often many with suspect goods, clothes and CDs). I had a small shopska salata (tomatoes and cucumbers), a grilled chicken sandwich, which marked the end of my vegetarian diet, and a lemon soda (Fanta). Coca Cola, with its red (for communist) color scheme, had made it big in Bulgaria; most of the cafes had coke signs, coke awnings, and coke table clothes (Pepsi, with its blue, democratic colors, existed in one or two markets but cost more — nothing was diet). McDonalds was muscling into the big city, but had not reached the towns under 100,000, that was to say, 99 percent of all towns).

At the book bazaar I tried to bargain for a 2-volume English-Bulgarian dictionary but failed; guess the accent gave me away. Rather than pay 45 Leva, I paid ten for a small dictionary. Maybe if I had had more than five minutes. Many of the volunteers spent large sums of money on clothes, music and books.

At the public toilets, three people at a table were selling toilet paper. I just pissed, so I saved money. Walking by a nice restaurant, I went in; the toilets were beautiful white porcelain, so I used them twice just to enjoy them.

On the bus, both ways, I had two seats to myself. I sat behind Joe, who talked a lot, and in front of Amber, with a high soft southern voice, who talked even more. I listened.

Back to Grade School Or Adventures in Listening
Language class continued to go downhill for me. Partly because I was blinded with conjunctivitis and partly because the traffic, rooms, and other students were so noisy that I could not hear. I had had one 15-minute tutorial, which was fun but too little too late. I expected to do better with the language, at least if I studied some more by myself

and talked more in the markets.

Thursday was more language and technical language; the technical language was not very technical yet. The language teacher was not a biologist and was confused when I used technical Latin names for his examples, e.g., *Canis lupis lupis*, or *Ursus arctos*.

Thursday night, for the third time, I had two dinners. I ate with Ilian and Rumiana at 7:30. On my way downstairs I was waylaid by Inga, the daughter-in-law, who thoughtfully asked me to meet their friends. They were eating dinner and I was asked to sit down. I did, but then I was asked to try everything, which I did: coleslaw, French fries, and sausage (hey, they're the younger generation) or *zele, persiani kartofi, i nadenitsa*. We watched Italy squeak by Netherlands in the semifinal soccer match. No one here seems to get exercise; they all watch TV, read, or play crossword puzzles.

Friday, *mein gott in himmel*, the end of June; the morning was spent on language, asking and answering questions on food, very basic and necessary. At One, we drove by bus to the Rila Monastery forest. We stopped in the monastery and looked at the wood used in the floors, which seemed to be from 30-40 inch diameter trees. I spoke with the State Forestry Board Manager, who had created the plan for this forest, and offered my services. He seemed mildly interested but said it would be two years before they would be ready for volunteers. The forest was mixed conifer/deciduous, with Beech dominating. I loved the small river, which was fast, but had an excellent riverbed with little erosion; many boulders, good pools, good riffles, and a decent percentage of meander. I got away just in time to allow my diarrhea to fertilize part of the forest floor. My body had not adjusted yet to the microflaura and fauna in the tap water or food.

We got back at Six, and I raced over to the internet cafe in the center of town and answered emails. Few people had personal computers; internet cafes were springing up in every neighborhood. Mostly they were used by young people to play games, send instant messages (to the computer across the room), and look at photographs.

Sunday the first of July I slept late, having told my hosts I would need no breakfast (*zakuska*). I woke up at 7:30 anyway, so did sit-ups for a while, then studied. At 10 Luboslav knocked and said that Rumiana and Ilian had food ready for me. It was fruit juice, yogurt with raspberries, and, yes, tomatoes. Then they tried to fix toast, so I had one slice. I knew that alone they usually ate about 6:00; on weekdays, they waited until 7:15 and ate with me. They were very sweet.

19

I found out that they were getting paid $180 a month to keep me here. That was about 370 Leva, which was over three times what they made for their retirement (Ilian had been a machinist and Rumiana grade school teacher, or *ocheatelka*).

Then, of course I studied all morning. For noon Dinner we had cold cucumber soup, chicken and rice (the chicken portions by the way were very small, possibly two bites or about one-fifth or sixth what we would serve), tomatoes, and leftover fruit salad made with the melons and raspberries. Afterwards, they invited me to travel to the old Baths outside of town to swim.

But, the car broke down. We coasted to the side of the road. Ilian opened the hood and cleaned the plugs, which were completely black and old, then reset the carb intake, then took apart the carb and cleaned and adjusted it, all on the highway. I basically handed him tools and screws. It started up fine, but then died after five feet. So, I pushed it by myself and we kick-started it downhill back to town, where it died two blocks from home. Rumiana and I walked back and got his brother to come and tow it back. They were embarrassed, but I was not; it was part of the adventure. Just as we were talking I came across a phrase in my language book, which now accompanies me everywhere; it was: "Thanks for a wonderful time." We laughed for five minutes.

Back to studying, I got tired and took a nap. Then studied more. Had now caught up on the language exercises. For dinner, a deep fried omelet with French fries, tomatoes (Yes!), and peanuts, which they discovered I liked. For dessert an excellent raspberry mousse. Oh, and wine and fruit juice, but no rakia. Then, after Nine back to the room to study, although I was writing this journal instead. I also wrote postcards to everyone and a letter to Moira, who was caring for my horse and wolf back in Oregon, which I had bought from her when she needed money last year.

A note on horses: Especially in the morning before Seven, I could hear the hooves coming down the street. Mostly Roma, but also others kept horses and use them to move hay, firewood and garbage. The horses all seem smaller here. One of the stalls in the market was selling horseshoes.

After the daily miracle yogurt treatment, my bowels seemed almost normal. I suspected that the local cultures had taken over and I could digest food again. I supposed that meant I would stop losing weight. I had lost fifteen pounds so far, mostly from walking and no donuts. But, it was nice to see and feel the muscles beneath the padding, and I could now wear the smaller jeans.

I saw a new house foundation being poured; the rooms were very small by American standards, only 8 by 10 or so. The concrete work looked decent, although many pouring levels were obvious.

The brickwork, however, seemed sloppy, as if they were short on mortar or on time — perhaps because it would be covered with stucco later.

Monday, the language classes accelerated. I could read better but the volume of words had increased. I could conjugate better, but still had trouble forming complex sentences. Skipped lunch as usual. Just water. Studied during lunch. After work spent an hour on emails. After studying at night, wrote nine postcards and one letter.

Another Birthday Or *Counting Solar Revolutions*

Tuesday July 4th. The Americans had planned a celebration for dinner at a restaurant. I was also invited to "Caesars Calpurnia's" birthday party; well, actually "GI Joe" invited me. I did not plan to attend either. More language and a medical session on safety. All statistics for the PC worldwide were shown; a good safety record overall. Drinking for men and walking alone for women seemed to be the most dangerous activities of volunteers.

After school I decided to go to the American Birthday celebration after all, since it was in a pizza restaurant, a rare place. I got there late, then sat with "Boss Jo" and "Dapper Dan." Jo was giving out American flags, which she had printed in town. We wore our gimmes (baseball caps) backwards and had our pictures taken — yikes, I was a red-necked American. The pizza was quite decent considering that the Bulgarians had no mozzarella or spices. I had two slices. A young buxom girl from Richmond came over and sat by me. She was a primary school teacher of good southern stock — very patrician with a soft accent. Joe shared his pizza with her.

Because Joe was going to Calpurnia's party, and he wanted company, I ended up going. Already there were "Mademoiselle Christine" Sailor, a French Major in college, and "Bold Alta" Strittland. We met the hostess, a vivacious brunette widow of about 45, who got cokes for us. Still no ice! Ice was more rare than pizza. We talked for a while and then gave Calpurnia her gifts (I got her a pen and notebook for $1). Then Amber came with her host mother, a vivacious blonde of about 37 who kept lifting her skirt to her waist to cool off — it was over 100 degrees that day. Joe was mesmerized by her and sat next to her. Her husband, a policeman, was late.

For dinner, we were served deep fried chicken patties (ground like a burger), fries, tomatoes, and coleslaw, which was quite good. Christine and the hostess started smoking so I did too. I was able to do a perfect French inhale and then exhale (best ever), thus impressing myself immensely. I blew smoke rings, but the others were serious smokers and could not be bothered with style or fun. Then the hostess made gin and tonic for herself so I had one; the gin

21

was very smooth and excellent, so I had another. The birthday cake had one candle, which Calpurnia had to blow out three times for the cameras; the cake was yellow with cream icing. Calpurnia got a new outfit from her host mother, which matched her own, so she tried it on. Almost twins. She was very pleased at the pants suit.

Calpurnia's hosts could not pronounce her name, so they called her "Cali." So, everyone started calling her that. She seemed confused, as if she had never had a nickname.

At dark I announced my intent to leave, and Christine and Alta asked for escorts home, so I walked them home. I was secretly pleased to be asked to escort two comely and vivacious girls through the dark streets (lights off to save electricity). I got home about 10, in time for bed.

On Friday, the seventh of July, we went on a trip to visit the Minister of Environment and Water in Sofia. The bus was slow and hot. I sat next to Amber, Tennessee Amber, who taught me Chinese for five minutes before changing the topic.

The Minister spoke well in a modern Euro meeting room. Then we had a presentation by a shy and self-effacing woman who was head of information. Afterwards, we visited the information center. I found a lot of good information on habitats, and asked for copies, which might get done in a week. We had a long lunch in a Chinese restaurant, which was quite good. The waitresses were Chinese and spoke worse Bulgarian than we did — that was nice to hear. I had sweet and sour chicken for $2.25. I could not afford the shrimp, which was $9.50 USD. I shared mine and got to try fried rice and other equally tasty dishes.

After lunch, we went to the Museum of Man and World, which could have been called Minerals and Women, since it was a display of minerals, based in an old munitions building near the new Hilton Hotel. It was hot but I listened politely, since the tour guide, who spoke no English, was clearly excited about minerals and went on in great and learned detail. I bought a piece of amber for Calpurnia, for her next birthday maybe.

Then we went back to the buses. Amber sat next to me and sang to me most of the way home. I was very pleased since she had a nice choirgirl voice and a good memory for lyrics, even Bread songs from the 70s. I actually sang some Mickey Newbury and some Elvis, but could *not* remember all the lyrics. It was very nice to be sung to, however. If only someone could get Amber to expand her attention span past three minutes.

Dinner was tomatoes, sausage, and fries, with melon for dessert. I had officially given up being vegetarian and ate some meat. Then I studied.

The room

Swimming in Low Water Or *One Size Fits All*

Saturday was a study day, although I went running and swimming around noon. The pool was Olympic size, but had not been kept up for years. It was only one-fourth full of water. A rusty pipe emptied water from somewhere on the hill above into the pool. The water was cold but a deep inviting green. There were a lot of leaves. The lifeguard yelled at me for not wearing a Speedo like everyone else. I told him it was an Amerikanski Kalifornia Baggy, then dove in and went swimming, careful not to rip my fingernails on the concrete bottom with each stroke. He was unhappy and followed me around, intoning the magic word Speedo and whistling, as if I would change suddenly to match the others. But, I had a good swim, then left, walking out the high end of the park.

Afternoon was more studying until Four, then I went shopping at the bazaar. I bought five tomatoes, garlic, and onions for $0.40. Then I went to the Market 2000, my favorite, new, faux-Italian market, and bought lasagna noodles, a bottle of Bulgarian wine (very smooth), mushrooms, olives, sausage, ice cream, water, cheese, soda, and eggs for $7.40 (I still translated the costs automatically). Then, I delivered the goods to the host family to keep for our dinners. More studying, more bread and tomatoes for dinner.

Met their daughter, Petya, a young, attractive doctor from Sofia, married to another doctor, Evol, with two daughters of their own. Immediately fell in love with her, too. She showed me pictures of their vacation to Sri Lanka and I showed them my animals (wolf and horses) and Oregon.

Sunday, after breakfast, Petya left and I started the lasagna. Alas, there was no mozzarella, spinach, cottage cheese, or a single spice to be found. I made it without those ingredients, substituting goat cheese for ricotta and mushrooms for spinach. For spices I used red peppers and black pepper. I tripled the garlic. I made my own sauce from scratch using several million tomatoes and large quantities of red wine. Rumiana and Ilian helped me prepare the garlic and olives. Turns out they hated spinach anyway, but I found some frozen parsley in the freezer and added that. Topped it with Kashkaval cheese. Cooked for forty minutes at orange-hot (the stove was color-coded, not numbered).

Tasted quite good. Very sweet, virtually no spices. Both

23

cheeses turned out better than expected. Gave half to Inga and Luboslav. Everyone raved, so now I was a famous chef in Bulgaria. Next week I would fix Tortellini, which I had found in the store also.

Took a nice nap, after doing laundry, then launched into a freelance study of my favorite verbs, clichés and bad language. Could not figure out how to say "asshole"" in Bulgarian. Things to write about tomorrow: View from my balcony, cars and drivers.

The next day, in class, I finally suggested that we use the PC brochure that we were making on Dupnitsa as a ecotourism device for Dupnitsa. The idea seemed well received, and I headed a small committee to meet with the City Mayor the next day. I found out that Jack's group also planned to meet the Mayor and suggested we combine groups for that purpose. We did and Dani, a Bulgarian teacher and a dance teacher, agreed to call to change the meeting and to interpret for us. She actually set it up.

Eating the Flag Or Salad Days

One Saturday morning, early in the summer in Dupnitsa, I set aside the day to catch up on my Bulgarian. So, I studied for three hours, then walked south to look for another Olympic pool I had heard about. No luck, so I went to the Dupnitsa Saturday market; it was twice as big as the market in Grants Pass Oregon, 30 miles from my cabin, and even had some permanent buildings for electronics and food. This seemed to have replaced the giant GUM-like central store as the place where people shopped. I observed many good electronics, athletic clothes and shoes, suspiciously cheap. Must be rip-offs or knock-offs.

I decided to buy the fruits that I wanted to eat, having gotten tired of mushy apples. So, I bought two melons, a cantaloupe and an unidentified something else. Then I picked out a few peaches and four pints of raspberries. Then a dried *plodovey* salad (fruits) and some peanuts. On the way home I picked up some water and yogurt. I couldn't read the labels very well, so I got three kinds — the third turned out to be chocolate pudding mixed with cream. Fortuitous errors entertain us.

At home I immediately ate both yogurts hoping to tame the ravages of the local bacteria, which had troubled me for weeks. I had been drinking local tap water to acclimate my body. The food itself was also quite a change; most of it seemed to be fried in pork fat.

So, I concentrated on salads. Shopska salata was like eating the flag. The flag was three horizontal stripes of white over green over red. The salad was made with white cheese and white onions over green peppers over red tomatoes.

The market

Death by Rakia Or *Drinking to Belong*

Saturday, after the main dinner at 1 p.m. — pork soup, tomatoes salad, French fries, with mousse for dessert and fruit juice, rakia, and wine to drink, I studied for another two hours, then went on another two-hour walk in the other direction, this time along the German River. I found many abandoned factories and an abandoned large hotel, that once had three fountains in front and a large garden surrounding it. But, no swimming pool, so I walked back. Studied for another three hours until the evening meal, which was chicken and rice, with a fruit salad for dessert, rakia and fruit juice, and of course tomatoes salad — fortunately I really loved tomatoes and these were fresh, local and quite good. After dinner I was able to study for a few more hours.

Sunday, had *nagosti* with my host family; their daughter Petya and her family, husband Boris and daughters Ralitsa and Viola, were here from Sofia again. We talked about medicine and soccer. We had kebabche, which was a special sausage made in Dupnitsa (hopefully not from the stuff in the dumpsters), fries, tomatoes and rum, rakia, whiskey, wine and beer (ohhh, my *glava*). Beer usually opens the parade of peanuts and appetizers. Rum and whiskey were rare treats before dinner, likely due to the high costs. Wine was served at dinner. Rakia was the only drink that was served before, after, and during dinners. It seems to be considered rude not to drink to a light stupor.

I tried to study afterwards. But my eyes refused to focus; so, I gazed over at the mountains from the balcony. I realized that my life seemed boring, between eating and reading, but it was boredom tempered by fear and strangeness.

Learning to Dance Or *Chalga Time*

After one of the first summer classes, instead of studying, I took a dance class with five girls from among the PC volunteers. I enjoyed that. Alas, we only did the folk dancing, which was a continuous line dancing or chorus line kind of dancing. Still, they were all young and attractive, as was the instructor, Dani. And, I was the only male (ha, ha, owaa haa haaaa).

The music itself seemed to be a cross between Greek, Turkish and Bulgarian, or at least showcase those influences. The music sometimes seemed almost monotonous in a way, although it did get faster and faster by tempo. The idea seemed to be to exhaust the dancers and or the musicians.

Some of the female volunteers were very sweet to me, but I figured that it was because I was actually older than their fathers. It was hard for me to figure out how to act towards them. The last time I had actually courted someone was in my 20s. I forgot that over thirty years had passed and I was white haired, balding and slightly paunchy. And so the summer passed, without me making or receiving any overtures.

I watched the volunteers start to pair off, thinking to myself it was premature, since they would probably be split up for sites. Not unsurprisingly, the women in their 50s and 70s seemed to find me attractive. I liked talking to Calpurnia, who had taught briefly at my high school in Virginia. I decided to be monkish for the next 6 months at least (sigh). She seemed to like to talk to me, but was very dignified and reserved.

Oh, yes, dance class continued every Tuesday and Friday. I finally started to master the steps, although Dani introduced new steps all the time. Anyway, dancing between Amber and Carman made up for any discomfort. It was always 100 degrees and we all sweated incredibly.

One afternoon in August, there was a visit to the cow village (what was that name?), where we were treated to a traditional Bulgarian marriage ceremony. I sit with Calpurnia on the way there. We talked about Bulgaria. I liked her hands, which touched mine accidentally. At the ceremony I met Filip. Svetla was there and also talked to Filip (I found out that she was the head of the program, not the assistant, as I had thought for two months, another cultural error on my part). I danced with Amber, Carman, and Julie; then Lillia joined in. It was a good wild dance. In fact, towards the end, I tripped and landed sprawled across the laps of three *babas* (grandmothers) seated on chairs. They grabbed me and everyone laughed (and they didn't let go until I laughed) .

The sponsor conference a few days earlier also had dancing. Joe and I were without sponsors, so we play acted as each other's sponsor, although we did not dance with each other. Dinner that night was at the Continental, a large basement disco in a large closed hotel in the center of town, which was actually quite nice. Scot and I sat together with Joe, Pentcho and Svetla. Scot and I had vegetarian food, which was stuffed peppers and potato cakes. Not bad. There was a live band playing the traditional music.

Calpurnia was at another table down the line, with her counterparts and their colleagues. I asked Calpurnia to dance by raising my hand and twirling it once; she answered by getting up and walking to our table, without speaking. Still without speaking, we walked to the small dance floor. We were awkward at first, but got better as we learned to move together. After dinner I asked her again. After the fourth dance we teased the "kids" for not dancing, so Marcus and Sylvia, Ben and Amber also danced. Then Bumpy and others, but it got silly fast. Calpurnia danced with Joe to ask him to ask her counterpart to dance, which Joe did; I had to dance with Bumpy, who was silly about it; half the dance floor broke up. Calpurnia and I walked her host to the bus and went back, but dinner was over so we went to the disco and danced for an hour.

Then we went to the Kino cafe and talked to others. Convinced a few people like Jenna to come back to the disco and dance with us. Lillia was there and Pentcho. We talked to Malcolm, who was DJing the thing and he gave us two slow tunes, which we use to hug as we dance. I was surprised, pleasantly, when she hugged me very closely on the last slow dance, but it was easy for me to do, since she felt so good.

After midnight I walked Calpurnia home. We kissed good night under the tree in the courtyard, then talked, then kissed, then sat, then sprawled on the bench, her legs over mine, and kissed.

As we were talking, a drunk come up and knocked at the door. We said good evening in Bulgarian; he replied something. Zlatka answered the door and was surprised first by the drunk and next by us in the background. The drunk was a friend of her fathers who did not know that he had died years earlier. Then the mother Petya peeked out at us and winked.

That reminded me of a joke. A couple went to the Rabbi to get instructions on marriage. The Rabbi says dancing was forbidden. The couple seem worried and the husband to be asks if can they make love. The rabbi says yes, of course. The husband to be seeks more details: but can we make love on our sides. Yes, of course, the Rabbi says. What about doggy style? Yes, yes, no problem. How about standing up? No, absolutely not! Too dangerous, could lead to dancing!

Daily Dumpster Report Number 1

The first day I was in Dupnitsa, I got off the bus next to a dumpster full of rotting fish bones and waste. I was surprised. Now, I see that trash was a real problem in Dupnitsa. Later that month I asked to see where the city put its trash. When it was collected, every month (or two or three, depending on who had fallen out of favor with the mayor), it was taken to a hill and dropped over the side; there an old Russian bulldozer pushed it over the hill. The valley was lovely, with small pines and a stream at the bottom — with only this one cancerous growth on one hill. I walked there on a hot June day. In the last mile, the amount of trash really started to increase — obviously people had been dumping at night by the road to the dump.

As I got there, I saw people going through the dump and collecting pieces of cloth and plastic bottle. Part of the dump was burning. As I started looking for things, upwind, I noticed that all of the people moved away from me. When I approached them to ask what they were collecting, they moved rapidly away. Finally they all moved into a large knot by the edge. One of the men moved towards me; I stopped and asked what they were collecting. He answered but it did not seem like Bulgarian (more like Romanian I think). I said that I was only curious and would leave soon. He did not answer. I looked over many thousands of medical wrappers from a nearby pharmaceuticals plant. I found very little glass, no appliances, beds, or anything large in fact. There were many broken bricks and blocks. Other things looked like food or some organic material not easily identified. Finally I walked away and waved to them. No one waved back, although they returned to work immediately.

In town, I asked my language teacher what had happened. He said they were gypsies finding things to sell or use; they also set the dump on fire in places where they had finished. Later on my walks into the forest I passed the dump regularly. It seemed to be larger and bleaker at each passing, with geological layers of ash underneath tons of medical wrappers.

I remembered that garbology was now a legitimate anthropological category. Normally, I ignored garbage, but one day as I threw away my empty bottles, I noticed a sheep skeleton in the dumpster. I watched that for days, as the local cats and birds removed any remaining flesh from it. That same week I was walking along the German river in Dupnitsa and found a whirlpool that had several dog bodies in it; they had been skinned. I was curious, so I worked backwards from the river talking to people (especially those who had some English), until I found a factory that specialized in animal hides. It seemed that dog hides made a nicer leather than cow, since dogs did not sweat through the skin, but panted (like foxes and wolves). Many handbags were made from dog skin and sold in Sofia and other big cities from here to Athens and Istanbul. There were also several hides that could had been fox or wolf.

Dumpster No. 3

Mafia Cars, Women, and Dog Leather

In Dupnitsa were many very new discos, apparently run by the Bulgarian mafia, a kinder, gentler mafia dedicated to the sport of weight-lifting and the consumption of coca cola (exclusively — and woe to those who dared to ask for pepsi cola). Oh, sure, there were a few violent public murders every month, but that was nothing compared to the violence and suffering caused by dishonest bankers. There were also a few local restaurants and stores that had suspiciously heroic incomes. These places always had large Mercedes and BMWs parked in front. In fact, now that Poland had cleaned up to join the European Union, the largest car-stripping operation in Europe had moved to the abandoned factories of Dupnitsa. Since the collapse of the Soviet Union, and the loss of subsidies, many of Bulgaria's state factories had been abandoned. Showing commendable initiative, the mafia found uses for those abandoned buildings. Alas, the volunteers were drawn to the nicest discos. Finally, the Piece Corn tried to influence the volunteers not to frequent mafia places. It did not work.

Filip and Kim were in town. I asked them over for a *nagosti* (visit) with the host family, the Ilievis. A good time was had by all. The Ilievis were pleased that the American guests had good Bulgarian language skills. We brought wine and chocolates to them, a fine tradition for visiting.

The next day, Kim wanted to see the mafia dog-skinning operation in Dupnitsa. We walked in ever-widening circles from the grade school until we saw a young man loading hides into a truck in back of a deserted building. From the hill overlooking him, Filip hailed him in Bulgarian, asking him pleasantly and innocently how was he doing. Soon they established a rhythm; Filip asked a question, like "was that a goat hide or was that a cowhide?" Soon the young man was answering yes, even to the final question: "Was that a dog hide?" Filip and I were smiling. Kim was hiding behind us taking photographs. After a few minutes, however, a large beefy man came out, sized up the situation, and had everything taken

29

from sight. He gestured dismissively towards us and we waved back socially. The visit was over.

Corruption was easy to understand, alas. Bulgarians only earned about $100 a month (we volunteers got $150 every month from the Peace Corpse for expenses, which was pegged at the national average, which may have included bankers, politicians and mafia chieftains); it was harder on teachers, doctors and police, who only got about $40-60 a month — in fact I knew three doctors who worked selling newspapers and waiting tables because it paid more. A *chalga* possibility: "Mama don't let your babies grow up to be doctors." Fake things, from computer programs to shoes and cigarettes, were much cheaper than brand names; they were almost as good and the only clue was usually a misspelling, such as "NTKE" for "NIKE." The mafia was very active, suggesting that people drink coke instead of Pepsi, for instance. Many political leaders had come out against corruption, a good idea to be sure, but unofficially, it was big business as usual.

Privatization was more complex and grey. State enterprises were being sold to private (usually foreign) companies; for instance, all of the banks were owned by foreign companies. Lands were being given back to families from whom it had been taken. This could lead to odd situations where, in forests for example, the government had been managing the lands fairly well, but as soon as they were privatized, the forests were liquidated for much-needed cash. In other instances, people had been given back part of their factories, but not any of the improvements or expansions made during Communist rule; this led to further unemployment since half or more of many factories sat empty while only the privatized parts were working.

Busted Buildings Broken Windows

Wednesday. More language. No letters from home. Spent an hour and a half writing email to professors, colleagues, friends and family. After dinner Ilian and Rumiana wanted to go on a walk to Rila park, so I agreed, thinking it was the Gratska park two blocks from here. I was wrong; we walked for 45 minutes uphill past the baseball stadium, past a burning house — the fire truck came, from just out of sight beyond some high rise apartments; the truck was probably a 1948 army vehicle painted red with a real siren — past the electrical plant, and past, I think, a crematorium.

The entrance to the park was ratty and abandoned. But, very green and lush with nice trails. Oaks and maples mostly. There was a huge wading pool, in use, and an Olympic sized pool that was not in use. This was the mythical pool I had heard about. The water was very cool looking but very green. I vowed to return on Saturday.

Thursday, more language. I did very well with grammar and tests, but was having trouble understanding and speaking. So, for lunch I had a tutorial with Lillia. In the afternoon sessions I was pathetic, but the lesson was childish and boring. So, I went with Joe to the Napoli Pizzeria and we were soon joined by Barbara, Carman, and two guys (oopps, forgot male names; maybe if I cared). We shared 2 pizzas, also very good. I finally went home to study. I tried to study with the host family, but they would get impatient and answer every question before I could. It did me no good to study with them, except for pronunciation.

Friday, we met with the environmental city officer who was just temporary since the permanent one left. We presented three ideas to her; she seemed most interested in the Rila park cleanup and actually suggested Rila Park itself. She promised to get back with us Monday and we would meet again to decide the final project.

On a trip to Vratsa, to visit a Natural Park, we left by bus for Sofia. Five *ekologs* and Hassan and Boris. Other groups were leaving about the same time. That night in Boris's apartment, I got email from my father saying that he could not open a savings account with my last paycheck because my social security number was closed and I was dead. I sent my number to him so he could check on it. *Et tu*. SSA?

I had to suffer through a long breakfast, long language class, and a long lunch at a cardboard pizza place. Then we took a long hike to the park. We got up the gorge and to the top by evening and were met by a Russian jeep, which drove us to the Ledenika cave, which was quite nice and very cold. I sang Ave Maria loudly to great effect. Then the Bulgarians sang their local songs — great acoustics. On the way back out I took a short cut and fell and banged a rib; it seemed better after a while, but it could had been worse. It was very dark, as they were turning out lights as we left. The jeep had broken down, so we ate or rather drank at a cafe nearby until a car came about 11:15 p.m. We had to double up on the seats, so Kailie, a nice quiet girl from Utah, sat on my lap. Given the speed and the roads, it was surprisingly intimate. I mentioned that she was not committed to bearing my children, but she said she was, according to Bulgarian automotive tradition.

Saturday, I studied all day, taking a walk to the bazaar at 11 and a longer walk to the Rila park, where I finally went swimming. I was the only one swimming. Afterwards I walked through the park, lushly overgrown and uncared for.

Early the next morning, we went on an Ekoklub hike up the mountain to a small park and nearby hotel, which was mostly just for weddings. I walked with Calpurnia, who seemed tired from walking and three Bulgarian girls, Yordanka, Kalina and Theodora, who was the only one who knew any English. Theodora had a bad knee from ballet and the other girls were her friends.

We got to the park and cleaned it up. Julie had brought bags. The rest of us found many bags among the junk and trash. We played frisbee, first Alexander, Bumpy and me, then two Bulgarian girls, a Bulgarian guy, and me. Alexander brought watermelon, so we shared it. Then we took the trash to the hotel dumpsters. Then we walked down. Calpurnia and I lagged behind the others. Theodora was our talkative chaperone. Cali seemed happier going downhill and took my hand when I offered it. Her voice was very sweet, so we talked, well, mostly she talked, but I liked listening.

Calpurnia and I had melbas (not raspberries and peaches but a fruit salad covered with ice cream and cookies and a paper parasol) at the Green cafe, which I remembered was Cafe Vienna. Afterwards she walked home, but I met Marcus and Sylvia who wanted to go swimming. I agreed, went home and changed.

I walked to the pool, waited for them, but then dove in to swim laps. There were many people in the pool, but none were swimming. It must have been 100 degrees. I swam around the lubbers, then walked back. As I reached home, a taxi sped by with Marcus, Sylvia and someone else. I went in and studied. I noticed that the entry way window was broken again.

Cali's Entrance

Teamwork Or *Ecological Connections*

Our Bulgarian language class went badly. I simply could not remember the verbs and pronouns to speak effectively. The afternoon was dedicated to technical teaching and language. I foolishly agreed to help teach an ecology course to the Dupnitsa Seventh-graders on Friday.

I stayed for the ecology club after school. We played a game of finding flowers and insects on the playground—our team won with the final sighting of a dragonfly. We would go together on a hike Saturday morning.

I was writing this in my sweltering room. The wind was coming from the burning trash dump on the edge of town, which made it far worse. The neighbors were loudly watching some kind of football game, and the traffic was as noisy and gritty as ever. This town did not need a piece-corpse person as much as a curfew, speed limit and traffic testing.

The demonstration in Ecology for the model school was in the center of town in a smaller, older grade school. The classes there were mostly English, but the kids had agreed to stay after their last class tomorrow at 11:00. Today, we simply participated in a game for showing how lost species put pressure on the remaining species in a food chain. A simple, but clever game of linking arms and drawing cards to see who dropped out. As each person dropped out it became harder to hold on to someone else. Back at Class Calpurnia, Joe and I decided to team up and give another presentation in ecology.

We worked on the presentation in the next morning. Then we walked to class where we waited an hour before it was time. I liked working with Joe and Calpurnia; Joe was like a younger brother and Calpurnia like a younger sister. They were very serious about the presentation, so we all tried hard to make sure it went smoothly. Joe gave the introduction, then I went into more depth about what an ecosystem was, using a larger example, the forest. I guessed I lost all but two young girls who whispered to their companions by way of explanation. So, I told them about how unique the flora and fauna here were, being in the crossroads between Europe, Mediterranean Europe, Africa, Turkey, and the Russian Steppes. That part went well. Then Calpurnia played a modified species game with the kids and with Joe and I, where each of us drew a card and then had to relate directly with species we needed to survive, e.g., a bat needs to eat a moth. After class Joe and I ate at a nearby cafe with Jenna and Dan.

Survival Language Or Marilyn Monroe was Our Mother

In school we spent much time learning survival Bulgarian. Mostly reviews. The next day, we had realistic situational exams, where we tried to buy tickets, stamps or food at "stations." My language exam interview did not go very well. The stations did go well: post office, restaurant, train station, party, and grocery store. Then at 10:40 there was an ecology interview for park sites, which I think went well. A package from my parents arrived with my pillow and a wool suit.

That day I had a pizza and salad at Napoli with Jo and Cliff. Language classes and technical sessions seemed dislocated. Went back to the internet cafe for more messages. Then I studied with Calpurnia at the Euro cafe (with the green awnings) and had a coke and melba, which was a fruit salad covered with ice cream scoops, a cookie and plastic umbrella—it cost about 80 cents. I treated. We were rehearsing saying the history of the Peace Corps, to recite to inquisitive Bulgarians. She had trouble with the word for 'founder,' which was '*suzdaden*.' So she suggested saying Kennedy was the father.

"Who was the mother then?" I asked.

"Marilyn Monroe!" she answered.

"And the first baby?" I asked, smiling.

"First volunteer, maybe?" she responded.

"And the goals?" I asked.

"To spread information," she started.

"Well, certainly, to spread legs, according to Will," I reminded her. "Remember him waving his passport and saying it was an aphrodisiac for Bulgarian women?"

"Yea, but I think he needed to use Spanish Fly, also."

After we were finished, she went to the internet cafe.

I went home for an hour to study, from 9:30 to 11:30, then went to Tiffany's birthday party. She was 23. I went in my running shorts and muscle shirt since the temp was in the 90s (and I had muscled again). Had a Cuba libre that the bartender had to give me the pieces to make since he did not recognize the name. Smoked and had a vodka Collins, which he did know how to make.

It was the end of July at last. I might survive after all. Two more language classes went down. We had switched teachers again, for the third time. Having had Hassan and Petko, I now had Lillia, the tall, pretty teacher, who was in her first year teaching and always seemed flustered and apologetic, causing her breasts to move invitingly in her peasant blouse. In the class was Barbara (again), Anthony, and Betty Lou.

After lunch we were bused to the hotel on the mountain for a conference with other volunteers from the ecology field, as well as with their counterparts, who would be staying at the hotel. We played frisbee during breaks. I got business cards from the Bulgarian counterparts.

Dinner was vegetarian for many of us and we sat at the same table, Michael and Marta for instance. I sat next to Calpurnia; we talked. I asked her for some of her French fries and gave her some of my coke — you can tell we were from the South, since we had coke with everything. Jenna and Tiffany were nearby. After dinner we played full-contact frisbee in the dark. I stood between Amber and Barbara, and was able to do quite well, at one point catching eight in a row. But I got over confident: while reaching for one I tripped, then Amber and Barbara jumped on top of me. A rock was under my chest and pushed in a rib. I was sure it was broken and it was hard to get up. I could not throw right handed anymore, so I foolishly played left-handed for another thirty minutes.

That night I had to sleep on my back while cursing my clumsiness and old age. The pain got worse.

The conference continued the next day, as did the Frisbee sessions, but I could only play left handed again. At noon we were bused back to the school, where we had language all afternoon.

More language all day. I liked Lillia. She was very polite about mistakes and helpful. More pain at night. I could not sleep. Now, I thought also I had broken a tooth, from eating peanuts from the bazaar, the peanut sack with pebbles added for weight. It hurt when I drank cold water. Arrggghhh.

Finally, we were offered our assignments for the next two years. The announcement was at 2:00. Tables had been set up with a giant cake in the shape of Bulgaria. The staff had drawn a chalk map of Bulgaria covering half of the playground. Drinks and watermelon were available.

The announcement began. Sylvia was first out of the hat and got Vratsa. So it went. I got Pavel Banya, the forestry unit. An ugly surprise since I was in the parks program, but everyone said it was a beautiful resort city with baths. I was to be working with the Balkan Park and the City, also (three masters, a bad sign).

Betty Lou, Marta and Ben, maybe Marcus and others, started a food fight. Malcolm was cutting cake in his wool suit. I was standing talking to Jo; I was wearing my black silk suit. Suddenly, cake flew everywhere. Jo and I left to look for Cliff, who was depressed at his assignment and had wandered off.

Jo and I went to have a melba, after failing to find Cliff. Jo went home. I changed into tank top and black jeans and went to the Underground cafe to talk with Amber, Tiffany and Jenna about the luck of the draw. We heard that this cafe might be run by the mafia.

Saturday. I studied. After dinner I went out looking for people to talk to. I found Joe, then Tiffany and Amber. Amber and I hugged and walked around hugging or holding hands. It was very sweet. I forgot momentarily that I was older than her father, at least for five minutes. Of course, I was very fit, strong, smart, and adventurous (cough cough).

Sunday: I studied, I walked. What a dull guy. A quiet day with the host family. More studying and walking.

On Monday, we prepared to visit our site, mostly with technical language about our past and Bulgarian environmental problems. We, that was Carman, me, and Milli went to Napoli for pizza and beer. Then I studied and packed two bags, one of clothes to leave at the site for September.

Saving Nature Or Please Shoot the Pigs

We met at the school at 11:00. I went to the bus station first with the
luggage. Very hot. Pace Car, I mean Peace Corps, buses drove us
to the train station in Sofia, where some volunteers got on trains.
Then, the rest of us walked to a chaotic bus station. Jenna was
going to Kazanluk, so we traveled by bus from Sofia together. She
was nervous, so I teased her gently. I got off at Pavel Banya, which
seemed run down, even by Bulgarian standards.

Two guys waited for me, Danny Devito and his younger,
inch-taller brother I thought; they were the director and assistant
director of the forestry unit, they were to be my counterparts. We
drove away in an old Lada, which turned out to be the director's
personal car since the official unit jeep was being repaired — he
wanted me to know this obviously — to a large hotel, which was
deserted except for three Bulgarian guys drinking at a small cafe on
the first floor outside. I was told to take my bags up to a room, any
room, and leave them. I went to room 800, as high up as I could go.

Downstairs, they were having rakia, so I joined them. I also
smoked with them. The maitre'd went in and cut up tomatoes for
us. I wondered if this was dinner. After an hour the three of us drove
downtown, a nice place with one giant hospital and many small
restaurants. We parked on the sidewalk and went to a beautiful
Italian restaurant, which the director immediately walked out of.
The assistant director explained it was too expensive. We went to a
second restaurant but did not go in; it was too cheap I was told. At a
third restaurant, very nice with a courtyard and umbrellas at every
table, we waited in the middle of the tables; the A.D. explained that
the director was deciding. He chose a table. We sat, and he ordered
wine. The waiter gave me a pack of cigarettes of the same brand that
I had bummed from the hotel earlier; they had noticed very closely it
seemed.

They asked me what I wanted; the menu had nothing but
meats. I said chicken; the director ordered three of the same. A band
came on and started to play chalga music, which was the Bulgarian
interpretation of folk music with rock-rap sensibility and timing, but
it was loud. The director motioned for them to quiet down, but they
played louder. He stood up and motioned again, but they played
even louder. He motioned to the owner of the restaurant who came
over and they talked. Then the owner talked to a woman by the
band. She went up the bandstand and started singing; the songs
were quieter and the director resumed a more normal human color.

We talked the entire meal about the projects of the forestry
unit, most notably about the problem of wild pigs feeding on too
many beechnuts and ruining the forest. Afterwards they dropped
me off at the lonely (heartbreak) hotel. I went upstairs and went to

sleep. Suddenly, a terrible noise awakened me. The disco, apparently in the hotel basement, started up at midnight giving me an instant headache, as the entire building vibrated in sympathy. Some while later, another disco, across the street, started. Both discos played until morning, around Six.

I was picked up by Lada about 7:30, after an hour of sleep, and driven to the forestry unit office in a small village about five miles away. The director entertained me in his office for an hour. His secretary brought in tea and chocolates. The tea had been gathered from wild flowers in the mountains. It was excellent and I asked for seconds and thirds. Afterwards the assistant director gathered me up and we went into his office. Across his desk, facing it, was a desk for me. It was completely empty. We sat for a few hours and contemplated the future. I asked for maps showing the unit and plans for harvests. Soon the desk was full. After an hour the director came by and took me out to see the official jeep, which was up on blocks and engineless.

After three, our official day ended and I was dropped off at the hotel and warned to be prepared for a signal honor that evening. I went swimming at the pool across the street, and found out that it was the second disco that started after midnight. The pool was Olympic sized but had only 14 inches of water. It was possible to swim but no tumble turns; no one else was swimming. A huge satellite dish was hanging over the pool; it said in English "Jolly American Satellite Royale." I sat down and had a coke. On a chance I asked if I could get a hamburger. The waiter answered in mixed English and Bulgarian that in fact I could. In fact, it was a piece of ham on two slices of bread with a strange bland catsup.

They picked me up after six. The "surprise event" was dinner at the local monastery. We drove for an hour and just before the monastery, we were flagged down and stopped at a small party at a colleague's house, a retired forester. His son was having a party and we were invited, me, the director, the *zamestnik* (vice) director, the lady forester, and another forester.

All of the foresters, except for the woman, had sidearms. We were standing having introductions when one of the foresters pulled out his gun and fired into the air. I started to dive for cover but noticed that no one else was. Another forester drew his gun and shot into the air. This went on sporadically for ten minutes.

I noticed the Zam seemed nervous so I asked him if we could walk to the monastery. He agreed, so we did. An hour walk up hill. I wondered if this was where we were supposed to eat. It was a small monastery with only 5 nuns, but 10 public rooms for rent to hikers or tourists. We peeked in the chapel, then a small nun in black, looking sort of like a barrel, ambled over and asked us if we would like to go in. We did. It was decorated, with a large painted dome. I lit a candle for Mark, Doris, and everyone else who had gone beyond the veil. The Zam lit one also. On the way out the nun asked us if we want to be blessed. Why not? I said. The old baba hit our heads with wet weeds then put the weeds back in a small barrel by the door. We thanked her and ambled back downhill, dripping water from our hair. The Zam seemed intelligent and sensitive.

The shooting was now being answered by guns from the other end of the valley. I wondered where all the bullets were falling. Dinner was ready; it was "elen" soup, from an elk that had been shot. I got a small bowl that I used to serve myself, not getting any of the meat or fat, which I think offended the cook.

So, I had bread and rakia to match the group. A woman asked me if I wanted to dance. I did, since I had been practicing twice a week. But, then her husband jumped up and wanted to dance with me. So she sat back down. We started a traditional horo, but he wanted to hold hands, which I was not ready to do. So, I stopped and he danced alone for a while; his wife never did get up again.

More gunfire, then some dancing, a little more shooting, and after a few hours the Zam and I were ready to flee, so we waited in the jeep for forty minutes while the director played to the retirees. The drive back was a relief and they dropped me off without comment.

The disco started again, from midnight to 6:00. I got up and looked at television, then wrote Bulgarian poetry about Bulgarian women. Later, when I showed it to Sasho and asked for his advice, he said I had used technical words, not romantic ones. No woman would like it. I wondered if Lillia would.

The next morning after a few hours of sleep, I got up and walked through the town. The old people were up already, so I exchanged many good mornings, "*dobro outro*s." I walked through the large and once-beautiful park, which was now overgrown and untended, the fountains dry and filled with trash. I saw a beautiful black squirrel. The municipal offices were by the park and also looked abandoned; in fact they had been moved across the street to a small old building — maybe the other was being renovated. I sought out the mayor and asked if I could talk about my responsibilities for the city and park. I told him I had already met with the forestry unit director. He looked at me very oddly, as if this was new information. He offered me tea, so we talked about Bulgaria and America. I never did get an answer about my responsibilities. I continued my walk.

Down a small street was the shell of a new hotel, but it was filled with hay on the lower floors and drying herbs on the upper

floors; a strange and actually pleasant sight. There were many
gypsy bands around, most were driving horse carts. They looked
different from the Slavs, who were blond, and the Bulgars, who were
shorter and darker — the gypsy features seemed coarser, almost like
aborigine features, and much darker.

At the office all day, we looked across desks at each other.
I was studying maps and a few plans. The plans were all made in
Sofia, and not by the regional foresters, so I could not participate in
that part.

Suddenly, the director came in and told us to come with him.
We drove to the hospital just by the center of town. We parked in
front and walked towards the dramatic steps. On each step was
seven or eight dogs; they seemed reluctant to move as we stepped
over them. I stopped counting the dogs at a hundred. The director
spoke with someone at an information desk, then we walked
upstairs to a room (the elevators did not seem to be working). In
the one room was a man with bandages covering extensive burns.
He spoke, and slowly reached under the bed for a large bag. The
director helped him. He handed the bag to the director, who handed
it to me. It was full of bullets, at least five different sizes. It was for
me to kill the forest-destroying wild pigs. I thanked him. I wondered
how many guns they would offer me.

On the way back to the office, we drove by a two-story
concrete building with many windows broken out. We stopped the
car and looked at it. On the brown, unmown grass lay a metal radio
that seemed to match one of the holes in a window on the second
floor. The Zam pointed to that window and said it was to be my
apartment. It was a forestry apartment, owned by the unit. But, it
would not be ready until December first; the rest of the building
seemed a wreck so my interest diminished by the minute. I asked
about where to leave my extra bag, but the Zam never answered.

That evening, I went swimming, at the lovely low pool across
from hotel. That night the disco finally destroyed me. I stayed up
and wrote all night. Before dawn I walked to the bus station with
both bags and waited for the early bus to Sophia.

Searching for Meaningful Work

In Dupnitsa, the next day, we changed instructors again. I got Lillia
again, but with Calpurnia, Michael, and Anthony as classmates. I
got debriefed as did everyone. I painted a bleak picture. Maybe two
others had times almost as odd as mine. I pleaded my case for a
new site at a park. The next day, Svetla, the environmental program
assistant, said that a new site was approved for me. Hugh, the acting
director, approved it that afternoon, and a new visit was scheduled

for tomorrow. Filip Hakel, a one-year veteran volunteer, gave an overview on nutrition at one class.

The next morning, I took the 7:50 bus to Sofia. Svetla was waiting at the bus station with Ivan, the driver and a new PC van. We drove to Aprilci, a village in the central mountains, which had an office of the Park.

We met with Iurka, the director of the Park, and Angelar, the head ranger, and Iurka's driver, Dimitar, at a cafe there. We ate shopska salata and fries. Then, we drove to the village of Stokite, where I would work in an office next to the mayor's office. It was remodeled, but did not seem to have a telephone or heat. I asked about living there in town but was told that there were no houses or apartments available. I noticed an abandoned movie theater as we left. I entertained phantom of the theater-type thoughts.

Then we drove to Gabrovo, the main Park headquarters, where we met in the office until 6:00 p.m. Filip and his wife Kim were there; they had a separate office with a door. We talked for a few hours; they gave me maps and booklets. These offices had also been remodeled and occupied the third floor of a water district building.

Svetla, Ivan and I went to a hotel at the edge of town. We each got a room, although I had to pay tourist prices, which were double the normal prices. I argued to no avail, in Bulgarian, that I was a state employee (technically true). It was a nice place on a stream next to a model old village, working, by the way, with a water-powered sawmill and clothes washer (a giant tub under a wooden waterfall). Svetla and I had a dinner in the village and then walked back. Almost like a date, but I was uncomfortable with her (I think maybe it would had been nicer with Calpurnia).

We left at Nine the next morning, after a mix-up about breakfast, where I waited for them outside and they waited for me inside, eating their breakfasts. When we stopped halfway for gas and snacks at a new Shell station, we got locked out of the car, that was, the battery on the car key alarm died. Every time the car was unlocked manually, the car alarm went off. I crawled under the car but could not find a way to disarm it. Svetla went onto the highway and tried to flag down motorists. Ivan tried to fix the battery. I kept clicking the dead clicker. Finally, one of the customers had a spare key with a battery that worked; we used it and offered to buy him lunch. But, he was in a hurry. We had lost only an hour.

Back in Sofia, I spent an hour at the PC headquarters, then caught the 3 o'clock bus for Dupnitsa. The bus station, actually two large vacant lots where buses parked anywhere, seemed less chaotic the second time. There were fruit, candy, magazine, and fast food stands clustered at one end. The fast food like sausages and bread.

I get back just as Amber, Michael and others were finishing early, so we went to the cafe together and exchanged stories.

The following day, Joe, Dan and I studied in the brand-new cafe, with a balcony. We sat on the balcony. Joe and I talked about our social lives, or lack of them; he suggested meeting with Amber and her family for a dinner; I suggested Calpurnia and her host family since they were close. We agreed to ask both sets later.

Monday, we had language simulation stations again. This test included meetings with the mayor, a professional colleague, and calling in sick. I did fairly well. At a "recess" Joe suggested having drinks Thursday instead of dinner, which could be expensive. I agreed but asked for Friday, so I did not had to worry about studying afterwards. Then we played serious frisbee.

More language. The teachers seemed desperate. Then, we found out that they believed that their salaries or jobs depended on our passing the final exams.

Saturday, with my host family, the Ilievis, we traveled to Sophia by bus and spent all day visiting (*Nagosti*) with their daughter, son-in-law, and their two daughters, in Sofia. Although the building seemed a little decrepit, their apartment was lavishly furnished. One whole wall was filled with books and music CDs. We returned to Dupnitsa at 6 and had a small dinner.

On Sunday, Joe and I studied again, then walked all the way to the mountain hotel, comparing our histories and tragedies. There were a few interesting parallels. Perhaps certain factors propelled people into the Peace Corps; perhaps not.

Finally, Calpurnia, Alta, I had the last scheduled tests. It went better than the first and I improved to an intermediate. Then, we finished the final language classes with the poster thing and another game about misunderstandings. We played a game with other classes, dividing up into two national groups, each of whom secretly got instructions that made it impossible for the other group to work with them. Amusing. Little did we know it was the most effective game to prepare us for Bulgarian life.

The day before graduation, our counterparts, except for Joe's and mine, arrived and we all sat in a classroom. I sat by Calpurnia, our hands and legs touching accidentally occasionally. She had to spend most of her time with her counterpart, including dinner. I invited her out for ice cream. We agreed to meet at 8:30 p.m. at the Cafe Mirage to have ice cream with Alta and Christine.

Our dance class gave a presentation of Bulgarian dances to the volunteers and guests (as if they had never seem them before). It went very well, although there were only five of us. We were rehearsed, coordinated and youthfully graceful, in our interpretation of traditional movements. For the last dance, we grabbed people sitting in the front row, Calpurnia first, and included them, until everyone was part of the line for 20 more minutes.

I walked to Calpurnia's room, a detached room upstairs in a house, to pick her up. We walked to the Mirage. Christine was drinking and so was Alta, but we shared only a Bailey's with ice cream. Then we went for a walk to the Continental, which was quiet, and to the Kino cafe, which was quiet, and then to the Underground, which was quiet. Everyone else must have been somewhere else. We went back to the Mirage, and met Christine, and had another drink; then the server said he had to go close up and go home. We walked Christine home, and then we went back to the garden and talked for a few more hours.

She asked me if I wanted to see her room. I said sure, since I was curious. We walked up the dirty concrete stairs and went in. She had two rooms; the first had a small bed and desk. The second had a double bed under a huge window, with a large dresser and larger armoire. She asked if I wanted to try the bed. I said sure and jumped on it; was not only noisy and unstable, but half the springs were poking through. I lay back and watched her. She undressed and started to get under the threadbare blanket, then noticed I was dressed:

"Hey, aren't you going to get undressed?"

"No," I answered, laughing, "this is more fun."

She turned a very attractive pink, "Hey, not fair."

"You'll have to take them off," I shrugged, laughing.

She tore off the shirt, and pulled the trousers down, saying, "Ouffff." The trousers got stuck at the ankles. One of the socks was jammed. I was trying not to laugh. She remembered something and said, "Oh, yes," pulling a condom from the dresser.

I reached over and pulled one from my pocket: "I see we both listened to the 'safe sex' lecture."

She had trouble getting it open and laughed. Then she had trouble getting it to stay on. Then we were both laughing, which tended to relax all the parts of a body.

I couldn't get the trousers off, but by then it didn't matter.

Graduation Day *Or Certified and Released*

After only an hour sleep, maybe, I went home and took a shower, then packed my bags. I dressed in black cotton with a black wool sweater — it had rained overnight and was cool — and my black Barcelona beret. Had a last breakfast with Rumiana and Ilian, donut-like things that I sort of liked, yogurt and tea. Alas, still queasy, from stress most likely.

Waited with Rumiana and Ilian, talking, then walked to graduation. Many people were waiting, so I scoped out the hall. I waited outside with the digital camera, armed with a new battery. Talked to Joe and Jo. The building was a more modern concrete block that housed a café and movie theater, where we would graduate.

Calpurnia arrived with her host family. We took photographs and talked. The doors opened and we marched in, the line splitting so the host families went to the chairs and the volunteers went to the stage. I sat between Calpurnia and Joe in a middle row, with Joe, Christine and Alta. Sylvia and Marcus were in front; Amber and Tiffany were in back.

The graduation took two hours because everyone wanted to talk and it was translated immediately. The American Ambassador was long-winded and slightly rude to Bulgaria (presenting it as a backward appendage to Europe). The new director for Bulgaria, Albert Foster, the happiest man I ever met, was slightly better but ruined his presentation with an American Christmas story, the moral of which seemed to be to whine for something until you got it.

There was Bulgarian singing and dancing as intermissions between talks. Several students also gave talks, as did a local actor, who represented the Dupnitsa families.

We took our oath, repeating the words to serve our country under God, but each saying our own names individually and sequentially. So, I was now a volunteer, broken body parts and all.

We went outside for a group photograph. I gave some of the girls roses, then put a rose in my mouth and tickled Cali, just as the picture was taken.

The Rose

Calpurnia, Alta and I and our families and counterparts got a table for lunch. We waited in line for 20 minutes at the Sole Mio, but

43

the vegetarian food looked good. We sat down to eat. I sat between Nicolai, Joe's counterpart, who finally showed up just as graduation was ending, and Calpurnia, who went to get drinks. I was eating my first bite, when Yordanka, Calpurnia's counterpart came up and asked where she was. I replied, and she said sarcastically in Bulgarian that they wanted to leave today. I told her that Calpurnia should return in two minutes, unable to add sarcasm, yet. But Yordanka was upset, so I found Calpurnia and took her place in line. After I got the drinks, I came back to an argument. They wanted Calpurnia to leave immediately, before she started to eat. So, I got Gaby (the daughter of Kosta, who spoke good English) to run interference with Yordanka, who spoke no English. They went to talk with "English Edward" and his counterpart, who were traveling to the same town, but who had not packed yet. Calpurnia was too upset to eat so we talked. The gang came back and wanted to leave immediately. Meanwhile, a tall slim ranger, Angelar, my never-seen counterpart, introduced himself and said that we had to leave immediately to fight a forest fire. We agreed to meet at the office in 30 minutes, since he needed his travel reimbursement first.

In graceful defeat, Calpurnia asked me to walk back to her room with the gang to help carry her suitcase. We did walk back and I carried her suitcases down; the seven women helped with smaller items. Calpurnia and five women left, and I was left with two crying women — her host family.

I walked back to the dinner to have a second bite, but it was time to go to the school to meet Angelar. This had been a dramatic introduction to a different side of the Bulgarian temperament. Later, Calpurnia told me that Yordanka's husband had ordered her to return immediately home because he suspected that she was having an affair (and she was, but it was not with anyone in Dupnitsa). The music started for those who were allowed to dine and celebrate.

Below the Fire

Excess in All Things

Fighting Fires with Coke

Angelar said we would be gone three days, so I grabbed the small bag quickly. We picked up Nikolai, then two more rangers, Boleslav and Pentcho, and headed out for the fires. First, however we stopped for supplies, mostly food. I bought a sausage, loaf of bread, pound of cheese, margarine, and a coke. Angelar insisted that everyone buy a two-liter plastic bottle of coke. This was for three days. Everyone had a beautiful red Swiss rescue backpack; I had my old brown German one. Everyone was dressed either in ranger uniforms, brown and green, or in waterproof red and black Swiss rescue uniforms; I had jeans, boots, sweatshirt and my black cotton jacket (which I had worn for graduation earlier). I was beginning to regret not bringing winter clothes, that was, what ones were left after I gave most of them to Goodwill.

No one spoke English, but I understood that this was the fire that started just before the graduation. We drove for an hour and stopped for coffee. No one seemed in a hurry. We drove another hour. It was cloudy and starting to drizzle. Angelar got a call on the mobile phone every five minutes it seemed. We finally reached the park; we had been traveling west on the north side of the park all along. In the park were inholdings of sheep and cows, and as everyone excitedly told me, the herbs that were used to make rakia. The skies cleared.

We pulled into a gated lodge. There was a huge home that was gated within the gated lodge. I was told this belonged to a television producer. The lodge itself was an old hunting lodge (*Loven Dom* — the word to hunt was "loveya" Yea, love you too, bang bang). We sat at the table under the awning in front and immediately had coffee and rakia. I asked where we were going next, since it was almost dark. Here, I was told, so I drank and waited.

After an hour we moved into the kitchen and started cutting up food. Dinner I guessed, so I cut my bread up, and the cheese. Dimitar cut up tomatoes. Boleslav put out some evil looking paste, which looked like catsup, mustard and toothpaste combined with peppers. There were three women there, one young one with a four-year old boy. We were not introduced. They seemed to live there. They disappeared in the back of the building, which was two stories. The back half of the lower floor was their home; the front half was a restaurant and bar. Upstairs was a large living room that opened out onto five dormitory bedrooms, each with three beds and a small wardrobe with no hangers. I put my pack on the bed by the window at the end.

Downstairs, the walls were covered with bear, wolf, and

fox hides (I was sorry they were not alive, but such was life with humans), as well as mounted antlers from the elen (*Cervis elephans*), and three other kinds of deer or sheep. We went outside for more rakia. There were two outdoor stonework barbecues, and a stone fountain with running water on one side and a faucet on the other. The water was cold and good.

Inside, about Nine, we finally sat down for food. All the food was presented on two plates each of shopska salata, which was tomatoes, cucumbers, onion, and syrene cheese — my favorite actually, peanuts, some strange canned meat, which I tasted but decided to forgo, and bread, and of course two more bottles of rakia, two bottles of vodka and a bottle of whiskey. To eat, we simply used forks to take from the communal plates. This was new to me, since at my host family and all other functions, we actually had plates from time to time.

A new, female ranger joined us, Nora, who looked 12 and maybe weighed 80 pounds; I guessed she was 30 though and possibly 90 pounds.

At 10:30, I went to bed, tired from trying to understand and speak Bulgarian for eight hours. I suspected the others drank until 2 or 3, but I was oblivious.

At 7:00, the chief, Angelar, came in and woke us. We all had slept in underwear, so we put on shirts and pants and ran downstairs. The restaurant was locked with our food inside. So, we packed up and drove to the fire. However, after five miles we stopped and had breakfast in a small cafe. The Lada Niva, although 4-wheel drive, was smaller than my old Subaru, so we were jammed in, three in back, three in front; Nora had to sit in Boleslav's lap, which caused numerous jokes. Boleslav by the way resembled George Clooney, ruggedly handsome with good teeth (good teeth did not seem very common, a full set even less so).

Cafes could be found every fifty feet in towns and every five miles in the countryside. I had apricot juice and went outside, where Dimitar was conversing with an animated, and slightly addled old man, Ivan, to whom I was introduced. We talked about Russia and our families.

Then we were ready. We drove up into the park, as the cafe was a detour, first on paved roads, then gravel, then mud, then on narrow foot trails. The roads had absolutely *no* culverts or waters bars, so they had eroded from one to four feet deep in the center or on the edges. I was surprised that we did not get stuck.

We drove through the forest, which was relatively young and mostly beech, and into a cloud. I heard bells everywhere. There was an abandoned metal barn, with no roof, looming nearby. We parked in the center of a field and got out. We were also in the middle of a herd of cows, maybe forty.

We packed up and walked up hill. After five hundred feet up we were out of the cloud and in the mountains, which were alpine pasture at this level and then bare rock at the peaks. I was told we were at 8,000 meters (25,000 feet). I was wheezing like an old man but kept up. Fortunately, Bulgarians could not walk for more than fifteen minutes without a cigarette, so at the breaks I caught my breath. At one point we stopped next to a herd of horses, also with bells. While the others smoked, I played with one of the horses, who was really curious. I used all my knowledge that Moira (way back in Oregon) had taught me, and stroked her with long strokes and kind words. I rubbed her upper lip and scratched under the jaw. As we left she started to follow — a new friend! But we were going straight up hill at 50 degrees it seemed. Finally, we saw the fires. Along the mountain ridge, for miles, it was black. The fire had started on the south side and came over the ridge. Fortunately it never reached the forest on either side, but it looked like thousands of acres were black. There were burning pockets everywhere, which we could locate by the smoking fumaroles.

The chief did not have a shovel, and they would not let me have one either. We had little water bottles, 1 liter each, and our shoes. I was starting to freeze so Milko gave me his orange overcoat from his pack. I made my own shovel with branches and a flat stone — it worked, and the rangers called me MacGyver for a while. So, we turned over sod, which burst into flame as the roots got air. We did this for six hours, gradually working uphill. The view was great. I wished my camera could be unloaded (the cable did not fit the camera, although it fit the computer perfectly).

At about Two, we sat down for lunch. I had a piece of bread. Others had meat and cheese with bread. Angelar got calls every five minutes on the mobile phone, either directions or reports. I sat next to Nora and we talked about her education; she was educated at the university in Sofia as a forester, as was Angelar. But, when the parks were formed, from uncut or regrown forestry units, many of the foresters went to work for the parks, where they made almost twice as much money.

Now, we went up the rest of the mountain, searching out pockets of fire. There were fewer now, although this was the end of the fire. At the peak we came to a fire line, obviously made with a tractor. We sat down and looked at the reserve. We were just near the Boatin reserve, which was one where I expected be working later. It was covered with pines at this altitude, which made me wonder if these meadows here were natural or were from grazing. In the middle of the reserve sat a large white shining lodge; it was one of the *hizhas* (mountain huts), I was told.

As we were sitting a group of four men with backpacks approached along the fire line. They were rangers from another park unit. Angelar went to meet them, then we all got together, smoked, talked, and ferreted out two more burning pockets nearby. We spent an hour inspecting the perimeter, making sure there were no active pockets. The fire had jumped the line only in one place so we ravaged the remaining plants to make sure. As we were working a horse and rider approached. The horse was loaded with four 10-gallon water cans. The saddle was a pack saddle and the guy was riding probably because he was tired. I stroked the horse, who seemed also very tired and preferred to nibble grass.

We left their crew who would work the south side and went back down the slope at the perimeter. Milko, Boleslav, and Dimitar had gone east and the three remaining of us went north, which was straight down. Angelar stopped to eat something from the ground. I noticed we were standing in a field of blueberries, very small, very blue, but past their sweetness. Who cared? We sat and ate blueberries, smoked and talked while Angelar answered the phone. It really was odd to see all the rangers smoking in a dry field which days before had hosted a very large fire, but they seemed to be careful with the butts.

After another hour or two of moving up and down, we stopped and sat down, the three of us. Angelar went down slope and Pentcho came up slope so we all exchanged information. I lay back and looked at the sky. The clouds were moving uphill from the north very quickly and dramatically. In minutes the sun was gone and it was much colder. Minutes later it started to drizzle. I sarcastically asked in Bulgarian if we were waiting for rain or to meet someone. Alas, sarcasm, like humor, was lost in translation, or rather the formation of words in a different language. Angelar answered seriously, yes, we were waiting for rain. As he spoke, clouds started forming down slope.

It did start raining, so we moved down slope, inspecting pockets. My legs were very rubbery and I was thinking about asking for another rest, but I did not. There were no breaks now, as we were all wet, even those with rain gear, so we hurried down. The horses and cows were huddled near the jeep and had mined the way with tons of manure.

We piled in the jeep and drove back to the lodge. After we got there, the women and a new man, the husband of the young one I thought, were waiting, drinking our rakia. So, we sat and drank and smoked, and the man and women made dinner, which was much more expansive than the previous night. I ate at least six tomatoes, with bread and cheese on the side, and tried one of the German-like sausages, which was quite good; in fact I ate another.

The rakia was good, although I preferred wine or vodka. Most of the rakia was homemade, so quality varied dramatically.

Again, I left to bed by 11:00 while the others drank and talked several more hours. There was no radio or television, although the bar had tapes of American singers, mostly bubble gum crap, too saccharine for me anyway.

Tuesday. Again, we were wakened early, dressed, and ran downstairs. This time breakfast awaited, but it was all the food left over from the night before, so I had tomatoes, bread and a sausage bit (so much for vegetarian resolve).

This time I grabbed a shovel and filled my coke bottle with water.

Again we drove to a cafe for coffee. Again, we hiked in and walked up the mountain to put out the remaining smoldering grasses. It had rained all night so we only worked for six hours putting out underground smolders. I could work faster with the metal shovel. The water only lasted for four pockets of fire, then it was back to stomping on them with boots. Not surprisingly, the boots got very warm very fast. We rested more this day, which was beautiful and sunny.

By Two we were heading to Aprilci to drop off the rangers. We did, but at each stop we had coffee and talked to them and their families. Angelar and I dropped off Dimitar at the bus station then we went to Angelar's apartment to sleep. His apartment was in Sevlievo, which was thirty kilometers away. It was in a quiet neighborhood composed of medium size blocks, about five stories each.

His daughter, Eva, 6, ran out to greet him. His wife, Ioana, was shopping; his son Bobi, 1, was asleep. Eva and I played soccer in the living room while Angelar walked out for fresh bread. I was surprised that we did not destroy half the furniture. Later we all talked for a few hours over rakia, coke, and tomatoes. Ioana called upstairs to ask the neighbor girl Alexandrina to come down. She was a university student with six years of English; tall, dark hair, could be the twin of my host family Ilievi's granddaughter. We were served soup, bread and a few cooked red peppers, which I could not finish.

I got to sleep in their kitchen. Woke up from the most comfortable Bulgarian bed so far, with a good comfortable pillow.

Finding a Home Or Heat is Extra

As Angelar drove I started to fall asleep regularly, but Angelar kept up a running commentary about the Park and other things. I only understood every third word; some of the rangers had trouble understanding Angelar, who had a heavy local accent.

Ahead of us was a pretty girl along the road waving to us. I wondered if she needed a ride. I waved and looked at Angelar, but he kept driving. A short while later were two pretty girls waving to us. I commented on how friendly these girls were. Angelar said that they were prostitutes, hoping for rich foreign drivers to stop. Nevertheless, I waved back at them, since they were trying so hard to be friendly.

We got to Aprilci in just under four hours by taking shortcuts. We drove to my new unseen house which was very promisingly located on the outskirts of town; it was a long town, up the hill towards the mountains. Many dogs were barking. Angelar pointed to the house, which looked like a Swiss chalet!

The house was locked so Angelar drove to the landlord Tsonko's house and got the key. Of course, we had to have tea and cookies first, but that was welcome, since I never got a chance to eat lunch.

The house seemed new, with three bedrooms upstairs. But, the kitchen had no fridge, stove, or heating stove. The bathroom had no toilet, but a huge hot water heater and a sink. Angelar showed me the outhouse outside. The house was on a half acre with old run-down gardens and fruit trees. There were three stories. The 2nd and 3rd had balconies with great views of the mountains. It was very quiet except for the dogs up the street.

Tsonko the landlord came over, also, so I asked about the stove and toilet. The fridge was coming Monday. He said it was too hot to have a stove. I reminded him that winter was coming. He answered oddly. The house would not have a toilet. He asked me if I wanted to use the outhouse in winter. I confessed that was the least of my worries, and he left.

I asked Angelar about another apartment. After a heated discussion, we drove to look at an apartment next to the landlords house. It was a second-story flat, with old fixtures but a roof that showed daylight coming through. It did have a double bed, fridge, stove and wood stove, but it smelled awful and was occupied for the next ten days.

We drove back to the house. I agreed to stay there for ten days. As I was writing this a mouse walked out then realized I was here and ran downstairs into the basement. I had the last piece of chocolate and the last of the coke that I had brought from Dupnitsa. I relished it. I went downstairs and looked at all the old building supplies and complex rat homes.

I went back upstairs. On the second floor there were three more single beds in two of the three bedrooms upstairs. I took the one that smelled the least and seemed to have slightly more padding and put it on the floor in the middle bedroom. I put a blanket on it, then the blanket cover then my sheets then another blanket.

It was dark and I was tired so I pissed on the bathroom floor and washed it down. I brushed my teeth, went to bed and slept for ten hours.

The sun came in the window and altered my dreams, which I promptly forgot. The bedroom faced east. I got dressed and decided to inventory the house.

House inventory: The house was situated in the south of Aprilci, which was a very long divided community shaped like a V and composed of four villages; each of which had it's own small center. I was in the south east end of the V. The house was halfway on a dead-end street close to the edge of all the houses. It was a three-story house, with a small attic. It was either new or, most likely, remodeled. The lot was about half-acre with six fruit trees, and it was fenced in. On one edge of the side was an outhouse, with a tile roof and a Turkish toilet inside; remember a Turkish toilet was simply a hole in the ground or floor, in this case a wooden floor. The house had a new tile roof. Red tiles, very Mediterranean, since it was white concrete on the outside.

Building techniques for these new traditional houses: First some guys frame columns and floors, then they pour concrete into the columns and floors, sometimes with rebar. The framing was done mostly with poles and small sheets of wood. Then, after a month or two they fill in the walls with hollow red bricks that were not mortared with much material. Then they build a pitched roof with the poles and beams (bigger poles), then slats, and on those the red tiles. Then the roof was closed in with wood for the sides. The entire house was plastered with stucco on the outside and plaster on the inside. The floors were a soft pine laid over the concrete of every floor. The ceilings were also the concrete pads. There was no insulation and very little finish work. For instance, the lights in this home were wires coming out of the ceiling that had a socket attached and a bulb in some of the sockets, maybe a half.

I went up to the attic the first morning. Some junk was stored in cardboard boxes that had decayed or been eaten by mice. There was a small chair and something that looked like a stove part. I saw light coming between many of the tiles, although it looked solid from the outside.

I went down the basement, which was really the first floor and had a long entry hall from the front, that came off the street at street level, and two large rooms. It was filled with building materials; some wood that I could use to build a desk I thought, and many other possibly useful items — a canning table with some jars filled with fruit, and covered with dust; many old tires and inner tubes, a good bucket, many empty wine and coke bottles, a motorcycle engine, some iron, etc. I planned to investigate further. There were at least two mice surprised to see me looking around. These mice seemed larger and furrier than ours. The rat may gave been hiding.

The second floor had a separate entrance on the north side. As you entered, there were stairs going down to the first floor on the east side. Then there was a small hallway going upstairs straight ahead. The stairs going to the third floor were on the right and over those going down (you know what I mean). The walls were all white plaster and decently done. In the small entrance hall the stairs were closed in with pine. Turning west there was a small hall with three doors on three sides. The first led to the kitchen (it was nailed shut); opposite that was a small bathroom with a sink — there was a place for a toilet and water and the drain pipe but no toilet or bath was there (it may not have been plumbed). The drain was in the center of the floor. Underneath an open pipe was a hot water heater made of raw iron and steel. The water was very hot. The walls were white ceramic tiles and very nice — if only there were toilet and tub!

The third door led to the living room which ran the width of the house facing south. Facing south was a large double window with a glass French door leading to the porch, which also ran the width. From the porch you could see the eastern edge of the old mountains (*stara planina*). There were curtains on these windows and door. In the center of the floor was a dark green carpet with black designs, looked like cotton. In one corner were two day beds which had red plaid wool blankets on them. In the other corner was a small desk (which I was using to write) with a table cloth — that morning when I came down I saw mouse turds all over the table cloth.

The kitchen led off the side of the living room. The end wall was all cabinets of pine. The kitchen was all white ceramic tile, even the sink was home made of the tile. The floor was red tile. There was no refrigerator, stove, or washing machine. There was only a small table with a red telephone on it. There was a place for a wood stove and a pipe leading to a small chimney, but no wood stove for heat either. In fact, every room had a connection for a stove for heat but there were no stoves at all. I could not understand the landlord's explanation for how I would keep warm all winter.

Going upstairs, the stairs were open and nice. The ceiling was open all the way, also. At the top, a small hall curved around to four doors. The first door held a small stair going to the attic. Two doors side by side were the front bedrooms facing east. They each had a large window next to a French door leading to a balcony; they shared the balcony. One room was empty; this was where I dropped the mattress on the floor. The other had two single beds and that was all. The third bedroom faced due south and had the best view of the mountains, from a small window. This room had a bed, sans mattress, with a toolbox underneath; the toolbox had at least five screws and several old magazines about British royalty and American movie stars. It was the smallest bedroom. The lights only worked in the large bedroom with the two beds.

I had been trying to decide what to do about this place. It was nice and quiet and large, but remote from the work office, which was in Stokite, three villages away, and from the mountains, which were about six miles straight up. I could walk in to the mountain park, but I also needed winter clothes and a good sleeping bag.

Hot Translator Or Baby Wears Black

Angelar spoke no English. He and the Rangers had decided that I needed an interpreter to help me to communicate to them. They arranged for the interpreter to spend the weekend with me and then go on my first rounds of the Park with the rangers.

So, Angelar and I drove to the bus station, where we met Ekaterina. She was tall and well-built with skin-tight clothes and a puffy jacket. Ah, my. She was as tall as I was, but then I noticed she was wearing 9-inch soles and 12-inch heels. Her face was very broad and Slavic, but she had large eyes and an engaging personality. We walked to the big department store in town. It had a great selection of televisions and radios, but very little in towels, which was what I needed. The women's clothing area was huge, also, and attracted Ekaterina's attention. I decided not to spend 11 Leva for a towel.

Going down the street, we passed a bakery. Ekaterina jumped up and down with excitement as we passed by, then said no to herself. I said that I would like something, so we went in and each ordered a slice of torte, about five layers each, and quite good. Ekaterina was very bubbly, more than most Bulgarian women I had met. She flirted with Angelar who was only five years older than she was. She was an engineering student at the university, which started in two weeks. We went to a hardware store and I got some hooks, clothesline, and extension cord.

Angelar drove us back to Aprilci to visit another possible house for me. It had nice bedrooms, but a wrecked kitchen and bath. It really looked good from the outside, like a Swiss chalet, but the kitchen and bath were very small. The sinks were falling off the walls; the toilet broke as I pissed in it. I was told if I signed a year's lease and paid today, they would fix it up and I could move in next week. The bedrooms were very nice, but small; they were all knotty pine, even the ceilings. It was heated with a wood stove, which was tiny. The living room was large, or rather wide but shallow; there was a new hi-definition television in the corner. I was told they would not leave the television. I could not decide. Everyone looked at me and asked if it was nice. It was, especially the yard, which had about 24 apples trees, with apples. It bordered on a mountain stream; it was near the elementary school. So, I said I would decide later.

The Niva broke down on the way to the next house. We waited in the rain, while Angelar got out and called for help. He walked down the road for another phone. Ekaterina and I waited and talked. An old Lada truck pulled up with Angelar and a guy with a heroic beer belly. Immediately they took apart the carburetor in the rain. Nothing worked , so he towed us back to town with a tow rope. At the bridge in town a herd of goats refused to move so we all braked suddenly. Then we could not get going, as it was uphill in the rain. Miraculously, we did get to the garage, after four of us pushed. I walked outside, while Ekaterina sat in the car and giggled. When I got back I asked her what was funny; she had never been in a broken down car before. I mentioned that such was life in Bulgaria, this would not be the last time (it was the fourth for me in three months — maybe I was the cause).

They rebuilt the carb and we were off, after a delay of only an hour. They dropped me off at the house, which was cold and dark. I walked in the rain to a market and got juice and pretzels for dinner. Then I worked on my laptop computer.

I woke up and it was light but without the sun. It was 8:30. I looked out the window, which faced due east and found that the sun was still behind a mountain, directly, so that the whole mountain was lit from the side. I walked down and got breakfast: a can of sardines, yogurt, and a loaf of bread (.50, .25, and .20). Took it home and ate it.

Angelar and Ekaterina came after noon and we drove to see the apartment, but we could not because the renter had not given back the key. He intended to keep it for a week. I decided that I would rent the hotel apartment for $75 a month. It had a beautiful bathtub and balcony.

I asked Angelar if there was a smaller house, closer to Aprilci, perhaps with a heater or stove. Driving through Aprilci I saw a sign in English and shouted to Angelar to stop. As I was walking, I saw the tourist bureau, which was advertising bike rentals. The sign was in front of the tourist bureau. We went inside and asked the guy behind the desk if he knew of tourist rooms or apartments. He had a room for $7 a night, way out of my budget, but I noticed a book on

the counter with pictures of apartments. I went to get Angelar and
we talked to the clerk. Why yes, they had an available apartment,
and yes I could rent it. It was $100 a week, fully furnished. We went
upstairs and looked at it; it had a heater, wood stove, cooking stove,
washer, sheets, television, stereo, Persian carpets, and a full kitchen.
In the front it overlooked the city square. In the back there was a
balcony overlooking a garden overlooking the Ostretska river; the
balcony had six clotheslines, also, and a grape vine the length of it
with ripe grapes. Also, a double bed, all linens, blankets, an electric
heater in the living room and a huge bookcase in the living room,
which had real couches and chairs, rather than the single beds
favored for such rooms. I thought it was a good deal since the hotel
room would cost $75 a month for a studio, although it had a better
bathroom and a good balcony. He repeated that it was $100 USD per
week. I asked if he would rent it for 100 for a month, if I signed a
year's lease. He immediately said yes. I agreed to rent it, wondering
how I could afford it if the Park did not approve.

Angelar called the rangers to see if one could take me and
Ekaterina into the mountains for a few days. I called Calpurnia's
office; there was no answer. Angelar set up a meeting with the
mayor. I went to the post office and got stamps, but the clerk
shortchanged me (just like the simulation station last month!), so
I asked for the difference. He refused but gave me another $3.00
worth of stamps. I could always use them. Then I went to the bank
to take money out. There was no bank machine, so I had to undergo
rigorous scrutiny in case the $50 was not really mine. I finally got
the money. Only one clerk in the bank could handle money, so you
had to take your receipt to the cash clerk. When you came in you
were met by an armed guard who asked you what you wanted (duh,
money). There was a large sign on the window that said: *No Guns*. I
noticed that Angelar was wearing his, but no one mentioned it.

Then we drove to each rangers house to speak with them.
The fourth one, Dimitar, was free and would take me into the park
on Saturday, Sunday and Monday. We would walk and stay at two
of the hizhas (mountain huts). We would look for the bears in the
shadow of Maragadjik, which was a tall peak in the central range.

Friday I got up early, went to town and bought a plastic wash
tub and a loaf of bread. I ate the bread as I did laundry using the
sink and the wash tub. Then I hung out the laundry using the new
clothesline from Sevlievo. Wrote a few letters on Ms. Ibook. Then
Angelar showed up with Dimitar and Ekaterina, and after a brief
discussion, I told them I had decided to rent the apartment in Novo
Cello. They agreed. We went to meet with the man, Vulko, who
was not there; the office was closed and a note indicated he was in
Ostrets, where we had just come from. So, we left for the Park.

But, first, we went for coffee. Then Angelar went to the mayor's office. Then we mailed letters, then we made various phone calls. I called Calpurnia again at home and office but got no answer at all. Angelar had arranged a meeting with the mayor, so we went immediately. The mayor, a thin man with graying hair and old wool clothes, was very polite and very interested. I used most of my repertoire of Bulgarian, but Ekaterina was there and helped translate — my own *prevedach*! The mayor called in the mistress of one of the four schools in Aprilci, this one was for poor kids from Russiya, a village to the northeast. I offered to work with the city and the school. The mayor kindly offered me the use of a car next week to show me the town; I agreed, more out of fear of displeasing him by rejecting the offer.

We went back by the apartment; no one was there, so Angelar asked in the hardware store below and they gave directions to the house of the owner. We walked there and talked with the woman of the house, a pleasant looking woman with beautiful eyes who was interested in my Greek name, since she had taken years of Greek. I agreed to rent if we could do it today and I could move my things today. She wanted to wait a week, but agreed. On the way to the apartment we met her husband, coming from the office. We all went to the apartment, which was still very nice. We went over the contract and signed; I gave him 100 Leva as down payment. They gave me the key. We all went back to the house and moved my things to the new apartment.

Angelar helped me move in, two small suitcases and my laptop. That night, after looking at the park plan on the CD, I called Calpurnia and we planned when to get together. I listened to music for the first time in three months; the apartment was stocked with bootleg tapes of greatest blues and rock hits.

The next day, I redid the laundry and hung it up; the porch faced south towards the mountains, so things dried well. I walked to town to catch the bus but did not see one to Troyan. I walked around a larger square with a giant concrete monument with raised rifles (celebrating the April rebellion against the Turks). I bought some wine and crackers. Then I ate lunch and studied the park plans. I thought the fauna plan could be improved, but was impressed with the flora plan, which seemed to be very comprehensive. I called Svetla at the PC to tell her about the apartment; she said I had to write to David Leigh, to explain why I spent so much — not a problem since only it was the only apartment to meet PC standards.

The park did not approve the apartment and refused to pay. I had to ask the PC. The PC would pay up to 150 Leva per month for apartments if the host agency could not pay; then we volunteers got a 270 Leva for expenses. So far I had paid L225 for housing, but it should be 200 per month (roughly $100 USD) from now on, although some of the hizhas only charged a few Leva for the night. Food seemed to be about L120 Leva per month. I suspected telephone would be about L100. Electricity maybe L35. So I was already over budget, not even considering internet, mail, clothing and incidentals. I would not be sending as much on mail anymore, and I would had to cut internet down to once a week. The PC would reimburse some travel, but I suspected that I would not be traveling much, either. The big worry now was warm clothing.

Beneath the Teeth of Pinups

Angelar and Ekaterina came back. We went to lunch and I foolishly treated with the last of my money. I wondered which day we might actually reach the Park. We all had soup and salads. Ekaterina and Dimitar wanted to leave immediately, another sudden decision. I agreed, although I would had preferred to enjoy the new apartment for an hour. Then Angelar announced that he would drive us halfway up the mountain. So, we started, finally. At the edge of town, however, we stopped at a house and had rakia (a strong plum brandy), tea and biscuits. I had no idea who these people were and I was not introduced. The man might have been a ranger.

We said goodbye to Angelar and started to walk. We were at the end of the paved road and met some gypsies loading firewood into horse carts; apparently they had cut the wood near the edge of the park and would sell it to homes. They were amused that we were walking up the mountain, then they left, and the three of us shouldered our packs and started uphill. Bulgarian trails went directly uphill, rarely being contoured or using switchbacks. I was gasping like a dog after five minutes while the two youngsters (Dimitar was 25 and Ekaterina was 19) raced ahead. Dimitar, the handsome young ranger, had captured Ekaterina's attention; she did not translate what they said. After ten minutes I caught up. Then Ekaterina got sick, vomiting up her tea and biscuits, perhaps the rakia, and had to stop. I offered her an orange, which surprisingly she peeled and ate. As we were sitting, I tracked birds flying through the beech forest. Leaves were starting to fall. The forest was quite awesome, a suite of white, grey and tan. We started out at a much slower pace.

For almost three hours we walked through an older beech forest (the trees may have been 150 years old). Then we were above it. The views of Aprilci were very nice. In the distance, above the tree line, we saw a large hotel-like building. Dimitar said it was a private old hotel that would charge us to stay, but we would stop for tea and go on to the *hizha*, which was only a mile past. The hotel was fenced in with wicked iron fencing and a dog barked loudly. Dimitar went in first to talk. An old — 55-56 probably, old for here but younger than me — man came out and greeted him. Then we were all invited in. Dimitar revealed that this was actually where he lived, not in the hizha, as he had told me last week.

So, we were asked if we wanted to stay. We sat around a small fire in the dining room, drinking a wonderful home-made tea (mountain blueberry leaves, raspberry leaves, mint, and something else) and rakia. It got dark and I noticed (duh) that there were no lights. Yes, the bank had foreclosed on the hotel, called the Agrotel, because this was where the Farmers Association vacationed, and taken everything valuable, mostly the radiators and fluorescent light fixtures; there was no money for electricity. Bulchru the guard lived there with his cat Hoy, dog Vixar and horse Doncho. Dimitar lived there when not with his parents in Gabrovo.

It was dark now and we started to fix dinner by candlelight in the large kitchen. Cold food, shopska salad, bread, cheese, and sausage kinds of meats. Back in the dining room, we ate, to music from a radio run by battery. There were no personal plates, only communal plates of food that everyone attacked with forks. Two odd things: Bulgarians always had music on in the background, this was true even in our classes, and the music was usually American bubble-gum music, which was mostly from Bootleg tapes made in Turkey or Taiwan (the wrapper looked original but the tapes were unidentified on the outside).

After stoking the fire, Ekaterina asked me. "Would you like to *sleep* with *me*?"

I snorted in my tea and said sheepishly, "Perhaps I should sleep alone."

Then she said, "Bulchru and Boris thought you would prefer to sleep with them."

I snorted in my tea, again, wishing she would speak English for a while. I realized she must have meant the rooms, "Okay, I guess."

Dimitar and Ekaterina talked about starting at 5 a.m.; it was 9:15 p.m. now. We all walked up to the third floor and started fires in the tiny stoves in two next-door rooms — this was the only heat, from fires. Ekaterina went into the first room, which had three beds and got in bed. In Bulchru's room, which was large, about 12x25 feet, there were three single beds, two tables and the stove. Above each bed was a calendar with a naked woman smiling through horsy teeth (I would be afraid to wake up underneath someone like that, in case she was a carnivorous man-eating horse). Each bed had two large wool blankets. I took the third bed by the door, furthest from the stove. We took off our clothes facing the wall; they had long underwear and I was wearing my running shorts, which I always wore in case I decided to go running at night. We went to sleep immediately.

Saturday morning, the sun shined in my eyes. This was September, so it had to be later than Five. We had all overslept, and it was 8:00. Breakfast was leftovers from the night before. Since there was no electricity, the food had been stored in a cabinet. The bread was older and drier, but I had bread and tea; everyone else had cheese and meat, also. Bulchru fed the animals, including the cat, crusts of old bread — the dog and horse devoured theirs, but the cat ignored his; I gave him my salami the next night.

I noticed that only I was carrying my pack (duh), so I asked if we were coming back, and was told yes, of course; unfortunately I was told yesterday that we were going to the next hizha, so I fumed about this for a while since my pack had all my clothes and food and weighed somewhere between 40 and 200 pounds. We got on the trail before nine. We were above tree line, at about 2000 meters, although I thought that it was an artifact of grazing, as there were still sheep, cows, horses, and wild pigs everywhere. In fact we walked past the hizha and an old cheese factory (it looked in good condition but abandoned) before going straight up the next mountain. The trail seemed to have been built in 1985, according to the markers. We passed some hikers coming from the next hizha and stopped and talked for a few minutes, short by Bulgarian time, then continued. After four hours of uphill, we stopped for lunch, which was bread, plums, tomatoes, and walnuts.

After a short lunch and rest, two hours, short by Bulgarian time, we hiked for another hour and reached the reservation, Singing Rocks, that I wanted to see. It had a small bear population and perhaps a pack of wolves (5-8). However, Dimitar pointed out that it would be another 6 hours in and back, so we stopped at a dramatic cliff, and look out over it for half an hour, occasionally throwing snowballs at each other (there were pockets of snow, although most of it had melted). We could see most of the Balkan mountains and into Romania from there. It was stark and cool.

There were many crows, so I called to them, "braakk braakk," but they ignored me. Perhaps I pronounced the words wrong, since many American crows would always answer me. There was one hawk circling for mice; the Bulgarian name actually meant mouse-hunter. There were also a few lizards, somewhat like alligator lizards, and a few black beetles.

Going back down, we passed many bronze grasshoppers, very large. Then, there was an entire hillside covered with ants nests. I looked at them closely but could not tell what species. I needed to know these things. The ranger did not know, either. On the opposite hill was a herd of cows. I asked about it and was told that during the summer, herds were turned loose to graze in the mountains, where in fact the cheese and yoghurt factories were located. This had been the way for thousands of years.

We took a longer way back, which involved more up and down climbing, but it was more scenic. Finally we took a ravine back to the original trail. My right leg thigh was aching somewhat and I wondered if I was reaching a physical limit.

We returned by about Seven, just as the sun was setting behind the mountain. Took off our boots and cooled the feet, which was easy on the marble floor. Bulchru had a fire going and had made potato soup. We had the obligatory tea and rakia for an hour, then chopped up food in the dark again. Mostly, the last of the meats, cheese and tomatoes. Bulchru brought out two more loaves of his bread; I hoped he did not run out of food.

He patted me on the head when I asked and said "Calm down."

I thought I might actually be much older than he was, but I was not sure. Dinner was very good, even with old bread. We went to bed as suddenly as the night before. My back ached from the frigging pack (an old military one) — I needed a new pack. Another night under the protective gaze of horse-toothed women (although the size of their other body parts was also quite large and shapely — must have been Playguy centerfolds).

Sunday, we were up at the crack of sunlight, 8:00 a.m. (the mountains altered the actual amount of direct sun). After a leisurely breakfast and discussion of the day, in Bulgarian of course, Dimitar and I walked due west today, up towards Mt. Botev. Ekaterina decided to stay at the hotel and rest, poor youngster.

After a few hours of hiking at high-speed through the treeless vistas, we located a red-book-listed plant, *Teantyava*, which only bloomed every 3-5 years, and had medicinal properties. Dimitar asked me if I wanted some — he said he would look the other way, since it was protected. I said no, I actually felt quite good. There were hawks all over today. Boris pointed out a nesting place for the Imperial eagles, but none were around. There were a few crows. We took turns shrilling for hawks but none answered us.

We hiked to the top of Maragadjik, which was the peak I could see from my new, untouched apartment, and looked down on Aprilci and all the other little villages that seemed to be spread every 15 kilometers. The weather was beautiful. Swifts were flying everywhere. We picked up some trash and carried it. I found a walking stick and used it. We rested and talked for a while. Dimitar grew up in the mountains, which was why he became a ranger, although his university degree was in social work with handicapped children. Dimitar wanted to know why I was here. I said to learn about new animals and meet new people.

Back towards the hotel, we veered to a hizha to arrange for a ride. Dimitar thought someone may drive us back so we did not have to walk for four more hours. We walked into the hizha, which had no water, but had electricity (a perfect complement to the Agrotel), into a large dining room, with about ten people having lunch, including the hikers we had met yesterday. Dimitar motioned me outside; after a few minutes he came out with a large fellow in fatigues, wearing a large hunting knife on his belt. I could not follow the discussion, which I suspected it veered off into other directions about making rakia or finding women. Then three other guys came out, wearing fatigues and Nike running suits parts. This seemed to be a regular dress. They were also wearing either large rubber boots or *maratonki* (running shoes).

While they were talking I looked at the three motorcycles by the wall. They were all three 1950s-era Bulgarian "IX" like old Harleys with low bars and no cowl. One of the guys pointed to a military truck and said that they would leave in an hour.

Dimitar and I walked back and packed our packs. Ekaterina was already ready. Then two women came to visit, followed by an old shepherd. As we were talking, my former landlord rode up on an old motorcycle. We all sat around with rakia and tea.

The truck announced its impending arrival with gasps of exhaust and revs. But only Ekaterina and I climbed in the back—Dimitar had decided to stay. There were already seven people in the open back and three in the front. They had been drinking and three of them could communicate only in shouts. This was only the third time I had seen Bulgarians drunk in public. The most garrulous invited me to live with him. I thanked him anyway. Then he wanted to buy me rakia when we got to town. I deferred until next week. He said something insulting and everyone laughed; Ekaterina said she would translate later. I said, in English, that I too could insult him by calling him a donkey's ass without him knowing it; Ekaterina and I laughed and the Bulgarians looked confused. Ignorance faces both ways, I thought. Then he suggested that I could not understand anything, so I answered in Bulgarian that I could understand many things.

The ride was backbreaking, as the roads were badly eroded and the truck was badly overloaded. We stopped for coffee just outside of town. Ekaterina was very irritated; she seemed more American than me sometimes.

Finally, they dropped us off at the post office and we walked a hundred yards to the apartment. I started to unpack.

Ekaterina said, "I need to take these off and take a shower. Is that okay?"

My eyes widened at the implied invitation, but I coughed and said, "Sure, I'll make tea." I could snort in it later.

Even 5 years ago, I might have offered to help her get clean; instead, I went to investigate the kitchen while she was occupied. When she was finished, I had two cups of tea ready. I gave her my Santana tape to thank her for translating. She was cute and energetic, but she sucked as a translator, as she did not understand English very well. How funny that I needed to explain my English in Bulgarian, so that she would understand me. Oh, well. She left to catch the bus.

Finally I was free to relax. I put on a Ray Charles tape—this apartment had a small stereo and about 30 tapes, 5 of which were American and the rest were Bulgarian music. I did a laundry, but I could not get the machine to do a final spin, so I had to wring the clothes by hand, and hang them outside under the grapevines. With my last remaining 60 *stutinki* I bought a loaf of stale bread—it was so stale I had only one piece for dinner with water. I made the bed and worked on my letters and diary entries. Then made a call to Calpurnia to see if she was having as much fun. She was!

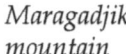

Maragadjik mountain

Finding Animals Or the Fine Art of Waiting

I worked on the computer in the morning, reading the park plan. Angelar came at about 10 and we went over a schedule for the next two weeks. Then we drove to Troyan to pick up the photos for my Park ID, which was what I thought he said that Vulko the landlord was going to do. As we got there, the film machine had just started working, so we walked to a nearby cafe to have a long break and wait. Finally, they were finished. We ate lunch, chicken soup for Angelar and shopska salata for me. I treated, since he drove. Then we waited in the car for a colleague, who did not show up, so Angelar drove me to a bank, where I took out money for the next week's expenses, a warm coat. We drove out of town and saw another Park car and stopped and talked; as we did another park car came by with the colleague, Krasimir, who was the infrastructure chief from Gabrovo.

The three of us drove to Vidima to a garage of the contractor who was supposed to fix the roads. Krasimir and I waited while Angelar drove off to talk to Boleslav about Monday. Finally the contractor drove up in a sporty Citroen, and the four of us drove to the park to inspect the roads, which we did for a few hours. I noticed that the roads were outsloped, but new work had been done to add a drainage ditch (unnecessary I thought) on the inside of the roads. There were no water bars; the culverts did not seem to be put in very well. One of the bridges needed fixing. The three discussed prices, 30 Leva to do the bridge, 40 to do two culverts.

We walked by a hunting blind for bears; it overlooked six feeding troughs, so the bears could be shot safely and easily. I imagined chopping them down later in the week (more realistic than my image of bears shooting hunters as they feasted on sausages at the troughs). No wolf tracks found. Angelar said Boleslav would take me out all day on Monday.

Then we drove back to Aprilci and I worked some more on the computer. Dinner was a strange tasting sausage, which I immediately froze, tomatoes, bread and tea.

On Monday, I took the 5:30 bus to Vidima and waited for Boleslav. He was a no-show, so I walked into the park by myself. It took two hours just to get to the entrance. Then I walked by gravel road for a few hours, then by trail, then along the river, then up to the head wall of the river.

From there I climbed an easy rock face, getting unbalanced several times with the pack and sleeping bag. I could not find the frigging hizha. It was on the map and I had seen it from Maragadjik, a nearby peak last week, but it must had been over another ridge or two.

I saw many birds but no bears or other vertebrates, no evidence either. Before dark I took an hour to have a picnic by another stream, which was coming off a higher peak and just beginning to wear the rock face. I drank the water, having forgotten water, as well as my thick socks. Then I lay out the bag on some good grasses under some beech trees and went to sleep.

The bag was quit warm although my bare head got cold. I did not sleep really well, but the ground was not too hard; the noises were new. I wondered where I was. Not having found Boleslav or the hizha I decided to backtrack to Vidima the next morning. I got up just before light and started back. A few times I get lost around the streams and ridges, but I found the first trail, which was marked by stones regularly. I had some trouble climbing down the rock wall. By the time I got to the trail below my feet had large blisters. I put on a second pair of sox and hiked on. Finally I reached Vidima at 1:30, just in time for the bus I thought. Wrong. First, the owner of a cafe where I bought *portocolo sok* (orange juice) came over to talk, then the retired postmaster, then a woman waiting for the bus; they all wanted to know about America and tell me about themselves, so we talked. The bus would be another hour they said.

Suddenly, it rained heavily and we all scattered to different shelters. At 2:45 I got tired of waiting for the bus and started walking. It took an hour to get to Novo Cello. I immediately went in to Vulko and we talked about my letters, all of which the post office had returned to him for more postage (this was ridiculous — each town charged different postage, so I decided to drop the letters off in Troyan when I went back there). The *lichna carta* (Bulgarian passport) was still not ready, but he would call soon. He has been extraordinary in helping me. Wondered how to pay him back. Then he offered to let me use the internet in the office the next morning.

I went home to do the laundry and soothe my blistered feet; this was the first time for that — odd, I had walked further in the mountains, so must be the gravel.

Just as I started to rest, Boleslav and Angelar came over and asked me where I had been. I said I was in the park, and asked where they were. It turned out that Boleslav expected me at 6:45 not 5:45, so I missed him by 15 minutes, since I waited for 45 minutes. I showed them my work on the Park plan. Boleslav asked me to come again on Thursday at 5:45 on the early bus and he would meet me.

Thursday, I took the early bus to Vidima and Boleslav showed up exactly at 6:00. We drove to the horse barn (a landmark in the Park) and parked the jeep, which he had for the day. After walking up the road he suddenly swerved straight up hill and we struggled in the dark for half an hour until we crossed a trail. It was a game trail for *Elen* (*Cervis elephans*). We followed this across the hill for a while angling up. I found a wallow, which was a good sign (we were examining the elk habitat). We kept going up until we were at the sub-peak below Maragadjik. Boleslav heard a bellow across a valley and we listened for twenty minutes until it was repeated several times; there were elk there.

On the trail we both spotted bear damage to a wild apple tree; some of the limbs were broken and there were small claw marks in the back of the bole of the tree. Boleslav found a hairball from a wolf beside the trail; his eyes were very sharp — I would had missed it. Then he found where a bear had clawed a pine tree, then rubbed against it, leaving hairs in the running sap. I found some dung with berries (probably blueberries). In one of the fields I found rootings from wild pigs, who tear up the grasses to get to the roots or mushrooms. It was a good day for observations. After 11 we started back down. We did not get back to town until 3, then we went to Boleslav's home where he offered me sok. I thought we might have lunch but then he said we needed to leave immediately. We drove to his old retired Bulgarian teacher and I arranged to have him for a tutor, although he said he just wanted to drink rakia. I got Boleslav to drop me off at the apartment, and we compared schedules. He planned to go back to the park from 6 to 8 the same evening, which was a good idea but my blisters were worse, so I begged off.

Then I went to see Vulko, who let me use his email for half an hour, then invited me to dinner. He is the hardest worker I have met. I agreed, although I would rather have rested; so I bought some red wine and chocolates as gifts. I met his wife, son and two daughters. We drank a lot of rakia, then had a dinner of shopska salata, kartofi and kebabche, my favorite Bulgarian dinner. I left at 10.

The Park

February Wolf Survey

The next day, I missed the morning bus to Vidima to my language lesson; I called Boleslav but got no answer; I tried to rent a bike but the shop was closed. Then, I made an appointment with Albert, who was out of the office, for next Tuesday. I called Calpurnia with that news. A nice leisurely morning. I bought bread and supplies (rice, coke, tomatoes, sausage, etc.). Worked on the computer on the Park Plan. But, at noon, Angelar showed up with two foresters, ready to go back to the Park. I put them off for an hour, while I try to reach Calpurnia, then I packed and waited.

We drove to the far eastern edge of the park and most of the way to Hizha Mazatla. We walked the rest of the way and got there at Five. At first we had rakia and cheese. We were the only ones there. Some tourists had just left and no more were expected. Then after an hour, we walked up the mountain to find some *Elen* (large horned elk). It was dark. We stopped every hundred meters to listen. We heard about six of them in the distance and searched for them with binoculars. Clever rascals stayed in the forest cover, bellowing out their territorial claims. Finally we rested in deep grass and watched the sun set and stars rise. After an hour we headed back in the dark, going through rock slides and trails up and down the slopes.

Dinner was the usual sausage, cheese, shopska salad, bread,

and of course vast quantities of rakia. About midnight we headed up to a bunk room. I had the sleeping bag which again was very warm, since the building was unheated. The kitchen had a stove and water; the lights were courtesy of a gas generator outside.

We overslept and did not get up until Seven. A quick breakfast, then we traipsed across the mountains looking for Elen. Good luck today as we saw six of them. In each case we had to sneak up on them from above, on dry leaves and a ground covered with twigs. We shared two pair of binoculars. As we got close to each, they stopped bellowing, and finally walked downhill away from us. It was quite enjoyable, but cold in the shade of the trees. The beech forest was more closed in than I thought, but more open than most Oregon forests. Perhaps because it was old-growth beech; the regeneration looked good only where trees had been cut; I suspected the seed bed was excellent and needed only light to grow,

Going down the hill we stopped at another blind used to hunt bears; we looked everywhere for footprints, but found none (except for a few Elen prints). So, we sat down. I sat right next to bear dung, which I showed to them; the dung was full of berry seeds. I walked around while they smoked and discovered many others. In the forest I found a rubbing tree where bears had clawed above and rubbed away the bark at about 18 inches. No hairs though.

Then we walked down through the forestry units to a large hotel lodge, where we had coffee and waited for Angelar, who showed up with Mikhaila, who was wearing a dress (so I gave her my coat and gloves). We talked for a while, then they left with Mitko, and Georgiu and I waited for them to come back. We checked into the hotel, which was a surprise to me (one in an infinite series it seems).

Mitko came back with the car, and we drove to another part of the park. We hiked uphill, then saw two Elen in an open field. We approached slowly but they bounded off (two young males). We walked to the top of the field and waited by a hunting blind. After an hour, after the sun had set, we had not seen anything else, so we hiked back to the car and drove to the hotel. A fox crossed the road in front of the headlights, looking like a very small coyote.

The next day, we drove out again. The roads were in bad shape; in some places the gullies were 18-20 inches deep and the car had to cross slowly; in others, the mud was 15-20 inches deep and the car slide around but made it through. The roads were even, in or out-sloped; sometimes they were graveled or rocked, but often just mud and twigs — it would be logical to make corduroy roads in some places, since there was plenty of cut wood everywhere. I could not imagine that these would be passable by winter.

We drove by a third harvest that evening. The trees were cut three deep on the upslope of the road, and one deep down slope. This seemed to be a very bad idea, since the roads would erode even faster, and probably collapse on both sides. I could think of no reason to log like this, other than laziness. In one place trees had been taken out in a narrow line about 10 deep; in another, there was a small clearcut of about 3 hectares. From above I noticed that in the past there had been larger clearcuts that had been replanted in Scots Pine, making an odd patchwork with the beech trees. The pines themselves were very close together and had dead branches still attached for the lower 20-30 feet.

In the first harvest, trees had been removed from the riparian of a small river. The second was quite like the third, that was, trees had been removed only from proximity to the roads.

The harvests were done with a cat with a blade and another cat without a blade used as a skidder. It looked like the cats made roads into the trees, which were cut on both sides. The logs were cut to 8-foot lengths and hauled with 2-ton trucks. The largest load I saw had nine 8-foot logs on the back and the springs were flattened by the weight.

Any remaining wood was cut for firewood and hauled out by smaller trucks or by horses, which had primitive wooden and leather harnesses. Two of the horses in the second harvest had raw chests from where the leather had dug in. There was no downed woody debris and the snags also been removed.

This was especially obvious in the park itself, where for the first time I saw many snags and a much downed woody debris. The soil in the parks was also much deeper and richer, but only maybe six inches, compared to two inches or less in the forestry units. By the way, all the forestry decisions were made from Sofia by forest engineers. All the foresters seemed to be forest engineers, whom I suspect, had even less ecology or biology than American foresters.

I had been outlining projects to measure forest productivity between the parks and forestry units. Alas, I had no equipment and had been unable to even locate any.

So, we got back to the hotel and the manager, who was also the owner, cook, and bartender, said that I had to change rooms because the toilet was not working. I agreed and he led me to a suite with a living room and bedroom with two beds and a huge wardrobe. I was worried that it would cost more than the $3,00 quoted, but it did not. Of course the toilet leaked but it flushed; the tank was mounted on the wall up by the ceiling, so when it leaked it dripped on my shoulder and back, as I was sitting on the seat. At least it was filler water and not waste water.

We brought our food to the dining room and Mitko took charge of fixing it. He made two shopska salads. I put out my

peanuts and bread, which the manager toasted in the broiler.
Georgiu and Mitko cut up a salami and a slab of kashkaval cheese.
We drank another two bottles of rakia. We ate until 11:30 at night,
about three hours. The manager sat with us and complained about
his situation and Bulgaria. He asked if I knew Bulgarian and Georgiu
said just a little, which allowed me to hear more honest complaints
I suspect. He went on and on about the business consultants from
New York, who helped him remodel the downstairs into a diskotek.
I asked him in Bulgarian when they did this and why. He responded
automatically, saying that they said business would be good (even
though this hotel was located many miles from the nearest village
and far from any city, although it was by the entrance to the forestry
units, but a good hour drive from the park). It turned out that we
shared the dining room with the local friends of the owner at one
table and a group of Bulgarian girls at another. The girls kept playing
American bubblegum music loudly and the manager kept turning it
down (they used the disco sound system, so it was very loud).

I went to bed late and could not sleep from all the tomatoes
and rakia. At 5:20, Georgiu woke me up to get ready. I went down
stairs in the dark and waited outside. No Georgiu and no Mitko and
no car. Finally I waited inside for half an hour then Georgiu came
down and the car showed up. We picked up another ranger named
Bulchru and drove to a third part of this region of the park — we saw
a small Elen standing by the road. We had been moving west each
day.

We drove for an hour straight up through another part of a
forestry unit having a small (and poor) harvest. Then we walked
straight up the hill along a spine until we got to a sub-peak. The
sun was coming up and illuminating the trees quite dramatically.
I enjoyed the hike since we did not have our full packs for once.
At the crest we observed for three hours, maybe hearing two male
Elen in the distance, although we heard capriols crying up on the
higher slope. I saw an Elen in the field where we were the following
evening. Before noon we drove back, dropping Bulchru off at
the hotel and going to Stokite to drop off Mitko. Then, Georgiu
dropped me off in Aprilci and we made arrangements to meet the
following Thursday in Gabrovo, where I need to pick up some Park
information and use the internet.

Again I slept late (8:10) this October morning. I burned the pizza
badly for lunch, but it was a bad pizza anyway. I called Calpurnia
and told her I would meet her in Sofia on Tuesday morning then
meet with Albert the country director. Then I decided to take the 3
p.m. bus to Sofia today and get to Pazardjik by 9 p.m. to meet her
directly. An impulse of course, since I was just going to work on the

computer plan Monday.

The bus was on time and only paused in Troyan before going on to Sofia; although it was a nice new bus, it was a local, like all of them and stopped three times at every (I mean every) village, once on each side and once in the middle. So it finally arrived at the north station at 7:45. I immediately ran to the Plovdiv buses and one left at 8. It made great time and went by the cut-off to Pazardjik at about 9:10, but I decided not to get off since there was no mileage to the town and I may not have been able to walk twenty kilometers or get a cab (it turned out to be a bad decision since it was only seven kilometers and I could had walked). At Plovdiv, I was dropped off outside a dark, locked bus station — the last bus had left at 9 p.m. I called Calpurnia and she said take a cab. I hailed a cab and asked him how much; when he said $10, I asked him to wait while I called Calpurnia. He said why wait, I could use his phone which I did. We make good time on a deserted highway and back roads to Pazardjik, going over 120 km/hr. I asked him to wait while I got $5 more from Calpurnia, since I only had $5 of my own. He refused but called her and asked her to come out. She refused, not recognizing his voice. I called her afterwards and asked her to come out. It worked out after all and I was only 40 minutes late.

We went back in and compared notes for our projects. Then we compared budgets. Then we compared beds. Then bodies.

Mean Paper Or *Infernal Passports*

Mid-September, the Peas Crops had warned me that I needed an official Bulgarian foreign resident passport. I always woke up when the bank opened at 8:00, not by design, but because the bed was over the bank vault, which opened with a resounding clang. I studied Bulgarian for a while and worked on my bank phrases. I walked downstairs and performed the extensive ritual to get the money to pay the rest of the rent. Then I walked to the police to ask for the *lichna carta* for living in Bulgaria, but I was told to go to Troyan, which was the regional center. I was too tired to face a bus, so I just spent 25 Leva on oil, wine, bread, tomatoes, and other necessities.

That afternoon I walked down to the tourist office. I talked to Vulko, who ran it. I asked if I could use his internet; he showed it to me and described how expensive it was. I offered to pay. Then I asked for the bus schedule, which he had. So, I told him about the passport requirements and he offered to drive me to Troyan, although we had to go to Lovitch first. Svetla, from the Peace Corps office, called back, and I told her about the passport problems; she said that she had called Iurka, at the Park office, who would call the tourist office to get official permission to use the internet in the office—the two offices were linked informally it seems.

More work, then another call from Calpurnia. In the bookcase in the apartment, I found a Tarzan & The Ant Men book in Bulgarian and started to read it. After two sentences I bogged down. Vulko called to say I had to wait until tomorrow.

Up at the clang of dawn, surprise, I had stomach-aches again. I ate a tub of yogurt, then went down to the bus station to wait for Vulko. I found him sitting with his wife at a cafe and sat with them. I thought we were waiting for a car. After fifteen minutes he got up and went to a car across the street, opened it and started it. We got in and left for Lovitch.

At Lovitch, he and I went to the police, who sent us to the passport office, who sent us around to the other side of the building. It took an hour and a half to fill out the frigging forms, then the head rejected the photographs as not being good enough; she also asked for my bank documents, and the rental agreement in Bulgarian—I only had the English version; Vulko had the other at home, but he talked her out of requiring a bank document since I had a bank card.

I treated them to lunch at a small cafe; we had bread, cabbage, and a sausage. Then I followed them as they shopped for a freezer, vacuum cleaner, and toilet paper. We drove to the tourist office in Troyan, where Vulko had business with the head of that office. We walked to the phone office to change over the phone records; after an hour of forms and arguments, the head refused to change it over, possibly because I was an unknown quantity. I asked them to call PC office. They did, but nothing was resolved. Vulko tore up the forms in anger; we thanked the head and left. I asked if that would be a problem; he thought not, but the waiting list for a new phone was three years, and he didn't want to risk losing their phone, which they paid for even when the apartment was empty.

They dropped me off at 4:30 and I had dinner—bread and tomatoes! With cola and peanuts. Then Boleslav and another ranger came to visit just as I was getting ready to call Angelar with a monthly schedule.

Three weeks later, when Calpurnia visited me for the first time, I had to go get my lichna carta or risk being fined for not having it. It had been finished in mid-September after the marathon of changes the chief requested. I had gone by bus once in later September to pick it up, but no one knew where it was. Calpurnia and I took the 8 a.m. bus to Troyan and the 9 a.m. bus to Lovitch. We walked to the police station annex and were escorted right into the office; the chief asked a subordinate to go get the card, which she did; the subordinate asked if I was a tourist and the chief said no, a volunteer. I signed the card. As we were waiting, however, Calpurnia and I talked in English about the house plant on the floor; the chief asked where Calpurnia worked and could she see Calpurnia's card, which Calpurnia gave her. The chief commented in perfect English (for the first time in that language): "Oh, my sister lives in Pazardjik." I created a mental image of her strangled body being eaten by ants. Before dismissing us, she told us that we had to renew our cards in Aprilci next year.

We walked to the internet cafe and worked on email. Then took the 3 p.m. bus to Troyan, got some food in Troyan (bread and yogurt), and took the 5 p.m. bus to Aprilci. Fortunately, we crammed on the bus in the first ten people; the bus filled to standing room only. By the third stop, people were refused entrance because there was no room at all. It was the most crowded bus we had been on. It was also old and creaked with the strain. It was dark for the entire trip and the landscape looked bleak and wintry. At home we had mushroom soup and fresh bread.

Stranger Rangers Or Ski Lift to Heaven

Angelar picked me up at 6:30, with three other rangers, and we headed to Karlovo for the ranger training conference. It was a two-hour drive, even though it was three and a half hours by bus; this was nice to know. One of the rangers, Tsonko, was sick (my former landlord in fact) and we had to stop twice on the way. Once there, we waited for 20 minutes until the ski-lift opened. The ski lift snaked to the top of the park on the southern edge. It was open and I froze on the way up. The vegetation was interesting. The rangers had paired rapidly, so I ended up sitting next to Tsonko, who vomited over the side regularly. I suspected that rakia was implicated, but said nothing.

At the hizha, about forty rangers were already there to meet with Iurka and the staff. Five rangers were brand new. Iurka talked for an hour and introduced me and the new rangers to the staff. Then we divided up into groups for the day; we were each given three questions to answer. Each question had to do with the activities of tourists and the laws of the park. I worked with three guys from our region of the park.

Dinners and lunches were huge, although as a vegetarian again, I only got cheese and tomatoes, although for lunch I had fried kashkaval, which was much like fried brie, greasy but tasty. I tried to buy coffee for the rangers but ended up having them buy me tea. The dinners were prepaid, but the drinks had to be purchased individually. At dinner, Bulchru and Boleslav had each brought two bottle of rakia. Our region sat together, eight of us at the table, which already had sixteen beer, one bottle of white wine (which I drank),

71

two bottles of commercial rakia (which no one touched), and six
bottles of very cheap soda (called Comfort, which no one drank — the
colors were very artificial and it was oversweetened and ghastly,
worse than the ubiquitous Joker Cola). We talked about the Park
Plan, or rather that was all I heard or understood.

The meeting was over; the staff collected the plans during
breakfast. Afterwards, we met outside then took the ski lift down,
then walked to the cars, then drove back. The rangers dropped me
off first at about 1:30.

I made dinner, which was stuffed red peppers, from the
landlord's garden. I learned how to burn off the outer skin by
putting them right on the stove burners (since then I have seen them
roasting on open fires or being fired with a blowtorch). I finally
bought a warm, waterproof (sort-of) coat for the mountains. It was
an authentic pilot's jacket "Made in Amerca," wherever that was. I
started to fix the porch doors off the living room and bedroom.

The next day, I took the 6:30 bus to Vidima to meet Boleslav. From
there we walked into the park. We reached the far western edge of
his region in only four hours. Just as we were about to enter the park,
we passed an active harvest in the forestry unit below the park. They
had set up a high-line (or skyline) logging system. The bottom cable
was wrapped around a large tree which was buried and covered
with boulders. The top end was tied to a large beech tree at the ridge.
The logs, which were only in eight-foot lengths were brought down
over a stream and dropped on the road, a fact that was obvious as
we had to walk around it uphill, carefully watching to make sure
a log was not flying down. The cut area went directly uphill and
seemed to be about sixty feet wide. As we walked up the hill, we
passed three more sites done with this kind of logging; each had a
sixty-foot lane directly up the hill (a perfect invitation to erosion into
the stream, which seemed okay so far this year).

Later, from a peak, we were able to look down on a hybrid
harvest. The right hand half was done with cable; the left hand half
had roads running directly up the hill. It was about twice as wide
and had a few damaged trees remaining in the zone; the tracks were
starting to erode and there were mud plains below.

Going back down I found a bear tree, again with claw marks
about five feet above the ground and light coarse hairs in the sap.
Not to be outdone Boleslav found one that has marks about seven
feet off the ground. Two different bears we guessed.

There were many footprints from Elen and a few rootings
by the wild swine (*dev svinska*). Boleslav found a wolf track — our
first — on the road below an old syrene-making house. We followed
the track which swerved to investigate two puddles with many Elen

tracks in and around it. There were two wolves, one much smaller. The larger track was my-index-finger-wide and long. We lost the trail in the dry grasses.

We were early and so took a short break on the hill in the grasses. Boleslav smoked while I lay down and dozed in the very warm October sun. A honey bee visited the clover around my head, quietly gathering but then buzzing madly to get to the next blossom (must be heavy with sugar). I noticed Boleslav was sleeping, but then we both got up as there was a crash from the beeches below us. Maybe a tree falling or a bear tripping.

We walked down the hill. Boleslav mentioned casually that Angelar would be waiting for us at the harvest area. It only took an hour and a half to go back down hill. Angelar drove us back to town about Four. I said that I really wanted to stay at Hizha Pleven and suggested that I walk there alone tomorrow. After a long conversation, Angelar said he would pick us up and drive us near the hizha.

I fixed left-over lasagna, then ate every cookie and bit of ice cream I could find. Listened to music, then called Calpurnia to see how she was doing, and went to bed early.

Immortal Buses of the Balkans

There were really a lot of buses everywhere. Most of them were Chavdars, made in Bulgaria from the 1930s to the 1970s I suspected. The new ones all seemed to be from Germany. At first, I was concerned about riding the Chavdars, which always seemed rickety and dirty, perhaps from the goats and ducks riding with us. But, now I believed that these buses were close to being immortal. Let me offer a few examples.

Calpurnia and I had decided to visit another volunteer in her town, but Cali was reluctant to travel alone, so I offered to go with her. The traveling began as I caught the 5:40 bus to Troyan; that cost 1.7 Leva. At Troyan I had to piss and there was no toilet at the station. Across the street fortunately was a nice cafe with great toilets, so I pissed and then bought water for the trip. The bus to Plovdiv cost 5.5 Leva and was old and rickety. It drove straight up the mountain for an hour then straight down, then rambled through Karlovo and other towns to Plovdiv, where I get my first surprise: No buses went south east or west from that station, which was the North Station. I was told to take another local bus to the South Station. Instead I went across the street to the Train station, but the same situation held there. So, I took a taxi for two Leva to the other station, which was newer but smaller. I bought a ticket for Pazardjik. While waiting I saw Mina so we talked for half an hour while waiting. Then a group of eight Mormons spotted us and buttonholed us with questions (the Italian word is "attaccabutonne").

At Pazardzhik, I called Calpurnia but got no answer; I called her office but got no answer. I walked around but lost my phone book with my numbers. I searched but had no luck. I called the number that I remembered and Calpurnia answered. We met in a nice square at 2:00 p.m. (the trip had been almost eight hours) and went back to her office and talked about the World Bank project.

The secretary told Calpurnia her mother called. No one else seemed to be working so we left so she could call from a public phone, which she did. Then we had a pizza and salad, sharing both — the salad had fresh corn in it, with tomatoes and cucumbers. We worked at the internet for a few hours, then went back to her apartment to pack for the trip.

The first time I saw it, I was surprised by the sad condition of the building: broken windows blind to the trash scattered around. Although many of the individual apartments were quite luxurious, the common areas of the building, including the roof, walls, entrance way, and grounds, were quite decayed. People owned their apartments, but I never understood who owned the building itself. I wondered if there was a committee, or maybe just no common money, but no one could say. The entrance was dark, because all the light bulbs were broken. It was cool, because the door was missing and some of the windows were broken. The elevator was making working noises, but we walked up one flight to her apartment. There was a bed, sofa, bookcase, and kitchen table with a chair. There was a miniature refrigerator and a similar stove with two burners. There were no blinds or curtains on the windows, which were cracked but unbroken.

I was packed but she packed a bag while I watched the Olympics. We had decided to visit another volunteer for her birthday. Calpurnia's apartment was plainer but larger. I slept on the comfortable couch.

One Immortal Bus

The next morning we left at Six and it was still dark, taking a taxi for two Leva to the train station at the edge of town. We bought tickets for Pleven through Sofia. The first train was first class and we had comfortable assigned seats for 1.5 hours. At Sofia we raced downstairs to see which track the next train was on, then raced back upstairs to catch the train which left after only ten minutes. After three hours, the first two standing by the window, because the train was crowded and there were no assigned seats, the last hour in a second class compartment with six others, we arrived. We walked across the street to the bus station and bought tickets to Iskra. There was no bus at the sector so we asked inside; she said sector 2, then we saw an information kiosk and it indicated sector 10 and indicated that it left in one minute so we raced over and got on. Fortunately the kiosk was right.

We were dropped off in a tiny town of 500 (the trip had taken over six hours by cab, train, bus, and walking). We went to the cafe to call Chris. No answer. The waitress asked who we were calling; we said the American; she got excited and walked me to the house, where I met the host family, who said that Chris had gone to meet us at Pleven at 2:00 p.m. So, we went to a cafe and had kartofi and a sausage; as we were finishing, Chris and George got off the 2 o'clock bus and came over. We went to her house, which was even more beautiful than any so far. Alta would be late, but Chris showed us the liquor supply so we started with rum and cokes.

Then Alta called to say that she had missed the last bus. We told her to come by cab and George would pay. She came by cab for thirty Leva. Calpurnia, Chris and Alta had become best friends over the summer; only in the last two weeks did I join them for the occasional melba or drink—they were an antisocial club trying to avoid the mainstream cliques. So the three of them talked and George and I talked; he and I were on a team together in July to practice Bulgarian by trying to locate things in Dupnitsa.

The evening progressed and we had bread and cheese. I stayed with rum, Calpurnia transferred to coke and the others started on whiskey. Chris opened her birthday gifts: Flowers from George, tortellini from me, a vase from Calpurnia, and jewelry from Alta.

Being the oldest, I faded first and went to bed about 11 on the sofa on the upstairs den. I heard the next morning that George slept on the kitchen couch, Calpurnia in the guest bedroom, and Alta and Chris on the king-size bed in Chris's room. Everyone overslept. We looked for food but nothing was open, so we went back to the house and had bread.

Time to go to the Park office again. Calpurnia and I left on the bus to Sevlievo and Gabrovo. It was snowing lightly and the buses were late. After missing the private bus in Sevlievo, we took the public bus to Gabrovo and got in around eleven, after visiting the many small villages between these two points twenty-three miles apart. I kept meaning to take a picture of the buses themselves.

All of them were old Chavdars, built here in Bulgaria. Aleksander mentioned that eleven years ago the bus service was fabulous, with many buses going to all cities and villages. Now, private buses went between the large cities (100,000 to 1 million), but state buses mostly connected the villages. The countryside was littered with old rusting bus shelters that were no longer used. The state buses had reduced service drastically but still went many places at least once a day (often at 5-6 a.m.). The buses were old but still ran.

Many were being fixed up; on the run to Sevlievo the bus had new seat covers — half were Playboy bunnies and the rest were Lion's Bank. The bus drivers decorated their buses with their choice of posters, calendars and decals. For instance, one bus to Troyan had Castrol, Shell and other decals all over the front windows. Another bus to the same town had the driver's window shades decorated with calendars of bare-breasted women — in fact, over half the buses preferred this motif. One bus to Plovdiv had blown-up photos of the driver sitting in front of his bus, with a smaller photo of his family. Another bus had a poster of the Tsar and one of the old President, Stoyanov — I hope he did not meet the driver with the poster of the new President, Purvanov.

These buses mostly carried old men and women who had bags of grain, old suitcases or backpacks, and assorted farm animals, mostly ducks or chickens. Many people carried large cheap woven-plastic bags called "baba bags." I had heard that one reason was to disguise what they were carrying; everyone carried these bags, so people seemed anonymous. Since the communist state forbad people to travel without permission or to leave the state, people used these bags as travel suitcases also.

Many people who worked in neighboring towns took the buses because the companies bought large blocks of tickets for them. Some students also took buses, but many students had cars now; as in the US, students seemed to have more money and things than their parents and ordinary laborers. In fact, the strangest dislocation I had was when a cell phone rang on the bus and nine different people reached for their phones; when getting near the bus stations they called their friends to meet them (cell phones cost about the same as the Russian Ladas you saw everywhere). Most regular phone service depended on the original phone equipment from the 1920s.

We decided to take the bus to Troyan to get food. The bus was late, because it was snowing again. But, this bus was newer (built after 1950 I think) and heated — this was only the third heated bus we had been on in eighteen months. It was a joy. The trip was slow, because the road was one-lane much of the way. Coming down the hill before Oreshak, we stopped behind some cars. A large double-length truck was stuck coming up the hill. A farm tractor had tried unsuccessfully to pull him. As we waited another larger farm tractor, with a snow-plow blade, took over the cable and started to pull. For a while nothing happened, then the truck started to move slowly. Surprisingly they both made it around the bus. As we went down the hill into the village, there were two more large trucks by the side of the road with cables attached to the front, apparently waiting their turns to be pulled over the hill.

In Troyan, we got off at a new gas station to look at the food in the gas shop; it was all pretzels and cookies, many were Danish. Then we walked to the Elma factory store, but it was almost bare, although it had a good selection of Russian and Bulgarian vodka. The public could shop in these stores. Most of the big factories had their own stores; usually these specialized in something, such as clothing or meat. We bought a few things and then took the bus back.

Going back, we had the old, unheated Chavdar bus, and there was standing room only as people were returning to Aprilci from the Balkanpharma and Elma factories. Many of these people were wearing old clothes (the kind of things I wore on the farm to clean out the stable every morning). But, a few of the women had large fur coats. One man had a suit, and a couple more were wearing the new Bulgarian costume, an adidas running suit and running shoes. Most women dyed their hair. If they were blonde, they dyed it black, if it was grey or white they dyed it red or black — the only problem was that the roots always showed through, kind of defeating the purpose I guess. There was only one blonde on the bus, and she had a short French-style haircut. The bus stopped at every village and a few places in between. The normal one-hour trip took two.

At home, we had leftover chicken and rice. It was pretty good. Then Calpurnia read Jules Verne and I read an old Vonnegut, *Cat's Cradle*. We were coughing worse now, but the bed was heaped with wool and cotton blankets and very warm. I took it apart and put the futon frame on the splints, and on the futon frame layers of cardboard; then on top of that was the thin layer of foam. For the first six months in Bulgaria I slept on the floor; for the past year on this thin foam. I saw a single mattress in the hardware store, but could not bring myself to buy it.

For the wolf surveys, I often took the 5:30 a.m. bus from Aprilci to Vidima, and from there I could walk to the national park. Most of the buses were unheated. One snowing morning, as I sat in the back, the back door fell off. The driver heard it and stopped. Me and another man helped him prop it back on. Nothing he did however could fasten it in place, so he called me and the other man over and asked us to hold the door as he drove. We did that swapping turns at the freezing end. When people tried to board, we waved them to the front. Vidima was the end of the line for the local, so when I left, we propped it on the floor inside. A few days later, when I took this bus, it had been reinstalled successfully.

Once, we stayed late at a service conference. Finally we went to catch the 4 o'clock bus. We actually get a fast local bus and got to the bus station for the Number 3 bus. Then we spend an hour at the internet in Sevlievo. For the 5:30 bus to Aprilci, we had to wait for it to get diesel fuel. He arrived without a label, but we recognized the driver and got on. The trip seemed too quiet, but at the third stop, black smoke billowed from the engine. So, the driver got on his large gloves and opened the door to work on it. Flames shot out and the smoke got thinner; maybe it was a gas line problem. I could not see through the crowd of advisors. The driver worked for half an hour. Some people watched from the bus; others went to a cafe; the locals come over and offered advice. But, then the smoke stopped, the driver restarted the engine, and we went through to Aprilci.

Holiday of the Week

A month later was a Bulgarian holiday, and I had told Calpurnia that I would help with her apartment problems. The bus at 5:45 said Sofia on it so I decided to go to Sofia rather than Plovdiv to get to Pazardzhik. It turned out to be a local so I did not get to Sofia until almost 11 o'clock. There were no buses going to Pazardjik from the north station; rather than travel to the south *aftogara*, I decided to take the train, which was across the street. I bought a ticket for the next train which was at 1:00 p.m., then shopped for supplies in the bazaar.

I got on the wrong train! It was going on the north tracks to Varna and not to Pazardjik and Plovdiv on the south tracks. The south train was the one directly behind this one (like I would know). The conductor suggested I get off at the next stop, which I did. Alas the next train back to Sofia was not for three hours, so I found the bus station; there was a bus in one and a half hours, so I walked around the town to wait. The bus took me to a local stop and dropped me off—I asked the driver where was the north station. He told me and I walked for twenty minutes to find it; it had no connections by bus or train, so I started walking to the downtown. After about six blocks I decided to take a cab to the Main train station (this cost 2 Leva). Then I had four minutes to find the next Pazardjik train, which I did; the conductor asked me to buy a ticket change but I said there was no time, and he motioned me on. I found an empty compartment and waited. I had to pay a two Leva fine for missing the first train, but at least I was on my way. At Pazardjik, I get a cab to the bus station.

For some odd reason, there were no connections between the bus stations in Sofia or Plovdiv; the north stations handle north traffic and the south stations the south traffic, and one has to use cabs or trams or buses to get between the stations. This was both difficult and annoying.

On the way to Calpurnia's apartment I called her then picked up tomatoes and vegetables for dinner.

Daily Bread Or the Will to Live Better

I looked around the town, which had many small shops. For Sunday dinner I cooked rice with tomatoes and Uncle Ben's Curry. It was quite good, with bread and wine. I left at noon to catch the bus to Plovdiv then to Karlovo, a new route, then to Troyan and back to Aprilci by 6 p.m.

Monday was a computer day, although I watched the Olympics a little on the old television; it was not able to pick up color signals, apparently. That night I called Calpurnia about our proposed joint projects.

Waiting for the park to arrange a survey, I worked on the park plans, writing, editing, and generally scribbling. Every night I fixed rice with curry and tomatoes, an excellent dish that I planned to eat every day. I worked on the park plan, did a laundry, and sat outside after hanging the laundry; the river burbled along under my balcony.

In fact, I had nothing to do but work on the park plan and on my plans for the projects for the next two years. I walked out for bread (a daily thing now, since it only costs $0.19 for a fresh loaf), to supplement the fresh tomatoes, then got back to work. Since I was in Aprilci for the day I walked a few miles to Zora the neighboring village, saying hello to every baba sitting on her bench. I passed a sawmill and a few restaurants and stores.

Over the days that passed I measured every experience, it seemed, by the freshness, availability, or the kinds of breads. I usually bought the small round loaf; there was a large round loaf, a long loaf, and a square loaf. Later, I found that each village had its own bakery. The bakery for Novo Celo, my village in the four-villaged Aprilci, was behind the police station. Each village made different kinds of bread. Since I came to prefer Novo Celo bread, I rarely bought bread at the other villages.

The bakers kept bankers hours, so to speak, so the first Christmas, we got caught without bread at all. Our neighbor said the bakery would not open for another four days. She said they were closed for every holiday, so you had to buy enough to last. I suppose that explained why there were crates of bread behind the counter, in front of the counter and on the steps. So, for Christmas day I made sweet breads, juice and tea; Calpurnia made coffee. We lay around and read, then had *persiani kartofi* for lunch again, using five potatoes. For dinner, I made soup and crackers, with pumpkin bread for dessert.

A few days later, we ran out of money. It seemed the bankers kept bakers hours and were closed for a week. We had bread for food. I made chocolate chip cookies, after spending our last Leva on flour, *testa* (which was dough for bread or *mekitsas* and only cost 30 stotinki), and coca cola.

Later, I baked apricot bread. I had tried to make regular bread, but it was hard and heavy as a rock, so I went back to my dependency on the local bakery breads. Shopping was an adventure in Novo Celo, because you never knew what was going to be in the stores (besides cabbage, potatoes, and bread). For instance, on my list was Spanish chocolate cookies, English granola, forest fruits juice, oatmeal, toilet paper, cheese, potato chips, light bulbs, celery, potatoes, apples, and chocolate. The Spanish cookies could not be found. In fact, my theory was that the Bulgarian food stuffs industry was based on opportunism or hijacking—some things came into the small mini markets (I call them all that now since most were less than 100 square feet in area) in large quantities, never to be seen again, such as the Spanish cookies, which were little fruit wheels coated in chocolate. Others, such as celery, maple syrup, granola, milk, or foreign cheeses, never showed up at all. I recently discovered that celery was grown for the leaves in gardens and the stalks were given to animals; this was true of corn also, which was grown exclusively for pigs (with one exception, usually in August, when an occasional vendor would sell corn on the cob, which was tough and tasted like pig food).

Ruffles potato chips, from Germany, made an appearance in August in every store, but vanished in September and never reappeared. The English granola, Harrison's, appeared in Sofia as a promotion last spring, but apparently never made it into production, or at least was ever sent here. The forest fruits juice was sold in large cities, like Pleven or Sofia, only, so I bought the local version, which was heavy on sugar and water. Light bulbs could be purchased, but you had to have the vendor at the bazaar try them each before buying—even then one out of two did not last out a day. The chocolates were mostly very good here; sometimes you could get Swiss chocolates; the Bulgarian chocolates had all been bought out by Kraft or Nestle; the Irish chocolates were only half the price as the Bulgarian, but were too sugary. The apples and potatoes were all local; sometimes, different varieties could come from Turkey or New

Zealand. I loaded everything in my old backpack, called a rucksack here, and carried it home. I was able to buy the last bottle of diet coke in town — I think it was ordered only for me and perhaps one person from Sofia who visited every third weekend, but she or he was only a theoretical presence at best.

At home, I made sandwiches for lunch. As usual, it took an hour to prepare, as everything had to be made from scratch. The bread must be cut, the cheese and tomatoes must be sliced, the soup must be assembled. I never had missed TV dinners, but I sure missed deli foods that were pre-sliced or prepared.

After lunch, I made more web pages for the city web site — I had almost 200 files for the site now. Then we went to Svetla's house to take more photos for her web page. Everything went fine, Calpurnia had the new camera for the Tourist Bureau, and I had the old Canon, but then Svetla did not stand still for her portrait photo, so we had her looking left, looking at her feet, moving her head — I thought we would use the working photos instead. She gave us tea and cookies and we talked about her correspondence with a man in Atlanta — he sent her photos of a swamp, cayman, and tropical garden. They looked like internet downloads.

Vegetable Stand

Among the Rangers Or *Waiting for Petko*
Friday the 13th of October. Wondered if anything good or bad would happen, remembering 1968 and 1972. Angelar was a little late but picked me up about 7:30 then we drove to Vidima to pick up Boleslav and Milko. The trip to the hizha ended at a dead end road with a small water-driven power plant. There were other vehicles there.

Each with a pack containing mostly food and a change of clothes, we hiked straight up the hill, going again right up the ridge towards the Botev peak. After an hour and a half we swerved west and went across the ridges, until we reached the hizha just before Eleven. The hizha was very large, the second largest so far. Most windows were south facing, which made for good views and good sun. We went around back to a large bar and restaurant; we had the usual: cokes and coffee (well, I had herb tea, *bilko chai*) and talked for an hour with the barmaid and her husband, who both wandered off regularly to cut wood or sweep floors. I borrowed the telescope and spent half an hour looking at the ridges for signs of movement but I suspected that all the animals were resting for the day.

Finally, they asked me if I wished to have lunch at this table or that table. I had trouble understanding the difference and tried to say that but then it became obvious that the table was outside in the sun down the hill from the hizha, so we took the packs and left without good-byes. The table had a good view of where Boleslav and I were hiking the day before. We each had a loaf of bread but I had cheese. Milko had mayo and catsup. Boleslav had sladko (sweet preserves from peach I think). We played with the dogs, a collie named Lassie and a German Shepherd named Rex.

We walked back down the direct way and got to the power station about Two. It was still a two-hour hike to town but we took a break with the people picnicking there and Milko tried to get a ride, unsuccessfully. We walked for an hour down the road to the main power station. Boleslav and I went inside and look at the generators; the three make 4500 watts from water power from the small stream. They were Swiss and were installed in 1946, but were beautiful and functional. Then after negotiating with another group unsuccessfully, we walked all the way to Vidima, where I caught the bus to Novo Cello and got back about 5:30. Dinner was lasagna again and crackers.

The next day, I worked on the park strategic plan to prepare for a meeting with Georgiu and Iurka. I read the entire vertebrate plan and parts of the flora plan, which was much better developed and longer. I could not find the data for the fauna plan, only one table. I did a laundry and made peanut butter sandwiches for dinner, risking the dreaded bread poisoning from eating too much fresh Bulgarian bread. Call Calpurnia about schedule.

A Decent Proposal

Calpurnia and Chris were visiting Saturday. Everyone slept late (after 10). Then we explored Aprilci and visited the local monastery, which was a nunnery that only had one nun left. She gave us a tour of the cirque. I lighted my usual candles for the beloved dead, but was told that in Bulgaria candles for the dead must go on the floor rather than the large stands, which were for the living. I declined to move them since they were living in my heart.

For dinner I made eggplant lasagna, but forgot the mushrooms. It was surprisingly good, even without the proper spices or ricotta cheese (I had used creamed *syrene* and eggs in its place). Calpurnia retuned the television and it received CNN. What a shock. I thought only two stations came in.

In the morning, Christine left at 5:30. Calpurnia and I cooked oatmeal for breakfast, then prepared letters for my landlord. Later that afternoon, we delivered the letters with my rent, but he was there and invited us in for coffee and a long talk (his sister had recently died and he looked haggard). Dinner was a mishmash of leftovers with a fine Bulgarian white wine.

The next morning, at 5:30, we caught the buses to Pazardjik and that trip went well. We got there before noon and went to Calpurnia's apartment, where there was still no heater after six weeks. We went to her office and talked to her counterpart, who explained that the city had problems. We arranged an appointment for me to meet with Tereza, Sonia, and Antonia on Tuesday about a new joint project. I worked at the internet cafe the rest of the day; this new cafe was in the basement of a bakery, so when I was finished I had a piece of chocolate mousse torte, which was light and way way too sweet.

I met Calpurnia at the reception area at City Hall, where she worked; we shopped for food, mostly fresh bread and spices. She helped me make fried chicken, which was a first. It was undercooked, but the mashed potatoes were excellent (especially since I tried to fry them first).

For the meeting Tuesday, no one was there in the meeting room. We found Albert first, then Sonia came in. I presented my ideas to her (I had worked to put them in order and had brought a resume), but she seemed uninterested. Tereza had suddenly gone to a meeting in another city. Then, Antonia came in—she had actually quit and started her new job in Sofia, but was writing the job description for her replacement this week. I repeated the discussion to similar effect. It was quite depressing. I could not decide whether they did not have a clue as to what I was talking about, did not care, or were unconcerned with my qualifications or what I would do. I suspected that I would not be working on any projects in this city; that meant that Calpurnia might be working with me on my projects in Aprilci.

Sonia said that the heater would be delivered to Calpurnia immediately. It was not. Calpurnia and I went to the Internet cafe and worked for a few hours then walked back to meet with Tereza, who did not show up.

We went back to her apartment and I made fresh bread pizza, with a Bulgarian sausage, which was quite good. We had ice cream, a real treat, for dessert.

At a restaurant in Pazardjik, as we were dancing, we were discussing our projects, how promising mine were and how frustrating hers were. I suggested that we start new ones in my area. She said that she doubted that the PC would let her change sites to be in the same city as another volunteer. I pointed out that she was already in a city with two other volunteers, and besides the PC was trying to emphasize small villages above large cities (where the volunteers tended to live like celebrities, with large houses and fine things). She indicated that she may leave if things got worse.

They did get worse. After a disappointing World Bank project meeting, we went to our favorite restaurant to eat and dance. During the first dance (I had asked the DJ at the disco for a slow one), I asked her to *marry me* and move to my village (well, how many times has *that* phrase been used in ten thousand years?). I gave her one of the fifty-cent rings from the bus station. Her only response was a hug that broke three of my ribs. Then while we were talking about it, not just as a romantic proposition, but as a business merger, I suggested that we could expand my carnivore projects to the entire country, not only working but also getting to travel across the country. She said her dream was to retire and travel; I said my dream was to have an assistant—her only response was to playfully punch my arm, causing a massive hematoma. We talked about how we could pitch this development to the PC.

The Secretary Wears a Gun Or Office Work is Dangerous

The next day, I left for Aprilci by bus. On the bus I ate all the peanuts and chocolate I had stored for the trip. Then, after the five-hour ride, I was back. I called the PC office to discuss projects with Svetla and Pentcho. At home I did a laundry, then had peanut butter sandwiches for dinner (first in five months—the peanut butter however was a cheap American brand). Then I called Angelar and Boleslav to set up wildlife surveys.

The next days and weekend were spent tracking animals in the park, mostly with rangers, sometimes alone, which was easier, since I could sit and observe without a schedule deadline or smoke break.

Soon, it was time to do some work at the main office. I got up before Six to try to catch the first bus to Troyan, but decided to take the 6:45 bus, and then went to Gabrovo from Troyan. At the bus stop I asked a baba if there was a bus directly to Gabrovo. She said no, that I had to go through Sevlievo. I wondered but then Bulchru, a ranger came up to catch the same bus to Troyan; he told me that I had to go through Sevlievo to get to Gabrovo, but said that the next bus there was at 8:30 so I went home and puttered around until 8:15.

The bus was on time and I went to Sevlievo. As soon as I get off there was a van to Gabrovo but it was full. So, I waited for the large public bus, which turned out to be new. So, I rode to Gabrovo and got there about 11:15. I called Filip at the Park Office, but the phones were not working, so I walked around the city and looked at things. At noon I had a small lunch of salad and fries. Then I tried calling the Park; someone answered then went away mysteriously and I watched my phone card subtract paid pulses for nine minutes before hanging up. I called the Open Society but Kim was not there. I called their apartment and they were there, so I walked there just in time for a nicer lunch of salad and bread with Filip and Kim.

We talked for an hour then they had to go on errands for their new secondary project. They walked me to the proper bus stop and I took the number Four bus to the edge of town and the Park office. I walked up to the third floor and went in to the Director's office. The Secretary was standing next to a desk in combat fatigues and wearing a gun. I asked to speak with the Director. She said the Director was busy. I asked about Georgiu and she suggested I wait in front of his office, to which she directed me. I wondered if the danger was greater in the office, since the rangers I worked with did not wear guns. Had my Bulgarian been better I might have asked. As I was waiting I noticed another blonde woman walk by on an errand. She was also wearing a gun with her camouflage suit (I later learned the office people got equipment first). I waited for half an hour, then I met with Petya and Georgiu. Krasimir was there so we talked (he was the infrastructure engineer for roads). Finally I talked with Nikolai, who was the GIS expert (but the computers were broken and the data was bad so we only talked for a while). Then I worked on the old plan in Kim's office for a few hours. I found copies of the plan in English buried in her bookcase.

At 4:45 I caught the bus back to the center and walked to the apartment. We sat there and talked for two hours waiting for the water maid to read the meter. She did not show up, so we went to the variety show across the street in the theater at Seven. The show traveled across Bulgaria, with songs and skits. The songs were sort of imitation Italian French and American rock (going back to Miami by a singer wearing a Riki Martin costume). The skits, however, were pure Bulgarian, making fun of Bulgarian and US friendship, as well as Bulgarian and USSR graduations and schools. I understood some of them. After Nine, after sitting on the steps because the seats were all taken, we left to find a restaurant. We went to their favorite and had chicken shiskabobs and fries. Not bad. Then we went back and talked before going to bed. I slept in their old sleeping bag on the couch. Not bad. Their apartment was on the 16th floor and had a good view of the river and park (and of the local dog pack, which was quite loud). The building had been designed by an East German architect; it was not the usual blok, but star-shaped with balconies looking in every direction.

Looking for Productive Work

Filip assembled a mighty breakfast; I had yogurt and orange juice.
We talked until almost 10 then left for the bus station. My bus was
scheduled to leave at 10:30—there was only one of course. I tried
to buy the ticket but was told I could not buy it until the seats were
counted after the bus got here. Outside there was a man asking for
people who wanted to go to Plovdiv. I asked him how much it cost;
he said eight Leva, which was the same as the bus ticket. Filip asked
what kind of car or van it was; he said it was a taxi, but he must
have three people to pay to go. Filip asked how many he had; two
he said, so I agreed. We loaded up then and I put my bag in the back.
Two women sat in the back. The car was tiny, a Japanese import that
could only hold four people with half a bag apiece. We made good
time to Plovdiv, getting there in less than two hours. As we got into
town the cabbie asked us where we wanted to be left off, the north
bus station or center. I said south bus station. One of the women
got out at an apartment building. Then the other woman asked, in
perfect English, if I was Canadian or English. I said American. She
said she had lived in Seattle for a long time. So we talked for the last
mile. She was an opera singer. We exchanged cards.

At the bus station I had a mekitsa, a giant fried donut, which
was delicious, then got the bus for *Pazardjik*. I called Calpurnia, who
agreed to meet me at her apartment. She went back to work and I
went to the internet cafe to catch up on email. The PC delivered her
heater (from Svetla's desk). I bought tomatoes and bread for dinner.
But we decided to have salad. Calpurnia was sick and went to bed
early.

Calpurnia had been frustrated by her work on the World
Bank project for the City. I never heard from Tereza or anyone about
my proposals. We decided to move to Aprilci to see if she could work
on projects there, either park or tourism projects.

We packed for an hour then went to buy a coat for Calpurnia.
We raced to the bus to catch the 11 o'clock to Plovdiv but it was full,
so we got tickets to the noon bus. We crowded on to the noon bus, in
the first ten people. The crowds in Bulgaria were lineless and chaotic.
You simply pressed forward and fought your way to the door,
pushing aside old ladies and businessmen (often the most ruthless).
At Plovdiv, we got two mekitsas and took a cab to the north station.
Once there we found that the 1:30 bus, that I had taken before, had
been canceled and replaced by a bus at Three. I was worried that the
bus would not meet the connection at Six in Troyan.

Outside the station was the cab driver who had driven me
from Gabrovo; he was soliciting rides. We asked how much to
Troyan. He would not go, as it was out of the way, but he found
another, noncab, driver who would take us for 40 Leva. We decided

this was too much and got the tickets for 3 p.m. The bus was a new large fast bus and made good time, but just near Troyan the driver decided to take a 15 minute break at a hotel, thus destroying any hope of meeting the bus to Aprilci.

In fact, we got in twenty minutes late and there were no more buses to Aprilci for the day. So, we went to the Mercedes taxi by the station and ask how much to Aprilci. At 15 Leva, we thought it was acceptable and left just as more people showed up looking for cabs. We practiced our Bulgarian on the driver and asked about his car, which had a lot of mileage. We got home and had toasted peanut butter sandwiches for dinner.

We slept until 8:15 when Svetla knocked on the door to talk about the meetings with the school and with the mayor. She came in as we got ready and went over the strategy for having Calpurnia hired to work for the city of Aprilci. At 9:30 we walked to the school and talked to the head of it, Rahil, who was sitting in a superheated office. The school was combined with a middle school. The children actually looked and acted like kids; the school was very clean and undamaged. So, we talked about tourism and Aprilci. Then Vulko showed up and participated. Then we all went to the Mayor's office, but were informed that he had left for the day (at 10:30 a.m.?). We decided that I would take Calpurnia to the park to talk to the rangers and regional heads.

Moving Out

It was a sunny November day. The park had decided to let Calpurnia work on projects. So, I had her accompany me on a short survey in the mountains. Having hiked all day, we stopped at Hizha Pleven by 7:30. We rented a small room with single bunk beds; it was possible to sleep in a single bed if neither of us moved. We were awake by Six but lay around and talked for half an hour, then got dressed and went out, where Rex barked his head off inches from my hands (and balls). One of the guards held Rex and we started down the mountain. After a hundred meters, the cook ran after us with a napkin with four slices of bread with bitter salty syrene cheese on them. We thanked him profusely, and continued down, leaving the syrene for birds but eating some of the toast. The trip down to the water plant took only an hour and fifteen minutes. Then we walked the road to the generating plant, which took another hour and a half. We stopped at the Vets cafe and had tea and coffee, and found the rangers, Boleslav and Milko there also drinking with two guys; we sat with them then called Vulko, who was not there and left a message that we were walking to the bus. We walked to Vidima, which took another hour and a quarter, picking up an escort of small dogs along the way (these guys had wiggled under their fences and escaped to see Vidima I guess).

At Vidima we had to wait forty minutes for the noon bus, but Vulko came barreling around the corner and we stopped him and begged a ride back. In Aprilci, we changed clothes and he drove us to Gabrovo for the meeting. We decided to go directly to Iurka's office without lunch.

At the office, trying to get through the locked doors, we met Nikolai, who got us coffee and sat us at the conference table. Iurka finally came out with Petya who acted as interpreter (sort of, since she was nervous and had trouble with both languages). Basically Iurka said that we could not have her permission to apply for the grant because it would contradict the park strategy, which we did not know about. So, we spent an hour or two discussing alternatives as well as what the park strategy was. We agreed to tell her about our funding plans and to call the ARD people in Sofia anyway. The meeting seemed to end agreeably, although Vulko was visibly frustrated and Iurka was not concerned at all; she asked Calpurnia to help with the hizha reconstruction project although Calpurnia would not be working in that area.

The meeting was over at Four. I thanked her and we left. I directed us to F&K's favorite restaurant and we had a good meal of chicken-kabobs and fries. We finally got back to Aprilci about Six and had a snack. We talked about the wedding dates and tried to plan the next few weeks with moving and projects. Calpurnia went to bed and I read about the biodiversity plan and their park plan.

Up at 5:30, we left for Pazardjik. The trip was uneventful, although we had to change buses at Troyan and Plovdiv, and each change involved buying a new ticket, checking the schedule, and waiting for the right bus, then crowding on with the herd — Bulgarians do not have lines, and tickets were sometimes oversold, so everyone crowded on the buses as fast and chaotically as possible. Several times, I had been left outside and had been unable to fit even with standing room. First, however, I counted the people waiting and if they were less than the capacity, I did not bother to crowd. This time, south of Karlovo, the traffic was backed up for miles. The bus driver drove in the oncoming lane to get to a police stop. There was a large bus and it looked like it might be an accident. Our bus had to park on the side of the road; we heard five minutes so we sat in the bus and everyone else got out and smoked. It was a protest march; they stopped traffic for five minutes each way. We did not know what the march was about (later we found that the gun factory workers were worried about layoffs). The bus driver made up the time by skipping Xisar (the village with the Roman aqueduct), and we arrived in Pazardjik before noon. I went to the Internet cafe and

Calpurnia went to work at the municipality.

Then I went to the City Hall and we informed Tereza that Calpurnia would be leaving and working with the Park in Aprilci. She acted dumbfounded, repeating how much they needed and wanted Calpurnia. Neither of us really believed her. We left and had pizza for dinner at the local restaurant. We had eaten there before; the crust was very good, and we had had different toppings each time, from corn and tomato to peppers and garlic.

It was Saturday. Phase One: Buy a cheap stereo that plays CDs. There were five stores in Pazardjik that had stereos. The one I had identified, a blue Aiwa had been sold of course, after I watched it for 5 weeks. It was $80. Most of the others were $100-400 USD. There was only one low-end one for $50. Most were bright silver or black or bright blue and silver. The black ones were all Thomson, which I did not trust. In the biggest store I had previously told them I only had $70, but they had nothing. Today I revisited each store and looked. In the large store I was told they just got in a stereo for $75 (I know that the same model in another store was $85), so we listened to it, then I bought it, although it was silver. It had a clock, alarm clock, and double tape player. We took a taxi back to the apartment for $1. The stores and cabs prefer American money, but one always has to make sure the exchange rate is good.

Phase Two: Work at the Internet cafe to do web searches for both internet in Bulgaria and funding for the projects. That night, as we shopped in the market I saw a Chris Rea tape and bought it; it was the greatest hits and very good — it was first tape for the stereo, then the six CDs I carried from America would get played. Dinner was my frozen pizza with salam.

Phase Three: Sunday was spent packing and cleaning. Dinner was frozen tortellini and any other leftovers. Monday was spent at City Hall, trying to smooth the feathers of Tereza and her colleagues. Tuesday, getting up at Seven, we finished packing. I went out and got money, then window shopped for a ski suit. I bought a small keefla for Calpurnia and then a scaler for measuring footprints for myself.

At 10:30 the PC driver came and we loaded the van in fifteen minutes; there were twenty two pieces of luggage, including the boxes of food and stereo box — we had thought there would only be about six. The van was quite full, with three passengers. We drove to Aprilci, which took almost three hours, including smoke breaks for the driver. We unloaded the van, which took only fifteen minutes and put everything in the bedroom. Then we treated the driver to lunch at 2:30. He had his typical lunch of coffee and coke; Calpurnia had a salad and I had fries.

That evening, we bought a few groceries and unpacked. Dinner was peanut butter sandwiches and shrimp soup. Two mailed boxes came with the van: one from my parents and one from Mike and Twila. M&T had sent peanut butter (organic) and tea and spices. My parents had sent long underwear, gloves, jeans, and spices.

Teaching English the Python Way

In Aprilci, I was thinking that I had never expected to teach English; in fact, nothing in my past, except speaking, had prepared me for this. Even my mother had said that English was not my native language; when I asked her if it was Greek, she said no, it was baby talk (maternal humor no doubt). Calpurnia had taught high school for a brief time, but mathematics, not English. Calpurnia and I met with Rahil, head of the tourism school (which was basically a vocational high school). She introduced us to Penka, who taught English on Mondays, having to take the bus from her home in Troyan; in the evening she taught an adult class in English, which we agreed to help with.

Monday, the day of our first English class, we worked all morning. Had our first tutorial on Bulgarian language at the tourism school. Taught the first English class at 2:20. We started with the alphabet, which was of course Latin. We described that future classes would be topic related. Then we helped with advanced class at 5 p.m. The plan of that class was pretty simple. Penka read from a book or article. Then the students tried to read it. Then they discussed the words, in English, if they could. The class had one older man, two younger men, two women and a boy. Apparently, they had been together as a group for some time.

Monday was our teaching day at the grade school. We worked to prepare for those classes. First, we took a Bulgarian Class, then stayed for the next English class, which was about Japan. Then taught our own class, a second class of young students. We worked until 5, then went to the advanced class, where we answered questions about conversational English. I kept wondering what strange things the kids might be learning. I imagined them turned loose in London, asking to massage people's parrots with a curtain hanger. I supposed that a generation of Londoners, steeped in Monte Python, might understand and offer to launder their clues.

Another teaching day! I worked on the lesson plans all morning, printing them off. Then I wrote scripts so that I could talk to Vulko and Angelar, as well as write a letter to Iurka about my program. For our Bulgarian lesson Penka came to the apartment and I served lasagna. We talked about foods, then about our lesson; she helped me with a script for the rangers. Then we rehearsed the lesson plans and went to the school. Only two students in Calpurnia's class showed up so we presented the class to them.

After class we went back and got warm. Calpurnia went to the evening class, but I stayed home and read in bed. That night we had soup and crackers and watched a little television.

Another Monday. Calpurnia went to work at the Tourist office. I worked at the closet office on scripts and notes. Then we walked to the advanced English lesson at noon at the center cafe, where we talked about the written alphabet. Then to the "Cannon" hotel for a salad and tea. Then, to teach our English course, but no one came to class, so we walked back to the center. It only took two months to reach zero attendance. Must be a record. Then, we went back to apartment to work until Five. After that, we taught the advanced class, a more dedicated group. The topic was giving or getting directions.

We took the 8:30 train, which was a nice first-class high-speed train (there were only two in Bulgaria, and I was on the other one to work to Vratsa in July), from Pazardjik to Sofia. We found good seats and rested. In Sofia, Calpurnia showed me where the Dunkin Donuts, Col. Sanders and McDonalds were, so we had a burger at McD's. Then on to the office to confirm the appointment with Albert. He was there and wanted to meet in ten minutes so I went upstairs and had my blood pressure checked. It was finally normal, well borderline, but at least no medicine or lectures.

Albert was very agreeable about our joint project proposal and an hour later, we were looking for camera cables in stores on Vitosha. We tried to find the new Vegetarian restaurant but finally agreed on Murphy's, a lush Irish bar (no pun intended). We both had rum and coke, then fish and chips, which was generous and good by Bulgarian standards. It was the most expensive meal in Bulgarian so far, costing $10 Leva for both of us.

Then we met with Mitko and discuss apartment costs and problems as well as paperwork. I told Mitko that I needed Calpurnia to visit Aprilci to meet my counterpart so that we could discuss our secondary projects; he agreed and the time was set. Then we walked to the Princess Hotel to meet Zlatka (aka "Lati," the daughter of Calpurnia's host mother), who wanted to go to America and had asked Calpurnia to hide the application in a letter to America to her sister.

The train ride back was interesting. Again we got a first class compartment (only six as opposed to eight or ten seats). This time, however, the other four riders asked us questions for an hour and a half and we struggled with our Bulgarian, until the girl I was sitting next to started to speak a little English; then the guy across from Calpurnia started using English words, which made for better understanding. The baba across from me asked if I had been anywhere else in Europe, and when I mentioned Norway, wanted to know all about it. She kept asking odd questions, such as "Did I think Americans were better than Bulgarians?" I had to make my answers as concise as possible. Better at what, I wondered?

Carpentry Beer Connections

Finished writing the letters for Venelina about plans for wildlife surveys and emailed them to her. Andrei asked me to visit him in the sawmill; there we talked with his worker about the futon that I had designed. They thought it would be too heavy, so we reduced the dimensions of the wood pieces. Then I walked back to help Vulko with the brochure on the Masters Organization. We all met from Four to Six in the afternoon. I introduced a plan to market the carvings and they decided to talk about the football team and weather.

The next day, I helped Vulko with the brochure and camera. I got a call from Nikolai. Looked for Trifon. After class with the advanced students, Andrei said the futon was finished. Would we like to take it? He drove us to the sawmill and we put it in back of his old Mazda. It fit together well, so we put it in the living room, and slept on it for the first time. We arranged to pay for it, but Andrei said to wait for a while to see if we liked it.

The next day, I started with calls to Iurka and Trifon about an antenna for the Internet Club. Worked on files. Then met with Trifon at 9:00 for coffee. Then we drove to Gabrovo to meet with Iurka. Most shocking was that Trifon used seat belts, because he had wrecked his car last winter and broke a rib.

We met with Iurka, Nikolai, Krasimir and Georgiu at the Park office. I thought that Iurka told Trifon that he could not put the antenna tower in the park without a scandal. Trifon either agreed to put it on Hizha Tusha or try another way; he did not seem too upset. Then Georgiu and I tried to plan wolf projects. Iurka signed my permission to go to Romania to train for radio-telemetry work.

Another day, another dolor. More computer work. Met with the class at the Center restaurant. Andrei said I could not pay for the futon frame. He said it was like the mafia. He was doing me this favor and someday, maybe in a month or year I could repay it. So, I asked if he wanted me to steal a car or kill someone, a lawyer maybe. He laughed ominously and said I would have to wait to find out.

After class we went with Andrei and Petar to the sawmill to have beer and wurst. I brought two cases of beer for the guys. Andrei stated that it discharged my debt. I drank coke, but we talked mostly in Bulgarian with mixed English, Andrei tried out his English. A wife of one of the workers, Vanya, had just gotten a job with the cable television station news division; Andrei said that if we needed exposure for our projects to call him and he would arrange it. After an hour she started speaking pretty good English. Calpurnia asked her where she had learned this, and she said she had a three-month course in Sofia. Back home, we went to bed by Eleven but could not sleep until after One.

Pledging Children to the State Or Getting Married

Our marriage plans had been approved. We planned on a Bulgarian civil ceremony. In a fit of enthusiasm and joy, Albert Foster, the country director of the Peas Core, offered to marry us at the Ambassador's home, and then remembered to call the Ambassador to see if it was okay with them. We were told it was okay and should meet later in the week with the Ambassador's wife, Margaret, the power behind the throne, so to speak.

We took the 7:30 train from Pazardjik to Sofia to meet with Margaret and Albert. We got in at 9:30 and walked to Dunkin Donuts to have a bagel and coffee, which was expensive and not very good (DD and McD were the first two American businesses to try to capture Bulgarian markets, although neither was very crowded yet and mostly Americans and Germans frequented them). Then we went to the PC HQ and talked to Albert about the Ecolog program. We gave him the letter we prepared making suggestions to improve the program. We talked about marriage plans and dates. Then we went to lunch at the Embassy with Filip and Kim. The home was blank walled facing the street with Bulgarian guards outside and American ones inside. We were brought upstairs by Margaret and sat in the formal living room for tea. We looked out at the sun room and nice garden with high wall around it. We talked about the Russian Embassy, which was huge, and the neighboring embassies.

Then we went upstairs to their private dining room, which was part of their family room. The Brit Ambassador (inconsiderate prick) was having lunch with the US Ambassador downstairs. I convinced Filip to sit at the head of the table so I could hold hands with Calpurnia. The maid poured white wine for all. Another maid brought a delicious vegetable soup and fresh bread. We talked about the cook, who was Bulgarian but refused to cook Bulgarian food and how he came to work for the embassy. Then, we were served a marvelous salmon salad. We talked about many projects including Kim's dog project and its new funding. Then we received Teriyaki chicken with rice—it was excellent. I suggested to Margaret that I would clean windows and carpets if we could eat there every day. It was the best food we had had in Bulgaria.

Finally we talked about the wedding. Margaret had offered to pay for everything as our wedding present. We talked about dates and details. Margaret offered us maple syrup from her basement. We agreed enthusiastically and asked for a dozen. Then, an hour late her 2:30 appointment arrived. As we left there was a small bottle of maple syrup on the stairs. We took a cab to PC HQ to meet with Hugh.

Hugh arranged for a car and we went to the Consulate to swear that we could get married. It seemed that no appointment was made so we had to wait an hour and a half. So, we went to a nearby student cafe and treated to coffee, then went back and waited some more. Finally we went upstairs and had to go through typical Bulgarian paperwork, where our names and dates were misspelled and mixed.

At 5:15 we were back at HQ and meet F&K for dinner. We were tired, and they could not decide between a good restaurant and a movie (which I wanted), so we went to McDonald's and had big Macs, which tasted better here since they were so rare (it was my first burger since early June). Then we raced to the train to Pazardjik at 7:30. We were both sick now from McNausea.

The following week, we took the 7:30 train to Sofia and repeated the DD breakfast experience, only with donuts instead of bagels. We met with Ilyana in the PC office, who transferred us to Marina, Albert's secretary. I talked to Albert by phone, then we went to the Bulgarian Consulate to get a stamp. We went by taxi and found a line of about 30 people ahead of us, down the stairs and outside in the courtyard. After waiting half an hour, we asked if there was another way to do this. Marina said that we could hire a group to stand in line for us and get the stamps. So, we decided to do that; she called the standing-in-line service and arranged it. Then, she took us by taxi to the wedding bureau to get a date and application forms. The bureau was deserted. The first room was a display of wedding dresses and paraphernalia; the second room was equally large but had a desk amidst the displays. We decided on December 9th but we were told that must return within seven days to pay. Also, it cost four times as much to be married on a Saturday, but that was still under $20. Then we took Marina to lunch; she asked to go to McDonalds so we all ended up with big Macs again (which we now refer to as BG Macs).

That afternoon we met with Sheila and talked about blood tests. The rest of the afternoon, we looked for camera cables and books. I bought two good wildlife books, which were very expensive compared with the US.

We met Joe at HQ and talked to him, after his dentist appointment, but he had a date. We agreed to meet at the Happy Bar. We went there and I had Kebabche and fries; Calpurnia had fried chicken with mushroom gravy, which we agreed was excellent. Joe didn't show. The Happy Bar looks like a Hard Rock Cafe. Then we headed for the train.

A week later, we went back again for a day. At 7:29, we left for Sofia by train; it was a two-hour ride, first class, which was quite comfortable. We walked down Vitosha street to the Dunkin Donuts for cocoa and coffee. Then to PC HQ for the paperwork, which had been delivered (we paid $1 for someone to stand in line for two hours at the Bulgarian consulate and get the papers stamped). Then we went to the marriage bureau and explain in halting and clumsy Bulgarian that we wished to be married and to change the date. We were eventually successful and had a new day, 22/11/00, in the Vitosha Hall of Marriage. We paid $5 for the date (instead of $20 for the Saturday).

We had a snack at McDonalds and went back to HQ, where we changed addresses, picked up mail, and had our blood samples taken. Then we took the samples to a Bulgarian lab for tests. That was exciting, as we used our sad language skills to try to explain why we were getting married here and what the tests were for. We paid the American rate of $10 apiece (regularly $8) and were told to come back for the results in five days.

After that we went to look at books, bought a wildlife book and a novel, then borrowed two books from the PC library. We had a small dinner at the Happy Bar and Grill, then walked to the train. The evening train back was the local; it had first class seats but they were indistinguishable from second class; this train also continued on to Istanbul.

Now, it was time for the marriage trip. It was Monday, the day before. We took the 5:30 a.m. bus for Sofia. Delayed by an accident, we got to Sofia late and walked to the PC office after a brief stop at McD's. At PC HQ we were met by Sheila who said that we must have a Bulgarian physical examination because the Bulgarian doctor at the PC had no stamps for the form. Venelina called to arrange it but the first medical office said that they would have to repeat the blood work at their labs; the second office agreed to do it at the Bulgarian prices. So, we walked over to the office, which was like "bodymed" and owned by a Greek. We presented ourselves in Bulgarian and waited for the exam. We were told that we must see an internist and a urologist. We took the paperwork showing that we had no syphilis or AIDS.

We were escorted into the office of the internist by the secretary, who stayed, standing against the door (perhaps to guard us from leaving before money was exchanged). The internist talked for five minutes and filled out the paperwork; she asked us if we had any diseases. I said that we were in whole health. She looked at us, critically, from her desk, and said, "Yes, Okay." She signed the paperwork without any further exam. No mention of the urologist. We paid the 36 Leva to her. She said if we were ever sick to please come see her. We went to find the Wedding Hall, but could not.

An hour later, armed with new directions and the name of the sign, we found the office. It was deserted, except for three secretaries. The wedding hall was in a small nook on the street with a small sign overhead; we walked down a small alley to a larger opening with matching staircases on either side and large wooden doors facing the hallway. We presented ourselves in Bulgarian, with our paperwork. All of the paperwork was complete, a minor miracle. But she asked us where we lived in the US and where we lived in Bulgarian and where we would live. Then she described the ceremony and we got lost. She said that we needed to have a translator; we agreed. Then we asked to change the wedding from 2 p.m. to 11:00 a.m. They changed it to 10:30. We left for the hotel.

The Hotel Niki was seven blocks from the PC; it was an old building that had been refurbished in the Euro style of rooms with Danish furniture and a small shower in the room; the toilet was down the hall. We checked in and went to look for wine glasses and the things we would need for the wedding. First we had a snack at the hotel bar, which was very nice; we had potato and chicken salads.

We spent an hour in the PC library looking for English books, that is, for books for teaching English. We found a few. Then we walked around looking for the Post Office. Then we went to the Chinese restaurant for a long quiet meal of sweet and sour chicken and vegetable fried rice. We walked back to the hotel and Calpurnia went to sleep while watching a television movie. I watched a special on Clark Gable, then fell asleep during *Mutiny on the Bounty*.

Who's the Boss Or Stepped On
It was the day! 22/11/00. We woke up about 8:00 and spent an hour getting ready. I was wearing my black outfit that I wore for graduation in Dupnitsa (it still smelled faintly of smoke from the forest fires); Calpurnia was wearing a green and black plaid cotton outfit with a blue turtleneck (that she had paid fifty cents for in Virginia at Goodwill). Then we went looking for champagne and wine glasses, as well as chocolates for the PC staff. At PC HQ we

talked to Marina and waited for the others, including Venelina.
We asked Albert if the entire staff could attend; he announced
that anyone who wanted to go could take lunch now. We gave out
the chocolates. We all walked to the Wedding Hall, which was on
Vitosha Boulevard six doors down from the McDonalds but only
two blocks from PC HQ. There were seven women and me. At the
hall, we met Zlatka, waiting outside with more flowers, champagne,
glasses, cookies, and chocolates — in case we had forgotten.

We all went inside to the first waiting room, through double
wooden doors. The room was about 40 by 30 feet. From there,
Calpurnia and I, with Zlatka and Venelina, went into the registration
chamber, a small office with three desks and a dressing room. We all
had to show our passports and give them the champagne, glasses,
rings, etc. Venelina and Zlatka (familiarly known as "Lati") were
assigned to be our Godfather and Godmother respectively. They
filled the glasses after cutting the cork with pliers (the cork hit the
ceiling). The four of us returned to the entrance room. Music started
from the wedding chamber, which was about 100 feet long and 40
feet wide; there was a dais at the end under a large wall-size metal
sculpture. The music was the Wedding March. Calpurnia and I
walked in first with Venelina by Calpurnia's side and Lati by mine.
The others followed in fours. We tried to walk slowly. At the altar the
four of us stepped to the first step, while the main Secretary presided
over the ceremony; the other two secretaries were standing by the
door.

She welcomed everybody, then asked us if we wanted to be
married; this took about ten minutes. She also mentioned the laws of
the state and our duty to have children loyal to the state. Calpurnia,
prompted by Venelina said "Da" and I said "Da, Az shtay." I was not
sure exactly what we had agreed to. We were allowed to kiss and
I lowered Calpurnia to my knee level for the kiss; she still had the
small flower in her hand, under mine. Then the Secretary presented
the 50-cent rings, and I put Calpurnia's on, and she put mine on my
finger. Then, she presented the champagne glasses and we gave each
other a sip. But, she said that we must drink all of it to "live forever."
That was what I thought was said. Venelina and Lati were so excited
they had forgotten to translate. So we finished our champagne. Then
Calpurnia and I signed our names into the big book; then the two
Godparents had to sign. Then we were told to live happy lives in
Bulgaria. And the wedding was over.

Teri had been taking pictures with Calpurnia's and Lati's cameras,
so we got pictures with Calpurnia and I as well as with the Godparents, then Teri, then the PC staff (all women). As I was thanking
the women for coming and participating, Calpurnia stamped on my

foot, which meant that she would be the boss of the marriage — in the excitement I had forgotten that little bit of folklore. I was teased mercilessly by the women.

The Kiss

We walked outside and invited everyone to the "reception" at McDonalds, but the staff had to go back to work. We went back with them to PC HQ and give out all the chocolates that Lati bought. Met with Albert and Annie. Saw Marcus and talked with him. Then we took Lati on a tour of the building, then took her alone to McDs where we each had hamburgers. We talked about the wedding, as Lati joked that she had been secretly married to Bruce Willis in Paris last week (she seemed to be wearing a ring on her right finger). Lati walked back to the university for her class, and Calpurnia and I went to PC HQ to pick up our baggage. We took a taxi to the bus stop by the Princess Hotel and get onboard the Troyan bus immediately, although it was only 12:40. The bus left on time at 1:00 and we got back to Aprilci by 6 p.m.

For our wedding dinner, we made spinach lasagna, with fresh bread from Troyan. I made a spinach salad with sunflower seeds and Italian dressing. The wine was a good Bulgarian wine from Ruse. Dessert was gingered apples.

After listening to music for a while, and unpacking things, we went to bed, on the living room floor. This was the warm room, with a view of the mountains and the river. It was also quiet except for the sound of the river. We slept until eight the next morning.

Standing Ecologist Seated Experts
After working on our papers, we got ready to go to see Rahil about the Public Forum on Friday. As we were leaving Angelar came with mail, but it was the mail that I had sent to him. The clerk had refused it, but had given it to him to give to me; so I handed it back to him to deliver it. We went to see Rahil but she was not there. We shopped for food and saw Angelar again. We found the announcements of the Forum, but could not get any anywhere. So, we went back and talked to Rahil who was arranging an interpreter for us (Desislava Karanova, the doctor at the hospital). We went back to work in the apartment on preparing for the Forum. For dinner, we virtuously

finished a heated up fourth-day left-over lasagna.

Worked all morning, 24 November, on the presentation in Bulgarian. We met with Vulko, who told us about the Forum, but then said he would watch it on television (or that it would be televised). We had peanut butter sandwiches for lunch; the peanut butter was almost gone, that is, the organic Oregon kind.

At 2:20, we met with Rahil at the old hall, which was a large unheated building at the end of the square in back of the city statue of gigantic rifles. We wondered what the building was for, although half of it had a barber shop salon upstairs. We were introduced to the doctor, a attractive woman of about 30 with black hair, slim, very Bulgarian looking. She seemed pleasant.

We walked up the stairs and to the back room, which has a very decorative ceiling. Calpurnia thought that it was the marriage hall for the city. There was a dais made of wood; sitting on it were overhead projectors. The sun was shining into the high windows; the carpet was relatively new squares of odd colors. There was a large closed square of tables and chairs. The side of the square closest to the dais was for experts, and we were placed there with the interpreter, and with three men from Sofia or the local construction company. The other three sides were for the Forum committee, who would hear testimony and then make recommendations for which projects should be funded. At the other end of the room, chairs were arranged for the public. Only five were filled when we sit down.

There was a camera in the corner for the local cable television. The committee was introduced by Anna, who also introduced the experts. The experts were invited to speak first, but we were seated at the other end and would speak last. The notes were elsewhere. There were only a few comments on the experts testimony at first.

Then we had a break after two hours. During the break Calpurnia spoke with the doctor, while I spoke with Bulchru from the forestry office of the city. Then we went up again. The room had been unheated and everyone wore their winter coats, except me. A kerosene heater was brought in and started, but it only heated the one speaker next to it, so I put on my coat.

I was introduced, so I gave my talk in Bulgarian, and everyone was quite helpful with my mispronounced words and strange ideas.

"I am not, like the rest of you, an expert. I am an ecologist. Being an ecologist is quite the opposite of being an expert. I do not know any one thing very well. In fact, I have kind of a professional myopia that prevents me from getting mired in details, which always seem fuzzy, contradictory, and really confusing. Because of this I look for large patterns. I see many patterns in a system and many connections between systems—the systems I mean are ecosystems, in size from a stream bed to our city of Aprilci nestled in the mountains here or the Balkan region.

"So, I do not have any solutions to the problems presented here today. I do not know the best way to rebuild the infrastructure of water delivery or how to deal with trash collection. I cannot match your expertise with plans for a water treatment plant or strategies to increase tourism from other countries.

"But, I can look at some of the things that were happening and connect them with other things. I can suggest some relationships between animal care and health, between trash collection and tourism, between advertising and market sales. For instance, I notice that many of you were coughing on this fine sunny day. I suspect that you stayed up drinking and smoking all hours, then went to the disco until dawn — neglecting your sleep — then went home to uninsulated houses heated with wood, and finally, to get here, you walked on roads traveled by all your domestic sheep and cattle, breathing in pulverized manure thrown up by cars driving over it. All of these things contribute to respiratory distress. Therefore, I would suggest a few changes in lifestyle, as well as new routes for domestic animals.

"There are many other links between our actions and our health, as well as between domestic animals and wildlife, and clean water and technology. We can see these links by examining the history of the area, as well as our human attitudes. We can think about how different models of thought or behavior could result in different, and hopefully better, lives for our inhabitants and communities.

"I was asked to describe the ten most pressing problems facing the city right now. Let me start with a few observations about what I had seen here in the past three months. First, however, let me say how happy we were to be living in a town as beautiful and prosperous as Aprilci — in a beautiful setting between two scenic rivers. We were still observing and learning about Aprilci and Bulgaria — and I trust you would forgive my slow and faltering Bulgarian language. Dr. Desislava Karanova will help me with the more difficult phrases. Thank you, Dr. Karanova.

"We recognize many of the same problems here that we had in America, and not all of them had been solved there, in America, either. Let me talk about some of these problems that we share and suggest some low-cost, labor-intensive solutions. I know we were all concerned with money, but much can be done with effort and ingenuity, based on thought and understanding.

"Number one. The worst problem is the indifference of people to wildlife and to their natural surroundings, which are more than just surroundings but are a complete ecological support network that provides air water, food, and even the deepest of enjoyments. The solution here is to have ecological education in school—I'm sure the kids would love to get out near the rivers and forests!"

So I continued listing the ten important things, from threats to wildlife to pollution, trash, industrial waste, inefficient water, phone and electrical systems, and indifference to health. Everyone was quiet and respectful, until I suggested keeping animals off the streets and having separate animal paths for them. Everyone roared with laughter at this funny suggestion. I tried to justify it by saying that the Swiss and the Americans did it, to keep people getting sick from pulverized manure. Then I concluded.

"The most important solution to any of these problems is an ecological education. That includes listening, not only to what people really need and want, but to the voices of all existence, from insects to cows. Television can help with that, by showing where things, like water, come from and where they go. Working and walking outside, looking, really looking, and listening lead to an ecological understanding.

"Another thing that can be done is to have an ecologist on the staff of the city, and just let her monitor the actions of the city and its residents. An ecologist could measure the exact conditions of the water and air, forests and fields, animals and people. For instance, I have seen dead animals in the river. Who puts them there?

"Ecological planning would be a great beginning. We need a complete inventory for the whole large community. We need to think of land use and maps. We need to develop partnerships in a complete community or industrial ecology, where the wastes of one group become the resources of another.

"Thank you all for your consideration in listening today. Thank you. Dr. Karanova, for translating my incorrect, mispronounced or new words. Thank you Madame Chairman, for allowing me to speak today. I will be living here for the next two years and would like to participate in the life of this community. Please discuss things with me and invite me to discuss things here. Thank you."

Finally I was finished and the public started to comment on the experts. At 6:30 we were all finished. We went home to have rice and wine, and the coleslaw we made earlier. We read until bed. I suggested that we mate like wolves, but we found it was too difficult on a soft surface. Think about it! When the male ...

Tracking Red Deer

After weeks of hiking and observing, it was December now. I woke at 6:30 to take the 6:50 bus to Vidima to meet with Boleslav and Mitko. Boleslav had the car again. Because Mitko and I went over the hill on Wednesday, I wanted to go directly into bear habitat today. We met in Vidima and drove the eight kilometers to the water works. Rather than leave this time Boleslav decided to walk on the other side of the river (Vidima).

Mitko and I went up the west side while Boleslav went on the east side about 300 meters away. We lost sight of him after five minutes because of the dense trees. The trees had lost all their leaves and their grey beech bark made the forest look ghostly as well as slightly dirty. The snow got deeper as we walked along animal trails. As we were walking we heard a bellowing, which was answered by another bellowing farther up the hill. Mitko thought that the first was Boleslav. We stopped and watched the opposite hill across the river valley. After about five minutes I saw two forms run down hill towards the river. I could not see them well. They ran well in the snow. I wondered if they were wolves or dogs, but was not sure. Mitko, who had sharp eyes, said that they were roe deer. We watched them until they were out of sight.

As we continued to walk, we came upon several sites where roe deer had bedded for the night (I thought because of the urine on one end; Mitko thought they had been eating there because of the nose marks in the snow and small bits of grass exposed. We could not resolve this in Bulgarian. Finally, we were all the way up the hill before the head wall of the river; no signs of bears. We went down the ridge and had to cross a rocky tributary and climb up the next hill. This was difficult and slow. I found a path down that let me hold branches at every stop; going back up however we had to pick across rock ledges in 16 inches of snow.

Getting near the top of the next ridge we found a wildlife trail with fox prints, which we followed. The paw prints for the fox were 4.6 cm wide and 4.3 long; at first we thought they were wolf, but seemed too small; the stride was small and only sank into the snow a third the way, so maybe seven inches. After getting off the game trail under the trees and into the opening (silver fir nursery and field), the tracks veered in and out of cover every 10 meters. Near a clearing the fox had vomited; in the vomit were one blade of grass, one leaf, two large bits of hide with fur (maybe roe deer), and stomach acids. I tasted it; it was bitter and sour. Bad deer?

The woodpeckers were active. Saw three at different times. Much smaller than I would have thought, with white and black but very few red feathers. They were able to find many trees to peck at. I think after 10:00 we started the end of the loop back to the car. We had gone two ridges away. The walk was easy at first because we were in fields with 30-38 inches of snow, but no rocks or trees. As we went along the ridge it got rockier. Then we went straight down through the trees for a few kilometers.

At the water station, Mitko set off a firecracker to let Boleslav know we were back, but Boleslav was in the building eating lunch. The stove had made it warm so we took off a layer of clothes and shoes. Mitko fixed a sandwich but I had only peanuts and tea. The guard, who lived there returned and we talked about the snow. The room had two beds, a desk, and a stove. There were shelves on two walls that had a stereo and some personal effects. After half an hour we decided to drive back to Aprilci.

Gabrovo Getaway Or Five Cold Offices

I walked to the Cultural Center by City Hall in Gabrovo and found the YMCA without trouble. I asked to wait for Joe who was still in a meeting. He arrived as I was on page six of a book on how to juggle — the pictures were entertaining. Joe looked sick and like he had lost weight (we had been roommates for two days in Chicago, and liked each other because we were polite and because neither of us snored). He said yes, he had been sick and wondered if I had lost weight. I said yea, but my cooking now included cookies, so I had stabilized.

We walked to the pizza restaurant that Filip told me about last July. We split an excellent pizza. Coke instead of tea. I wondered if I could get rich making good pizzas in this country. I wondered if Craig would be interested. Joe and I exchanged stories about our new lives. Then we talked about our projects. Finally, he gave me a key to the apartment, and we went over there. Joe worked in Dryanovo but expected to work in Gabrovo two days a week. Georgiu had arranged for him to use Mary's old apartment, which was quite well stocked with furnishings and even a television with cable. I had arranged through Albert to use the apartment one or two nights a week, since I worked in Gabrovo for the Park directorate. So, Joe would be here Wednesday to Saturday, and I could have Sunday to Wednesday if I wanted. Joe went back to work and I went out to the Park.

The apartment was on the 12th floor of a 16-story building designed by an East German architect for the city. It was quite different from the concrete cubes of normal Bulgarian buildings. It was a concrete tower, with an octagonal floor plan and balconies. Inside the front door was the bathroom, with the toilet and sink; the water heater was hung on the wall and a shower head was nearby, above the drain in the floor, which was raw concrete. A hall ran the length of the apartment to the bedroom; it had a washing machine, which emptied into the bathroom, bookcase, clothes tree, and vanity. The first left was the kitchen, which was very oddly shaped, with nooks too small to hold a refrigerator or stove. There were these things, as well as a sink, small counter, and spice rack above the sink. There was a separate doorway going into the living room, which was rhomboid (or some shape). The living room had a large window and a door leading to the balcony. There were two overstuffed chairs and a matching sofa bed. Against the window was a table with three chairs. Two tables and an old refrigerator sat against the wall shared with the kitchen. In the corner was a telephone table with the nonworking phone. The indoor-outdoor carpet was in good repair. There were posters on the walls (the famous artists series seen in every college dorm room).

Weeks later, we checked out the YMCA, where Joe worked (he had gone to Paris for holiday — these young volunteers were so rich!). Then we shopped for gifts for men at the Park, mostly knives and decorative bottles, but waited before buying them. Then we shopped for food, and got fresh bread, chicken salad, potato salad, coke, and peanuts. At the apartment, we relaxed. Then had dinner and watch a taped Saturday Night Live show from October 2000.

The apartment was very warm, even without the two electric heaters. The city only turned on the heat after Seven on days with below freezing temperatures, but it had been freezing for over three weeks. Calpurnia called Christine who had been working in Stara Zagora; she wanted to visit us so we agreed and she would visit Friday night.

Friday night, the apartment was too hot and too dry. But, we made cereal and yogurt, then went out and look for knives and hats. At noon, we had yet another pizza and then headed for the Park Directorate, my reason for being here (but playing hooky was so much fun, especially when you were not paid and no one helped you with anything anyway).

Surprisingly, Georgiu was working there and we met right away. We discussed the surveys and plans for monitoring, then he became agitated and asked Petya to translate. He always did this, although we ended up talking in Bulgarian and Petya ended up listening. Afterwards I talked to Nikolai about the GIS system, which might be ready for loading data in January and the web page, which was still languishing (making it the fourth web page I was working on, sort of). After 3 p.m. we caught the local bus back to the center, and waited for Christine at the bus station. We called her cell phone and she answered that the bus was just entering town, so we waited. Cell phones had almost replaced all the old land lines in this country.

We dropped off her bag at the apartment and immediately went to the pizza place (she did not seem to want Bulgarian food, although we knew of the good Serbian restaurant nearby). After dinner we returned to the cafe at the theater and had tea and chocolate. Then we saw *Moulding Rouge*, a cartoon pretending to be a period piece interpreted through modern songs as tragic poetry presenting the comic talents of — oh, never mind. After an hour of interesting sets, we left. I never realized that the lyrics were so banal.

As we walked back to the apartment, the door was open. I rushed in and saw Ben and Seth and his surly (I thought she must have thought she was sultry, but was missing a t and all mixed up) Bulgarian girlfriend. We discussed the situation with them, that Calpurnia and I were working and stayed there two days a week. We offered them the living room with the double sofa bed, but they decided to take a bus back to Dryanovo, five miles away, where they worked. We suspected that Joe was lending or renting the apartment to anyone who wanted to visit on weekends; I left a note for him suggesting that, when he returned from Paris, we at least make another schedule. We watched more SNL and talked about the strange desire of volunteers to goof off (not us of course, well, except for a day every ten months). Christine took the living room and Calpurnia and I the bedroom.

At 11:30, the apartment upstairs issued loud music, live music as a band started to tune up. I wondered, did they work until 11 and then decide to practice, or did they get kicked out of another apartment. The piano and organ were fair, but the vocalist sucked; sounded like funeral music with a sick dog. After an hour the pipes and floors start banging from angry residents. They threw the vocalist out the window or down the stairs, but they started again with just instruments. The banging restarted. After a final pause, a final set, all was quiet in Gabrovo, except for the screeching cars (and this was hard to do on icy streets) and 8,000 barking dogs. We decided to go back to work in Aprilci on Saturday.

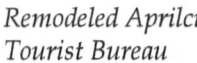
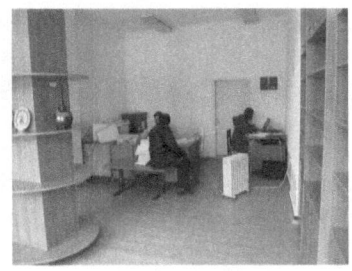

*Remodeled Aprilci
Tourist Bureau*

One Step Closer to Death Or *Down Please*

Later that week, I worked an hour in the office, during which we went over the script with Vulko. Then I went back upstairs and worked on my proposal. Angelar came at 11 and asked me to wait until 12. Hmmmm. I worked some more.

At 12 Angelar returned with two rangers, Bulchru and Tsonko, whom I had met before. We drove to Stokite and unloaded the jeep into the garage. Tsonko went to wait for a bus. The rest of us drove to the Rosaritsa hotel bordering the forestry unit. They explained that I should take a *pochefka* (rest). When I asked when they would be back, they said tomorrow at 7 a.m. I asked when we would return to Aprilci and Angelar said by Four the next day, then I asked if I could go make evening observations; they said okay. After they left, I put my pack in the room, which was very small, had a small electric heater, and a hot water tank in the bathroom, which had running water.

Wearing my new ski pants and long underwear I walked up the road (the same in fact that Georgiu and I had walked down from Hizha Mazarat after observing red deer in September). After 2 hours on the road I cut uphill on a game trail to the top of the ridge. It started snowing. I walked down the ridge recording my observations (including a spine and two hooves from a roe deer). It got darker, the snow became thicker, but when I turned down to the road I came within a few hundred meters of the road by the hotel. I was back by Seven. No one else seemed to be staying at the hotel, although there was a coat on the sofa in the hall. I had sweated gallons in the long underwear and new nylon ski pants, so they were all soaked, but I did not get cold. I went to sleep.

The next morning, Bulchru was right on time. I was waiting outside in the snow, which had continued overnight. I was wondering if the jeep was going to make it up the trails. Bulchru was ready to go immediately, so we did.

We drove to the west road, which I had not been on, and saw deer and capriols. We drove for an hour finally to the field where we had watched for red deer in September. But, then we parked and walked up into the beech forest. We walked for a few hours along the side of the mountain through deepening snow.

Suddenly, we started an *avalanche* — the whole hill broke loose with us on top.

We saw the snow moving below us and started grabbing any branch or tree that we could. We bounced over rocks and trees but could not get a grip on anything. Finally at a rock shelf, we slowed enough to each grab a small tree. We clung and waited for the snow to stop moving.

I peeked over the edge and watched the snow cascade down

the mountain; it was not as large a path as I had thought. But, we had survived. Bulchru was feeling himself for cuts or broken bones; I did the same. My watch had been ripped off by a sharp rock or something. There was a thin cut on the underside of my forearm that started below the wrist. It had almost been surgically removed. Bulchru asked if I was okay. I nodded and asked about him. I held my wrist up and mentioned the watch. He asked if I wanted to climb up and look for it. I laughed and then so did he. I was curious about it but decided to wait until spring to look. We carefully edged our way horizontally along the slope until we were in the thick trees and felt safer.

Then, after a rest we cut up hill to the top of the ridge and walked down to the jeep, returning about 12:30, in time for lunch I thought. But, Bulchru said I should go back to the hotel for a break until Four then we would go out again. I pointed out that I had no more money or clothes for another day. We tried to discuss what to do; I agreed to stay if the park would pay the hotel, which was 5 Leva a night and if I could call Calpurnia to tell her I would not be back until Thursday. He then drove me to Aprilci without lunch or explanation. I wondered if he was upset by the avalanche.

Back in Aprilci Calpurnia was finishing lunch, so we talked and then went to work in the Tourist office until about 5:30. I tried calling Angelar but only left a message. I had peanut butter sandwiches. It finally stopped snowing about 2 p.m. More work that evening. We tried to get on the internet from the apartment, and almost succeeded, but the phones were bad and we got kicked off too many times. Angelar called back and we set up an excursion for the following Tuesday.

Skiing with Corn

On Tuesday, I took the 6:50 bus to Vidima and was met by Pentcho and another guy (not a ranger). Then Dimitar picked up Boleslav and the four of us went to the Forestry unit by car (4WD Lada Niva). The snow was melting and very icy; the car got stuck a few times and we pushed it out (I pulled a muscle in my chest doing this). Then we made it to the hunting blind and put out some corn. There was already corn there and a dead sheep, which had been dragged onto the road by some animal but not eaten. I found no bear, wolf, or dog tracks.

Pentcho and Dimitar put on skis and Boleslav and I snowshoes — new hi-tech fiber shoes (I pulled the same muscle putting on the shoes). We slogged up the hill for an hour easily beating the skiers. We dumped our rucksacks full of corn on the snow, near the salt lick. Going downhill the skiers easily beat us. It

107

was hard to breathe because the muscle was red hot and expanding my lungs makes it worse.

At the car, we drove down to Vets, and there put on chains. Then drove up towards the "water source" (the Bulgarian name was very long). The car almost got stuck several times but pulled itself out. Finally, we unloaded at the old barn, which had finally fallen in under the snow load. I got the food pack and the others divided the hundred-pound load of corn. We hiked up to the last hunting blind there, which was next to the Park, and put out the corn. Then we hiked up to the water containment, went into the small house, started a fire and had lunch. I had brought peanuts, sunflowers seeds and chocolate, Pentcho bread, Dimitar half a bread, and Boleslav an entire kitchen, including jars of meats, cheeses, cabbage, mayo, milk, and the ever-popular pure fat cubes. The other guy from the morning was there; he would stay there for a day or two. Apparently, he was an employee of the water company. After lunch we hiked down for an hour, drove for 40 minutes, then took off the chains at Vets. We talked to the water plant workers for an hour, then drove to Aprilci, where we had tea and talked. I told them I could not go tomorrow until my muscle settled down — they laughed and said I must work on the computer, my curse. About Three I walked to the apartment and they went shopping (I saw the Niva sitting there as I walked away).

At home, I worked on another article, on pet ecology, for the *Sofia Echo* newspaper. I helped Calpurnia with her article for *Eko Planeta*, on eko-trails. I planned to track animals by myself for a few days. I told Angelar; he reminded me I should not go alone, so I said Calpurnia was coming with me. I told Calpurnia the rangers were going with me. Everyone feared that a lone person would be eaten by wolves.

In the afternoon, I decided to go on a walk to the north ridge. Tracked a dog (or wolf — would not know until I calculated the footpad ratios), then a fox. Crossed many roe deer prints perpendicular to the road. There were mouse prints also in the snow by the side of the road. This road went up through the hills towards the state microwave tower on Black Peak. There was a small settlement of houses. I stopped to talk to a man working on his car. The weather was beautiful and sunny. I wanted to talk about wildlife, but he wanted to know where I was going. Going back, I played tag with a black woodpecker.

Our Second Marriage

After three weeks of a working honeymoon, we took the bus to Sofia for the religious wedding at the Ambassador's house. In Sofia, we spent an hour getting books in biology, tourism or teaching English; the selection was not good, but we found a few. I donated my urine samples for Sheila. She checked me out; my stomach had been ravaged by some microorganism for weeks. The cause remained unknown, but she suggested I try to eat since I could always stay in sick bay after the wedding. A suggestion met with amusement on my part.

Calpurnia and I went to the Hotel Niki to confirm things, but we could not check in, so we went to the Cultural Center to find the internet cafe there. A small one had bad service and we could not even get on. Looking around the building, we found a huge internet gaming center and went in. It was fast, but as we found later, very expensive at three Leva an hour. We caught up on all the email. At 1 p.m. we went to the hotel to check in, holding for a room for Alta and Christine also. We went back to the PC HQ and talked to Albert, who told us to come to the Ambassador's house at 3 p.m. tomorrow, to get the final instructions.

We went to Murphy's bar and had lunch. Calpurnia ordered the New Yorker, which was three open sandwiches, one with roast beef, one with smoked salmon and one with Gouda cheese. I ordered the Leprechaun burger, which was small but hot and seasoned well. After lunch we looked for flowers and film. Went to the Sheraton to check our reservation for the one wedding night. Then we took the luggage to that Hotel. At the hotel we had tea and fries. Then we walked to the Train station to pick up Christine at 6:30. We finally saw her, possibly the last person off the train. She had dyed her hair a deep mahogany. We took a taxi to the Pizza Hurt and had an excellent dinner there. I had chicken soup, a chicken pasts salad and a coke. Calpurnia and Christine had pizzas, which seemed good but unremarkable. Then we took another taxi to the Hotel. Each of these taxis cost about 1.30 Leva, which was very cheap.

At the Niki hotel we saw Chris's room, which was in the attic and has a 2/3rds bed and a balcony; the ceiling was done with knotty pine. We traded rooms so she could have the shower in our room and so that Alta could have the other single bed. This room was the one that we had when we were married last month; it had high ceilings and a small shower in the corner and a large wardrobe next to that. The single wooden beds were catacorner; under the large window there was a table with a television set on it. We went down stairs and sat in the crowded dining room — the hotel had three small dining rooms and all were crowded with students. We sat at a table and had screwdrivers, except Calpurnia who had a Baileys.

Ciaran

Back at the room, Calpurnia and I went out on the balcony and looked at the cute Japonoiserie courtyard, which had picnic tables around the raked gravel. We went to sleep.

Wedding Day! Again! We woke up and dallied for a while, then dressed to go to get Alta on the 6 a.m. train. We waited on the landing instead of the stairs, where we were supposed to wait. So, we missed her and went back inside where we found her waiting on a bench. She had dyed *her* hair blonde. We took a taxi to the Hotel and dropped her off in Christine's room. Then we went back to bed and dozed for an hour. At 8 a.m. Christine and Alta wanted to have breakfast at DDs and then to the train station to buy their return tickets.

At DD we each bought three donuts, which were 1.35 Leva each (yikes, the cost of weddings these days). I had hot chocolate; others had coffee. Then they went to the train station, while we looked for a blouse for Calpurnia. This was hard because no one opened until ten or eleven, but I found a cheap pair of ski pants to wear in the woods, which we bought. We each get another 100 Leva cash from the bank machine to pay for the expenses of the day.

At the Hotel Niki, we packed for the next Hotel, the ultra-expensive Sheraton. When Alta and Christine returned at 10:15 we went to the Sheraton, taking their luggage also. At the Sheraton, we found that the room would not be ready for a few more hours. Also they gave us the old reservation. Then we found that they had the new reservation also, but it had *not* been paid for, only guaranteed. They promised us a junior suite on the second floor, which was not ready either, but which we took out of desperation. We put it on Calpurnia's MasterCard. Calpurnia, Christine, and Alta went shopping for a blouse for Calpurnia. I waited a while but nothing happened so I went on three different expeditions: One to get a knife and workman tool, then to get a watch, then to get a battery for Calpurnia's new Wal-Mart watch and a book for her (Jules Verne). At 12:30, I complained that we needed our suite *now*. This room was our big extravagance for one night; we had made the reservation six weeks ago. Then I went looking for the girls, who of course were on their way back from the opposite direction. Then Calpurnia complained to the manager, who gave us the junior suite to use and promised to have the Executive Suite ready when we return from the wedding.

In the Junior Suite, 258, we all took showers and got dressed. This took two hours. Calpurnia was laid out on the couch like an actress. Calpurnia was made up and her hair put up by Christine. But, her hair was too thick and it fell down, so they went with a modified sweep. Alta performed the required fussing. They were all wearing mudpacks as I went around and brought them the complimentary champagne and cake from the Hotel. There was also a basket of fruit. I packed all the suitcases as the girls finished each getting ready. About 3:15 we were all ready and ask for a cab. The hotel offered us a complimentary car, which took us to the Ambassador's residence at Veliko Turnovo Street.

As we exited the car, Albert, the PC Chief, was waiting in his robes. We were escorted upstairs, where Joe was already waiting. We met with Margaret and talked about things. We gave out our gifts to them, which were wool scarves, a vase, a bell, and a book of poetry. She gave me another jar of maple syrup (after I begged)! Then we were cloistered while Albert instructed us on how to act. The piano room had been set off with a screen, so the girls and I and Joe were kept there. Michael and Marta came in also. I had a cuba libre to relax and got a small one for Calpurnia, but then I started to drink hers. She was already partially catatonic from stress, but outwardly calm at least.

We went out to greet the host families for a few minutes, but Albert herded us back in. Marina and her husband were late, as was Vulko, so we waited another five minutes.

The actual procession seemed very fast. We were last after Joe and Alta and Michael and Christine. I tried to match our left and right feet but give up after three steps (I should have used pieces of hay and straw and showed her how to march). Then, we were standing before Albert, who started the service. He talked about good things that we should be for each other, then he asked the Ambassador and Margaret to read alternate passages that we wrote; they read the poems well. We were given away by our host families (Ilian and Rumiana said in English "We. do."). Then he gave us six instructions from scriptures and other books. Then we gave each other the rings—these were the fifty stutinki rings that I had bought at the train station—and Albert blessed us with holy oils. We were pronounced man and wife and I got to kiss the bride. We did our sweeping low kiss.

Then we mingled and met people, many of whom gave us gifts anyway, against our instructions—we asked for none because we did not want to have to carry them! We each talked with our counterparts. Angelar had a new haircut and a nice jacket and tie. Vulko looked tired and lost. Iurka was there with her boyfriend and father of their three-year old daughter. She was smiling and looked excited and happy to be there. Annie and her fiancé were there; Marina and her husband. Lillia the language teacher was there. Jo came in with David Leigh as her escort; she was wearing a large diamond ring and expensive clothes. After forty minutes of greetings, we then were called to the buffet, which had caviar on crepes, chicken pasta salad, Caesar salad, and many other salads, all of which had meats in them. We mingled and talked to various families and people. I make sure to thank the Ambassador at least three times.

Then it was time to cut the cake. It was a beautiful heart-shaped, single layer white cake with silver things on it and flowers of icing. It turned out to be white chocolate and dark chocolate mousse with a cracker layer in between layers, like a White Russian cake. Calpurnia fed me and I fed her. After mingling for another fifteen minutes I begged for a second piece of cake. Many pictures were taken, although we had forgotten Calpurnia's camera at PC HQ.

It seemed like it had gone on for many hours, and some people, Albert first, started to excuse themselves. We tried to go first but ended up last, waiting in the basement for a cab to arrive. We took the cab for 1.4 Leva to the Sheraton, where our new suite, 543, was finally ready. We, including Christine and Alta, went up. They each took a photo of me carrying Calpurnia across the threshold. I carried her to the bed and collapsed dramatically. We took photos of each other in the suite. In the excitement, we left the gift bags outside the room for an hour, until a hotel guard knocked and told us. We all relaxed around the large living room and had the champagne. The suite, however, looked exactly like the junior. So, we wondered if we were in a junior or executive suite.

Then we went to McD's for the final post party. We each had a big Mac or nuggets, except Calpurnia who had only Sprite. We went back and the girls left with their luggage. Calpurnia fell asleep, while I prowled around. She was stressed out and was disinterested in eating or watching television. We thought we might go out to a movie, but decided not to. After an hour I came to bed also.

We stayed in bed until 11:30, although we did get up for the breakfast. The breakfast was the simple vitamin breakfast, with fruits, yogurt, and breads with jams.

We checked out at 1 p.m. and left the luggage at the desk. The check-out brought more problems as we asked about the suite. When they gave us the bill it was for 711 Leva, so they had charged us $260 for the suite instead of $250, then 26 for breakfast, 5 for one coke, and 33 or so for taxes (20%); we decided to pay now and complain later about the constant miscommunications.

Then we walked to the bus stop and checked out bus times, but could not find anything early. We went to the PC HQ to get the books. We rested there for a while. Then went looking for food stuffs but the Oasis was closed. We looked at music and then went to the Capital cafe under the Sheraton for tea (I had a Japanese cake, which was two mousses, like White Russian cake). Finally we rested in the lobby then asked for a cab. As we were leaving the car driver said it would be 5 Leva; we refused, get out and then found a real cab, which cost 1.28 Leva. At the bus station we got on board and paid 12 Leva for the trip to Troyan. The trip was the fastest ever at two hours and forty minutes; the driver actually skipped many local stops. At the cab stand beside the bus station, one cab was waiting. We negotiated well, and agreed to pay 14 Leva to Aprilci and home.

Being slightly nerdy and addled, we both unpacked and hung things up, then put our presents, the wool blanket, plastic clock, and other treasures, on the dining table, before making the bed and getting in. Calpurnia went to sleep and I read a book. Well, actually, after ...

Eating Cake

Drinking to Live

It was mid-December now, and another busy Monday. Calpurnia worked in the Tourist Bureau in Aprilci while I worked on grant proposals upstairs in my small unheated office (formerly a janitor's closet). We had a quick lunch of soup and went to teach our English language class. Language class was writing Christmas cards. Then we waited half an hour and taught the beginning conversation class. This class had no advanced members but three new beginners. Calpurnia took the four girls and I took the three boys and we gave them similar lessons. Then, we went home at 2:30 and worked at home until Five. Calpurnia then went to the advanced English class at the Pepsi restaurant, where everyone could drink during class, an intriguing idea, and I went to the Hotel Ceramic up the hill in Aprilci for the annual ranger banquet.

When I got to the hotel, I looked around and found Angelar in the bar. I treated him to coffee, then he went to find the others traveling from Gabrovo, while I went to the billiards room and watched people play. The conference started after half an hour. In a small *zala*, the assistant director gave a rambling note-free speech and then introduced one of the finance women, who talked for a while about reducing travel expenses. After an hour they gave out calendars and notebooks. I talked to Petya for a while in line. Then we went to the main dining room (restaurant) where four large long tables had been set up. I sat with our rangers (of course each branch sat together but toasted the others regularly). Angelar gave out pay, paper money in small envelopes, and some rangers gave him back

113

twenties (Leva), possibly advances. We had peanuts, shopska salads, and bread, as well as the ubiquitous and lethal rakia for several hours. Then the main course came, which was turkey breast, stuffed and rolled with mashed potatoes and gravy, and quite good actually.

I talked to Angelar about plans to go out with the rangers later in the week; he said to be ready at Nine tomorrow morning. I talked to Georgiu about my letter and projects but he asked that I send it in English to Petya soon. Before eleven, I excused myself and walked, err, stumbled, down the hill in the dark. The streetlights were out as usual, as an energy conservation measure by the mayor, who needed the money for gas to visit his mistress in the next village over.

The shortest day of the year, the solstice, was yesterday. Shopped for tomatoes and gifts, mostly cigarette lighters for the men and chocolate for the women and childers.

Starting with a Bang
New Year's Eve, 2000, we got on internet early, before 7:00 and wrote more email, mostly work on grants. Went to the bazaar to get fruits and vegetables; saw Mariya's sister several times and talked. While fixing potatoes for dinner, Vulko called and asked if we wanted to come to dinner with his in-laws. We agreed to go, somewhat surprised by the timing.

At 7:30 we arrived at his house and waited with their two girls, who were busy making dinner for themselves, sandwiches with grape juice. Then we left and walked across the street! Mariya was already there, helping her sister cook. We took off our shoes and put on our new booties, presents from Mariya.

The first course of dinner was a plate of meats from the pig, including brains and stomach, along with cabbage, a hard-boiled egg and homemade syrene. I could not eat the first, but had several helpings of cabbage. We were served rakia to start, then Fanta limon, and water. The next course was sarmi, rice stuffed grape leaves and also rice-stuffed cabbage leaves; with lemon it was wonderful. Then pieces of chicken, with mashed potatoes, also good with lemon juice. We were served white wine, Bulgarian of course. Then the red wine came out, which everyone mixed with lemon soda to make a spritzer; not bad. We had been eating and drinking for about four hours when the last course came out: Fried steaks. I was too full to eat one. Then, before midnight the champagne came out and glasses were poured. During dinner the stereo had been on with classical music and some popular songs. At the same time the televisions (one in the kitchen and one in the living room) had been showing new years celebrations from everywhere else — ten-second clips from other countries and live shows from around Bulgaria.

We toasted with the champagne and then loaded our pockets with fireworks; we walked downtown to the central square. A restaurant was playing music in the square. We stood around and met other people sharing drinks from bottles of champagne. Then dancing started so Calpurnia and I went with Mariya's sister and danced a wacky horo — no one was in synch at all. Dancing was a large part of Bulgarian life. Virtually every celebration included dancing. For instance, the New Year's party ended with a long dance. Meanwhile all the men were throwing bangers (fire crackers) into the crowd, which deafened all of us.

The crowd started to break up so we went back. As we walked back, we put the remaining firecrackers in broken steel sign posts and watched as the flames blew out. Back at the house, we had desert, which was a great raspberry torte, with Austrian cookies and fruit. Just before 2:00, we staggered home and went to sleep. But we were up within hours from rakia poisoning.

The day after, we were invited to Vulko's family home to participate in killing the winter swine. We got there before 9:00 and Vulko, three butchers, and his father were stoking the boiling water (I was hoping that the pig had already been killed, but she had not). Calpurnia and I went in with Mariya and her two daughters, where we were treated to tea and cake; then she brought out a plate of mekitsas and I had three of them. Calpurnia ate a piece of cake, which was like German chocolate with walnuts.

Then, Vulko asked if we wanted to see the pig killed; we said no, then I changed my mind and went outside wearing rubber flip-flops. Dyado brought out the very large swine (maybe 300 pounds) on a rope; he led her in a circle, so her feet did not get tangled. Then, the four men each grabbed a leg and upended her on her back; she squealed. One of the front-leg men plunged his knife into her throat and she screamed; he cut like a hara-kiri cut and backed off. The other three held her down as she gouted dark blood; the screaming stopped as she choked on her blood. After she stopped kicking and struggling, the other three let go. There was a lot of blood pumped out. One of the men kicked her in the hind leg. The rope was used to bind her hind feet, then they all pulled her out to the front. My job was to open the gates. If it was so easy to kill an animal, I wondered why people thought it hard to kill a human being.

She was dragged to the front patio, next to a table and two sawhorses. She was still moving sometimes but obviously not consciously. The breathing slowed and stopped. I touched her ear, but did not try to catch the last breath (as I always did with my animals as they died). With Vulko, we lifted her onto the table top then lifted the front of the table onto a sawhorse; urine squirted out the back for a few minutes. Then the others lifted up the back. Vulko and I carried boiling water from the drum (with a fire under it); the fire was so hot that my shoes started to burn as I got two teakettles of water each time, and the smoke was so thick that I had to be sure to be cautious and not dip too deeply. We used the water to heat her skin as the three butchers started to shave the hairs off. That took an hour.

One of the men fired up an industrial blowtorch and used it to burn and blacken the skin. When this was finished, we took a break and had hot rakia and cabbage salad. Then the city water went out. No one seemed surprised. Vulko and I walked to a neighbor's well and carried back about ten buckets for the boiling drum. Then we poured boiling water on the blackened skin again and the butchers shaved her again. This took another hour.

Completely pink and clean, we turned her on her back. The butchers went to work. First they cut off the feet and head; the feet were taken inside to the baba and the head was hung on a tree. Then they cut out the entire belly. The skin, thick with fat was taken to the basement where it was salted on a table. The intestines were taken out; one of the butchers worked on the intestines for the next hour, separating the small and large intestines, then emptying and washing them. Another butcher carved out the heart, lungs and liver, and hung them up under the grape arbor. Then all four legs, haunches actually, were removed and hung in the basement. Meat from the back was removed in long strips and taken in the house to be cooked first. The rib cage was removed and divided and hung in the basement. During all this my job was to wash things with near boiling water, including the knives and everybody's hands. Other meats were removed and put on trays, which were taken into the house. Finally, the entire skin was divided in two and the halves were taken to the other basement (in the old house, the one his parents had built first) and salted with the belly. We spent half an hour cleaning up, washing down the patio, and giving a few scraps to the dog. Nothing was left of the pig, and every part had been kept for eating later (except the contents of the intestines, which were put in the garden).

The day started out cold and cloudy; it was just above zero when the pig was killed. Then the sun came out and much of the snow melted. Calpurnia and I sat on the porch and watched Dyado put away the teakettles and rope. Then, we were called inside, where Mariya had set a table with salads and bread. We sat down and quickly were served scraps of pork tenderloin. The butchers came back in clean clothes and we all started drinking rakia. Calpurnia and I kept to the hot rakia, having learned to nurse half a glass for hours. Then mashed potatoes came as well as more cabbage salad. We all ate small portions. People came and went on various errands, then the Dyado and Baba came up from the basement and sat also. Then Mariya brought out large servings of tenderloin, but by then we were too full to eat much.

About 4:30, after she brought out cake and peanuts, also. We made our farewells and left. We went on a long walk to try to digest the food. Back at the apartment we had tea and worked on the computers.

Driving off Ghosts

A few months later, we had a typical Sunday to start: slept late, then, went to the bazaar for fruit and vegetables; spent about eight Leva. Then in the afternoon, a truck with a tree drove across the back gardens — we watched three guys unload a telephone pole and put it in a shallow hole. Then, they left and came back with about twenty car tires; then they left and returned again loaded with evergreen branches. We thought they were building an addition to the old building out back. But, then they hung the tires from the pole, then hung the branches from it.

As it got dark we heard a voice calling us. I was not sure who it was, so I did not answer. Then Vulko came to the door and asked if we wanted to participate in a celebration. We said yes, we would be down in ten minutes. Once down, we noticed about nine men sitting in the rain under the eve eating the strange canned meat things that Bulgarians love to eat. On asking, we were told that today was the day to celebrate Old Bulgaria. We wondered if it may have been suppressed by the Communists.

I went back up and brought vodka down, but there were gallons of rakia, so Calpurnia and I had a glass of rakia — immediate headache! Then we tried bread, pickles, pork, and smoked Elen meat, but declined the fat and canned meat. One of the butchers played a trick on me by asking me to identify the face on a glass, which looked like Stalin. I thought maybe I should not say Stalin and said Vasil Levski, but then he laughed and said it was Stalin; everyone laughed. At least I erred on the side of ignorance rather than political incorrectness. He filled the glass with rakia.

At dark, we saw two other bonfires start in the hills around Aprilci. Calpurnia and I got up and went on a walk to look at them closer. When we came back, the bonfire was ready to light. It was hard because of the freezing rain, so we went inside and watched from the balcony. Someone kept throwing gasoline on the flames until the tires started burning, then the whole thing went up and burned for several hours. The flames were about fifty feet high; the black billowing smoke was tremendous. The sparks lit up the sky over the river. We went inside rather than breathe that stuff.

The next morning, the pole was still smoldering, but no flames. Everything, grass, buildings, and roads, were covered with black soot. If it hadn't scared the ghosts, it certainly would have poisoned them.

Celebrating Spring Or *Mother March on Horseback*

Two months later, on a Sunday, we got up late (8:00) and rushed to the internet to check on messages. The British Wolf Group had offered to fund more research in Bulgaria, so I answered them and thanked them! The *Echo* had asked if they could profile me; so, I asked Calpurnia if she would like to be profiled instead. She said no, so I told them I was too busy with surveys, unless they would be willing to do an email interview.

Around 5 p.m., we cleaned up and left. Calpurnia and I walked back to the apartment and got ready for dinner with Vulko. The sky had high bright clouds and a cool breeze. After an hour of working on the computers, we left for dinner at Vulko and Mariya's.

Vulko was waiting for us in the garden; he was dirty and sweaty. We gave him the wine and rum, and he said that he had a surprise for us, an enormous pizza. We followed him to the shed by the doghouse; there was a clay oven with a clay-straw door, which he lifted off. He said it had been cooking for three hours. It was in a deep metal pan, covered with aluminum foil. He took the foil off and revealed it was an entire lamb. He asked Calpurnia if she liked lamb and she said yes, very much; he asked me and I said no, I had never eaten it. I had been a vegetarian too long.

We drained the juices and took the lamb over to the garden table, which was set for dinner. First we had "koktaili" with rum and coconut. Then rakia. Mariya brought two salads, a green cabbage salad and a tomato/cucumber salad. We ate those, then she brought out two more. His parents sat down—this was a second rare time we had eaten with them; we were surprised that we had not done so often before. I had once asked Vulko if he liked living next to his parents; he only rolled his eyes. We talked about the politics of Aprilci. The mayor, again, agreed to accept money for a heating plant next to the school. The city council had suggested water treatment as the first priority, but the mayor decided without their approval. Then, we discovered that the grandfather had relatives in Chicago that he had not heard from since the 1950s, so we agreed to search the internet to get a phone number and address.

Mariya served the lamb. I asked for a small piece with mostly rice (it turned out to be a stuffed lamb). The rest of us were served while Vulko and Mariya continued to poke at their salads. We now had wine and beer also. Desert was strawberries, from the garden, with ice cream, that Monika, who was now only in half a body cast for her spine, walked out and picked up. It had been three months since her operation and she had another three months to endure in the cast.

About 10:30, after the parents had gone to bed, we also begged off and walked home, having eaten a week's worth of food in one day and expecting to take a week to digest it.

March first, we slept late, but we were surprised by Vulko, who showed up at 9:30 with Baba Marta ribbons. After he gave us two, I gave him three, for him, Mariya and Alekka. Then he asked us if we wanted to go to the elementary school to see Baba Marta — we said yes and got dressed, unable to take time to drink the hot tea Calpurnia had made.

We drove to the Edelweiss Day Care School in Ostrets with Vulko and his daughter Alekka, who was spoiled and had not had to go to her day care school for three months, preferring to stay with her grandmother, who lived in the basement of their house. As we got out of the car, Alekka started to cry, but Vulko assured her she would get to see Baba Marta.

In the school, which was not only warm, but richly decorated, the classroom was already filled with about thirty children; more came in, with a few teachers and a few mothers. We knew the head of the school, who was the sister of my landlord. She greeted us warmly. We sat in the back with Vulko (and I prayed that I would not have to give a speech in Bulgarian, even to six-year-olds — Bulgarian children did not start First grade until the age of Seven). First, the director made a speech, but the camera man, from the local cable, made her start over again, after he fixed the sound; she started over but was less loud then her first attempt — she must have been nervous about her Bulgarian, too.

Then two older children came in, dressed all in red and white; two girls, one dressed as a boy. They recited a memorized passage about the meaning of spring. Then two younger gypsy kids gave a memorized talk also. Then an older boy, maybe eight, gave a short talk. Then the director took up her accordion and all the children sang songs of spring. After the first two songs, various teachers led their classes in dances, including one that I had learned to do — I wanted to dance with them, but I was behind too many chairs. After fifteen minutes of dancing the children were called to the window to see that Baba Marta had arrived and was decorating trees outside with ribbons. She was outside doing just that. She was a woman of about sixty with very long braided hair, wearing a traditional peasant costume in red and white; she was carrying a large basket of red and white ribbons.

The children were asked to run down and greet her, which they did with great glee and noise. Only the adults and Alekka were left in the classroom. Then, they came back with Baba Marta. She sat in a corner and a large basket of popcorn was placed in front of her. Then a tray of rolls was placed next to her. She was greeted by the teachers, who brought the students up one by one. The students each recited a poem and in turn were given a pin with a ribbon on it; each pin was plastic and had a dog or cat on it.

When she was done with all the kindergarten children she stood up and walked to the older children and gave them each a ribbon from her dreidel. Then she gave ribbons to us and the other adults. The director thanked her for coming and a short ceremony closed the morning. As we were leaving one teacher rushed over with a roll for Alekka, who started eating it immediately. We drove back to the center.

For lunch I made falafels, using the Arabic mix and a Bulgarian flatbread. They were excellent. Now, we had to get more somehow in Sofia.

Off to the Races

Two days later March third, we woke up and cleaned the apartment. Then, got ready for the horse races. At 10 a.m., we walked to the central square and waited for "the guys" from the advanced English class. We spotted Aleksander first and waited with him, then Closimir and his son showed up, so we set off across the foot bridge and up the hill past Kosta's house, then continued up hill until we ran out of street, right by a vacation house with a nice swimming pool (empty now).

Then we started up the muddy trail. In fact it was so muddy that we walked on the upper bank. The trail went straight up the hill past old orchards and cow pastures. At the top of the hill there was a large pasture with an enclosed section for raspberries. We walked along the ridge as it changed to an old orchard, in which the lower half of the trees had all been cut and only branches remained on the ground. Down the hill on one side was brush and pines, on the other side it was a hunting lodge (for wealthy German tourists), which also sold Christmas trees. In the distance we could see the large pottery factory, on whose grounds the race would be held; we could hear people, then rising over the people was the same ultralight craft we had seen for the first time on a trip to Troyan — it was flying over the race area. Many cars were parked along the road and by the factory; the two most popular brands were Lada and Mercedes.

Beside the factory were many grills selling hot kebabche, fries and bread. There were also a few bazaar merchants selling jewelry and clothes. There was a large flatbed truck with speakers; a tape was playing of Bulgarian music. There was a microphone. We arrived and stood on the hillside overlooking the track and directly across from the flatbed. Closimir asked me if I would like to race—I said yes, but I would prefer to know the horse first. I thought he was kidding, but then he asked if we wanted to go down and meet his friend who was racing.

There were about forty horses and riders milling about, including the wild priest (the only one who was a bachelor, has a long hair and beard, and rode a horse apparently—the other two priests in town wore the Cossacks, but had homburgs and briefcases when they walked around). Closimir's friend was on a large black stallion. We took a few pictures, but no one asked me if I really wanted to race. I did, but these horses were all nervous and had metal bits in their mouths, not a single hackamore, which was what I was used to using, so I was nervous. Then the mayor was introduced to a few claps and a few boos. He introduced a musician who sang a little. Then all of the riders and horses were introduced.

The Great Race

The Great Horse Races

We got confused because it seemed the owners names were also mentioned, as well as the towns they were riding from. One of the riders had a traditional British riding apparel, another was dressed like a cowboy. There was a whole group of kids on ponies. There would be seven heats with five horses each and then the winner of each would be in the final. The race committee had cleverly made one heat with all of Aprilci horses to ensure that Aprilci would be represented in the final.

We were standing around talking when the first race started— there was no gun or other loud start. In fact some of the horses left the starting gate long after the others. It was quite confusing around the starting gate. Two of the other heats had false starts, but the first three horses ran all the way anyway. Calpurnia and I took turns with the camera. Zhan, Krassimira, and Petja, from the advanced class, also showed up. We saw Vulko and talked with him for a while. Towards the end of the races Angelar showed up with his family.

His wife had bought a martinitsa for Calpurnia (to celebrate March). Angelar and I talked about my plans and work for a while, then I promised another letter and calendar.

The final approached. Two of the horses were very fast, including Krusthew's friend. The race started and the friend on the black horse was behind. He tried to catch up but the chestnut held on to win. The prizes were handed out by the Vice mayor and celebrities, including our very own Gameyski, who probably owned some of the horses. Closimir bought a dozen kebabche and offered everyone one. Calpurnia and I shared one. Quite good actually, like a sausage.

We watched a while longer, then Aleksander asked if we wanted to go. We said whenever they did, so we walked up the hill again. The crowd broke up. We walked back, talking about Aprilci history and the cable station, which received satellite stuff and shipped it to everyone's house or apartment (although many places had large satellite dishes of their own. Aleksander suggested that the dish was the national flower, although Calpurnia noted that West Virginia had beat them to it).

In Aprilci, we went back to the apartment and rested before going to the advanced class. I had set up a series of questions and Calpurnia had selected a portion of the business English book. At 1700, we walked to the center, met Aleksander and went to the Center (Pepsi) Restaurant. Andrei and Closimir showed up. It was obvious that Closimir and Andrei belonged to different political parties and had difficulties talking to each other. Nevertheless the evening proceeded for a few hours and we had a good discussion. At home, we read and relaxed.

We caught the 8:20 bus to Troyan and Aprilci. The people ahead of us were trying to figure out the schedule; since they were speaking English we helped. They were from North Carolina and sold crafts at bazaars in America. So, we sat together on the bus and told them about Troyan and Aprilci. The bus was only a third full but slower than normal.

In Aprilci we raced home, called Vulko about dinner that night, then went out and bought food. Calpurnia cut up the tomatoes, cheese and onions. I did the mushrooms and assembled the sauce and tortellini. It did not look like enough so I made pizza also. Then, because we had bottled green beans, I made a mushroom, bean, tomato salad with oil and balsamic vinegar.

Vulko and Mariya arrived, with a bottle of wine and a present (a cotton shirt). We had drinks. Then Christine called with birthday wishes. Then Dr. Vulkov called to set up a meeting about his book.

We set out the food in courses. Then tried the Cuban rum.

We talked about the things in Aprilci, as well as their family, and what we thought we might do once we were back in America. They left about ten. There was a lightning display, which I watched in fascination from under the eave of city hall. I went back in and called. Then we settled down to watch a movie, but five minutes into it, the electricity failed, so we went to sleep and watch the lightning over the mountains. The rain hit and was tremendous. Much more involving and dramatic than a small electronic screen.

Moonshine & Sunlight

A while later we had a full day at the Tourist Office, finishing grant proposals and moving pictures from the zip drive to Vulko's computer, which now had USB ports and could handle the zip drive and the camera disk port. We waited for the Bulgarian class, our last for the summer, with Penka, but none of our students showed up. The evening class was also canceled. Then at 5:00 Vulko invited us to help him make rakia, so we walked over to observe this mysterious process.

When we get there, we went directly to the barn, where Vulko pulled aside an old wool blanket to show us the barrels and still. Alekka, the youngest daughter, brought cookies out. We started to transfer the rotten plums (sleevee) from the fermentation barrel to the copper still, which was embedded in a brick fireplace. After about five buckets full, Vulko added a gallon of weak rakia from a blue barrel (like a modern plastic water barrel). Then we started the fire. The top was added and cemented with a mixture of flour and ashes. The transfer pipe was then fastened to the top linking it to the cooler barrel, in which a large copper pipe was centered in a gallon copper barrel; at the bottom was the outlet pipe. The remaining pipes were sealed. The fire was slowly fed with twigs and broken branches, from pruning it looked like, with one large block of wood in the back.

Mariya brought out tea and we stood around. Then it was time for the goats to come home, rather one milk goat and two large dirty, long-tailed sheep. These animals had been collected in the morning by a shepherd and herded around town to eat grass and weeds, then returned. About fifteen minutes later Vulko's father brought home the cow, who has also been collected by another shepherd and taken up the hill to a pasture. The cow smells us and was uncertain, but was slapped around by the old man until she goes into her barn stall.

The first drops of rakia started to flow. Vulko cupped his hands and tried the first. He blessed it. I tried it and almost fainted. He suggested that it was weak, but we collected a bucket and put it into a small barrel by the house. We hooked up the hose to the cooling barrel so that the new water cooled it; the water still got very hot. The runoff hose ran to an open pit by the house; this was where the sewage from the toilet and grey water from the sinks collected before flowing on its way to the Ostretska river by our apartment. For every subsequent bucket, he measured its temperature and alcohol content by using a combination thermometer and gizmo (sorry, I just could not get the Bulgarian name for it), which also had a copper sleeve. All the other buckets were poured into the water barrel which was a fourth full of weak rakia from the last batch. As we were stoking the fire, or cooling it so it did not get too hot, I told Vulko that this was illegal in most all US states, even my native Virginia. He laughed and said it has been illegal for a long time in Bulgaria; then described how they hid the tanks and vats and barrels with curtains across the barn.

Mariya came out and filled a maple syrup jar with rakia and then went back in the house to work on making salads and potatoes for dinner. I tried the rakia again and said it was perfect. Vulko tried it, laughed and said it was just water now. Well, I thought, that must account for my liking it. I wondered if Vulko thought all Americans were as weak drinkers as Calpurnia and I. So, we took apart the fire by pulling out the burning wood and watering it. Then we took apart the still by rubbing the seals with hot water, and cleaned the still of all the remaining plum pits and garbage, which was collected for the chickens, goats and pig—nothing was every thrown away until there was no value left in it. The manure was collected for the garden, which was the source for most all vegetables and fruits, which were intercropped with the trees.

We had a brief rakia-soaked dinner, then went for a long walk, before we shuffled home. We passed my favorite horse, Red.

Red waiting

Exciting Cross-cultural Miscommunications

Dancing. As I went to Bulgarian language classes in the elementary school, I read over the biographies of the instructors. One attractive woman named Lillia said in her bio that she loved to dance. After school, at the cultural exchange, I asked her to dance; she said no thanks. Later I asked another instructor, Aleksander, what that meant; he said that just because she liked to dance did not mean that she wanted to dance with me! Aleksander suggested that I take dance classes. I did and by August Lillia and I got to dance together in a horo—a Bulgarian folk dance with 50 people in a line dancing for 45 minutes to a rapidly increasing tempo, until the old and weak collapse; in fact, near the end I tripped and fell into the laps of two grandmothers, who were resting; they were surprised but friendly. I wondered if they were older than I was.

The meaning of being vegetarian. My host family made a wonderful meal of pork, chicken, cabbage and potatoes. I remind them that I was a vegetarian. They said that was why there was no meat from a cow. I sampled the food and it was good. I tried to describe what vegetarian meant.

The next night there were small pieces of chicken, which I ate. But, I explained that being a vegetarian meant no meat from any animal. The next night there was chicken soup, but with no pieces of meat. It was very good. I reminded myself that I was an ethical vegetarian and figured that I should be a good Buddhist and just accept what I was given. Somewhat later, on New Year's day, I drew the line at fresh raw pig's ears.

Good Housing. I showed up for my first day at the Central Balkan National Park. My colleague Angelar drove me to a large three-story, four-bedroom house that had been rented for me (it cost $65 a month, but my living allowance was $130). The house was completely empty, with no furnace, no stove, no toilet, no refrigerator, or no furniture; there was a sink in the kitchen and one in the bathroom, and on the second story there was a single metal bed with a cotton mattress over layers of old magazines.

I asked him what happened. He said that Americans liked large houses (and in Bulgaria, large was synonymous with beautiful) and this was the most beautiful available. I asked about a furnace; he said I would had to buy one. I said that I had no money. That night I slept on the mattress on the floor (the loose springs had made the bed into a hammock), listening to the rats walk around. They were still walking around in the morning and I saw they had nice furry tails.

I asked Angelar to help me find a place with a furnace and

stove (having lived in rural Oregon, toilets were optional). He showed me many large places without furnaces or stoves. Then, he got a call that the rangers had located a beautiful apartment for me in an old hotel that had been converted. Also, an apartment downtown Aprilci that we could see the next day. We got to the hotel by Five, which was located on the very edge of the village of Vidima. The apartment was quite nice with energy saving large windows overlooking the mountains, and with a beautiful bath, with a tiled tub, but no kitchen. When I asked, I was told that they would put a small fridge and tiny cook stove in the corner. The living room had three single beds in it, but the bedroom has a double bed, plus a huge wardrobe. There was no desk or table. The balcony was great and had plastic chairs. I looked up and saw another balcony above, and asked about it. It was the attic, I was told; they did not think I would be interested but I could see it.

So, we did. It was slightly smaller with only 2 windows, but the same bathroom. It was laid out a little better. I was told that the lower apartment was 300 Leva a month and the attic was 200. I said that I would decide the next day, and I liked the idea of a bath, especially since I was black with smoke and ashes from fighting the last forest fire. But, I could not decide. Finally I screwed up my courage and went looking for myself (asking to rent places in Bulgarian was a challenge). After three days I found a small apartment with furnace, stove, fridge, toilet, and real bed — even dishes and carpets. Angelar asked why I would want to live in such a small place.

Time. I took the 5:30 bus to Vidima and waited for Boleslav, a ranger. He was a no-show, but I knew he said the early bus; so I walked into the park by myself. It took 2 hours just to get to the entrance. Then I walked by gravel road for a few hours, then by trail, then along the river, then up to the head wall of the river. From there I climbed an easy rock face, getting unbalanced several times with the pack and sleeping bag. I could not find the mountain hut, where we were supposed to hike. It was on the map and I had seen it from Maragadjik, a nearby peak last week, but it must have been over another ridge or two.

I saw many birds but no bears or other vertebrates, no evidence of them either. Before dark I took an hour to have a picnic by another stream, which was coming off a higher peak and just beginning to wear the rock face. I drank the water, having forgotten water, as well as my thick socks. Then I rolled out the sleeping bag, lay on some good grasses under some beech trees and went to sleep.

The bag was quit warm although my bare head got cold. I did not sleep really well, but the ground was not too hard; the noises were new and strange (I found out later it was wild swine). I wondered where I was. Not having found Boleslav or the hut I decided to backtrack to Vidima. A few times I got lost around the streams and ridges, but I found the first trail. By the time I got to the trail below my feet had large blisters. I put on a second pair of sox and went on. Finally I reached Vidima at 1:30, just in time for the bus I thought. Wrong. First the owner of a cafe where I bought orange juice came over the bus bench to talk, then the retired postmaster, then a woman waiting for the bus; they all wanted to know about America and to tell me about themselves, so we talked and listened. The bus would be another hour they said.

Then it rained heavily and we all scattered to different shelters. At 2:45 I got tired of waiting for the bus and started walking. It took an hour to get home. Boleslav (who resembles George Clooney) arrived an hour later and asked where I was. I told him. He said that I took the first bus, at 5:30 a.m., but the early bus was at 7:00 a.m. and that was the one he was waiting for.

Driving Rules. I got a ride to Gabrovo for a Park meeting. Vulko was driving. It was a sunny day. He asked me if I wanted to drive. I said yes, but I could not. He stopped and said I could if I wanted. I explained that the Peez Core forbid volunteers to drive. He asked if any other volunteers had ever driven. I said yes, but no one knew it. He asked if they were thrown out. I said just one. He asked me again if I wanted to drive. I said I could not. He asked would it be bad if I were sent back to America. I said yes. He asked why, because he would like to go there. I said I had to finish my assignment. He shrugged and drove on. We were not wearing seat belts, which was considered a sign of distrust in the driver; in fact, there were none in most cars. There was a seat belt law on the books but it was not enforced, although once when we approached the police Vulko fastened his seat belt, unfastening it when they were out of sight.

Invitations. A Bulgarian colleague asked me to give a brief talk on wolf biology for his course in Gabrovo. I agreed. On the appointed day, I showed up at the appointed time. He asked me where I had been, why had I missed the banquet. I said I did not realize that there was one or that I was invited. He said there was; it was the March banquet and everyone knew about it. I apologized and said that I did not know.

Then we went into the lecture hall. It was not to be a brief talk after all but an invited lecture and training for two hours for the students who were studying to be rangers. I had no slides or handouts, and my prepared talk was only ten minutes. So, I gave an informal training, by describing my research and giving anecdotal information. From then on, I required a written invitation with a written schedule.

Spying. After working with Trifon for several months on an internet center, we got funding from USAID. I helped him remodel the rooms and we installed the computers. As we were working, he asked if I was CIA. I said no, that no Peace Corps volunteer could had any connection or experience with certain agencies. He asked FBI? I said no. He asked how we got funding. I replied that he got the funding and all I did was help with the translation. He said that the Mayor had told him I was a CIA spy, furthermore that all the volunteers to Bulgaria were trying to get her secrets to use against her. I asked him how the Mayor thought that. He said the Mayor was communist and resented Americans being here. I asked, how could that be, since the Mayor was elected in a free democratic process. I asked what secrets. He said guns and goat cheese. I pointed out that America buys both from Bulgaria, especially the machine guns which were very popular in some states.

I asked him what could I do. He said I needed to tell everyone that I was not a spy during our conversations. A few months later, during a television interview, I announce "Ne sum spionen" and laughed. No one else laughed but I was sure I heard several sighs of relief.

Later, I asked Aleksander, a language student, why people thought I was a spy. He said that it was because I was an American and everyone knew that we were always spying for oil or gold. He said he told his friend Aleksander, who also thought I was a spy, that there was nothing to spy on in Bulgaria, except for sheep and abandoned factories. But Aleks said that we were in constant communication with spy satellites that told us where to spy, and as for what, it was a secret. If he told me, I might find out. I could not argue with that.

Secrecy. A colleague asked if we could had a secret meeting. I said sure. So, we went to coffee at the largest coffee shop (of three in town). I said why was it secret if everyone could see us. He said all the meetings were in the coffee shops — that was where every decision was made. What made it secret was that no one told the Mayor what we were talking about. He told me that he wanted to go to America and wondered if I could help him. Since I had found out how from the embassy, I said that the only way I could help him was to send an invitation to him after I was back in America. For now I could do nothing.

Body Language. I went into a mini market to ask for orange juice. The clerk nodded yes but said no. I asked her where it was. She said they did not had any. Then I remembered, embarrassed, that in Bulgaria, moving one's head up and down means no (and sideways means yes). I kept forgetting this, although later I closed my eyes and listened to the words. When I talked I just bounced my head on my shoulders for any communication, regardless of what I actually said.

Money. One day one of my students (from Advanced Conversational English — the Peace Corpse told me I was on duty 24 hours a day and should not refuse any requests for help) asked me if we could have class in the hotel of a friend of his (Aprilci was only 1100 people but had 10 working hotels — many of which were factory hotels with names like "Ceramic," "Biochem," and Cattle Breeding."). I said sure.

At the hotel the owner sat down and asked if I could get funding for his hotel. I said I would be happy to look, but I was an ecologist and didn't know much about funding businesses. He pointed out that I had gotten money for the internet, library, craftsmen, and National Park. I admitted that was true, but it was just a few thousand dollars, not the $85,000 that he wanted, and it was from small humanitarian or research groups.

He gave me a tour of the place and I got him a few addresses from the Web. Then he asked if I could get all PC volunteers to stay at his hotel. I said that I would ask then to do so, if they came here. He asked if I could had a conference for them at his hotel. I said I would ask. Later, I got requests from schools, hotels and restaurants for financial help. I tried to show them how to look for help on the Web.

Banking. One day I went to the bank to take out money to pay my rent. The bank said they could not give me any money from my account. I went home and got $50 USD to get changed to Leva. They again refused. Finally I asked to speak with the manager. She told me I could not get anything for the next two weeks because they were doing the end of the year accounts (this was mid-December). I asked why they were open. She said in case anyone needed anything, like an account balance. I asked if I could see mine; she said no, it was in Sofia and they did not know what the balance was.

I took the bus for an hour to another town and used a bank machine, called a bankomat, to get my rent money. I bought some English cereal and went back and paid the rent.

Hotel Rates. I checked into the Niki Hotel in Sofia and gave the clerk 20 Leva. She said it was 40 Leva. I said no, the posted rate was 20. She said that was for Bulgarians, that Americans and Swiss had to pay double rates. I said how did she know I was not Bulgarian, since we were talking in Bulgarian. She said my clothes were non-Bulgarian. I said I bought them in Aprilci where I lived. I said I had a Bulgarian passport and a letter from the Minister urging hoteliers to give me Bulgarian rates. She said she did not care, I was not Bulgarian. I said, as a volunteer, I had less money than Bulgarians, not more. She said I had made more in the US (this was true of course). I said everything cost more there, where I had to pay the equivalent of 6 Leva for a loaf of bread rather than 0.40 Leva here. She said I had to pay the highest amount. I said I would go somewhere else. She said that was fine; she was just a clerk and would earn the same amount either way. I said not if the hotel closed for lack of business. She shrugged, and I went to the local youth hostel and paid 16 Leva and got a free breakfast as well.

Got Milk? One day, I was hungry for milk (after 15 months without). I had not seen it in any of the stores. So, I asked Iva, my favorite proprietress, for milk (she had been able to get pickles and Greek ice cream for me). I described that I wanted cows milk that came in glass or cardboard wax containers. She asked if I had a cow. I said no, but the neighbors did. She said she would have some tomorrow. I assumed that she would order it from Troyan, like she did the yogurt or bread.

 The next day I arrived early and a man was unloading a white substance from a plastic bucket from his Russian car. He took it in. I followed. Iva poured it into an old coffee container and said it was a gift. I took it home, boiled it and drank it. Next week she had irradiated milk in boxes from France. I went back to eating yogurt.

Connections. A friend of mine was working for a one-woman NGO near the Black Sea. She had nothing to do for six months and wondered if I had a project she could work on (she helped me contact shepherds later). I asked how she got assigned there—she said "vruski" (connections); her director was friends with the woman in the capitol who made assignments and who owed her a favor, so she got a Peas Core volunteer to baby-sit her kids.

 I didn't think much about this informal economy of connections until I needed a window for a winter night blind I was building in the mountains. I asked one of the rangers, Dimitar, for help. He took me to a local sawmill, where the operator made a small window to my specs. When I tried to pay, he suggested that bring the beer to the next party that Friday (which I did, and it cost about

$4 for a case of 24 bottles). Then we went to the hardware store, and argued about hinges; again, I did not have to pay, and I found out that Dimitar gave the owner two bottles of rakia from his home still. Then we went to another ranger, Tsonko, who had a chain saw. The three of us went to the mountains and finished the blind in a few hours. I think Dimitar gave Tsonko an old car axle for his help. The next night I sat up and watched the green shapes of pigs, deer, wolves, and mice through a nightscope that I had bought in Walmart the year before.

Biology. I told the forestry unit that I was a biologist and ecologist. I had experience studying the relations of plants and animals. I went into gruesome detail about the breadth and depth of my experience, with trees and animals, from porcupines and coyotes to black bears. I asked them in detail about the kinds of problems they had in Bulgarian forests, listening to the special problems with the unique beech forests, the largest extent in Europe. Finally, after three days of assessment, they assigned me to kill pigs in the Forestry units in the mountains, even providing me with a gun and many kinds of bullets (the shotgun shells did not fit the rifle).

Information. Today I saw the clash of an information culture (USA) with a culture that values anonymity (Socialist). Heather asked the Bulgarians at the conference to collect data for the telecenters, including name, address, id number, telephone and email. They did not like the idea. I suggested collecting only information about age, sex, time and maybe income. I understood that the US was supporting the initiative and it wanted to know if the help was being used. And the Bulgarians wanted to use the technology, but they did not want their names or numbers on lists or databases.

Nagosti Or *the Fine Tradition of Visiting*
We had decided to return to Dupnitsa to visit our host families after a nine months. We took the 5:30 bus to Sofia and had a small lunch at Murphy's, an Irish bar, which was not very good this time. The weather at least was warm and beautiful, unlike the food.

Calpurnia and I looked at the trams, which were crammed with students, and then took a cab to go to the Southwest bus station (it cost 4 Leva). In the dark, we found the bus to Dupnitsa; the ride was mercifully brief, then we walked to Petya and Zlatka's house. We had brought them gifts, a Bulgarian tradition for visiting. There we were treated to a chicken and pork dinner, which we nibbled at, along with gin and cola. But, mostly, we exchanged news of our lives over the past year. About 10 we climbed up to Calpurnia's old room, with the double bed with the broken springs. The heater was going full blast and the room was very warm.

It snowed over night, and we woke to six inches of snow on the ground. Everyone overslept. Petya made mekitsas, which were very good. Zlatka and I scarfed down many with yogurt. I walked over to my host family, the Ilievis, and had a long lunch with them.

By Two, I was back at the other host family; we wiled away a few hours and then drove to Blagoevgrad. Zlatka's boyfriend (number Nine?) had borrowed a car, a Volkswagen rabbit, but we got stopped in the city by the police at a roadblock and the boyfriend paid a 10 Leva fine for not having his registration. We then walked to a large coffee shop on top of a building and had coffee. We walked to the American University, which was across the square from the city hall; they got a big kick out of showing the university to us and we took many pictures with each other. Then we walked around the town and drove back to Dupnitsa in the snow. That night we took Zlatka to a Chinese restaurant in Dupnitsa; the food was okay. Chinese restaurants were almost as popular as Irish pubs and somewhat more exotic, especially since only Chinese people ran them. Afterwards, we had dessert at home, a chocolate crème cake that we bought in one of the new grocery stores in Dupnitsa. A few obligatory drinks, then to bed.

We slept late again as Petya and Zlatka always slept late on weekends. A small breakfast of yogurt and syrene biscuits. We talked until Three, then it was time to walk over to the other host family to stay for a day, so we packed up and walked, then gave up after a block and took a taxi.

At the Ilievis, we unpacked and gave them their presents. Then we went to the internet cafe for a while to answer emails. It was slow compared to Sofia. Then back for an early dinner. We talked and showed pictures for an hour. Luboslav made many kebabche on the grill in the garage. We started with soup, peanuts, and salad. Then the main course of kebabche and fries. We had vodka and wine. Talked and watched a little television until about 9:45. I had never been so tired of talking.

Breakfast was apple strudel. We talked for a while, in case some topic had not been covered adequately, then packed for the bus station, taking a taxi there also for about a Lev. There we took another bus back to Sofia. Once there another cab for three Leva to the South bus station, where we were two hours early. We walked around looking for an internet cafe. Then had tea at a hole-in-the-wall cafe. Walking back to the bus station in the snow, we spotted a larger restaurant and spent five Leva for a good lunch. The bus was on time and the snow did not slow down our return.

Animal Schedules

Finally, we had scheduled formal animal surveys for the Park.

Up early, I had cereal (well, Musli) for breakfast, with yogurt and grapefruit. Then immediately went to the internet office and read the mail. Beverly has generously offered to send books from Arizona, for the local library, but I tried to talk her out of sending more than one box (at about $50 per box for postage).

Calpurnia ran over to the office to tell me that Angelar was early. At the jeep, I asked Angelar if Calpurnia could go with us; he said okay but then added something I could not quite understand. Cali and I came down with our sleeping bags, wearing the winter ski suits. She had to sit on my lap in the front seat with three rangers in back—that must have been what Angelar said! The seat was very small and Cali had to double over against the window.

After an hour we stopped in Stokite. Angelar had to work on his report for an hour (maybe that was what he said; I need more vocabulary for complex situations). Anyway, we walked to the two stores and asked for bread; there was no bread. Could this be the legendary town without bread? We bought cheese, crackers, and chocolate, then had tea in a small cafe. The snowplows were racing through the town (large farm tractors with blades actually). We waited in the office. Another ranger joined Angelar and the other three, and they were doing their trip reports for the end of the year. Calpurnia heard them say something about a Christmas party and not a survey or ranger training.

After another hour of reading bird books, Angelar asked Dimitar to drive us and Dimitar to Lugat. That took an hour. We got there after Ten, but were kept awake until Two anyway. The room was cold. Calpurnia slept in her sleeping bag, with mine on top. I braved the wool blankets, and any resident wildlife.

We were used to bread with every meal; sometimes it was the entire meal. For example, today, breakfast was cheese and wine, with bread and tea. After an hour of joking about drinking the wine, we all wandered around while waiting for the annual photograph. Iurka, the Director, did not show up, so someone decided we should take the photos anyway. Since I had one of two cameras I got to take many photos outside in the snow. Immediately afterwards, we all jumped in the jeeps and left. It was still snowing and the trip took a few hours. The roads were mostly one-lane, which slowed things a bit. The streets of Stokite were cleanly plowed, unlike most other villages, including Aprilci.

In Aprilci, we picked up a package two magazines and a Christmas card. I had an article in one of the magazines, on wolf populations. We worked on a few projects. I went on a walk to the new soap store (every store was named by its characteristic specialty;

they do not have names), which rented old movies, some with subtitles, some dubbed. I got Godzilla with subtitles. Going back to the apartment I saw the afternoon bus to Sofia. It was pulled over by the bread store — the driver had just used his lighter to ignite a rolled newspaper and was crawling under the bus. I asked if I could help; he grunted no. Perhaps he was just melting snow buildup from the brakes, or igniting the boiler. It was still snowing.

Woke up to another nine centimeters of snow. After a healthy breakfast of German Musli, Bulgarian yogurt and British tea, I started to work on the web page. I had had to redo it as the craftsmen decided that they needed new pictures or new text or new layouts. I had still not been able to find a Bulgarian counterpart to finish it.

After a long coffee with Petar, Vulko came in (apparently he asked someone in the street where we were — everyone always knew where we were it seemed) and invited us to his daughter Alekka's fourth birthday party. I was about to say that I was going to the forest when Calpurnia agreed. It snowed all day. I continued to work on wolf model. Then, I walked in blowing snow to get margarine, toilet paper, corn flour (there was no corn meal, no sweet potatoes, and no chocolate chips, but plenty of fresh bread), fresh bread, and oranges from Turkey.

Before dinner we put a few ornaments on a tiny palm plant, our make-believe Christmas tree. Then made corn bread and baked a pumpkin. Our present to each other this year was a tea kettle, which was badly designed (burned the fingers), but was blue and looked nice. We distributed small gifts to the neighbors, especially the baba next door, who was very happy. The little girl from upstairs, later brought us a Royal Cake, a branch with three paper stars, and a small plastic toy, wrapped in a matchbox, but decorated by her, we thought. It was the first time we had been given something for Christmas, which was still not much celebrated here. I made cookies. It snowed all day and all night.

This was the second holiday in two years that we had forgotten to store up bread; we had not had fresh bread for five days. We walked to the store but there was no bread — we were told the bakers were taking an extra day off. The stores were all virtually empty, except for preserves and detergent. Bulgarian small markets seemed incapable of planning for big sales days, such as Christmas or New Years. I understood their caution; they may not had enough money to risk getting goods that could spoil. Still, at least once a month, we had to eat frozen leftovers for a few days.

This day was not officially a holiday, but only a few

shopkeepers were working. Calpurnia and I went on a short walk around the village. The internet cafe was having trouble with the signal, so the internet was no good.

It had been freezing since November twenty-first. All the rooms were closed off except for the living room, where we slept on the sofa bed, ate, and worked. There were no kleenexes, so we each had a roll of brown toilet paper by the bed; in the morning the room looked like it had been struck with large pieces of brown paper snow.

Finally, two days later, I was able to buy fresh bread, finally, although the stores were still bare. We had butter and peanut butter, as well as some cheese and salami, so the food of the day was sandwiches.

Calpurnia went to class in Bulgarian, while I worked on an article for the newspaper. This was the series of ecological thought experiments that I convinced the editor to run, although he refused to call them that and always retitled each one in awkward Bulgarian.

I contacted the Park again about my monitoring. That night we rented a movie dubbed in Bulgarian. It was a Jackie Chan movie. However, only one voice played all the parts, and the volume seemed different. I guess that each voice was dubbed separately on a different track by the same person—even the women's voices were a flat male monotone. At least the kicking was not dubbed.

I met with Aleksander for coffee and to proof his latest letter to America—he was now writing to four women in America, one in Ireland, three in Japan, and one in Italy—this one was to Lynda in America. After making a few corrections (he either had way too few words or way too many, depending on the Bulgarian original), we talked about the COOP in Aprilci; they owned four or five stores, including the main bread store. I mentioned that there were new clerks in the store, and Aleksander said that they had to fire the three clerks who were working there; they had done the inventory for the year and came up $1300 short—since none of the women confessed, they fired them all! This was a ridiculous travesty. I asked if it could have been just miscalculation or waste. He said no, they kept records. I pointed out that they wrote down the amounts on paper, but Aleksander said at the end of the day, they put them in an adding machine. I said it was the only store in Aprilci not to give receipts. Then I suggested the possibility of reconciling the books monthly or weekly rather than once a year. Aleksander said they always did it once a year, all businesses did. Two of the women were really nice and always gave me the correct change—and they understood my Bulgarian well. I supposed in America, all three would had sued, but here they just looked slowly for more work.

Always in Motion

Travel by Train Car & Plane

There are a lot of cars. Most were small Ladas or Fiats, but a few were BMWs and large Mercedes, Many motorcycles. To drive them, Bulgarian drivers simply push the accelerator to the floor and aim. This made for many close calls. There seemed to be as many cars here as in southern Oregon. The Bulgarians only seemed to have two positions for their feet: Both on the accelerator or both on the brake; this was odd for a country that was supposedly poor, could not afford gas, and had 20-40 percent unemployment.

Planes: Forget it. They exist only to get people in or out of the country. Although there was a small airport in Varna for rich people, I had heard.

Trains: Although most of the trains seemed to be vintage, there were two new ones that traveled from Sofia, either northwest or east. The vintage trains offered first class seats, if by first class you meant a slightly higher quality than low class or peasant class.

For a Piece Corpse training meeting, we took the bus to Kazanluk, which was just over an hour from Aprilci. We walked up the street to the hotel, which was a gigantic block, like Shumen and Panagyurishte. The rooms were okay but with single beds. There was a new small television and small bar refrigerator. We went exploring and bought vodka and Baileys, as well as peanuts, chocolate, and orange juice, the requirements for a balanced diet. Dinner was a decent pizza at a modern pizza restaurant called "Burger King" oddly enough. Back at the rooms we drank and talked.

Morning was dedicated to language training, but the afternoon tested all of us, then we had to endure one-on-one for questions and help with language. I drew Mila for my language exam. She led me through the standard questions and I did quite well, only misunderstanding a question about factories selling things in the bazaar. The one on one was quite helpful. Finally, I went to a political class but I was the only participant. Dinner was pizza again.

The next day, we were in the Language training all day. I took classes in eco-words and animals, Calpurnia took verbs and pronouns. For lunch we had a good chicken, but for dinner really awful food downtown in a run-down restaurant, in which we were the only patrons; we missed meeting Filip and Kim in a comedy of errors. Although I later heard they found a wonderful place to eat.

The last day, after more language classes in the morning, we asked permission to leave the conference early. Getting it, so we walked to the train station and bought tickets to Burgas, the four of us, Calpurnia and I, Alta and Chris. We sat in second class by mistake but took up the whole compartment with our luggage. The train took an entertaining four hours to get to Burgas on the coast of the Black Sea. We walked downtown to look for food — then stopped looking after Chris spotted a McDonalds (one of five in the country) — these girls all had junk food tastes but I was grateful for non-Bulgarian food, even if it was McD's. Then we took a taxi to the west bus station, where we picked up an intervillage taxi to Sredets, Alta's village.

At first glance her building was a wreck. It was a raw concrete block; every third window was broken; the outside door was hanging on one hinge. On second and third glance it still was a wreck; the light bulbs in the halls did not work; the elevator barely worked, missing the floor by six inches. The hallways were dirty and littered. Her apartment, however, was clean, had the standard pressed wood furnishings, and a new television, that she had bought. She gave us the bedroom; we put the mattress on the floor and unpacked.

At the Eco-Tourist Convention

Saturday morning we returned to Burgas by taxi, where we spent a few minutes at the Internet, then the girls went to shop and I worked for another two hours on the web page for a Serbian wolf site. Then we met at McDonalds and had lunch. Sometimes it was embarrassing to eat mass-produced food, but at least, if it was not great, it was also not sickening. We shopped for books and presents, then checked out the bus and train station for schedules. After lunch we walk to the sea and spend a few hours walking to the dock and back to the city. We left for Sredets about Four.

Sunday was a quiet day in Sredets. Calpurnia, Alta and I walked up to the forest. We ate out every meal at the various cafes and had traditional Bulgarian fare.

Monday and Tuesday were quiet days in Sredets. I made pizza and Italian food, with Bulgarian ingredients. After working on school projects with Chris, we all read and took naps.

Wednesday, it was back to work. We were up early to travel to Varna, up the coast, for a Tourist show, where we represented Aprilci. We got the usual cab into Burgas, only directly to the bus station for an extra Lev. We could not buy tickets at the booth, but had to wait at Sector 12 for a minibus. The first chased us off and we waited for a second; both buses took twenty minutes to fill up with passengers then both were off to Varna within minutes of each other. This was a new thing, small private buses to supplement the schedules of the state buses; they were also new and more expensive.

We sat in the back.

The ride was comfortable, sort of, as the bus driver seemed to regard the entire road as his to use. Chris kept commenting on the country for not having more modern amenities. Cali reminded her that things were more difficult in many other countries, such as Uganda, where she was originally scheduled. I reminded her that the people were thoughtful and hard-working, despite their economic setbacks. We both reminded her that many Bulgarians spoke or understood English and she should temper her criticisms. She snorted and kept suggesting improvements. At a break for gas, the young man seated in front of her turned around and asked her, in English, why she came to Bulgaria if it was so primitive. The ensuing conversation was quite interesting.

Getting in by 10:30 a.m., we took a cab to the Sports Hall, which was hosting the Tourist Show. Vulko met us at the booth and hid our luggage for us. Then, as the first item of business, we abandoned the booth and went to coffee for an hour. He returned to the booth with people from Gabrovo and Troyan, while we investigated the Tourist Convention, picking up information on other cities (to remodel for Aprilci naturally). After noon we went to dinner at Happy's, which we found about six blocks towards the harbor. An excellent chicken lunch. Then back to the Convention. We walked around until 4:30, then Vulko told us that the man from Troyan was returning immediately and could take three passengers. We asked him if he needed us; he smiled and shook his head. So, we went with guy from Troyan. That solved the problem of looking for a cheap room for the night and then having to spend eight hours on the train the next day.

He drove a new Ford, considered much sexier than BMWs or Mercedes, and turned out to be quite a character, from being a Communist elite student to radio entrepreneur. He dropped us off in Aprilci after a four-hour drive and a detour through Veliko Turnovo and the walled city. We were over 15 hours early, so we went to bed early. Chris took the bedroom and we set up the futon in the living room. We had traveled through half of Bulgaria in a week, on every kind of vehicle except airplane (there seemed to be no intercountry air flights at all, not that we could had afforded it).

Chris caught the 5:30 bus to Pelovo. We stayed up and did two laundries, then worked on the computers until midnight.

Rich Communists Or *Return of the Ruling Class*

After lunch we walked to the Computer Club to meet with Trifon
and his partners. We waited there and talked for an hour and then
moved to the Caprice cafe and drank tea and waited another half an
hour. The group from Sofia did not show up; there was no call from
them. We sashayed back to the apartment and worked on a wolf
proposal. Finally at 6:30 p.m. Trifon came by and said they were on
their way, and we should meet at the Gameyski Restaurant in twenty
minutes. In the street we were met by Dorian, a partner and also a
member of the craftsmen guild. We walked to the restaurant and met
the evaluation committee for AED from Sofia, who were deciding the
fate of the Telecenter applications. The group was led by John Caine.
Dora from USAID, Floyd from AED, and Jivko, their driver, who
used to be a driver for the Please Corps, completed the group. We sat
in the front smoking section and ordered dinner. I ordered for John
who said he had no Bulgarian — he was stationed in Washington DC
but spent six weeks at the Sheraton the previous fall. He had pileshki
sheshchi and persiani kartofi, and I had kebabche and persiani
kartofi. The others ordered large dinners, except Trifon, Dorian, and
Floyd, who each had coffee and persiani kartofi with syrene.

The restaurant was owned by a Mr. Gameyski, who also
owned a cattle-breeding facility in the next village. We were told that
he got his money in an unusual way. After the fall of the communist
system, the rich communists decided to give large sums of money
to others to hold for them until things settled down (presumably
in cash), then they would buy the most profitable businesses still
existing. Mr. Gameyski was one of the "holders." Apparently, he
bought several profitable businesses for himself, and now lived in
a large walled compound, with seven houses, on the top of a hill
overlooking Vidima. I never did hear what happened to the men
who gave him the money to hold.

Many of the privileged were able to buy the most profitable
businesses, usually relating to food. Most other factories collapsed
without the Russian subsidies. Half the Mayors in our circle of
small cities had communist Mayors that people elected because they
recognized them — and had some nostalgia for Communist times.

The News Stand

Daily Dumpster Report No. 163

In Aprilci one day I noticed a really awful smell coming up the street
from my flat. The dumpster was burning. I raced to the landlord
and asked what to do; he laughed and said "nishto" (nothing). It
seemed that the grandmothers in the building often cleaned out their
stoves and threw out the ashes, even if there were live coals. The fire
burned itself out after two days, consuming all of the plastics and
materials inside, doubtless contributing to respiratory ailments so
common.

When President Stoyanov was coming to visit Aprilci, all the
dumpsters disappeared for a few days. The day after he was here,
they reappeared, but were all moved alongside buildings instead
of in front of them. This looked better but caused several problems,
since it made them harder to get to — you had to plow through
mud and weeds. It also made them harder to empty and to clean
up around. Recently, after I dropped off my bag of plastics and old
toilet paper (which could not be put in the toilet), I saw a woman
come from the cafe with bags of what looked like old lard and throw
them in the dumpster. The next day, as I was putting a few wax
cartons out, I stepped on a pile of short sheep hair, dark grey.

In its new site, the dumpster seemed to be acquiring a halo of
garbage, such as cans and plastics. The new vegetable stand packed
the dumpster with boxes and left-over vegetable matter. The babas
and others took the cardboard for their fires. The woman who ran
the vegetable stand set fire to the dumpster every week to reduce the
volume of garbage. Her timing had something to do with my clean
laundry hanging downwind every week. The mayor was supposed
to have the dumpsters cleaned every two weeks, but had not paid
the company, so that he could use the money to have his hair coiffed.
That meant the dumpsters were only replaced every six to eight
weeks.

These dumpsters contents were taken to a site between
Aprilci and Troyan and dumped over a ridge down into a creek.
The gypsies there also regularly went through the garbage, taking
out any plastic or glass bottles. When I went to inspect the dump,
the gypsies there all moved to one side and waited until I finished
looking, then moved back.

Some things in dumpsters were conspicuous by their absence:
Plastic and glass bottles were all used for making home-made wines
and brandies (rakias). One day I saw loaves of bread sitting on top of
the dumpsters, so I sat down by the river and watched; after an hour
a gypsy with a wagon pulled by two horses showed up and took the
bread. Maybe once a month someone left extra bread (I gave often
my extra bread to my landlord for his pigs and chickens).

One day, as I was throwing out some plastics and rock-hard

bread, I was approached by an elderly woman in black. She asked me haltingly, as if she doubted her language or mine, if she could look in the bags first. I leaned over the dumpster and retrieved the two bags. She carefully unwrapped them, leaving the plastic, but setting aside the bread. I asked her where she lived; she avoided answering. Over the course of twenty minutes, we talked about her family and mine, about my projects, which she thought were strange and funny — why would anyone care for wolves? — and about bread and plastic. I was pretty sure that she was a gypsy who lived by the river in a wagon. So, I agreed to leave any bread and potential valuables on a box by the building, under the eave, rather than throwing it in the dumpster.

Sickness and Health, Balkan Style

In our first December here, I got sick first. Of course, I always got sick around the solstice, when the weather changed rapidly. When it did not clear up after a week, we called the PC medic, Sheila. I told her about my wolf poisoning and asked if it could be flu or nerves or an ulcer — she suggested it was flu and told me what antibiotic to ask for at a drug store (prescriptions were not needed to get drugs in Bulgaria).

The antibiotics did not seem to work, so I called Sheila again; she suggested that we could stay in the HQ sick bay so she could see me in the morning. We decided to take the 3:00 bus, which we did. It was a Trans5 directly to Sofia. It took four hours to get there with all the local stops. We walked to HQ, stopping at McD's for a burger for Calpurnia. I got one also, since I would be in sick bay.

At HQ, the guard let us in, and we climbed upstairs. She had left a towel and some stool sample kits for me. The beds were firm innerspring things, how rare, and the room was heated. It was a small attic room with two beds and a night table. We were looking at books as Sheila came in, so we talked, then Calpurnia and I went to bed and slept until 8:30.

We got American antibiotics and took the bus back the next day. A day later, I seemed fine. A week later, however, Calpurnia was sick. It must have been a contagious bacteria. I prepared for the big community meeting for the Craftsmen, which had been advertised the last week. Fifteen showed up in the Center Restaurant. I gave the opening talk in Bulgarian. The Craftsmen decided to start an NGO and wanted a small SPA grant for their group. We set the next meeting for the following week.

The next day, I helped Calpurnia in the office. We went out for coffee after Four, with Vulko. We were both getting sicker. We were out of the American medicine, so we got more Bulgarian medicine. We stayed in bed and read. Calpurnia was sicker the next day, so I walked to the bazaar alone and bought tomatoes and apples. The following day, we were both sick and stayed in bed, although I worked on the web page. I pushed to finish the web pages in January, but had to sign on seven different times because I kept getting bumped off. The phone lines were 1927 analog lines and very bad (that was 1927, the height of American civilization).

The bug seemed to be bouncing between us. A call to Sheila and we decided to take another bus to the capitol and stay the night. We left on the 1 o'clock bus to Troyan to meet with Judi Benyus. We intended to take the 4 o'clock bus, but were surprised when the tickets said 2:30. I raced to get money and supplies, while Calpurnia met with Judi. A friend of Judi's, Rada Gankova, helped us try to change the tickets and then sell them, but we could not, so we went early, just as well since we were sick. The bus was very fast, considering it was a state bus; it made few stops and we arrived in Sofia about 5:30, over 2 hours early. So we ate at McDonalds, then got film and spent a few hours at an internet club. Just before eight we got to PC HQ and checked in for the night.

We were in Sofia, the big city, so European, so big and busy, except that in the morning there was hardly any rush hour traffic. The cars were already parked on the sidewalks though so we had to walk in the streets. We ate at Dunkin Ds. Then went back to meet the doctors. Calpurnia got new meds. I got eye drops and the verdict that I had a viral throat ulcer and instructions to gargle in salt water. Lunched at Happy Bar. We had chicken and shishkabobs, and met Ben and his girl friend there. Afterwards Calpurnia collapsed into sleep at PC HQ. Sheila said stay another day. I wandered over to the internet cafe and admired my web page, with a few changes. I got back at six and we snuck out to dinner at Pizza Hut, with chicken soup and chicken salad. Then we found ink cartridges. Excellent. Back early, so I read. Unbeknownst to us Joe Mance had come in to pack to go back to America; he worked down in the basement until after midnight.

A January day, I worked on the internet, and on the Small Project Assistance (SPA) handbook changes and questions. This was all computer work—surprising how much of it was to show Bulgarians how we worked in America, with plans, calendars, assessments, grant applications, and so on. Sent email to the committee. Worked on web page graphics. Finished the quarterly report on the SPA grant for the craftsmen. Talked to Vulko about hiring a local guy to finish the web page. Got home for lunch about 12:30, a sandwich with tomatoes and pepper.

That evening, started preparing dinner for Vulko and Mariya, our landlords. Had decided to fix my summer salads, chicken pasta (with baby corn, a rare treat, and tomatoes and pickles) and potato salad (southern American style, quite different from the German-Bulgarian style). Then made sugar cookies for desert. Calpurnia suggested that we had the traditional Bulgarian antipasto, so we cut salami, and both kinds of cheeses (remember there were only two, kashkaval and syrene, yellow and white, or cow and goat), set out peanuts, wine, rakia, and vodka. It took five hours to cook all the pasta and potatoes.

Our guests were fashionably late. Vulko showed up first with rakia (another home-made batch in a coke bottle, although I had to admit that his was better than most). I poured screwdrivers for us, using the more expensive Danish vodka rather than the local brain-killer vodka (the Bulgarian was about $1.20 and the foreign was about $7.00). Calpurnia had wine, from an expensive Bulgarian bottle, about $1.10 — there were very expensive Bulgarian wines that went up to $2.50 or so. Mariya arrived and we had another screwdriver.

We stood around and talked about politics and schools for a while, then about the wolf projects and tourist projects. We sat early and tried a few peanuts with our drinks. I explained the summer salads dinner and then put them on the table. Surprisingly, they refused the Bulgarian food and ate only had American food, about four helpings of each over the next three hours. I added cooked salami and peanuts to the potato salad, which really spiced it up — of course, the cayenne pepper and the Bulgarian red pepper and garlic contributed to its piquancy. Calpurnia and I each had our dictionaries out to look up the difficult words. We tried to express complex concepts, just as in English, but needed the wretchniks for Bulgarian words. Sometimes it did not work at all and we all gave up. Then we talked about grapes and food.

It was snowing lightly this January day. After the early bus to Sofia, we met with Albert Foster, Head of PC Bulgaria, David Leigh, head bean counter, and Pentcho Dachev, new head of the Environmental section, regarding the fact that I had had to set up a local office and pay all of the support costs for it. David had been denying us help for ten months, and had Pentcho signed a letter saying his decision was final, but then Albert had Pentcho visit us to assess the situation and now he supported a supplement. Albert approved the supplement and David agreed, but not very graciously (it was a pyrrhic victory, since I had paid out for sixteen months and I only would get a supplement for the next six).

At Nine the circus of the applicants for SPA money began. Alta, Christine and I were on the committee, with two others, which

essentially meant that we could approve anything. I interviewed
two applicants and took notes on one. We approved the first two,
but got bogged down afterwards in problems with bids and the
completeness of applications. Then it was noon and Calpurnia and
I had to leave. We took the city bus to the Natural History Museum,
near the Parliament and Palace, where we met Dimitar and Hikmet
(the biologist and veterinarian who were heading the wolf survey
project, since they conducted the previous one four years earlier). We
all drove to Aprilci, where we dropped Calpurnia off, then continued
past Stokite to Lugat, the forestry unit at the northern edge of the
Park. It was snowing very hard and the driving had been hard and
slow — fortunately there were almost no other cars on the road.
Dimitar said that if it was like this tomorrow, we could forget about
having a good survey.

There we were met by a ranger who led us to the hunting
lodge hotel. We were the last to arrive. The others had started
drinking the rakia and eating salads (shopska of course). We sat
and drank and smoked and talked for a few hours over salads.
Dimitar and Hikmet lectured on wolf tracks and measurements
(the handouts were from the Biodiversity plan and were of interest
because of the claim that the proportion of tracks can be used to
determine sex and age). I added color commentary. Afterwards
we had kebabche and persiani kartofi with wine, beer, coke, and
homemade rakia. Although I excused myself before midnight, the
group carried on until after 2 a.m. The room was very warm because
the floors were heated (in fact the radiator was off); the sleeping bag
was too hot. The bathroom, however, was freezing cold and there
was no hot water. But, then the rakia kept me warm and awake.

We had now identified many sickness vectors. For instance, water
sickness: The electricity was off for a few hours, again. Must have
to do with the rain. When it came back on, we made water with the
distiller. That took six hours to make two quarts. The water here
made us sick every week or so, for some reason, so we had switched
back to distilled water again. I thought the spring runoff scoured all
the micro-organisms from the reservoir.

Then there was food sickness: One Sunday I made fried
donuts for breakfast, french fries for lunch, and more French fries for
dinner. Was sick all night. Served me right. Sometimes it was from
bad food or badly prepared food.

Oh, of course there was rakia sickness. It was just too strong.
I learned to sip without every finishing more than half a glass,
knowing that should the glass go below half, it would be instantly
filled and I would obligated to drink more. I identified my limit as
two ounces. If I ever went over that, I would get sick for a day. I

thought Calpurnia's limit was one ounce.

Four weeks of hard work in perfect health! Much more computer work. Finished and mailed article on forestry to Don in Canada. Drank rum, made cookies, got sick. Old age has transformed me into a delicate old fart, who cannot drink without getting sick, and who must have his porridge before 6 p.m. or risk another upset stomach. Old age was an adventure, but not the kind you want to have or to pay money to have.

Then everything was normal again. We were healthy for months. In the shower this morning I realized that, due to the strange arrangement of Bulgarian bathrooms, I could piss, shave, and shower at the same time standing completely still; this must have been designed by men for the comfort of men. The toilet and sink were very close, and the shower was directly overhead, and drained on the floor, as did the sink — the toilet at least drained directly down to the river, bypassing the bathroom floor. These bathrooms were universally unheated, and since everything, even the washing machine, drained onto the floor it was always wet. No wonder people got sick all the time.

I spent all day reading, evaluating, commenting on, and summarizing the SPA applications. There were only ten this time, but each one was about 20 pages of text, statistics and budgets.

At 12:30 Zlatka and Petya, Cali's host family from Dupnitsa, arrived to visit us for the first time. Lunch was sandwiches, dinner was tamale casserole and apple kuchen. All we ever did on these visits, coming or going, was eat and talk.

Then, the next day, up at 5:00, we had to leave for Sofia for the SPA meeting. After walking to the PC HQ, we both saw Sheila and Dr. Todor for minor medical irritations. Then, we took Venelina, the sublimely attractive SPA Coordinator, who had attended our wedding, for a two hour lunch. I was careful not to talk about the SPA project, since she had cut the funds and I had to fight to restore part of them. She, like her arch-nemesis Svetla, was acutely sensitive to imagined or real insults, formed instant decisions, and then held grudges it seemed. Anyway, lunch was part of my effort to restore the balance, so we could work together. She talked about herself and her history, which was fascinating. Lunch was good, but expensive, in a small garden cafe off Vitosha Boulevard. We rarely got to talk about our experiences, although all three of us had been teachers at one time or another.

The details of lunch and so on did not survive the delay to record this a week later. But, the afternoon was spent in the unheated office beside the Telecenter. It was another way to court ill health I

145

suppose, that and walking all over the mountains, tracking wolves in thin cotton clothing (mine, I mean, not theirs).

After another dinner of leftovers, Calpurnia and I packed for our six-day trip to Pleven for the In-service training. Usually we would not want to go, but being in Aprilci for a month has been tiring, and this would be the last time for us to see some of the volunteers.

We woke at Seven, having decided to take the 8:00 a.m. bus and risk getting there late (the 5:30 bus would had arrived at 8:30, too early to use the internet or check-in). The gods of transportation had smiled on us though, and the three buses took three hours — each time we literally stepped onto a waiting bus.

At Pleven, we walked to the hotel, which was across town, but it was only 11:00 and we were not supposed to check in until 3 p.m. At the hotel, we identified ourselves as having reservations and asked if we could check in early. The clerk agreed, so we did; perhaps the hotel was still empty, as often was the case. The room was on the eighth floor overlooking many blocks and streets. It had a double bed, single bed, desk, and television with cable. The bathroom had a tub and apparently limitless hot water — so many new treats and luxuries. We dropped the bags and raced out to lunch.

On the way downtown, we met Gabriel, a volunteer teacher in a small town in the northwest. He had been a prosecuting attorney in Atlanta before joining. We suggested pizza, but on the way there, saw a good Bulgarian restaurant. I had *pileshko shishche* (chicken kabobs), which were excellent. Calpurnia had soup and Gabriel had a salad and fries, having been sick the past few days. Everyone we knew, including us had been sick the past few weeks. Not really sick but with a nagging headache, upset stomach, sore throat, or something.

After lunch, we shopped for a camera battery, printer ink, paper, and all the things that only concentrated in large cities. We went back for a nap, but before we could lay down Christine and Alta showed up. They were starving, so we walked to the Chinese restaurant near the hotel. The service was typically Bulgarian. The waiters were surly, confused, resentful, slow, and forgetful. But, the food was good. After dinner the three girls decided to get their hair done, so I returned alone and read the mail.

Calpurnia got back about nine; she did not had time for her hair and arranged to have it done the next night. We went to bed early, but I was sick with an upset stomach. As long as I sat up I was fine, so I watched cable television all night. Many movies were in Italian and German. One channel was French. Many were Bulgarian, including one of the cartoon networks. At one a porno channel started up. So, I switched between jazz, Bulgarian music, two Italian movies, and the porno channel, amused by the strange juxtaposition of images and words. Around 5 I slept for a few hours.

The hotel offered breakfast, which was mostly toast and tea, with a little fruit. Then we trundled off to the sessions. The sessions were the same as last April, with two exceptions, one of which I had begged for, which was making words with prefixes and suffixes. I visited the nurse and told her I was sick and drinking only water; she gave me some Bulgarian antibiotics. The class I attended first was on emotions, which was sort of a mime class with Bulgarian words. Then it was lunch time.

Christine and Alta wanted me to go with them to lunch. Calpurnia took a nap. We ate again at the Bulgarian restaurant and I had the same food. Afterwards we picked up three bags of kitty litter for Christine's cat, as well as a bag of cat food and a leash. They expected me to carry it while they shopped for make-up. I asked them if they would treat their father this way. They informed me that this was exactly how they treated their fathers. Bowed but not quite broken, I carted the cat stuff. Even borrowed children can be trying, I thought. We got a key made for the Gabrovo apartment. They bought make-up and other supplies. Then we returned to the hotel for the rest of the afternoon sessions. I attended sessions on finances and medical.

Dinner was at the Panorama restaurant at the hotel, which offered us ten percent off. We shared a bottle of wine. We each ordered a different chicken dish. The restaurant only had one other set of customers, four teachers from the day. Then, Calpurnia went to get her hair done but Alta and Christine went to watch.

The next day was meetings. At last I went to the word-building class (the very one I suggested last year and was told there that there were no rules for prefixes and suffixes in Bulgarian). It was advanced, so all the young people who had had four years of Russian or other languages were there, but I did well because I had been playing with many of the words for the past few months. I loved it because I could make six times as many words.

Lunch was fries, soup, and chicken filets. After lunch there were more sessions on politics, pronouns, and dialogues. Dinner was at another restaurant downstairs, where they gave us 15 percent off. But, the dinner was not as good. Alta ordered a chicken with mushroom sauce. I told Calpurnia that Alta was what was known as a "good chooser." In every group of animals, one was always a better chooser than the others, whether of food, mates or routes. I suggested that in the future, we let Alta order first and we just get the same thing. I knew that I was a bad chooser (with a lifetime of experience in bad choices — even my enemies were dickless gits).

Renewing Stamps

A year later, we had to renew our "guest" cards. At Nine we went to coffee with Vulko. Then we went to the police station to renew the lichna cartas. They said we had to go to Troyan. So, Vulko drove us to Troyan. After going to the camera place, we were too near noon, so we ate at the Chinese restaurant, which was called Sezchuan (in Bulgarian Seshuan), and had sweet and sour chicken and rice with vegetables and tea. Then, they told us, after about twenty minutes of calling that we needed to go to Lovech and get a residency permit notarized first by the police in Aprilci, proving that we lived there. The clerk gave us more papers to fill out. We got the Mayor's office to sign papers for the residency. Getting back to the office, we worked until 5 p.m.

The following day, we left for Lovech at 9:00, but Vulko said we did not need the rental agreement, since we had the residency permits. In Lovech, we encountered more trouble. The clerk did not like the new passport photos; she did not like the residency permits and asked for the rental agreement; finally she kept mentioning Pazardjik for Calpurnia. We went to a new office store to get another copy of my US Passport. Then we went to the Kodak store and got new passport photos. Then we went back and paid sixteen Leva for the new forms. Then we had to have the official typist fill in the forms, trying to get the names spelled correctly in Cyrillic. Then we were told that we must have the rental agreement after all.

Back at Aprilci, we asked for the PC to fax the forms. They did but the fax jammed. I walked over to the Telecenter to use their fax, but Trifon wanted to set up the office hub for Ethernet first. We could not get it to work, after reconfiguring the computer again. So, we tried in his office and it worked—I could reach my email. But, that meant that the hub to my office did not work. Calpurnia came over to work on her email, and I walked home to make pizza and oatmeal cookies, a balanced diet for stressful days.

A day later and we were still working on the rental agreement. The fax did not receive anything, so I sent email and asked for it to be emailed. When I got back, Vulko had it by fax, so we filled it out in triplicate, then he took it to the city for the official seals to be added. It could not be mailed to Lovech because, we were told, the seals were too important to be in the mail, so Vulko arranged for it to travel by car to Lovech.

I worked in the internet, on one of Trifon's new computers. I set up the Aprilci account on Yahoo and Geocities. Christine called two times to discuss the SPA proposals, which she had received today. Eventually, we got our official cards, which no one had ever asked for and which seem to have no value.

Hiking and Walking in Mountains

Spotting Vulko outside this late May day (today was a special holiday — to get it, however, everyone had to work last Saturday), we asked him if he would drive us to the Park, so we could hike (it would save two hours of walking on roads to get there); he agreed and we left in fifteen minutes. Five-year-old Alekka was in the car, but was still shy around us. At the entrance, past Vidima, we got out and they drove back. We hiked up the road to the forestry enterprises, then I took the photos for my article. We hiked to the Park entrance and took more photos of the river and landscape. Then, we returned, hiking back to Vidima and across the hill to Aprilci, getting back about Five, tired but happy.

A week later, we took the bus to Chiflik to work with the Park on marking and renovating the mountain trails through the park. At Teteven, we walked downtown to buy supplies for the week. We bought cheese, salami, tea, and cookies for the team. Then we walked uphill to a Mexana (bar) for lunch. An earlier wedding had cleared the hall of chicken, but there were still salads and kebabche. Quite good. Many beers and rakia, ouzo, a unique wheat drink, and a strange yogurt drink. Then we trooped down the hill after three hours to meet the rented van to the hizha. The van took another 2 hours in sweltering heat, stopping every 20 minutes to cool the radiator.

Finally, we arrived at the Hizha Vezhen and met the other rangers and hosts. The hizha was large and had been rebuilt in the late 1930s. We had a room with three beds, and took a short nap. Dinner was just coleslaw and tomato salads. After dinner, we talked about the last week and the next week. We agreed to start at 8:00 with breakfast, then leave at 8:30.

The next morning at 8:00 a.m. everyone was already leaving, so Calpurnia and I grabbed some tea and bread then started out after the last group. After ten minutes we left the road, came to a fork in the trail and took the south branch, which went into the woods, and then downhill towards Chiflik. We could not find them, so we decided to conduct an animal survey. After two hours of counting butterflies (not a single animal print or scat) we turned around and went back. At the intersection we took the other branch which also said it went to Chiflik. It went through a pine forest down by a stream. After an hour we turned around and went back, getting back just before two. We were the first to return and spent time talking to Dimitar, the project coordinator, who had stayed behind to fix dinner. He described how he assembled the group with web advertising in several European countries. We were impressed.

With nothing much to do, we took a nap, then the others

started dribbling in about 3:00. The rain started again, with much thunder and lightning. So we had lunch, which was rice and chicken with chicken soup and cucumber salad. Afterwards, we went for walks around the hizha in the rain.

Too late and wet for more work, we sat around and drank tea and ate fresh goat yogurt with honey, which was very sweet and good. Then we played more cards and talked — the universal form of entertainment before television. The second day, we were first awake and ready. So, we took the blue paint and went with the blue trail team all day.

We were the earliest up the third day and sat around drinking tea and eating musli. After 8:00 we broke up into teams. Calpurnia and I went straight uphill with the boundary painting team, but were left behind after an hour (we had heavy packs, they had a pint of paint and a brush). But, it could just be age, as the others were 18 to 25 years old.

We walked through the pine forests, Macedonian pines and Scotch Pines. Then at the intersection, instead of going up to the Vezhen peak, we went east towards Botev. From the forest we broke out into the high meadows. The trail skirted the mountain, but always angling up, through many vodapods (waterfalls) and streams. We took photos. At the next peak, we caught up to the team, who were painting the poles that marked the trails. I raced up the cliff to meet with them, blowing loudly with effort, while Calpurnia went straight to the next ridge. We said good-bye and headed east; they headed west back up to the Vezhen peak. Our trail went up and down the peak line towards the Hizha Exo, which receded from us, either like Tantalus or due to continental drift. Finally after five hours of hard hiking we approached the elusive hut. A woman was outside with two large black dogs; she was picking "Grandma's soul" for tea. The dogs were named Caesar and Cleopatra. They did not bark at us.

She invited us in for tea. We had cokes as well, and she offered us tea cookies with the tea. We looked over the hizha, which was a split level, and decided to stay. We were also the only people within miles. The kitchen had about five large tables, as well as stoves and a sink. She put down a table cloth and served us on a silver tray. After our snack, she showed us to a room with eight beds and gave us sheets; the beds were cheap and sway-backed, but the sheets were clean. The living room was very nice, with a fireplace and built in seats around the room (all carved woodwork). We asked if we could take a shower, being used to cold water. She asked if we wanted hot water. Cali swooned. We said yes, but were used to cold. Then she took coals from the kitchen and started a fire in a small room. We came back in an hour and looked into the room. The fire was in a metal box under a water heater. She brought in a kerosene lantern for light, so we had an interesting but very hot shower. It was too small to move around easily; the spray from the shower sizzled on the water heater and coal box. We had to be cautious to avoid parts of our anatomy sizzling as well.

We went for two long walks up to other peaks and looked around. Found an old church, which was being restored. The foundation had been redug.

Back at the hizha, we heard a strange sound and followed a trail around the peak; there we saw the ski lift bringing food and supplies up. We helped unload some, carrying parts of a heavy iron stove and giant bags of grain, then went on another hike (hiking fools that we were), towards the east and a trail that wound around a strangely shaped peak (like a ripped loaf of bread).

Back at the hizha again, we asked if we could use the stove for food, then if she had a menu. She said she had just made hot potato salad and would make us shopska salads as well, with tea. The food was great and we had a nice quiet dinner. After dinner we went out and talked at the picnic table and watched the sky. The outhouse was large with two Turkish toilets and four 50-gallon barrels of water. The flies were legion. Then to bed about 9:30, or dark.

We were up before 7:00, due to the old navy kind of bunk beds. We heard her in the kitchen and went down and had tea and a croissant. After paying the bill (only 8.50 Leva, she had refused to take money for the beds), we started out up the next mountain and over to the trail down to hizha Xaidyzka Pesen, which we reached after five hours. When Cali got tired I took her pack and carry it on my chest. It was only difficult going down the trails, not up. The trail had skirted the entire side of the Reserve Kazya Stena, so I had now circled the entire reserve and been through the middle twice.

From Hizha X.P. we walked down the road to Chiflik, past a large resort and swimming pool, to the bus stop at the Park edge of the village. There we got a coke and asked for the next bus to Troyan, which was at 1:00. We decided to have lunch and ordered shopska salata, kebabche and bread. As I ordered the clerk said in halting English that he had worked in the Bulgarian Merchant Marine in the Pacific. We switched to Bulgarian because it was faster! He learned to cook in the Navy, and for seven years he had worked this restaurant. He showed me his signature book and the article on him and his veal soup in the Sofia guide to regional cuisine. He gave me a bowl of fresh yogurt which was very good. We ate dinner, then he offered us an excellent Creme Boulez. We talked some more about food and things. He invited us back. We agreed to come back as soon as we could.

While waiting the last five minutes for the bus, a van driver offered us a ride to Troyan. He coasted downhill, then decided to visit a friend of his who owned another cafe outside of Troyan. We ordered coke and coffee, but then he raced off with his friend to fix a garage door somewhere. We watched a funeral procession go by — the plain wooden coffin had been put in a Volkswagen bus and covered with a sheet. A few women were in black; there were no cars following for the group. About twenty people walked behind, and behind them was a long traffic jam.

They turned off the road, and we saw the bus stop down the street. So we paid for the drinks and ran to the bus. I doubted that he would miss us.

Shopping in Bazaars & Magazines

Breakfast was good fresh bread from the big empty market, yogurt, orange tea, Peanut butter, butter and jam for the bread. I worked on the computer all morning, for information for the World Wise Schools in Oregon and the park information.

Today I started setting up grant materials on the computer. Calpurnia got ready to work downstairs with Vulko, who had ordered a desk for her for the office (an old one from the school we thought). As was usual, I went out to get fresh bread between 7:00 and 8:00. After trying all of the markets, I had found the place with the best selection and freshest bread — it was the large empty Coop store under the empty textile store. The bread only cost $0.19 for a small loaf. Sometimes I got a $0.10 mekitsa, which was like a donut.

The food here was very inexpensive for native things, but incredibly expensive for imported things. For instance, a pumpkin large costs about $0.15 and 2 pounds of tomatoes was about $0.30. Greek chocolates however, were $6.00 for a single one. English teas were about $2.00 a box, and American peanut butter was $3.50 for the cheap brands.

It was the start of a lazy day. We had the usual breakfast, then went to the bazaar and look at things (since we had no money). We met Kaloti, whom we saw in Troyan coming back from Sofia. He insisted we have coffee with him for an hour and we talked about the excursions into the park with him, to start next week. We bought corn and cookies with the last Lev. I worked on my letters and Calpurnia worked on her lesson plan. Then we made soybean casserole with the soybeans from Sofia and the local corn and tomatoes. The afternoon was devoted to lessons and computer work.

The next Sunday, we slept late and then went to the bazaar about 10. The bazaar got set up later as winter progressed, it seemed. There seemed to be shifts of merchants also. Many more tire merchants. Christmas toys and wool winter clothes had begun to

appear. Many of the toys were violent children's toys and weapons —
that looked quite like real weapons in fact. We bought a new plastic
measuring cup, but found it had a hole in the bottom later, which I
plugged with tape.

The afternoon was spent preparing for class and work in the
Tourist Bureau. We watched a movie on television. Sad to say, the
television comes in better than the video movies, so we do not rent
any more movies.

The following Sunday, we had pancakes for breakfast, then a
leisurely stroll through the bazaar for fruits and vegetables, apples
and oranges. Made pumpkin bread. I bought a pair of wool gloves
for three Leva — nice to finally see woolen things for winter wear.

For lunch I made rice with Thai sauce, which was quite good.
Then over the next few hours, we ferried Alta and Christine to their
buses. After Alta left we did two laundries and cleaned up the dishes
and living room. Then, worked on lessons and paperwork. Worked
on park stuff.

And, the Sunday after that, the usual, again, we slept late then
had a leisurely breakfast and went to the bazaar for cheese and fruits
and vegetables. The rest of Sunday was devoted to preparing for
the SPA presentations the following week. I spent my time trying to
finish up the wolf proposals for PCPP funding.

The next week, off to the bazaar again. The strawberries were gone,
ruined by the rainy weather; it was too early for raspberries. The
frogs were massing to attack again. At first, exactly 32 days ago, I
thought they were strange ducks, but after going down to the river
I saw them in their true amphibian beauty and awesome size. They
were huge and noisy; and they made love verbally all night long.
Fortunately it was cool enough to close the windows to enjoy them
as mere background noise. Tonight however, I thought it was an
army of cats getting closer. Perhaps the disco could not compete and
that was why it closed.

Off to the weekly bazaar for tomatoes and cucumbers. Then,
chocolate and eggs. Work on the computer. In the afternoon, we
had a 2-hour English class for Andrei and Aleksander. For dinner,
Desislava Karanova was coming over. We made peach cobbler and
Tamale casserole, which was quite good with the black beans from
the US and kashkaval cheese from Bulgaria and the spices from Italy
and France — quite Mexican actually. She did not show up (again), so
we ate at Eight and listened to music. Prepared for Monday.

Sunday number 100 I thought, and the usual trip to the bazaar for
vegetables. The afternoon had a class at the Pepsi Garden restaurant,

called the Draganovski Restaurant or the Center Restaurant. A rest day Sunday, except for all the cleaning, shopping and laundry. I was getting rather tired of shopping this way. Having to buy one thing at a time from a different vendor or minimarket, then carry it home. Aleksander asked us if we would come to the raspberry field and take photographs (we thought he was jealous of the attention given to the Telecenter and the mill). So, we all walked up and took photos of him working and him and Calpurnia talking; then I put them on a disk for him. Aleksander talked nonstop; either he was lonely or really wished to practice his English, so we heard about his work, businesses, politics, and email correspondences.

Agrotel Market

The Meat Market

The following Sunday, we slept late. Even the bazaar got started late, after 9:30, so we did not miss the excitement. Only half the merchants had come. We asked why of one of them, who said maybe there was another some event somewhere else. We bought the usual tomatoes, apples, cabbage, and stuff. Lunch was more pizzettas. The rest of the day was reading, computing, and cleaning. Calpurnia made mashed potatoes and gravy! So many of our dinners were based on bread and tomatoes (or potatoes and cabbage) that it was a rare treat. I was able to read a novel every three days. I was still working on the new book of essays, and I now had my monthly newspaper column on ecological thought experiments (wondered how long that would go on?).

The bazaar was the biggest social event of every week. Every one met and sat and drank tea or ate kebabche and bread. We got to wave hello and stop and talk. Everyone wanted to have tea at the cafe, but it was hard when carrying packages of vegetables, so we usually postponed it until afternoon, if we could.

Although I liked the stores here, I missed the variety in the US. I recently read a book on the web, called "Falling Light," in which the author described grocery stores as the modern image of heaven (a highly recommended book for other reasons). That was my memory of American grocery stores: clean, bright, full of novel things, neatly packaged in a great variety. It was not like that here in Bulgaria. There were food stores (*xranitelno magazini*), which were very small hole-in-the-wall places; the slightly larger micromarkets (maybe 100 sq feet), minimarkets and markets (maybe 180 sq feet), and supermarkets (maybe all of 220 sq feet). I had heard of large stores coming into Sofia, like Super Wal-Mart's or Costcos but I had not seen them. Every city seems to have either a permanent bazaar or weekly bazaar that moved from city to city, for the smaller cities.

The selections were roughly the same at every store, but the larger ones had more of each item. Many stores had local foods, such as cheeses and yogurts and breads; other stores had locals things and commercial; the larger stores actually had packaged breads and things. When I bought them once they seemed stale and tasteless compared to the local stuff.

Many of the boxes were partly crushed or broken. I figured that many supplies were from crashed delivery trucks (maybe the entire supply network relied on accidents or hijackings, who knew). Often times, there would be twenty or thirty packages of the same thing. I wondered if the stores were supplied by people who simply bought out the last stocks of things that could not sell. Those things that had expiration dates seemed to bear this hypothesis out, since they had been expired from one to three years usually. I ate the expired sardines, but decided not to eat the 1998 cereal that I had bought earlier in desperation.

Today at the weekly bazaar, we saw avocados for the first time. Large and hard as rocks — reluctantly did not buy one. The potatoes had disappeared and the cabbages and tomatoes were scarce. But, citrus fruits were well-represented. Had kebabche and the last two potatoes for lunch. I started to rewrite a grant and get frustrated, so I decided to read a few stories by Mark Twain and Edgar Allan Poe.

Hotels & Huts (Hizhas)

Catch-up day. We slept late, then made pancakes with the maple syrup from Mrs. Ambassador, Margaret; pineapple and chocolate pancakes, not the normal combination, but not likely to be repeated soon either. The morning task was to clean the apartment. Afternoon tasks were writing, computer work, then a long walk towards Ostrets. We found Aleksander at work and talked to him about the language meeting on Friday in hizha Vidima. Lunch and dinners were the leftovers from Tuesday and Wednesday, except that the apricot bread was new (and burned on the bottom and too dry). In the evening I read the Clarke novel and Calpurnia read the *Rough Guide* to Bulgaria.

Friday at 4:30 we walked to the bus stop and met with Aleksander and Closimir. We talked while we waited for the Vets bus — and found out that Vets meant water and electric power station. On the way, the bus picked up the two girls from the class.

Then Closimir talked to the driver who drove us further towards the hizha Vidima. From the arch we walked up the hill to the hizha, which was in very nice shape, although only the front of the bar was heated, and by a kerosene blaster (the same kind used almost everywhere). We took our food into the large unheated kitchen and unpacked. All four had brought rakia and potatoes, as well as cheeses and salami; we added ours to theirs and made shopska salads, persiani kartofi, and potatoes salad in huge metal bowls.

Then Penka came with two cars of boys from Troyan (her Troyan class). We all started drinking. The hostess, a middle-aged woman who lived there with two dogs, took us up to see our room, which was nice with a new tile floor. As usual the room had a wardrobe, two bunk beds and a night table. An electric heater was plugged in to get the room warm. Then we went back downstairs. The hallways were also marble but with long oriental carpet runners.

One of the boys had brought a new Sharp stereo which he plugged in; he had many CDs, mostly either hits of the decades or disk jockey specials. Calpurnia and I danced, then she danced with Closimir, who danced with all of the women. One of the boys danced with the youngest girls from the class. Penka shared her lemon vodka with me and I stayed away from the rakia. We started eating the salads and fries. Then the boys cooked sausage and "roast beef," which looked like sausage. After many conversations and dances, we decided to go to bed about midnight.

I turned off the heater and gave Calpurnia the sleeping bag. My shoulders got cold but otherwise I was warm and she was very warm.

The next morning we went down with Closimir and had the apricot bread and other bread for breakfast. We found that everyone else had partied until after 4 a.m. I had tea and Calpurnia had coffee. Then Calpurnia and I went for a walk up the eastern trail by the stream. We sat by the stream and talked and took photos and then walked back about 11:30. Just in time for more breakfast—the leftovers from last night mostly. After eating for an hour and talking, Closimir, Zhan, K's son, Calpurnia and I went directly up the hill in back of the electric station. Calpurnia was tired so we lagged behind. About two thirds the way up, Calpurnia was too tired, so I went a little further then tried to convince them to go all the way to the reservoir, but they decided to go back down, also. With no snow there it was very slippery with the dead leaves and everyone fell several times, even me, once.

Back at the hizha, we sat down and talked to everyone while they tried to decide whether to stay. Finally Zhan wanted to return so we asked to return, also. Just as we were leaving a new car came with five girls. At home, we did a laundry and then relaxed.

One Thursday, I decided to go with Calpurnia to Severen Djendem, for some animal tracking, so we packed, then asked Vulko for a ride to Vets, but he was busy and Mariya had the car. So, we waited an hour for her—she was going to garden with her parents in Vidima and agreed to give us a ride to Vets.

From Vets (the 1946 water power generating plant), we walked for an hour to the foot of the Pleven hill. Then went the long way around. It was as steep as the short cut but took even longer. Finally at 2:30 we reached the hizha and decided that there was not enough time to reach Botev Peak. So, we rested for two hours then went straight up the hill towards Botev. We saw the sheep being brought into a pen nearby the ski lift. In a nice glade of beeches, we rested for an hour, watching various birds. We were back down to the hizha by Eight and asked if there was a menu. To our surprise there was, so we had shopska salads, tea, persiani kartofi and a kebabche. It was a nice dinner on the veranda overlooking the sheer wall down from Botev. We talked to some Bulgarian students from Gabrovo and to a couple from Belgium, who spoke Flemish, German, English and French, but were interested in learning more Bulgarian.

The next morning we had tea and a croissant at 7:30, then went down the short cut which only took an hour. From there we went directly into the reserve, following the old basin road. It was a quiet walk for two hours and we saw hundreds of birds, but no mammals. Then we reached the basin that supplies Vets and walked directly downhill for thirty minutes. From there it was a very hot, sunny walk to Vidima, where we wait only ten minutes for the bus.

For dinner I made pizza, green beans and giant oatmeal cookies. Trifon did not show up for the internet at 6 or 7.

Another month passed and we entered the winter holiday season. After the new standard breakfast—Bulgarian yogurt, British tea, German cereal, and Greek (or African) grapefruit—I went to the forestry department at Aprilci City Hall. Closimir was waiting next to the stove. The city hall was heated with one wood stove in every office. We talked about a joint park project with his friend from Lovech; his friend had not shown up for the meeting, however. After we were finished, he showed me his English vocabulary program on the computer. Then we went over the forestry plans for the next two years. I offered to help, as usual, and as usual he said that we would see. Earlier I had given him the *Ecoforestry* book, but he said he did not need to read any of it because he knew it all anyway. I wondered if I should take it back and give it to a potential reader.

On the way back I bought vodka for Andrei's sawmill party. Then we walked to the party, half an hour late. Of course, we were there first there. Four of the workers were playing cards while the rest were rounding up chickens and potatoes for lunch (already cooked, however). We gave out the leather work gloves as presents. Andrei arrived with karnache and cakes. Then the two guards arrived, then the glazier (in other words, the usual gang). We sat down and ate. One of the boys cut up the four chickens. Another started a grill outside for the karnache (which was like one long thin beef hot dog 15 feet long). Andrei tore up the bread. Ivan dished out the cold potato salad and the dry terator salad (yogurt with dill, but without water). The rakia flowed freely and we had a glass, then some vodka. We gave an envelope with twenty Leva to Andrei, for Emil's family (he was killed driving drunk last June on his unlicensed motorcycle, without a helmet, passing a car which was passing a slower car — to avoid a head-on collision, but he hit a trash dumpster; he left a retired mother and handicapped younger brother). Andrei announced that we would have a larger collection, and the guys donated another thirty Leva; I asked them to all sign the card, and then we had ten signatures. We all drank to Emil (with a certain self-conscious irony, since drinking had killed him). Andrei gave a long and ringing toast for the old year, which was bad, and to the new year for the factory, which should be better. He introduced us to the new guard, who was a homeless gypsy who wrote political poetry, and who in fact recited some for us, in praise of Mr. Stoyanov, the outgoing President. I liked this guy; he looked like Chico Marx. I thought Andrei and the two guards lived in different rooms in the building next to the mill — each with a bed, stove, light, and television. But, Andrei protested that he had a house in Sofia and a secret apartment down the street.

Iva and her daughter Antoniya arrived, bringing more vodka as a present. We made jokes about the political leaders, for instance, Ivan was a communist and he had threatened to put Mr. Purvanov's photo inside the double-pane windows for Iva's shop (which was the blue party headquarters). I took a picture of all of us drinking and threatened to put that photo in the window. Andrei said he would tape a photo of Stoyanov over any of them. Then Andrei and the glazier got into a loud spirited discussion of the sizes of those windows (they were too large for the frames). Iva had been remodeling her little food magazine at night, to avoid the attentions of the mayor who liked to tax such things; she joked that it was an incognito remodeling. Ivan took a burning chicken out of the stove, outside to the grill; he had stored it in the bottom of a roaring wood stove. No one even glanced as he blew out the flames and threw snow on it.

After three hours of food and drink, Calpurnia and I left to check out the post office and bookstore (but mainly to walk off the rakia and food). As we were in the bookstore, the post office clerk ran across the street and told us that we had a package (does that happen in any other country?). I told her we had picked it up last week. With awe in her voice, she said that we had another new one. With surprise in my voice, I said "*Kakvo*?" (what?). The package was from Greg and Linda Thomas, who had sent boxes of Market Spice Tea and boxes of chocolates (bless you, my children). Rushing home, we heated water for tea and ate chocolate. Skipping dinner, I worked on my mathematical model of wolf populations. Then, finished the reports for the SPA and quarterly Park report.

Iva's Market

Cleansing for the New Year

It was our second New Year's Eve in Aprilci, 2001. After my new new breakfast, German cereal with Bulgarian yogurt and French milk, I worked on more computer stuff. A trip to the internet Telecenter yielded the first email in a week (Yahoo had been clouded and many other providers did not work at all).

After a lunch of peanut butter sandwiches, we wrapped presents and watched a French movie on television (thus confirming that the folk wisdom on "use it or lose it" applies to high school languages, as well as to muscles).

After six we walked to Vulko's house; the two daughters (Monika, 13, and Alekka, 4) were there, as was his wife Mariya, who taught German at the grade school. We gave Alekka a chocolate and sat and started drinking rakia with Vulko (knowing that rakia poisoning was shortening our lives as a result). After half an hour Iliana (the head of the kindergarten) and her husband Ivan (a bank clerk) arrived. We refueled and were served Russian salads (peas, potatoes, pickles, in mayonnaise). Over the next five hours the courses come: sour fermented cabbage salad, wine, surmi (cabbage leaves with rice), broiled cow pieces (honest that's what they were called, not steak, but not too tough either), persiani kartofi, baked chicken pieces, coke, and finally champagne.

We had been watching the various concerts on their nice large cable television. The old President gave a four minute address then the fireworks went off. We toasted and drank the champagne. We made a list of ten things that we would like, e.g., house, car, job, health. Then we trudged out into the raging snow to celebrate in the

square. Father Christmas was there, and most of our acquaintances —
altogether about sixty people. People were throwing firecrackers at
each other, as well as in car exhausts and pipes, which caused the car
alarms to go off. This year a dance (horo) did not start, so we walked
back after half an hour and had banitsa (filo dough with goat cheese)
in which nine number and one coin were hidden. Calpurnia got the
coin, which meant money, and I got number six, which meant a new
job this year.

We got home by 2 a.m. but were too woozy to sleep. So,
we watched television for a while and then read. I worked on the
computer until dawn. After a breakfast of tea and toast, we went for
a long walk. It was snowing strongly. At Iva's new store, we bought
flour and vanilla (which was dry and came in little packets). Outside
some kids with sticks hit us and wished us health — the sticks were
called *surovachka* — but we had to give them a Lev (50 cents) each.
The sticks were decorated with tinsel, popcorn, and paper. This was
an old Bulgarian tradition that we missed last year because the kids
were afraid of us. This year it was still snowing, as it had all night,
and the going was tougher. The plow roared by us; it was a farm
tractor with a blade in front.

At home I made tortellini, which we had been saving for four
weeks, with sauce and bread. I felt less sick, and started to work on
the web page, praying for it to be good enough. Dinner was leftover
tortellini. We watched a Bulgarian concert on television (we only got
two channels, National TV and Fox TV, with Fox Kids in Bulgarian).

Teaching English the Amoeboid Way
It was a new year, new January, new Monday and a new English
class. Teaching day, however, was the same as always. The lesson
was on finding our way downtown. Eight children show up. Due
to the fading of the class last semester, Rahil, the head of the school
had promised that these students had at least eight years of English
(however, that was only 40 minutes a day, one day a week, and 24
weeks a year, including exposure to television programs. We had
more Bulgarian in two months). Rahil pointed out, also, that the class
was an optional, after-school class that did not count.

At the evening lesson I read from a novel and the students
wrote it down — they all failed! But, they tried, so I was happy. The
class was in the rich Gameyski restaurant, because the school was
too cold. We had to buy drinks and food, usually tea and fried
potatoes.

Still January. Penka did not show up for our tutorial in
Bulgarian. Another teaching day, also. I taught alone. No heat in
Tourist Bureau. No heat in the classroom. The lesson was going to a

hotel and registering (very apropos since the students were in hotel management). The class had six students. It went well I thought, the better students helping the less prepared. Then I went back to the office and worked on grants. At five, we went to the cafe and met with the advanced students. They explained to us that the celebration on Sunday had to do with scaring away the ghosts of winter and it was a very old celebration. Afterwards, we went back home and worked on grants.

For the next Please Chlor training day, I had been asked to teach a lesson on ecology to the new volunteers. I agreed, since I could talk about ecology for days before needing a sip of water.

Then, that day arrived. After getting to Panagyurishte, we walked through town and saw the volunteers at the cafes. We talked to Malcolm and Stephen, who told me Mitko was looking for me. We went to dinner at a small pizza restaurant and saw Aneta and Dimitar, who said that Mitko was looking for me; they told me where his apartment was. The pizza was okay and we went to see Mitko about the lecture. It turned out that I was expected to team teach with Bob, who was working with vulture populations in southeastern Bulgaria.

The next day, I meet Christine, then Bob and Milli at a place near the hotel. Bob and I figured out a teaching plan. Christine and I went to the internet, but it was worthless. We went to the school and Albert Foster was there with Rod Bisson, a consul from the State Department. We talked a while, then Albert addressed the new recruits outside in front of the school. The school was very nice and well-cared for. Christine and I went for lunch at a nearby cafe, but could not avoid Milli. I had yogurt and coke; they had chicken.

At 1:30 I went early to the classroom and prepared my drawings. At 1:45 we started. I asked for definitions of biodiversity, as well as the values of it and threats to it. I introduced the biodiversity of Bulgaria and the reasons for it, then Bob talked about birds and vultures. I talked again, this time about wolves. We summarized, then answered questions. We were finished by 4:00.

I went downstairs and got my reimbursement for the travel. Then hiked back to the hotel and met Christine at 5:00. She wanted to go shopping so I looked for blouses for Calpurnia. They were all small and tight, made of spandex or something. Dinner was at the hidden restaurant, but the food was not as good as it was last time. We had coffee at a cafe.

Today I had been asked to assess the results of an English class and the library of English books at a school in Troyan, supported by USAID and a PC SPA grant, so I took the bus to Troyan at 8:00.

161

At 9:00 I walked towards the school, stopping to get a small pastry first. The internet cafes were not open, except for one, which had no internet. At the school two hours early, I went to the principal's office. He was in. I said that I was just making sure where everything was and could he confirm the appointment for noon. He said, thankfully, why wait? We talked about the program, then teachers started coming in. This was in fact Judi Benyus's old school. The interviews went well. The counterpart was there, as well as two colleagues and one student, who was very well-spoken and probably the token student at all the school assessments. After further tours of the school and library, I told them I was giving them high marks.

Later that afternoon I walked to the internet cafe and wrote for a few hours. I had a small pizza for lunch. Then I shopped for writing supplies and for food, especially granola (no), Fruit juice (no), grapefruit (yes), and radishes (yes). Then, I waited at the bus station for the last half hour before the bus. Back in Aprilci at 6:00 Calpurnia met me and we tossed a lettuce salad. Then received monthly calls from her parents and mine. Then, I wrote up the assessment.

Today, a beautiful day, I foolishly worked on the web page all morning then went to coffee about 11 a.m. with Angelar—I never understood why coffee leads into lunch, but it did. I invited him home and we had the first peanut butter sandwiches in a few weeks. It was the last jar, so we would have to be slower with it.

In the afternoon, I read for an hour. Then, Mariya came over with several sets of scissors and buckets, and we all cut grapes for half an hour. We had been watching the grapes since April, when the leaves started coming out. They grew around the porch and framed it; by August they actually cut down the sunlight to the porch. But, now the leaves were falling. The porch itself faced due south and so had good winter sun and good summer sun, which was so high, the overhang blocked much of the heat. For the past two weeks the smell had been heavenly as they became more purple and started to turn alcoholic—the birds discovered this last week and made runs on the grapes, then collapsed dizzily on the porch floor. Our reward was a large dish of grapes for our table.

The advanced class was at 5:00 in the Pepsi Garden restaurant, aka the Center. We showed up and waited. Sometimes Calpurnia or I would teach alone, but with the adult classes it was much easier with two. Aleksander showed up, so we started by asking about his letters and then about the problems with the municipality. Aleksander was a good source of information because he worked next to the city offices and knew everybody. He told us about the mayor, an unemployed communist clerk who got elected by a coalition then screwed everyone. He refused to pay many employees whom he did not like, including those in the tourist office and the library, but he spent his own full salary and his full allotment on his car and telephone (about $150 on each).

Then, Andrei showed up and contributed to the info-fest. The mayor was being tried in court tomorrow in Sofia, for violating his agreements, so we might, with luck, have a new mayor next week. Trifon had told us that the mayor reneged on his promise to trade internet for the city for the rent of the internet cafe, which Trifon owned. Trifon went to the City Council and they approved the trade (even though they were bargaining with the Swiss at the same time to give them internet through the cable television). Tonight, I was tired and had a hard time focusing on the discussion. The Bulgarian way of doing things was truly a foreign way, influenced I think by the 500 years of Turkish domination as well as a Mediterranean influence from Greece. Everything was done in secret and at the last minute, and competition displaced cooperation almost completely—I had given up trying to get them to cooperate on things like internet and school heat.

At home finally, we had milk for dinner. This was our first store milk since last November. It was radiation-treated milk from France, which was sold in cardboard cartons and only needed to be refrigerated after opening. There were two cartons in Iva's magazine. Then we watched a sci-fi movie about large aliens dominating primitive earthlings in the far future; ho hum, it might be more fun if the Pillsbury dough-boy aliens were mean and the sharkish ones were wise and benevolent. The television lost color and the old video player had trouble keeping the tape smooth. Of course, at least we had these things that many volunteers do not—oddly enough, all the Bulgarians we knew had new Sony large screen televisions.

Tuesday—as always, I liked Tuesdays, even though they always contained a class now. Morning was spent on email. Afternoon was preparation for teaching English to inquisitive adults. We meet at Gameyski's this time because the Center was closed; I did not mind since the food was fresh here and the gas heater was warmer than any other cafe. This was the second week of talking about verbs. Unfortunately, we both were in over our heads, never having been trained to use English very well, much less teach it. I teased Calpurnia about her distorted southern accent, holding mine up as an example of genteel learning (although there was not much left anymore); she ignored me, being polite and lady-like. Nevertheless, we tried and once the class settled into a rhythm, it was quite entertaining and worthwhile. Tonight, four students were here and we talked until after Seven. Then, we went home for soup and whatever rerun was on television. We had now limited our television consumption to Sunday evenings and Tuesday, after class, to relax and rewind after an 11-hour day.

The adult English class had started another night, on Wednesdays. Class tonight was at the Center restaurant. A new student from Troyan, who had been a student of former volunteer Judi Benyus, asked to join because she hated her new Bulgarian teacher of English. The class was on advertising; we made up series of ads for the businesses, including Andrei's sawmill, which he refused to use because it would imply that he was better than the other places. I said that was exactly what he should convey, and he agreed, but he still refused.

The next Tuesday, I finally slept late, for eight whole hours. Then turned on the computer and worked all day (my ass was getting huger from sitting half the time) on the new web pages for the craftsmen. I met with Vulko for half an hour, then we left for class. Sava was there, with Aleksander and Andrei. The topic was slang, so we talked about slang for two hours, and learn many valuable things (i.e., in Bulgarian it was horrible to say "damn" your mother, but it was okay to say "fuck" your mother). We decide to avoid profanity until we learned better normal language. After class, we had a small dinner, watched the news and then a movie.

On Wednesday, we had class in Iva's café, on fixing pizza. All morning was working on the computer, entering data and notes, finishing articles, and starting the last round of funding applications. We finished a laundry between work, as Calpurnia or I came up from the office every hour.

That afternoon we prepared the materials at home for the pizza course at Iva's cafe. At five we went over; no Iva, no Andrei. Calpurnia called Andrei, and I searched for Iva. She was working in the back of her magazine. She came over and started to assemble the pieces, flour, cheese, yeast, water, salami, spices, etc. Then she showed us a new pizza maker, which she had bought in Sofia. It was kind of like a sandwich maker, but with heating elements on both sides and a ceramic plate in the middle.

We went over to her cafe, from her food magazine; the place was tiny and we had to disconnect the coffee maker to plug in the oven (that meant that no customers could had coffee while we were working). There were three tables inside and eight outside under a canvas tent in front of the street. All the outside tables were filled; one of the inside ones was, so I set up the other two, and started to cut the onions and mushrooms for sautéing. Iva, a short taciturn-looking woman, who was a good democrat and friend to Andrei, came over and started adding yeast to the flour in a large banitsa pan. I added the spices for her and let her finish the dough.

Calpurnia cut up tomatoes, which we added to the sauté, with wine and our last can of puree. More spices. Iva and Andrei were amazed that I added the same cheese, spices, and wine to every separate part of the pizza. I then reiterated my laws of Italian cooking: Cannot have too much wine, cheese, or garlic. Or tomato or hot spices. Only the pasta can be excessive.

Anyway I decided to cook this the old-fashioned way by double baking the crust. This however seemed to kill the yeast, especially since the oven was not hot enough. We all split the pizza and ate it. Then made a second, but without the extra cooking step. The crust was much better, lighter and crunchier, so we shared that also.

By seven, Iva gave the last of the sauce to Andrei, reminding us that his wife was in Sofia and he was a poor bachelor. We gave Iva the rest of the slices and went home to plan the next day.

The adult class has now moved to a Thursday as well. Aleksander jokingly suggested we just start seven days a week. Being a class day, Calpurnia worked out a time line for verb tenses and I proofed and printed the pages. At the Center restaurant, the students themselves however were confused by the concept of a time line and it took us two hours to explain it. Dr. Vulkov was there the whole time and listened attentively. I thought that he only wanted to ask us a question, with Aleksander's help. The restaurant was not busy, thank heavens. The Gameyski restaurant had already asked us not to have classes there because we did not buy enough food, and we disturbed the other customers, I was told. The brick police restaurant let us go there sometimes, although it interfered with their card players. So, we tended to go to the Center restaurant, even though their food sucked and we got sick there just drinking bottled water or Pepsi— must be their glassware.

Expecting Dr. Vulkov to show up with a local history book, this late Friday afternoon, I found Angelar at the door. He had answered my emails and letter about the wolf survey. He told me I could go out either on the wild goat survey next Tuesday or with Boleslav on a Park round on Monday. I agreed to both; he would call me Sunday evening to say which. He said Georgiu had not set a date for the last wolf survey this month. I reminded him that I was writing the reports already since I only had twelve more months left to work before my two-year hitch was up. He asked what a hitch was and I said it meant job commitment.

Like Sunday, Mondays were meticulously plotted and always the same. Calpurnia worked with Vulko at the tourist office while I prepared the lessons for the day. Calpurnia did her homework then

I finished what she did not do. After a peanut butter sandwich for lunch — thanks to Mike and Twila, we were again flush with this southern delicacy — we had our language lesson. Today, Penka was forty minutes late because she stopped for tea with the advanced class who met her at the bus and asked if she was okay (she had missed the past three weeks). So, we had a brief lesson. Then we had our beginning conversation class. Six regulars, but two new girls, showed up — we thought this had to do with the chance to go to Italy for hotel work if the students could pass proficiency exams in English and German. The subject was hotels and we had games for them. The first game was so hard (underline the words that had to do with business), that we switched to a crossword puzzle in which the students not only found all our hidden words, but also words that we did not *know* were in the puzzle, e.g., sex, fuck, shit, and ufo.

The afternoon was more SPA work, then the adult class. To which we brought magazines in English.

The next Monday was as above, as always, except that only one girl showed up for the beginning class so we gave her the new lesson on tourism. The adult class was held in the Gameyski restaurant, since the owner was out of town. The evening class had only two, Closimir and Aleksander. Vulko came and gave us the wedding rings and we paid him the final Seventy Leva. But, he could not stay for class (we knew he knew some English, but thought he was too shy to make errors). Nice rings, engraved in the inside with our names and the date. No one would guess that we had several wedding dates already and maybe another to come in the States!

This following spring Monday, no students showed up for class, not even Tatiana, our best student. So, we talked and left early. Penka did show up so we had our own short Bulgarian class on adjective/noun agreement. The class that evening had Aleksander and Closimir only. That was the adult ramble class, where we talked about anything, political or cultural, by far my favorite.

The classes at the school faded away again. Was it lack of interest or bad teaching, I wondered? The evening class continued, mainly with Aleksander and Andrei. We had good discussions on politics.

The end of May. Christine and I went to the morning English class with Trifon, Aleksander and Andrei. Christine asked Trifon about her dating dilemma. This was a popular topic and everyone offered her advice in English. Then Trifon called her the taxi to Troyan to catch the Troyan to Pleven bus. Trifon left the class shortly after Andrei started to talk (this was a pattern it took me months to notice; must be bad blood somewhere). I agreed to see him later.

The class was pretty good, as Andrei and Aleksander improved our Bulgarian as we asked questions about prefixes and suffixes. The class continued to 11:45. I went to see Trifon but he was not at his internet office. After going back home, I heated lunch, tamale casserole, which was excellent.

The adult class had now taken over part of Saturday, also, although only Andrei and Aleksander attended now. I worked on the last grant and letters while Calpurnia cleaned and did a laundry. I joked that since the neighbors always saw me do the laundry, they might think something was wrong if she did it.

Andrei and Aleksander, the loyal core of our English Conversation class, came for dinner in the apartment this Saturday evening. The class was about eating. Aleksander brought a glass elephant in front of a mirror as a gift for us; Andrei brought chocolates, and they each had a flower for Calpurnia. Dinner was the crusty soybean casserole from the *Diet for a Small Planet* cookbook, which I had modified for Bulgaria, by cooking with massive amounts of red pepper and garlic, as well as my Italian tomato sauce and a small amount of salami on top (like pepperoni); the dish was now eaten with peanuts, yogurt, and fresh bread. Andrei went wild and had fourths. We drank the bottle of white wine, and talked about the elections.

This summer Saturday, more computer work then class. The class has entered a phase where I did not have to prepare lessons. We simply talked in English about pressing issues and I corrected their mistakes. Sometimes we talked in Bulgarian and they corrected my mistakes.

Monday, I called Dimitar, but he was not working until Sunday, so I left a message that I would be going into Severen Djendem. Finished translating. Met with the map guys from Troyan at the Tourist office. Had a class at the Pepsi Garden. Today's subject: the change of politics after Simeon, and whether he would make any difference to the Bulgarian economy.

Wednesday — I had no idea what happened to Tuesday, must have been a rakia vacation day — we worked on the computer and internet. Then hosted a class at Center Cafe Garden. Christine joined us for a lively discussion of words. I had made a list of prefixes and suffixes, but Andrei said there were none in Bulgarian. Nevertheless, I had made a list and it worked surprisingly well, that was, I could add the fixes to words and make new words that already existed. Dinner was shopska salad, with corn on the cob (tasted like animal feed, which it was), and rum (the bottle had no name on it but RUM). Inexplicably, I became really nauseous and could not sleep — sinuses and teeth ached to touch, so could not lie down.

Thursday, five minutes before class, I outlined a lesson on punctuation and found some good examples of amphibilogia (it's your turn to look it up, lazy readers). There was the usual confusion about where to meet. Trifon took Calpurnia back to the internet and gave her a flower and a bottle of wine for me. Aleksander went to the Center restaurant to talk with his friend from Canada for five minutes before class. Andrei and I went to four cafes, but they were all crowded and noisy. We found a new small remodeled one by the Police Station and had tea. After ten minutes I went to find the others, gathering them up one at a time and sending them to the new restaurant. The class started with discussions of letters and verb tenses; we ordered more tea. Then we dealt with punctuation, which in Bulgarian was in a different order often, e.g., the comma comes before the preposition (or whatever).

Sunday, we sleep late; had German cereal and Swiss yogurt, with African orange juice. Went to the bazaar for grapefruit and onions — the tomatoes were bad and not much else was available. Prepared for English class, which this week was business plans, so I used the outline for an old defunct business Laughing Coyote, then prepared sample ads again for Aleksander and Andrei. The ads were interesting; they each made an ad for their business, but they never used them later.

For the class Monday night, Calpurnia suggested a new topic, arguing and debating. There were many good words and an agitated discussion. Aleksander and Andrei broke out in an argument, which proved to be a good example. Never got to the new less-competitive ads.

After lunch, Thursday, we prepared for class and made handouts on descriptive words for people. The class had Sava as a regular now, so there were five of us. We now always went to the pizza restaurant by the Police station; it was quieter and less smoky. I read some news and then get ready for class, which was a continuation of slang phrases. Sava did not show up, but the other two fanatics were there.

It was one of those Sundays where everything started to come together. After the new normal breakfast of cereal and tea, I emailed letters to Venelina, then worked on the wolf project schedule. Balkani had set the traps, but we would have to take them down in late March so no pregnant females would get caught, and then reset them in May. The Park survey should start in late March, also, and we should get more outdoor time.

At the bazaar we got very little since we would be leaving again in two days. We had kebabche and potato salad. Then the Sunday class. Two hours of speaking English was welcome, so it balanced out. Class was on travel words. Showed photos from Sandanski and Greece. I was always amazed at what words they do not understand, e.g., hint, belly, sky, or basement.

Thursday was cold and cloudy. Too much to bicycle to the Park, so I worked all morning on the computer. Wrote out my three-month schedule for the park office. Now had a weekly job mailing for possible jobs. The English class was today. We talked about sentences, their parts and order, Despite the fact that the class says word order was the same in Bulgarian as English, I differently showed them.

The advanced class

Money & Banking Or Come Back Next Week

One day I mailed six letters and paid almost six Leva. That didn't seem right so I went back to the window and asked for more change. The postmaster, also Director of the Post Office Bank, looked at me, but gave me eight more stamps, which I accepted with a shrug. A week later, I gave him a twenty Leva bill to pay for five Leva of stamps. He gave me back five Leva, so I stood at the window and asked for the rest of my change. He again gave me change in stamps, as if I had asked for them. When I mailed letters in Troyan the following week, I found that I had paid about half as much as I did in Aprilci. I went back to the window and asked what the normal postage was. I was told that it was what I had just paid. Later, I asked Andrei about mailing and he said each town could charge different amounts, especially for tourists. After that, I determined that it was cheaper to take the bus to the next town, Troyan and mail letters from there. I saved the cost of the bus ticket and more.

In late November, we went to catch the bus to Troyan at 8 a.m. but found that it was only at Nine on Saturday, so we bought bread and went back home, then ate breakfast and went to wait for the bus again.

In Troyan we found that the PC had not put our monthly allowance in the bank, so we were soon to become moneyless. We went to the internet for forty minutes, then bought two pumpkins for twenty stutinki and went back to Aprilci. After a lunch of tomato sandwiches, we took a long nap.

Ciaran

Three weeks later, we had a surprise with the Aprilci bank as they said we could not get money until after the new year; we went to the nearby Hebrosbank, but got the same story. All we had was a few twenty-dollar bills of American money, which we could not cash. The PC would not get the monthly allowance in until after the 28th, but we could not get to it anyway.

After working in the morning, I started fixing food for the big dinner with Angelar and his wife, Iona, and Vulko and his wife, Mariya. It snowed lightly all morning, but it was a cold light snow. Spinach lasagna, shopska salata, pumpkin, and apple crisp. The first couple was slightly late and the second later, so we started sitting down about 7:30. We spoke in Bulgarian and had a good time. Finally after nine we started showing photos and offering coffee. Suddenly at about 9:40 Angelar and Iona had to go and so did Vulko and Mariya. It was sudden, but both couples were parents with small children.

The next month, I waited all morning for Angelar who did not call or show up. I remembered that he said the rangers met in Gabrovo at the end of the month to get their travel expenses, so maybe he was waiting there for me. But, I could not get my travel expenses without traveling there in person. I gave up and worked on the computer all day.

The next day, we had fried mekitsas, which were good, like donuts but larger. Worked on computer. Internet failed, so wrote letters. In afternoon I took the bus to Troyan to take out money — there was no money, so I had to use the coop card to get 150 Leva. This was very tiresome. Then I found some Uncle Ben's Thai sauce, which I used with dinner after getting back at Six. All of the factories were off by noon for the holiday, so the buses were not crowded.

Today, we finally picked up the box from my parents, which had food, such as apricots and bread mixes. Had to pay additional postage, naturally. Worked on wolf project and predator projects for the park.

In March, we had to go back to Sofia to pick up the money for one of the projects. Because the bus ride was so long, we always stayed at a cheap hostel overnight and returned the next day. This morning, we had breakfast with Jo then shopped a bit before the 13:00 bus to Troyan. We picked up the money for the SPA grant for the craftsmen project. In Troyan we worked at the cafe for two hours.

Back at the office the next day, we worked for a few hours, then deposited the cash into the special Craftsmen bank account. Calpurnia accidentally added her own secret stash of American bills to the total, but figured it out just in time.

In late August, after only two months of getting expenses from the Park, I decided to call and make an appointment. Then, I decided to take the bus to Gabrovo to turn in my expenses. This was risky because the Park had never paid my expenses from September to July. But, if I did not go I would not get paid for the August trip to Gabrovo and the later trip to Sofia to pick up the grant money for the wolf monitoring.

The bus was on-time at 8:20. We got to Sevlievo at 9:30 and the minibus was waiting. Calpurnia and I got the last two seats. The bus dropped us off at the central bus station, where Calpurnia had coffee and I a keefla (roll filled with dates). We caught the tram to the Park office at the end of town.

Nikolai was sitting at the secretary's desk, talking to Georgiu. We adjourned to the meeting room and went over the monitoring project for October. Georgiu gave me the monthly wolf data from the rangers, which I had not received since January. After an hour we went to lunch at the local cafe. Calpurnia had chicken soup and I shopska salad (tomatoes, cucumbers and goat cheese).

After lunch Nikolai said that Angelar was on his way to get the jeep insured and could give us a ride back. We were concerned because, with the bus schedule, we could not get back until 6:30 that evening (after three buses). Then he helped me get reimbursed, but one of the receipts did not had two stamps and another did not have the amount (in fact it was the wrong kind of receipt that just showed that I had stayed at the Hostel but not that I had paid), so I was not to be reimbursed for my lodging. However, they gave me per diem for food that was more than the lodging, so I did not complain. Then the secretary unclipped all the bus tickets, which were in order, and asked what was what. So, I had to go through them one by one. Then she said that Calpurnia's could not be reimbursed because she did not have the proper form. I said that it was only her secondary project, but we were told that we could speak to Iurka about it. Iurka, alas, was on vacation this month, so we could not be reimbursed at all for hers since the Park only reimbursed monthly.

Then we had to wait for Angelar who finally showed up at 4:30. We unloaded the car (of old tires) and drove down to the insurance agent. The car had also been waxed. Then we drove to Ostrets to drop off Dimitar, who was working the next day. We picked up another ranger and dropped him off at his father's house and had coffee with the father, who was also a ranger, and the mother. We finally got back home at 6:25, just in time to welcome the bus from Sevlievo. Bread for dinner (pizzettas).

The next day, I had an exciting time defrosting the refrigerator. Then made five different shopping trips to replenish the tomato supply, as well as olive oil, peanuts, salami, cheese, coke, fruit juice, ice cream, and flour (among other things). Many trips were necessary due to the fact that we had to walk with small plastic bags and because each store only had a few things that we could buy. I got on the internet for half an hour. The afternoon was spent doing laundry, cleaning, vacuuming, and the reading. For the evening, we rented two bad movies in Bulgarian (only $0.40 each), but spent most of the time reading.

A busy catch-up day. I spent a few hours on the internet, then met with Trifon. Then Calpurnia and Vulko wanted to have coffee. Then I met with the librarian. After lunch I went back to the library and gave them the next installment of books, mags, and money. They had a phone now. Then raced to Andrei's mill to take photos of the sawing of the logs from the forest. Then raced back to Trifon because we were going to see Atila Petkov about the web page. We looked at the variety of Ivan's art, which ranged from metal sculptures to paintings and wood work. He showed us the new Telecenter USAID sign that he was carving. It weighed at least 100 pounds. After a strange and fruitless discussion of who would do what when and how, we went back and had a chicken casserole that Calpurnia had made.

Novo Celo Library

After a small breakfast of yogurt and tea, we caught the 8:30 bus to Sevlievo; the trip was slower than normal because there were branches and trees blocking the road occasionally, and the driver got out and sawed them off and pushed them into the river. This was also the local bus, which meant we stopped every hundred meters to pick up a baba (grandmother) or dyado (grandfather). We got to Sevlievo fifteen minutes later, where we barely made the van to Gabrovo. The van was direct and saved about forty minutes of winding around the hills.

In Gabrovo, we decided to forgo the apartment and dropped off the film. Then we went to the new supermarket and bought rice and pasta. Then back to the Pizza Tempo, the only wood-fired oven in Bulgaria perhaps, and had mushroom garlic pizza which was excellent.

At noon we took the local bus to the Park office to meet with Nikolai and Georgiu. Georgiu was not there; he had gone on the owl survey that I thought I was supposed to help with. So, Nikolai helped me give the grant money to the treasurer, who did not make out a receipt and only put it in an envelope and then in the safe. So, I gave her one of my pre-made PC receipts but she refused to sign it. I got Nikolai to sign that the money had been received. I ask for my *commanderovka* (travel voucher), but I was told that there was no money for travel and that Iurka had to approve everything in advance. I said that I need to be reimbursed for the buses to Gabrovo to give the money to the Park. I was told it was hopeless.

Back in Nikolai's office, I told him that I was afraid this would happen since I had not been paid since October, so I had withheld $35 from the grant to cover my travel. Nikolai smiled and said that I was becoming a Bulgarian at last. We talked about projects, calendars and the computer work at the Park.

Mediterranean Work Style Or Why Do it Now?

At first, we thought nothing ever got done. People got to work late, then they took long breaks, three-hour lunches, and finally left early.

At the beginning of an incredibly busy and confusing March day, Vulko drove us to Gabrovo at 9:00 and dropped us off at the Open Society. We met Kim and Filip there but there was a note on the door postponing the meeting for an hour and a half, so we left a note saying that we were going to the Park public meeting. I went, but Calpurnia and Chris went shopping and then to lunch.

The Park meeting was quite impressive; there were displays and banners. The meeting room in city hall looked like council chambers but seemed small, maybe only sixty people and sixty-one chairs. Vulko and I sat up front. Presentations were made by park officials, including the chief and Allen Hertz. Then many questions were asked, including many from the Balkani and from the forestry enterprises, but few answers seemed to satisfy the askers. I left at 13:00 with Calpurnia and Chris, who had returned.

Vulko dropped us and our luggage off at Open Society, where we met for an hour and a half, going over the plan for the Incubator project and Calpurnia's questions about it, such as 'why was it located out of town in a private building?' Then we went for coffee for two hours down the street. The project smelled like a front for the mafia, so we opted out of it immediately.

Sex in the Balkans

Bulgarian women, mostly instructors by the way, keep telling me that Bulgarian women were the most beautiful in the world. I supposed this might be true, but then all humans looked alike to me anyway. Nevertheless, keen scientific observer that I was, I had identified three distinct phases of Bulgarian womanhood:

(1) thin, sylph-like waifs wearing skin tight clothes (I mean really, I can identify muscles and bones, as well as hairs, nipples, and tattoos, under those clothes); ironically, volunteers were asked not to wear shorts so that no one would think Americans immodest or underdressed.

(2) modest middle-age, where the skirts went to the ankles and the blouses were loose (although unmarried women at this age sometimes wore miniskirts and tight blouses), usually darker colors.

(3) stocky peasant women bent-over and stout, with black blouses and skirts. Some of these women had a 90-degree angle at the knee, and waist, probably from not enough calcium.

One day, I went for a short walk in my running shorts and shirt, to get more yogurt. On the way I passed three young girls, who started giggling. I supposed that meant I was underdressed, but on the other hand, I could easier count their assets through their extremely tight clothing, more than they could see mine in shorts and t-shirt. Confusing.

The young women had also appropriated the strangest form of Italian fashions. This included boots with nine-inch heels and soles. This made women taller than most men. Of course, it made their legs seem far longer and few men would object to that. This was okay but it lead to perceptual problems when the women wore flats later. The first time I saw our language teacher, Lillia, without her giant clogs, I was worried that she had been sick and shrunk.

Flirting: I just thought everyone was really friendly. One of our language teachers, the sublimely attractive Lillia, often stood very close in language class. When she bent over, in her white Italian peasant blouse, to assist with some difficult written phrase, her well-formed breasts would try to get a peek at the problem, also.

Party No. 84.

Most of the flirting took place during dances, which were group line-dances with hand-holding and not couples (although close-couple dancing took place in discos, on slow tunes anyway).

At breakfast in the hotel restaurant in Pleven, I asked the buoyant coordinator Nadya, if we could leave the language conference early, to catch the 3 o'clock bus. She agreed, but seemed heartbroken that we would want to leave early. This was the second time this year. So, we went to morning sessions on holidays and cities.

After lunch the girls raced to the bus station, buying food on the way, while I waited for the auction at 1:30 p.m. Calpurnia and I got everything we bid on, except for the adapter. She got jeans, blouse, tablecloth, and I got a jar of peanut butter. I arrived at the bus after it pulled up, so we got on. This was the direct bus, which skipped the villages between Pleven and her village Pelovo. After an hour ride we descended into Pelovo and walked to her house. She was one of the few who had a house. It was right next to the school.

We unloaded groceries and started to prepare dinner, which would be Italian chicken. Dinner passed well. After dinner, they talked and I read the Oates book, *Blonde*, which was disappointing, too much Oates to be a psychology of Monroe, but clever, but uneven. Dessert was a large chocolate cake, with screwdrivers.

Petya's daughter, Sasha, came over for cake and cigarettes. She was 16 and let Alta and Christine borrow her list of men to date. So, Alta and Christine went to a bar with Sasha, and waited for men. They returned after half an hour, and we talked. One of the men that Sasha thought would be good for Alta had no teeth and no job—I was sure Alta was not interested, so we teased her, asking her if she would date her 300-pound neighbor instead. Calpurnia and I got the unheated guest room, and Alta had to sleep in the kitchen, on the floor, but next to the large heater, a fair trade.

Christine later went out with a handsome sailor named Danyel. He was home for a few weeks, before his cruise ship left port again. Okay, not a sailor exactly, perhaps gigolo on a love boat. Anyway, Christine met him every evening at the same small bar for a few vodkas or rakias (tourists, please note, good Russian vodka was cheaper than American or Finnish; on the other hand Bulgarian vodka was cheaper than air). One evening, Danyel was sitting with another woman whom he introduced as his girlfriend. Christine was surprised since she thought she was the girlfriend. Hmmm.

As a side thought, I was told once that because divorce was impossible under communist rule, people simply took lovers quite publicly, even sharing holidays with sometimes two sets of families. This history has resulted in a refreshing openness that sometimes confused the Americans or Swiss.

175

Always Looking

Looking for Wolves from Windows

I decided to hike up the east branch of the river to the reservation to look for wolves, alone this time. Early, I walked by the new path directly to Vidima, then to the Generating station (Vets), then to the road leading to the waterfall. The new path cut directly over the ridge and avoided several miles of roads. It was drizzling. I saw six trout in the river pool. I ate bread most of the way, since I had stopped for a new loaf at the bread store. Before the waterfall, I went directly up the hill in a westerly direction and almost immediately was on a game trail, which I followed over the ridge and up the next hill into a nice old-growth beech forests. There was no snow and the leaves were about six inches deep and wet.

It started to rain heavily, so I walked back. My feet hurt by then, since I had only been doing this once a month instead of once a week. I walked back down the road past a logging operation, then towards Vidima. I was picked up for a short ride by one of the logging trucks. I asked what the wood was for, firewood or furniture — furniture I was told, for Troyan. I then took the short cut over the hill back to Aprilci. I had been thinking about the wolf data I had gotten from the Forestry Unit. The sightings were clustered oddly, as if around waterholes. When I looked at the topo map, I noticed the clusterings were on ridges. Later, when I saw a map of mountain huts, I realized that the clusterings surrounded the huts. Either wolves were massing to eat hikers at night or the observers were seeing wolves everywhere through the hut windows.

In Aprilci, I bought a coke, then went to see Calpurnia and Vulko at the office. But, I ran into Bulchru from the Agrotel, and he said Iurka was coming to town in ten minutes to meet with the mayor. I took a shower and went back to the Mayor's office. No one was there. I waited in the lobby until the Vice Mayor invited me into his office to wait. I waited for almost two hours, but was given decent Polish raspberry tea. Finally the Vice Mayor suggested that I go home and wait to be called. I thought this an excellent idea and started to do so. One the front step I met Closimir, a forester with the City and we went to tea at the Caprice cafe. Closimir talked about the *Ecoforestry* book, which he did not read. He said that their forestry was very advanced, so that he did not need to read it. I kept quiet. He said he was not able to write a letter of support for wolf research, either. My guess was that he was communist and could not afford to look controversial. So, with nothing to lose, I decided to critique his forestry techniques. We started with the lazy approach of cutting trees only near roads. He said that it made sense, because it was easier, more efficient and did not damage the forest floor. I pointed out that eventually it would leads to a 96 percent road cover, with hardpans such that no forest could recover. This exchange continued until he decided to go back to work.

Back & Forth Back & Forth

At a Park conference, Angelar dropped me off at the Rosaritsa hotel next to the state forestry unit. The entire hotel was empty. Usually, the rooms were divided into all male or female, usually having three to ten beds in them. This time I got my own room. I dropped off my pack and took a hike up the hill, looking for animal signs. Passed eight horses and nine cows, but found no other tracks. It was snowing steadily. Not even a crow or roe deer. Returned by mid-afternoon, but not many people had arrived. The other rangers from our region were there, however, drinking, so I sat down and talked and drank with them. Around Five the salads were served. The homemade gallons of rakia appeared on the table, dwarfing the commercial bottles, which were less preferred and drunk last, if at all.

I talked to the owner (this was where I stayed during elk surveys earlier); he was still unhappy with business, and said the disco was closed permanently. The hotel had 50 rooms and they were all filled for this conference. Penko, who was sitting across from me gasped and looked into the kitchen. The cook was putting food on the plates with her bare fingers, lifting cold French fries and chicken kabobs and arranging them; I looked but no one else bothered (I doubt if that was the worst thing that ever happened to our food here, since this place was closed 350 days a year). Then the owner's dog came in and begged at every table.

Instead of a formal meeting before dinner, Iurka, the Park Director, made a few comments and gave out presents to the children of the rangers. We ate and drank until about Ten, when the dancing began. For the first time I decided not to dance (partly due to the immense cabbage salads I had eaten, but also due to a complete failure of confidence in anything physical, from speaking Bulgarian to doing the endless folk line dances).

I admired Svetislav's new coat. He said that each ranger got one; they were from Austria and cost 600 Leva each. I had asked for a winter coat for myself and was told there were none. Oddly, I had never paid over $50 for a coat in my life and that was for a long wool dress overcoat in Oregon. And just last month I paid $32 for a Columbia knock-off to wear during blizzards in the park. Since the Park had ten new jeeps, 40 new cell phones, and 66 rangers, I could see that they were paying a lot of money for things. Just last week, I was told that there was no money for wolf surveys (even though the legislature now required monitoring for biodiversity). I was depressed. Everyone was better dressed and better equipped than I, the supposedly rich American, was, but doing less work. Nikolai gave me a lecture on not trying too hard to change things.

Howling to Communicate

On Tuesday, a late spring day, I biked to the Park, to the water station below Hizha Pleven, intending to walk through the Severn Djendem. But, as I walked into the edge I heard Boleslav and Valeri. They wanted me to go with Valeri to look at the bear den on the mountain. I agreed and we left immediately. We walked behind the plant and went directly uphill for an hour and a half. Valeri pointed out that I was weaker and slower. I pointed out that I had to bike for two hours to get there while he rode in a car (he was also thirty years younger and trained daily). I asked for a brief break from our uphill race. He granted it begrudgingly. I did not ask for another, but after forty minutes he flopped down on a mound of grass (ha, I thought, I could outlast him in the long-run). I scanned the hills with binoculars; we talked a little about hunting.

Finally we were at the end of the forest; the slope was very steep. As we neared the cave, he pulled out a metal whistle and whistled, then we walked closer. At one point we climbed straight up the rock face, stopping to whistle every three meters. We found a very large pile of dung, very healthy with berries in it. Finally near two pines on an outcropping, we were at the cave. I climbed in head first and took photos and Valeri climbed a little higher. The cave was very nicely appointed with freshly dug dirt and dried grasses. There were no hard or sharp surfaces. It seemed warmer than the outside air. So then I climbed above it and took a panoramic snapshot of Aprilci. We were just below the tree line. I could not figure out how the bear got up and down this slope. After an hour we climbed back down, then went another route back, one that paralleled the river, which was just as hard to walk as the ridges that we climbed. At the plant I biked back to Aprilci and get back in time for evening class.

Breakfast was leftover blueberry muffins and yogurt. I called to the Park about a ride to 10th anniversary meeting in Kalofer. Told to ride with Troyan group, but to call first. Worked at office on internet for first time—finally figured out how to connect the hub, and so it worked now, but only from computer to computer and not using an uplink; must explain that to Trifon someday.

I had a quick lunch of peanut butter sandwiches, then biked to Severen Djendem, near the water station at the foot of the Pleven ridge. Met Boleslav and Dimitar on the way; they were cutting firewood from the park near the road. We talked, then I continued. After leaving my bike at the station, I walked up the hill past the Hizha. With the pack, this was still arduous, although I made the two-mile hike in under an hour. The Hizha seemed deserted. As I was walking down the hill towards the sheep pen, the owner came out with Rex, who barked up a storm. I showed him my hands so he barked into them at tremendous volume. Nice German Shepherd, in fact a rescue dog, but he did not like strangers (I had only known him for a year now). The owner was hunting mushrooms, so he walked a way with me. When he saw the horses on the old ski slope (which had not been used for ten years, but the towers and cables still stood), he made a loud crying like a mountain lion and the horses raced into the woods. He found mushrooms to pick and I continued on towards Mandrata.

After an hour, on the middle ridge, I stopped and started my fourth howl survey (where I pretend to be a wolf communicating with young wolves—I know it works in Alaska, but here it does not seem to fool them or inspire them to answer even if they know it was a real wolf). After three sets and no answers since July, I walked on. The walk was very nice. The beech trees were dropping their leaves and last nuts as I walked under the canopy. Then, after fording three streams, I was out into the fields. I could see Mandrata from two ridges away. So, I slowed down, as the sun still had an hour on its metered descent. I walked by a herd of horses grazing near the cheese factory. Then I was at the night blind.

I left my pack inside and went to an old roof (from a cow shelter I think) and took a long piece of rubber—the roof was rubber nailed like sheets of asphalt. This I used to put on the springs of the steel bed in the blind (from an earlier foraging expedition). I put the sleeping bag over that. I went for a walk to the spring and counted footprints, then walked up the hill to watch the setting sun. It had been a while since I had done that. I lay down on the grass and watched. It was very sudden since it went behind a mountain, but the light lasted for another hour. The fog and clouds were rolling up from the north and covering everything. A large hawk swooped down for a mouse and glided off into the fog.

I walked back to the blind and napped until dark. There was no moon that night. I had the binoculars, night scope, flashlight, candle, matches, camera, and penknife laid out on the edge of the bed. The night was uneventful. The night scope did not work well beyond 100 feet in a dark night. I saw movements and heard sounds but was not able to make positive identifications. I did see *two wolf-like shapes* moving past the spring. The owl was back. The stars were very bright, unusually so.

Naturally, I was up early, despite alternating hours, dozing

179

and observing. I observed for another hour, then cleaned up. Breakfast was an oat bar. I met the trail back up on the hill. After an hour of walking through fields, as I was about to enter the beech forest I heard moans, as from an elk. Not having heard an elk in weeks I wondered if it could be a bear. So, I walked directly towards it. In the woods it was quiet; he had heard me, whoever. Then after a ridge, I heard a light barking, like a fox or small dog. But, it became quiet also as I approached (so it must not have been a dog). The rest of the walk was quiet. Except for some fox scat, nicely placed on rocks for me to see, and a little horse manure, there were not many signs this day.

At the Hizha by late morning, I tried the door but it was locked so I walked on (without my tea or break). The trip down was tiring but quick. I retrieved the bike and went down the hill—my favorite part. Immediately I met Angelar, with Boleslav and Dimitar, still cutting wood. We talked about the meeting and about my getting a ride to Hizha Tuzha to investigate another part of the Park. Then I got back to Aprilci. The rest of the day was making calls, checking email, and starting the brochure for the Craftsmen.

Today I took the long walk to Vidima and back looking for animal signs. Then I worked on Wolf Proposal. When I went outside, a small group of people were already waiting. We were to clean sidewalks for President's visit. We used brooms and shovels to clean up. One fellow used a sickle, then a weed whip to cut the grass.

Some days later, Vulko was in Gabrovo, so I borrowed a bike and rode into the Park. It took about two hours there uphill. Walked all the way to the waterfall, but veered off into the ridge when I heard and saw a group of boys with a man (they did not see me, as I was stalking them from above).

On the next ridge, in a small clearing, I sat, but no one came to show herself. Maybe I should fast for a few days to see visions at least. Going back it only took an hour, down hill. I unloaded photos of scat and tracks directly onto the computer. Then met with Vulko and a map maker, who had driven to Aprilci. This was to be the first ever map of the town, since the military never allowed one to be made (this was to be an evacuation center in case of war with Greece, to whom Bulgaria lost much territory in 1913 and 1918). Vulko agreed to hire a boy to ride around and record the street signs. I would try to find aerial photographs in the library or at the Ministry.

Up at 7:30, without daylight savings, I bicycled to the Park, to the water station. I decided to cross the whole of the reserve with the bike, so I rode on the trail in. Surprisingly, I could ride because it was relatively level. For the over the ridge climbs I had to portage the thing, which was easier uphill than downhill. Not much to see, dead salamanders and fox scat everywhere. The entire circuit took almost exactly five hours, even though I went about five kilometers further. Surprisingly, it was quieter and faster, so I had expected to surprise more animals. Not quiet enough I guessed.

Another quick trip to the park, Severen Djendem. Bicycled to the water station and walked west into the reserve. Not much was visible. My legs were tired; these trips, that used to take eight hours or more on foot, only take five with the bicycle, but used different muscles, especially for the uphill ride into the Park. The downhill ride, however, was worth it. It took me less than an hour from the park to the apartment (instead of three hours by foot or two by bus and foot). At home by 2:00, rested and read. Before dinner, I worked on my animal reports and on the wolf proposal for the Balkani wolf group in Pernik.

Looking for Wolves on Foot Or *Play Another Track*

Foregoing the 5:30 bus we took the 8:00 bus to Troyan; it was much more relaxed. Then waited an hour in Troyan and took the 10 a.m. express bus (only 2.8 hours) to Sofia — it skipped about four villages and two towns. We had become more sophisticated about minimizing our bus time. The bus was slightly late; we jumped off at the Lion's bridge, a landmark on the way to PC HQ, and walked, jogged and ran to meet our 1:00 p.m. meeting with Albert, the chef d'instituti. He was waiting and said he was too busy to have lunch with us, but he heated coconut tea in his office instead. So, rather than having lunch for an hour, he served us coconut tea we talked for two hours about politics and PC problems.

Then I raced to the Natural History museum to meet Dr. Russinov. Calpurnia and Christine rushed to meet Alta (Alta, Christine, and I were on the PC Small Projects Assistance or SPA committee). At the museum I asked for the good doctor and the receptionist called him — he would come down to meet me. So, I waited by looking at the exhibits of South American caymans. He arrived and we walked outside to his office, which was above the museum but at another street entrance; the hall was shared with the astronautics group oddly. In his office, he gave me his chair and pulled up a folding chair. The office had three desks and floor to ceiling bookcases. Papers and books were everywhere, as were old skulls and bones. He related that he was most interested in paleontology and evolutionary changes, but liked to study bears and wolves. We talked for an hour about the observation program; I would secure some funding and six volunteers; he would provide one vehicle and three biologists, and the park would give us twelve rangers and four vehicles and additional funding. We scheduled a follow-up survey for February, as well. We could have concluded this in fifteen minutes, but everyone felt it necessary to repeat everything at least six times.

Then I raced back to the PC HQ and all of us walked to Pizza Yurt for salads and a pizza. Then Calpurnia and I walked to the Balkani Wildlife Society office by the American embassy. We were fashionably late but they still had not started! We talked to Desislava about the wolf project in Western Bulgaria and the foresters/hunters survey in the south. The meeting was informal, but we covered a lot of issues, including possible funding for radio-telemetry. Then after another hour, we went back to Hotel Niki, had coke and chocolate — hey, we're in the big city — and slept (as well as one can with coke and chocolate-filled stomachs).

The Hotel Niki advertised rates of 35 Leva per bed. Calpurnia and I reserved a room with one bed, but they insist on charging us 35 Leva each. We decided that this would be the last stay at Hotel Niki, and told them so.

The SPA meeting started at 9:00. This day we spent three hours on the handbook, rules, regulations and such, then we broke up for lunch. Venelina, the sublime diva of all things SPA, brought me some expensive Greek cigarettes to try. Very mild and elegant looking, with good packaging. For the afternoon, we reviewed all the projects, lined up our questions and discussed problems with some of the applications. We actually finished before six. We bought groceries for the weekend, as well as things one could get only in the big city.

Christine had heard of an American cafe, so we walked there, and had burgers (dry) and Mexican food (wet), as well as alcohol (dry, wet and expensive). The place was in a basement, with a large American flag above the entrance. Everyone there spoke English, although we spoke Bulgarian.

Reading Wolf Signs

At the Park, we had finished the elk and goat surveys. I had started the wolf survey, but there did not seem to be much interest yet.

This typical Thursday, we walked in the park looking for wolf signs. As usual Dimitor walked too fast for me to see signs, so I slowed down and then caught up later. He was looking for poachers or fires and was on a tighter schedule.

The next day, Angelar picked me up at 9:00 and we drove to Vidima. Boleslav and his son were waiting there. Then Angelar and the son drove off (to their house I think), while Boleslav and I walked up a new road (that was, one I had not traveled on before). Then Angelar and the boy came back and picked us up.

We drove past a house and up in back of it—it was an old logging road going into the forestry land. It was badly eroded and we only went about five miles an hour. We bottomed out twice and had to inspect the suspension. The road was really badly eroded. It looped along the ridge overlooking Aprilci, so we could always see all of Aprilci including Vidima, Zla Reka, Ostrets, and the center, Novo Celo.

Finally at the top, we were on another ridge where Boleslav and I had seen a lot of wolf prints earlier last year. Now it was drier and there were fewer prints, one from a wolf and maybe two from dogs. I photographed them all. The dog prints were smaller, with shorter nails, and wandered more. The mud holes were drying up. Boleslav said that it marked a major wildlife trail going west into Severen Djendem. So, I looked in all directions and saw two places that might work for a night blind. The first was a beech tree on the side of the hill about 100 meters away; we walked there. The tree had three stems, the third of which was broken off about 3 meters in the air and would hold a platform. The second candidate was an old shepherd's house about the same elevation. On a concrete pad, it was fairly clean; the roof was made of rubber overlapping tires. It would need a window to see the trail from that angle. I reluctantly agreed that it would be easier to fix up that build the *chakalo* (blind) in the tree.

Then we drove higher to a cheese factory. Three guys were making syrene and yogurt. They asked if we want some. We all said yes. Boleslav started helping two younger men rinse curds through cheese cloth. The older man led Angelar and me into the building, which had many broken windows. I saw four rooms with beds. The fifth was set up with a stove for cooking. The fire was hot and soup was steaming. We sat at the table, which was long like a picnic table; on it was a bowl of soup with dead flies. In fact there were hundreds of flies in the room. Other bowls were overturned on the table. Bringing the yogurt in a blue plastic bucket the guy ladled out a liter for each of us, into two of the dishes that were overturned. It was quite good; I was told it was from sheep. Since I had seen about ten cows on the way up but no sheep, I asked where they were. I was told there were about to hundred and they were at a higher pasture.

Boleslav and the guys came back with a bowl of burned fat and a bowl of tomatoes. Boleslav cut the tomatoes and one guy dowsed them with salt then olive oil. Two loaves of bread appeared. I had a hunk of bread with water. Everyone else dived into the fat and tomatoes. After an hour of gossip or talk about the park and the weather, we said we had to go to work. So, we thank them and left.

Ciaran

The trip back was just as long and slow. I invited Angelar for coffee but he said he had no time. I was home by three, and working at the internet cafe five minutes later.

On Saturday at 6:50, I bicycled to Vidima to meet Boleslav. I waited at the small cafe by the post office and he arrived a few minutes later on his motorcycle. I invited him to coffee but he said he just needed cigarettes. He suggested I ride to Vets (the energy plant) now and he would catch up. I agreed and started. This whole part of the trip was uphill, so it was tiring. About halfway he passed me. He was waiting there ten minutes later, and we stored the bikes at the plant, which was now closed for remodeling. Then we hiked up to the water basin about an hour away.

From there we went straight up the hill towards Botev. There was a trail partway, but then we were without a path for an hour. I was very tired and had to stop often—maybe the sinus infection made me weak or something, but it was very uncomfortable. Finally near the tree line, we found the path that went from Hizha Pleven to the Waterhole. We walked to the Waterhole, which was a large natural cave and the headwall for the Vidima river. We explored the cave and sat for a while. Then we struck overland towards the hizha but got off on a large trail, which used to be the main trail to Botev. It was so wide it looked almost like a road. It lead directly down to the hizha trail intersection and the water basin. We had lunch on a fountain made by Valeri; he had carved a roe deer into the rock.

Then we returned to the Vets. After a break I bicycled off. He passed me halfway again, but I had another forty minutes of biking to get to Aprilci. Dropping the bike off at the apartment, I went to the English class that Calpurnia and Alta were teaching from 3 p.m. Svetla, a talented weaver, was there for the first time. We talked about various things. Then the guy and his wife from last week showed up and wanted to join the class. We scheduled one next Saturday at three so they could make that.

On a day trip I went to the Park with Boleslav. I took the 6:50 bus, then we jeeped to the water works, ditched the jeep, then hiked to another water works. On the same trail as with Mitko in December. Same fox prints maybe. Saw six elk.

The next day, Calpurnia wanted to go out. We took the 6:50 bus to Vidima and walked up to the forest road. Along the way we picked up a dog who would not stay home, a friendly large shepherd. We passed a new gypsy camp with three trailers pulled by horses. The horses were saddled for hauling wood. Their dogs, about seven, started to attack our new escort, who acquitted himself well. We shouted and the gypsies came out and shouted, and their dogs retreated. We talked with them a while. The men were getting ready to bring out firewood by horse. We said goodbye and we walked on.

Along the river we were passed by several trucks and a tractor. On the back of one of the trucks were Boleslav and Milko, who waved and pointed ahead. After another hour of walking we caught up to them watching the logging operation. The skyline had been moved from its November location. We tried to take a photo but the camera battery died. So, the four of us walked up the same path that Boleslav and I had taken in November. I fell crossing the stream and cut a knee and palm. Then Calpurnia got tired going straight up a hill, so we told them that we would just go more slowly then return to the camp the same way.

We had a picnic in the beech trees, giving the dog some bread and salami. Then we walked down, along the trails and finally on the road to Vidima. At Vidima, we had a coke and walked around waiting for the 14:30 bus. We talked to a guy that I had talked to Wednesday (who was he?), and he invited us to his house (oh, he was from Sofia), but we had to get back for a meeting with the advanced English class.

On Tuesday, I worked on the wolf model. It looked bad for wolves; the model shows extirpation by 2006 at current levels of growth and hunting. Only no hunting and above-average births would save them I thought. I worked in the internet cafe (my office was still not ready, no hub but much junk as it was a temporary storeroom). At noon, we met Aleksander and Iliana, who was head of the kindergarten in Ostrets. We drove to Ostrets and toured the school. It was coal heated with wood stoves in some rooms. She wanted twenty thousand dollars to redo to gas heat. She had been turned down by Japanese for financing, and asked us to find money. We agreed to try to search the web and contact funding groups. She would also like toys and food for the children. The school was an NGO, founded by the parents four years ago.

At Five we had a class with Aleksander and Andrei; the topic was politics and my continual inability to write a letter in Bulgarian colloquialisms.

The next day, I bicycled to the Park again to explore the new trail. I was now taking the camera every time and was able to get photos of signs. I took the new trail, which did go directly to Vets. It was where the water was collected from small streams and then sent to the reservoir above Vets to power the electrical generators that make electricity for Aprilci. From there it was a simple downhill climb to the plant. I bicycled back by 2:30.

I met Angelar and told him the window was ready, but he was too busy, and so apparently were the rangers. He said they

were going to a GPS course for the next three days. I mentioned
the Telecenter Grand Opening, and he said that no one could come
because of the course. I told him that I had been going into the Park
alone for the surveys.

Afterwards Andrei and I picked up the window for the night
blind. He drove me home with it. We discussed how I would pay the
two cases of beer for it (the barter system was alive and doing well).
He said I could not bring it before Friday or the workers would get
drunk and not come to work, as happened last Wednesday, when we
celebrated the new driers working).

Three days later, Angelar arrived at my door after 9:00. I
showed him the window. Vulko came over; we all went into the
hardware store. Vulko asked for hinges. I said that I wanted to slide
the window. Vulko looked at all the hinges, showing Angelar how it
could be hinged. I repeated that I want to slide it because I needed
to look out without glass and the window was not designed to be
hinged. Finally, I picked out nails for the frame. Vulko thought they
were too small and picked out spikes. Angelar reminded me to get
small ones for finishing. Neither of them liked my nails, so I put
them back and got larger ones and the finishing nails. I asked about
galvanized, but was met with confused stares. The woman put all
the nails in one wrapping of paper.

Then Angelar said he did not had any tools, and he did not
know if Boleslav did, so Vulko and I walked to his house to borrow
a hammer and saw. Vulko did not like the hammer his father gave
me and went to the workshop to find another. I thanked the father
for the keyhole saw, saying it would be perfect, but Vulko thought
I should take a larger saw and made his father go to his house and
bring over a (rusted) set, which I thanked him for. Then, he found a
cardboard box for the set; then he found a cloth bag for the hammer
and saws. Then we returned to the hardware store.

On the way, we stopped at Andrei's sawmill to find some
scrap wood for the frame. Andrei was not there so I told the boys
that I was just taking some scrap wood from the pile—they thought
that was okay. Then Andrei returned and insisted that I take better
wood (although it was finished on only two sides). Then he said that
he would make a new frame right now with hinges! I said that I only
wanted to slide the window. Angelar was respectfully silent. Then
Andrei finished a few pieces of wood that would work to slide the
window on, and we loaded the jeep.

Angelar and I drove to meet Boleslav at his house. He was
waiting with a new Husqvarna chainsaw and a giant ax. Then we
drove the goat/forest trail, with the 4WD in low, past the meadows
near to the night blind. The roads were very eroded, except for the
deep puddles and mud, which we had to plow through; top speed

was about nine miles an hour on the straight-aways. Rather than build the night blind in a large broken beech tree up the hill, Angelar suggested that I convert the shepherd's cabin, which had been abandoned for ten years, into a blind, using only the window. So, we reconnoitered the cabin, which had two small rooms and two small windows facing an old cattle fence. Then, on the side overlooking the watering hole, we sketched in the window with a pencil. I had measured it one inch too large to fit within the bracing. Boleslav chainsawed the outer wall to fit the window, then did the same to the inner, pressed wood, wall. His eye was good and he had barely touched the frame.

I started to hammer the nails into the bottom part of the slide frame, but Boleslav took it outside and trimmed one of the unfinished sides with his ax, so that it would be more square. Then Angelar finished nailing it in. I started to cut the slide piece but Angelar said why bother, so I put one nail in to hold it. Then Angelar took over the hammer and finished the bottom slide. I started the top piece but Boleslav took it away and nailed the other slide piece to it (which was a good idea). Then I held it while he nailed into the frame (but I held it an eighth inch above the window so it could slide). Then Angelar started to cut up the old outside wood for a sill, but Boleslav suggested doing the sides first, so I cut one and they cut the others. It fit surprising well together and looked very good. Then we took pictures of each other.

Boleslav nailed up a piece of wood to block the old stove exit, and he wanted to put boards over the old windows or openings, but I said that I would put plastic on them. We went over to the spring and had a picnic. I had bread and peanuts, Angelar had bread, and Boleslav had bread, cheese, tomatoes, apples, fruit spread, canned meat, and water. Then we drove back to town, which took about two hours on the trail.

Angelar &
Boleslav at
the Chakalo

Blind to Green

The next night I packed to try out the blind. But, first, paperwork had to be finished. I wrote letters to Albert and Venelina about funding, and on grant applications.

Finally, I took the noon bus to Vidima and walked to the *chakalo*. There was more snow that last month, so I was bogged down, but, since I left two hours earlier than last time, I made it just before sunset. The usual assortment of tracks went along the road, but this snow was very wet and heavy. One set of wolf tracks crossed the road and went into the forest; I followed a ways until the vegetation got too low, but it looked like a regular trail.

Approaching the chakalo, there were more prints around the water hole, which was still covered with snow, mostly wild pig and roe deer. The plastic curtains were still up over the holes at the night blind (chakalo). The candle was still there as I left it, so Boleslav had not been there. Dusk took forever to get to dark. I took out the binoculars, nightscope, knife, camera, and water and lined them up so I could find them in the dark. Immediately I heard the owl, who had doubtless come to see if I scared out any mice.

There was surprisingly little activity that I could see with the nightscope. The moon was out, but behind clouds. There was a little snow coming down, but not too bad. The *chakalo* was too far from the water hole, I thought. With the binoculars I saw shadows that later I knew were several wild pigs. These guys were very large and more worrisome than the brown bears; their tusks came about mid-thigh level. I managed to doze for an hour every hour, sleeping on the wood part of the floor, using my coat as a pillow. I remember all those wildlife videos I had seen and wondered if I was ever going to get any good photos, much less a video.

Not being able to sleep much, I left about 5 a.m. at first light and walked downhill. I did not stop to take photographs since I saw no new tracks (except for fox and roe deer, which were the most active). I got to Vidima in time for the 7:30 a.m. bus, which got me back to Aprilci.

After a shower and change of clothes, I started working on email. Georgiu canceled the survey for this weekend and postponed it for a few weeks (which was why I always did what I wanted before asking when the rest were going to go). Nikolai approved a volunteer meeting at the Park office in April. It started snowing.

On Saturday, I hiked to the chakalo. Roads were covered with snow, especially the large potholes now filled with cold water. So, I finally learned to walk along the edges. This was the first time I had walked this way, along the road, as opposed the trails. It took longer but the grade was gentler and there was no chance of getting lost. A few tracks of mice, deer, and fox.

More tracks around the pond. It was cloudy, so the night scope did not work well. That meant that I got more sleep. The sleeping bag was quite comfortable and warm. But, I only stayed in for an hour at a time, and observed for the other hour.

On Sunday, I walked back the same way. It was snowing gently. Got back in time to buy two *tikva* (gourds like pumpkins but smaller). Then Trifon and his coworkers wanted to be let into the Tourist office to hook up the cable for the grade school. I let them in and started to help, but they didn't need any, so I read, and then worked on the internet when the cables were all connected.

Got back to the apartment before Three, just in time to write down a dozen sentences using prepositions, for homework assignments. Then we went to class at the Caprice cafe, which had been sold to one of the partners. It was crowded, noisy and smoky—all those tough 10 year-olds smoking and cussing—so we went to Gameyski's after half an hour. There we exchanged uses of prepositions in English and Bulgarian. Back at the apartment after 5, Calpurnia worked on translating the Operating Plan for the Tourist Office. I did computer work.

Back to the *chakalo* on Wednesday, I found that the nightscope had definite limitations. If I defined the focus the field was much narrower and seemed brighter. Perhaps I should have bought the more expensive model, but the grant did not cover the scope so I had to use my own money, which was severely limited. I saw a horse go over the hill, into the trees. I saw the ground squirrel trying to stay out of sight of the owl, who was late coming out of the lower forest, where she lived. Couldn't see her, but did hear her arrival at the edge tree. Slept for an hour at a time. Before light saw one green shadow moving smoothly by the waterhole and down the west slope. He looked like a wolf, but it was so fast, I was not sure. I remembered the tail, straight back and down.

In the light I looked for prints. I found only two wolf prints near the hole—he did not stop to even look at the hole or the other prints—and a few roe deer prints circling it. The horse prints led up the hill. I took photographs of the prints. Next time I would try to take a photo at night, if I could turn off the flash.

The Deification of Christ(ine)

What can I say. Every year, one volunteer was so loved by her hosts that the town renamed itself after her. This year it was Christine. When her landlord was mean to her, the school and town remodeled a house next to the school for her. It had everything, including a wet bar. When she donated her books to the school, they named the room for her. When she left, they all got drunk, even the ones who were ordered to, so Christine's feelings would not be hurt.

For Christine's record-setting farewell party in Pelovo, we took the 5:30 bus to Pleven, through Troyan and Lovech. Then we took the 10 a.m. bus to Pelovo, which as luck would had it was direct and new. Walking to the house, Christine and Alta hail us from a cafe, where they were drinking cokes. We sat and talked, then headed for the house. We changed into good clothes and walked to meet the head of the school, who gave us a tour of the school, including the new teaching lab, paid for by USAID, and the new computer lab, paid for by Christine. The Head was a few months younger than me, but with white hair and smoker's wrinkles. Christine had a crush on him.

About One, we headed to the Center restaurant, which was only open for special occasions. There was one long table the length of the restaurant and five small four-person tables up on the riser above it. Then there was a small three-person table at one end; this I found out was for the students who read a poem for Christine. The small tables were filled, but the long table was empty; the director and his wife insisted that we sit at the head of the long table. Christine refused, suggesting that the mayor sit at the end. So, we sat at the three places on one side near the end and the director and assistant director sat across from us.

The table was now filled with sodas, beer, wine, and rakia bottles. Small shopska salads were served. A long line — of the mayor, vice mayor, school head, students, and teachers — gave Christine flowers and gifts. She got at least three tablecloths, an ounce of real rose oil in a carved wooden figure, a diploma, lace curtains, table runner, music CDs, dolls, and a book on Bulgaria. Each was accompanied by more flowers. In a surprise, Calpurnia, Alta and I were each given roses and a small vial of rose oil extract.

The music started and Calpurnia asked me to accompany Christine to the floor for the first horo, which I had almost forgotten how to do. Many other dances followed, most with Calpurnia, but a few more with Christine and one with Alta, in which the music stopped so we stood on the floor and talked. Then more horos. Then Christine played her own CDs, mostly Me2 and Stink. The Bulgarians could not dance to that, so when I got tired Christine danced by herself. Eventually the math teacher and music teacher danced with her to the strange popular music.

We drank and danced until after Seven, which meant seven hours of drinking and dancing. Finally I suggested to Alta that we were tired. She told Christine, who agreed. As soon as we left, all the Bulgarians fled immediately — later we heard that the director told them to stay as long as we did; and that Christine wanted to stay longer than the longest celebrations, which were usually only five hours. Calpurnia and I walked the girls home; they were really oversudzed and collapsed immediately. Calpurnia and I cleaned up and then went out for a walk to buy food.

We had heard that the Director of the school had set up a shrine to her in his private office, and knelt before it daily, praying for new funding for computers and projects. We did not think the rumor was an exaggeration.

Wily Craftsmen of the Mountains

One good idea for a business would be to start an ecotourism group, I thought. There were many hotels at low capacity, even the ones in the mountains and the Rila park. Someone could get a contract with their college alumni to have them visit Bulgaria. We would arrange the travel and accommodations at the hotels — even roughing it for students maybe. The Bulgarians were acutely aware of other ecotourist schedules, but seem not to have been able to capitalize on their beautiful mountains and quaint houses — perhaps due to the poor reputation of the Balkan countries as good places to travel.

After seeing the crafts displayed for sale in stores in Sofia, the next big idea was to organize the local craftsmen into a guild to increase their income and exposure. So, we started working on craftsmen materials at the Tourist Office.

Later, we went with Vulko to a cafe and had coffee. He thought the idea was ripe (I thought that was what he said; maybe he meant rotten). Then, Angelar drove by and I flagged him down. We all sat and talked about projects and the conference; he gave me the wildlife observations from the rangers, and we talked about the form for Svetla for January. We also talked about the rangers banquet next Monday at the Ceramic Hotel.

After lunch, which we satisfied with soup and toast. Vulko took us to visit two woodworkers. The first one was directly across the street from our apartment. Tsonyo Velev had a small shop in back of the house. He used almost Linden wood exclusively, although he said he also used some cherry, apple, and walnut when he could get it; he carved out dishes, picture frames and wall ornaments by hand with old woodcarving tools, then dyed the wood dark like walnut. Wood was ordered in a quantity of about five cubic meters, which lasted for two years. The things he sold for 8 to 100 Leva, were finished and resold in Troyan and Sofia (Tsum!) for thousands.

The second craftsman, Stefan Radef, made pipes from wood, also Linden. He had an old electric lath. The pipe blocks were only about 12 inches long, which was about the maximum for the lathe. Each pipe had four parts including the boll. He paid about 15 stutinki for each part but gets about 3.5 Leva for a single pipe. He showed us the papers that proved his father lived in America from 1922 to 1934.

For dinner, we made eggplant Parmesan, sans Parmesan, sus kashkaval. The topic for dinner conversation was how to get the craftsmen together.

We started the next day by meeting with Rahil, the Head of the Maragonzov school, about our disappearing English class. She explained the problem — it was a voluntary class after the buses left, which meant the students had to walk to their villages, something we did not know. She decided to reschedule the class for 1:50, due to the new bus schedules. She reminded us that the next community forum would be about the privatization of forests on January 19th.

At the office Vulko took us to see a weaver. We only had to walk three blocks. She made wool rugs or bedspreads, each one taking from ten to sixteen days, each costing between 160 and 250 Leva. She sold directly to people who ordered them. She was working in a basement of a house (her extended family most likely); the room had a wood food stove, single bed, the large loom, then a sink, washing machine and counter. The wool came from the sheep of her family; she spun it herself and cut it to length.

For the afternoon, I worked on the computer with the wolf data. For dinner, rice Szechuan with pineapples and tomatoes, as well as oatmeal cookies.

More work the next morning. First though, I walked down to the store to buy fresh bread and a mekitsa, which I heated in the oven. Bread was a wonderful habit. I met the same people every day; we waved hello or talked about constantly rising prices — the bread suddenly went up three stutinki last week! As I walked back by the news vendor a woman asked me where she could see a tapestry — I suggested that she visit the tourist bureau. The news vender reminded me that his wife makes *goblins* (tapestries), now that she was no longer employed as a medical doctor, so I suggested that the woman ask the news vendor first, which she did.

There were snow flurries all morning. That afternoon, we arranged to meet with Kosta and Ivana, the ceramicists, to discuss the possibility of a craftsmen NGO in Aprilci. Vulko was not there so we went over about 1:45. We sat down and talked to them for a while; his English was good, but hers was not, so we mixed all of our Bulgarian with all of his English. Then Vulko showed up. The snow came down thicker. We continued talking, finally having tea and chocolates, and playing with their dog, a black setter, Bullet, with a gift for walking on sofa backs.

The business over, we asked if we could buy some more gifts for our host families, so we selected two bells, two candles burners and one candle stick. We were able to pay with 20 dollars and get 23 Leva as change. I noticed they put the American money away in a vase, not with their Bulgarian Leva. We said our good-byes and walked across the river in the snowstorm. The snow continued all evening.

That night I read Verne's *20,000 Leagues* (Calpurnia fell asleep early — poor trophy wife, three years younger).

This morning as I went forth to buy the daily bread for 43 stotinki, the news vender asked me if I would like to see a tapestry that his wife made; he told me that his wife spoke English and German, and that they would come by our apartment tomorrow morning early; I said that we would wait for them. Then we went shopping with our 23 Leva and only spent 13 of it on butter, flour, eggs, sugar, cola, and cheese — the basics for cooking breads and cakes.

The snow continued. I tried to get the final wolf proposal finished for Georgiu but could not get it in the proper form. The rest of the afternoon was occupied with laundry and reading. Hardly any work was done. We sat on the balcony for a while and watched it snow on the river. The mountains were invisible.

The day before Christmas, we slept late, then got up and went to the bazaar, where we got apples and tomatoes, and one orange. The news vendor said that they would come by after noon. At one we went to the new bazaar which had a display of local crafts including weaving and pottery (Kosta's). Then as we went back, the news vendor said they would come by later. At home, Calpurnia made persiani kartofi, which was excellent although greasy. We had salads with it. Finally at Three we went for a long walk to Zora and around. As we were waiting at the bus stop trying to decide which way to walk the clerk from the torta store stopped and offered us a ride, which we declined gratefully, although it was our first such offer, ever. Then we walked back and I made brownies for Christmas. There was no sign of the news vendor or his wife.

After New Years, Vulko took us around to look at more artisans and craftsmen. Then we went to a new hotel to have tea and look around for an office to display crafts.

The next day, Calpurnia worked with Vulko and visited

another set of craftsmen, such as the knife maker, clock-part maker, and others. I went to the mayors office to meet with him but he stood me up — the only time I had met him was in September with only five minutes notice — so I met with the Zap mayor, who called in the head of the other schools to attend the meeting about the craftsmen.

I worked on reports for the PC: Quarterly travel, utilities, and educational materials. I finished the Defense grant for a roof for the hospital and emailed it to the contact at the Embassy. I prepared and printed the SPA grant for the craftsmen NGO. We printed a few other materials, then packed for the Dupnitsa visit and the In-service training.

Time at last for the day of the SPA presentation for the Craftsmen, at 7:30 we walked over to Kosta's house. We all sat and had tea while Petya's father warmed up the car, which was a Volkswagen Passat station wagon, a really new car for this area, one of the few. Then, we were off to Sofia.

After a relatively fast trip (2.5 hours), we were dropped off at the Cultural Center, while they went to buy glazes for their pottery. We walked with our bags to Hotel Niki and dropped off the bags. Then we went to the Peace Corpse to make copies and talk to Pentcho in the environmental office. Svetla was just back from America and we talked to her about her trip. Then we raced to McD's for junk food lunch. The SPA meeting and the application went smoothly. Kosta and Petya represented the craftsmen for one grant and Vulko represented the Tourist Bureau for another. After 6:00, we went shopping at the Oasis below the Tsum Mall. Looked around for a watch and gifts.

Tired we ate at the Chinese restaurant, but it was Woman's day and the restaurant got very crowded after we sat down; in fact, we were asked to share our table with another couple. Then back to the hotel to rest.

We were back in Aprilci and back in class at 2:00. We met with Aleksander and Andrei in the Capris Cafe. Went over Andrei's politics and Aleksander's internet letter. He was writing to five women on the internet (in Italy, Ireland, Japan, and America) — I suggested that he start files on them or he might forget to whom he was writing. Now, Svetla, one of the crafts makers, was also writing to men in Italy and America. I jokingly suggested that Aleksander ask Svetla out. Aleksander ignored me. Svetla is attractive, but I suspect she is now considered too old for marriage by the local men (she might be 35 if that).

In order to discuss difficult issues in Bulgarian, I had to make scripts that covered most possible topics. So, today I worked on scripts for Vulko about the Masters and the tourist bureau. Then, we helped Kosta and Petya set up the craftsmen exhibits for the Folk Fair. Rahil asked if I would take photos of the fair. I agreed. I started by taking photos of the preparations and the theater, which we had not seen—it was quite large and dark, with a good stage. We took many photos of the preparations for the fair. It seemed that only Kosta and Petya were working on the set-up. I helped them put up burlap for a while, then old brown wrapping paper, as backgrounds. Then we hung five of Atila's paintings. I arranged some of the bronzes, and Petya placed the pots. After a while, since we were only talking, I drifted away and took more photos. Back at the apartment, I sorted, sized, and named the new ones.

On Saturday, the Fair began at 10:00. I started taking photos about 9:45. The festival was well orchestrated, every group getting ready then going up to dance or sing. Every group wore its traditional costumes, which most people could tell from the fabric patterns, just like Scots clans. I learned our regional design, which had four vertical stripes. We watched and shot until about One, then had lunch, which was a few kebabche from Gameyski's restaurant, with bread and tomatoes. In the afternoon, I took photos of the craftsmen when I could find them, then of interesting faces, then of friends who wanted their pictures taken.

Tuesday, we met with Vulko about the Craftsmen (and I used my Bulgarian scripts). Afterwards, at the internet café, I searched the web for funding for the schools. Found and wrote to several, but they answered that they could not fund, even the solar power project was only for telephones and not for heating. I found a few crafts guilds on the web, also. I wrote up the addresses for Kosta or someone to try to contact about possible partnerships.

Wednesday morning was more work on the computer. At the office the internet was down, so I helped Aleksander edit a letter to Lisa, his second American pen-pal. Then we walked down the street to the leathersmith to try to set up an appointment for me—the father and son were both craftsmen, a rare combination, but they were busy and asked to meet on Saturday.

Lunch was potato and chicken salads, left over from Monday. Afternoon was devoted to working on the SPA application for wolf teleporting, I mean, telemetry, using the new information received from Desislava.

After Saturday English class, Aleksander and I walked to the leathersmiths, so that I could interview them (using the new form for the craftsmen) and take pictures of their work. They were a father and son, who live in adjoining houses (that also were connected to the barn and hay sheds, like most Bulgarian homes). The father had his diploma as a Master from 1947, but the son did not, being trained by his father. Most of their work was for horse harnesses. They invited us for rakia, but I declined due to a sore stomach (and in fact dinner would be only milk and soy powder). They offered to host me later and I accepted gratefully. Finally I went back and rested after Six.

Up at seven and out to get fresh bread, I walked to Iva's market, and she was getting crate after crate of bread. I only bought one, but she wanted me to buy one for Sunday, since no bread was made then. I politely declined, saying that I had a freezer full of leftover bread, but I did buy extra yogurt.

Basically the rest of the day was devoted to the web pages. I now had one for everyone, but I would had to take more photos of some of the craftspersons, so I made temporary construction pages for them for the moment. The photos were resized and laid out for each craftsman. I also created pages for Aprilci, the city, businesses, and organizations. I would need a lot more information for the entire city.

We went to bed early and read. Then watched the movie Waterworld, with Kevin Costner speaking mean Bulgarian, and then a Clint Eastwood movie speaking strained English. Calpurnia fell asleep, but I was fascinated by the television station, which has been purchased by Fox this year and had changed in many awful ways. For instance, instead of one commercial every hour, with normal sound, there were now eight commercials at every break, with tripled volume, and there were three or four commercial breaks per hour. Most of the commercials were for shampoo, beer, soccer, and cell phones. I remembered the first time I watched television in Dupnitsa, the television station played cartoons between programs, which often ended before the hour was up.

Wednesday after lunch, we meet with Desislava and Vulko and called the masters to make arrangements for interviews and photos. Only one, Valeri, the gun maker, was willing to be photographed. So, we drove to his house and looked over his gunstocks, all in walnut. He worked in the garage in back of his house, where he also had his weight-lifting equipment. His wife came out and asked if we wanted tea. We thanked her but did not had any. After looking at the three guns he was working on, including his own, he brought out bear and deer skulls, then all of his photographs, some of which we borrowed for the map and brochure.

On the way back to the central village, Novo Celo, where the office was, we stopped at Dyankos, the knife maker, but he was out cutting hay. Then, Vulko remembered the coppersmith, so we went to see him, but he did not want photos or to talk much, which was good, since it was almost Five anyway and I was suffering from a language headache. Then we went for tea at a new store in Evil River — the old restaurant being remodeled. Vulko decided that we should then visit the Two Rivers Hotel which was run by the head of his NGO.

We went and took pictures. The owner returned and asked us all to tea and beers. He complained for an hour or two about having no business. We sat in the empty dining room in the empty hotel and believed him.

The following Saturday, Calpurnia and I waited in the square for the bus from Gabrovo. There was to be a wreath ceremony at 9:15, then a hike to the Maragadjik monument. But, we saw Vulko and sat with him at the Caprice cafe. He said there would not be a ceremony in Aprilci, because the mayor was a bad man. Then the bus came and he asked us if we want to ride to Maragadjik; we said no and he left. So, we went shopping for cheese and kleenex. Nothing ever happened quite the way you think it would.

Finally, on Tuesday, after weeks of arrangements and postponements, we had another meeting with the Craftsmen to decide on the name of the NGO and elect officers, but we did not do either. We went back to the freezing Tourist Office and translated the summary and forms.

Wednesday, we worked all day on presentations. I finished my wolf proposals and printed them out. Then we had a board meeting with the Craftsmen to discuss final particulars about the project. That night was the final preparations for the other grants.

Thursday and Friday, more discussions. We worked on the internet, then did a laundry. Alta arrived at 5:30 and unpacked. We discussed the projects with the Craftsmen NGO and the possibility of forming another NGO for the Park. She would be working here for two weeks, interviewing crafts people and translating, with her superior Bulgarian ability. In fact, Alta and Christine both spoke Bulgarian better than any other volunteers, so we were grateful for their help.

The next three days were filled with work on the craftsmen brochure in the Tourist office with Vulko and Calpurnia. I was working on the web pages trying to finish them before the meeting of the Craftsmen tomorrow. All day I wrote HTML files to present the craftsmen, but I also had to dummy up the files for Aprilci and the city, so the craftsmen fit into the whole web site.

Then the meeting took place. I made my scripted presentation. The participants voted and decided to have an NGO. The rest of the meeting was dedicated to the forms. Vulko and I took photos. I agreed to get the final samples to Kosta by Monday. The meeting had

197

lasted one hour and forty minutes.

At 4:30 Aleksander showed up to escort me to one of the craftsmen, a leathersmith. Calpurnia was too sick to go. At the house, which was in a family compound of three houses, we went upstairs to a living room next to a kitchen; the television was playing Bulgarian Folk music from a cable channel. We started talking about leather work; the craftsman was a teacher of German at the school, which I did not know, and had followed his father into the business — they had a small studio on the street in front of the houses. The snack was a 14-course snack, with rakia, beer, coke, juice, potatoes, cabbage, peanuts, kyufte, pork fat, salami, beef jerky, chocolate cake, cookies, and candies. We talked for three hours and filled out the informational form together. At home, I entered the data on the computer.

Friday. More Web page work. There were problems attaching files to the new web name. I started to rewrite the web page, but got frustrated. Then lasagna for dinner, but I forgot to mix the cheese with eggs and mushrooms, making a strange cheesy mess. Then more internet work. Wrote letters to host family. Made notes for lectures. Made more changes to the web page for the masters. Reloaded pages to the web. Ad infinitum. Was becoming weary of HTML. I could not convince Trifon or Ivan to learn it, although Trifon took copies of my photos and maps. Tried to find someone to maintain the web page.

Craft Meeting No. 9.

Next week, we went (Calpurnia, Vulko and I) to interview the elusive and cantankerous Dyanko Dyankov. But he was not there (in Sofia, where he told me he would be, but Vulko wanted an early appointment). Then we went to the Red Andrei, but he was in the mountains gathering wood. So, we finally gave up searching for craftsmen.

Because the Tourist Office has been closed since early January, Calpurnia worked at home on her funding matrix for our last class on grant-writing. We were driving each other slowly crazy. I cussed when things did not go right. She sat and ate peanuts with her mouth open. The Tourist Office was an interesting case study. Vulko let the phone, electricity, and internet be cut off for nonpayment rather than spend the last of the Swiss grant money. So, he had worked at home for the last month, as had Calpurnia. He had the money to pay the old bills, but did not have a commitment from the Swiss for future bills.

I heard from Georgiu and Russinov that we would have the next wolf survey in two days.

Vulko drove Calpurnia and me to Troyan. I downloaded the files for the craftsmen and we looked over the design. They suggested ways to improve it. They decided to come to Aprilci on Saturday, if I could get separate files for the craftsmen. I agreed. After coffee, we went buy some dolls from the dollmaker. He wanted us to drink rakia with him, but we begged off until next time; we had tea instead and talked to his wife, who ran the business side of their partnership. Then we spent an hour looking for medicine for Vulko's father, because the hospital did not had it. The sixth drug store did have it so we drove to Troyan to give it to the hospital. Then home, and more computer work.

This day, I prepared a web page for the craftsmen. New names. This afternoon, we visited four more craftsmen, for one hour each. First was Dyanko the knifemaker. We take pictures of his rakia flasks, knives and gun stocks; he was going to Sofia again soon for a display for the Chinese. He agreed to make two knives for me. Wanted them to be gifts but I said they were gifts for my friends and wanted to pay twenty Leva; he said five; I said twenty-five — not sure what the price would be. Then we located Gos. Vrabetsov, who made wooden plates and plant stands. We bought six plates for seven Leva and he gave us two. We gave him ten Leva, saying that we had no change.

Then we went to Teodora, who paints. Took photos of all her paintings and a few sketches. Then off to the famous Red Andrei (because he had red hair, which was now grey). Took photos of him working. Drank rakia with him at the picnic table in back of the clothes lines in his yard. Offered to buy a barrel for drinking rakia, but he wanted to clean it up or make a new one. We agreed on a price of twenty-five Leva (I offered twenty, so he knew his value better than most I thought).

All this information was also going into the new brochure. So, Calpurnia and I had to prepare Bulgarian translations for the brochure. The brochure printers from Lovech drive down and met us at the Tourist Office. We worked for three hours on transferring the files from my computer to Vulko's by zip disk, then Vulko burned a CD and we loaded it on to their PC. The translations were not quite finished, so I gave them the original interview sheets — which may have been a bad idea.

Wednesday I fixed a good breakfast (African grapefruit, Seattle tea, German cereal, Bulgarian fruit juice, and cinnamon bread), then started to work directly on the computer. Had to finish the proposal to the park for a meeting with all parks and send a letter to the Minister of Environment, asking for a wildlife inventory and countrywide monitoring. My fingers hurt from typing. Translated Bulgarian from Vulko into English for two new craftsmen. Worked on web pages with new photographs. Vulko drove us to the furniture factory in Ostrets — two doors down from where I lived that September (2000). We waited and watched them for a while, then meet the owner at the Tourist Bureau, where he showed us samples and took measurements (this part of the grant was for display cabinets for the crafts. I sent the web information to Georgi in Lovech.

All morning I finished the web pages of the craftsmen, so that I could take the pages to Vulko so that they could see and criticize them. Finally it was done before noon. But, I had to empty a zip disk of photos to stick on the web page files, then load them onto Vulko's, which I did.

Monday, April Fool's Day, was also Vulko's birthday (46). I worked in my office next to the internet, slowly freezing because of the cold air (the window next to the office door was broken now). The usual searches for grant money were now spiced up with the first searches for a job back in America. At 8:30, Calpurnia told me that the furniture had arrived for the Tourist office. So, I went help them unload it while she searched the cafes for Vulko. The furniture arrived in pieces and had to be screwed together; my specialty was holding things together while two of the guys drilled and screwed. The furniture was made of pressed wood with a faux plastic cover; it looked okay from a distance (at least thirty meters). It was cheap and necessary, since none of the craftsmen had time to build displays, even though we had three different designs. It took about four hours to put together.

Calpurnia came back from the post office with a large box of books from Darien Book Aid. I put them upstairs. Kosta came over and wanted to make a CD for his ceramic work, but we were all too busy. Of course, we immediately went to coffee for an hour, with Kosta, who understood that having coffee was part of being too busy. Then Calpurnia and I had lunch (left-over potato salad). After lunch we worked on the final final draft of the brochure, since Vulko has written new Bulgarian text for the history of the area. Then Kosta came back and we all make a CD of his crafts, which he wanted to send to Spain to generate interest for sales. The computer acted up and had difficulty finishing the CD.

Then, about five we took Vulko out to dinner. He would not eat or let us pay, but we ordered vodka and whiskey and drank it.

Calpurnia and I got fries (persiani kartofi) to eat. Then we offered to buy him a cake, so we went to the next door sladkarnitsa (sweet place) and each ordered a small slide of burned sugar cake, with coffee and tea. We gave him his present, which was a card and bottle of red wine (which he never bought himself because he could make it if he had grapes, but did not because he did not have any grapes left).

I had only four days now to finish the craftsmen project. In the morning, Vulko and I looked at tiles and floor coverings. The materials alone were more than our budget, so we did not know what to do. I suggested linoleum, but no one knew what that was. I suggested wool carpets but they laughed (seriously, it was a good idea because the city owned the office and any permanent improvements went to them, whereas a carpet could be taken out with the computer and desk, although the carpet would probably get dirty in the winter). No decision was made. I noticed on Vulko's desk copies of the class notes for English class. Sometimes he came to class but was embarrassed by his speaking, so he got someone to give him copies of the notes and practices alone. I tried to convince him to come anyway and talk, since there were only five of us and he knew everyone.

I went back to work on the computer and the electricity went out. Most Americans thought it was nice living here because I had a shower, stove, and television, but nothing worked like it should: the shower handle could not keep the water warm, so cold showers were normal; the television only got two channels on a good day and zero on a bad — it was old and lost color even on a good day; the stove only had one burner that worked and that burner was much hotter on its left side, so food had to be stirred constantly, making one item at a time. The electricity went off regularly; since the heater was electric, if it was off for more than six hours, it started to get cold very quickly. The buildings were made of concrete and stayed colder all the time (which was nice in the summer, but not in the winter). The water went off regularly, but most often on Mondays, after weekends of heavy use. Transportation was only by bus, which was cold and slow (but almost always on time), or on foot, or by begging for a ride (maybe once every 40-50 days). Still the apartment was dry and the blankets were wool.

When it came back on, it immediately went off again for an hour, then repeated this cycle until mid afternoon, when it stayed on for the rest of the day. Dinner was leftover pizza. At the plant store, which had some videos, I find the Mummy II, which we rented and saw (as the color on the television went out naturally and the sound kept booming and fading).

Another day of dedicated work. I started by spending an hour at the internet Telecenter, answering email (internet had not worked well for a week because the engineer had been away taking a course and no one else could reset the server or control the bandwidth distribution). Vulko came up and laughed at my office—I was wrapped in my winter coat and sat huddled over the computer for warmth—and asked if I could translate the craftsmen's bios for the brochure. We sat at the computer for a few hours, then he called Desislava (Dr. Karanova) to come over. She came at 1300 and we retranslated everything from the English back into the Bulgarian, so the two matched better (which I did not want because then the English was stilted).

Dyanko's Knives

At 4:15 Calpurnia, Vulko and I drove to Lovech to turn over the disks to the brochure people (an advertising firm). We met with them and went over the design, text, and photos again. Then I paid them 900 Leva in advance for the brochure (I had to pay out my own money before Friday, when the grant money might be available). At Seven we went for coffee, then Vulko drove to his sister's house. She was a teacher at the local school. We had more coffee and talked about the brochure, which she would proof for errors in Bulgarian, and about Vulko's family. His father had eye problems and was being moved from the Troyan hospital to the Pleven hospital. His oldest daughter had a spinal disease and starts a six-month hospital stay next month; his wife would stay with her in Sofia for that time, but had no place to stay herself. His mother had eye problems. We suggested cooking food to help them. Calpurnia lent her portable stereo to his father so he could listen to news.

At 9:00 we returned and fix soup and sandwiches for dinner. No computer work. Just sleep early. Up at 3:00 to read, due to flaming stomach ache. The book was good enough to keep me from whining.

Onto the poor computer again to work on the final report for the craftsmen's project. Talked to Trifon, who said that the library has gotten a grant for two computers, so he would hook up internet for them. The internet was fast so I checked my email and searched for funding for wolves. Get email from Venelina saying that another of my wolf surveys got funded, this one by the Global Fund. The money would be sent directly from America to the Park bank. Unfortunately, that would bypass me, and I would have to stand in line for any reimbursement of expenses.

The computer battery ran out and I had to plug it in. I now had to recharge it twice a day due to the heavy usage. Prepared for class; the lesson again was slang phrases. Spent 2.5 hours in class, teaching phrases to the guys. At home afterwards, tried to watch television, but the sound and the picture died. So, we read then slept.

Roughed out budget and completion report for the Craftsmen project. Met with Kosta and Aleksander B. about the final stages of the project. The money all had to be paid out now, but some of the work could not start until later in March. The paperwork was taking up all my time, now, except for weekend trips to the woods. I had vowed to finish it all by early March and then only do things that I wanted to do, such as a Bulgaria-wide wolf survey.

So, I immediately went back to the computer and finished the wolf report for the first survey, drawing two detailed maps of the wolves tracks around the mountains.

Friday, I worked on Ms. computer all morning for web pages. Then drove to Sevlievo with Vulko to meet with Georgi about the web page, which he had transferred to from my site "aprilci.net" to "nat. bg/Aprilci." It looked the same. We both paid for his consulting, but reminded him that we still needed to send changes to the pages. We drove back with Vulko, but did not get back until around seven, in the dark.

Saturday, worked on all Piece Corpse forms, such as the quarterly report, Craftsmen project completion report, and the last SPA paperwork. Translated the English report into Bulgarian. Had class early and asked the class to help with translation. This was a can of worms, which results in five different conversations. After class, went back to work on computer, but decided to hike up to black peak and look for wolves. No wolves, only dogs, ravens and roe deer. Extreme exhaustitude set in.

After a quiet day eating and sleeping, Monday continued the work on making a draft brochure for Calpurnia and the Tourist Bureau. Just as I finished Vulko came in and said we could go to Lovech now to meet with the brochure makers about the final Craftsmen brochure.

We left immediately, e.g., without more than fifteen minutes at coffee, and drove to Lovech in Vulko's faithful Lada. We were presented with two models of how the brochure could look; each young lady at the office had created a model. I could not choose between them (the models I meant) and said they were both good. Vulko decided, but later switched. We paid the balance of the money and chose the paper.

We worked a little on Calpurnia's brochure, then left for lunch. I wanted pizza, Calpurnia wanted Chinese, Vulko wanted coffee, so we decided on a small Bulgarian place with a French name, Bistro cafe. They had a buffet of cold food which could be microwaved. I had salad bread and a coke, Calpurnia a mishmash of potatoes and meat, bread, coke and coffee, Vulko soup, bread and coffee. The entire lunch came to $1.20, half of which was the two cokes, so I paid. At first I thought they imported the coke bottles from the US, but now I know they were trucked from Germany.

Then we went to the local school to get a check on Vulko's translation. Then we raced back to Aprilci to have the final Craftsmen meeting with Kosta and Aleksander Bakerdjief. We signed all the forms and made sure the money was accounted for. Just as we finished the bank guard came in and said the bank was flooded with water from our apartment. We asked if it was toilet water or sink water; he said sink and we all sighed. We went upstairs and looked, then returned and said the apartment was dry. Then the neighbors were asked to come down, but each said the problem was not theirs. Too bad the bank did not just hire a plumber. No one could trace the water. Dinner was leftover pasta. Then back to work on mister computerhead.

Then, we spent a few days re-editing and re-translating. We asked Vulko to drive us to Lovech; he agreed. Vulko picked us up at 8:30 and dropped us off in Lovech for the meeting with Samir and Desislava, the brochure printers. Because we were four hours early, they were not there, so we met with the computer specialist, who made the changes to the brochure as we found the errors and suggested corrections. The German paragraphs did not look right, and in fact, no one had corrected my rough translation. So, we said that we would have Mariya proof them in Aprilci.

It was noon when we finished so we went to eat at the pizza restaurant and then walked up the hill to the bus station. We took the 1:00 bus to Troyan, where we shopped for our favorite juice and cereal, then spent a few hours in the crafts museum there. It was in an old revival house and a very good exhibit; it also featured two craftsmen from Aprilci, although only one current one was mentioned and that was Dyanko, whose works were on the cover of our craftsmen brochure.

Then we had a salad at the bar in Troyan. It seemed to be less carefully prepared than usual, but better than most. We went to the bus station and took the 5:10 bus back to Aprilci.

All morning I worked on reports for the new projects. Then a classic American lunch with German peanut butter, Bulgarian raspberry jam, Greek potato chips, and Italian coca cola, which had to be rationed here because it was so expensive (three times as expensive as the Bulgarian Joker cola, which was not potable).

Then Vulko said that he must drive his father to Pleven, again, for the eye operation. We asked him to describe it and it sounded like a herpes infection, rather than a lens transplant. It was still a mystery. Anyway, Vulko dropped us off in Lovech, where we found that the printer could not print the brochure because of the fonts. So, we stayed and worked on one more pass through the text. Unfortunately we found a few mistakes and decided to rewrite some of the text. Then we noticed the "all rights reserved" paragraph had never been translated, so Calpurnia translated the words and I rewrote in readable English. After Six, we walked around town and found a pizza restaurant that Andrei had recommended. We had an 'okay' pizza, then walked back. On the way we found a small magazine with cereal and bough a box of German granola, as well as a small piece of chicken and some raspberry juice.

Back at the designers, we tried to help the owner fix the font problem, but he was using programs, such as Coreldraw, that I had never used. After an hour of helpless finger ringing, Vulko showed up and we all argued in that unique Bulgarian voice that was not quite a shout but not very pleasant either. Then we left for Aprilci and returned after Nine.

Friday, after the usual international breakfast, we worked to finish the brochure. Calpurnia made a list of hotels in Bulgarian and Mariya and I translated them into German. Ditto with City offices and important sites. I sized all the photos and loaded them onto the zip disk. As we were working I saw a group of school kids with bags, picking trash out of the river. I was amazed; we had talked to the teachers about cleaning the river, but no one told us if or when the students would do it. We went down and helped and took digital photos. We suspected that this was a good example of how the city kept things from us by not telling us of events, such as library poetry readings, forums, meetings, or cleanups, until afterwards. We had tried not to get between the warring factions in this little city. We had been told that the Mayor and many counselors resented having Americans in town. This had caused some schisms to widen, since a few people were curious about us and wanted to know more about what we were doing. Since we had other projects in the park and other areas, we were not much offended or disappointed by this attitude, although it could be frustrating.

Then, with the photos and program disk, we took the bus to Troyan and then to Lovech. It spanned two hours and two buses, but we make the connections.

We walked to the ad agency and set up our computers and theirs. It took an hour and a half to transfer and test the files, which was made more difficult due to the fact that Samir had no word processing programs, only page formatting or graphics programs such as PageMaker and Coreldraw. But, with ingenuity and perseverance, we transferred the text (without the formatting). He now had all the pieces and they would start working next Monday. He asked us if we wanted to take more finished brochures (another 1400 in boxes), but we said would wait until we could load them in Vulko's car. We took a few to admire.

Then, we looked for more cereal and juice, and walked to the bus station. At the bus station was a celebration fair, with many rides and many people. It was sunny and warm, really welcome. We looked around and then went to buy tickets. Surprisingly, we could catch the Pleven to Aprilci bus, but it left twenty minutes after the bus to Troyan, so we decided to take the risk. Every other bus left at Five, and we almost died from the fumes. The Pleven bus reached to Aprilci ten minutes before the bus from Troyan. We bought some food and relaxed and ate.

Spoofing the Corpse

Famous Detective Stories from the American Foreign Legion of Peace (fortuitously combined with a vocabulary-building exercise in English). As told to and recounted by Everett Saylor

1. The Case of the Missing Volunteer
2. The Case of the Second Missing Volunteer
3-71 The Cases of the Missing Volunteers
72. The Case of the Inadequate Allowance (" I must speak with the Director. I simply do not had enough money for my daily costs at my site. How do you expect me to get to Sofia every day week? ... What, oh all right, I guess I can wait a week. Can he see me when I get back from Paris?")
75. The Case of the Missing Counterpart
76. The Case of the Unbathed Counterpart
77. The Case of the Lecherous Counterpart
78. The Case of the Abandoned Counterpart
79. The Case of the Demulsive Drugs Episode ("Who? No, I don't know. Sure, I doubt if it would happen again. Jeez the stuff was from Turkey — that's how good it was. Had to move to a new place now though")
80. The Case of the Dedal Driver ("But, how did he get from the city to the project? No buses, no rides ... had to be bicycle, but no bikes. Couldn't be a car — that's not allowed.")

83. The Case of the Missing Toilet ("There was no toilet in there I tell you, just a hole in the floor")

87. The Case of the Emergency Depression ("But I'm hysterical because I lost my speech! Again! Send me back to America please! I'll be fine after 4 weeks there!")

88. The Case of the Emergency Reservation ("Please Ani, my Bulgarian was not good enough, and my parents and 47 relatives and friends were visiting me next week and I do not had hotel reservations for them." "Oh, thank you, and by the way, could you arrange for taxis and dinner reservations at the Hilton, for 36?")

91. The Case of the Vacationing Staff (in 96 parts)

92. The Case of the Inflated Market Survey ("In my town, cheese does cost 19 Leva a kilo [it's made from homeless dogs]. You said to calculate the cost for 40 kilos.")

97. The Case of the Simultaneous Sites ("I need to be in Varna to consult. I need to be in Sofia to see the Minister. I need to be in Pamporovo for meetings on business development ... I need all three sites, but I'll only be in one at a time, maybe summer or winter or ...")

102. The Case of the Overused Medic ("You're the only one I can talk to; you speak English and I don't feel well anyway."

105. The Case of the Pestilent Business Consultant

107. The Case of the Tortured Teacher ("12 hours a week? You must be joking? I need to have Monday, Wednesday and Fridays off")

115: The Case of the Uninvited Guests ("Hey, I want to visit you, see your town. When are you there? Can I stay for a week?")

122: The Case of the Double Standard ("As an American you had to pay the double price for the room. If you want to eat here, use a separate menu, double plus extra gratuities and taxes.")

123. The Case of the Big Entertainment Allowance (for Sofia volunteers only. "I need this extra money to buy dinners for, uh, influence peddlers. It's, ah, for the good of the state. I hope you didn't think I would, err, benefit.")

124. The Case of the Moneyless Employer ("No money for my employees this month, cause I bought an Alfa Romero, to add to my fleet of Mercedes. It's okay, they are used to it.")

125. The Case of the Important Meeting (a 1 hour meeting followed by a 2 day party)

128. Illinois Smith and the Temple of Tsum

130. The Case of Beer

131. The Case of the Unimportant Cases

Test for Stress in Bulgaria
By Boris Badenuv

Directions: Circle the letter that resonates with your inner chord.
1. Being a volunteer was:
    a. an important source of entertainment for your town
    b. an important personal commitment to world peace and
        understanding
    c. constantly saying "I am not a spy!"
    d. a form of career advancement for the desperate, challenged or
        confused

2. The Pre-service training was useful:
    a. to get acclimated to the local party scene
    b. to understand true cultural differences
    c. to employ more Bulgarians
    d. for testing your reaction to stress

3. The Bulgarian Language is:
    a. The basis for Russian and other more modern languages
    b. A challenge because there were too many words to learn, but not
        enough to describe what you want to say.
    c. as useful as "uheeri" or "bangole"
    d. Something you would torture your children with years from
        now (or Bulgarians moments from now)

4. Your primary assignment was made:
    a. based on a thoughtful match of your experience and skills with
        the needs of a site
    b. according to an intricate pattern of social connections, favors,
        and paybacks
    c. as a direct challenge to bring out the most in you
    d. as a result of your partying sophistication evidenced during pre-
        service training

5. Your primary responsibility was to:
    a. hold a spot in the social order for a Bulgarian not quite there yet
    b. provide advice and examples to your colleagues
    c. serve as a source of amusement for colleagues, who insist on
        tellingl you things immediately after you had to know them
    d. justify the overhead of the main office

6. The P'lice Cars office was:
    a. Your best resource
    b. Your worst enemy

c. A place to visit in Sofia after McDonald's
d. A strange and exotic government institution

7. Your counterpart was:
    a. A lifeline to everyday life and work
    b. Missing — out for coffee
    c. An effort in social contracts requiring patience and tolerance
    d. Your babysitter

8. Secondary projects were recommended because:
    a. You should do something besides party
    b. You should do everything you can to help Bulgaria
    c. There was too much to do for 70 volunteers
    d. The primary babysitter needed a rest

9 Teaching English:
    a. Was what we all ended up doing
    b. Was what most of us had no training to do
    c. Was what our hosts wanted us to do
    d. Was a good way to explain the American Way of partying

10. It was okay to travel away from your site on weekends because
    a. everyone expected you too — you were a rich American
    b. your expenditures were boosting the Bulgarian economy by 2%
    c. there was nothing to do in Celo Phane
    d. you do not want to party with another weekend horo

11. Parties were an important release of stress, since
    a. a wide spectrum of drugs and alcohol were available
    b. everyone spoke English
    c. they contributed even more to the economy
    d. they kept you happy and a happy volunteer was productive

12. Kebabche was:
    a. A new and exotic food
    b. What you ate every day with persiani kartofi
    c. The act of snapping your fingers
    d. A furry animal living under snow

13. Breakfast was the:
    a. Foundation of an active day
    b. Meal before lunch and after nightly rakia
    c. Foundation for a day of meaningless meetings and coffees
    d. Most effective cure for a rakia hangover, if it included vodka

209

14. Fresh bread was:
    a. a necessary part of your diet or 90% of it
    b. a source of nutrition for many others after you discarded it
    c. a really neat cultural treat
    d. useful for insulation around broken windows

15. Your apartment was:
    a. a place to hide
    b. your hovel away from home
    c. probably the most luxurious place in your town
    d. the mean in Bulgarian housing (really mean)

16. A warm apartment was:
    a. A fading memory of long ago, in a country far away
    b. An unfair comparison with Bulgarian standards
    c. Possible if you spend 200 leva a month on your 4 heaters
    d. Required for EU membership

17. An automobile was:
    a. What you drive to work, praying no one sees you
    b. A dream of a past life
    c. What everyone else had but you
    d. An accident that would happen

18. Rakia was:
    a. a paint remover
    b. ambrosia
    c. essence of rotten plums
    d. the mainstay of the barter economy (tripling effective income)
    e. all of the above

19. Mobile telephones:
    a. were necessary to replace the 1928 telephone lines
    b. provoked violence in theaters
    c. should be owned by everyone, or no one
    d. were a better way to spend money than on pirated CDs

20. Chavdar buses
    a. were the missing link between 1915 Ford trucks and 2006 mag-lev trains
    b. were immortal (they just keep rattling on, like the energizer warthog)
    c. killed more people with cold air than all viruses and bacteria put together
    d. were on time and that's what counted

21. The Bulgarian Mafia was:
    a. a group of fun-loving guys who lifted weights, had scantily-clad girl friends, and drove really nice imported cars
    b. a social menace that may prevent early EU accession
    c. your main source of things you absolutely needed
    d. rated "BG," less violent than the Russian or American mafias

22. Gypsies were:
    a. a discriminated-against, socially-deprived group
    b. a separate nomadic culture who like their lives as they are
    c. a secondary project
    d. a critical component of BG society to tell fortunes and redistribute wealth

23. The end of your commitment means that:
    a. you can really go shopping now
    b. you can relive this experience and share it with others who spent the past two years shopping
    c. you can pursue a lucrative career using your intercultural communications skills
    d. you can reenlist in the PC to teach computing in Samoa

24. Chalga music was:
    a. the natural evolution of folk music
    b. the cultural answer to rap hip hop music, used in mating rituals
    c. used to power trams or fill silences
    d. a sensitive expression that mirrored universal harmony

25. The best thing about Bulgaria was:
    a. the friends you made or bought
    b. that it would survive volunteers from the US, Britain, Germany and Switzerland
    c. that your new friends will all visit you in the US
    d. that we have given them more to complain about

Calculating the Results:
If your answers spell "cab" then it is time to take one. Too much stress. If your answers spell "baa" then you had settled into the proper Bulgarian mentality. If your answers spell "aaa" then you should not be doing what you were doing right now. If your answers spell "dad" then you should not have done what you did to get warm 9 months ago. If you answers spell "bad" then you do not have the proper attitude to be a volunteer. If your answers spell "ccc" then spit it out before you swallow it. If your answers spell "eat me" then you had cheated. Congratulations.

Ciaran

My Life among the Wolves of Bulgaria
by Castor Thrice

I had heard that wolves in Bulgaria were few and secretive, that
after 3000 years of being hunted they had become nocturnal. I had
heard that they were giant fierce creatures with hard claws and sharp
fangs, who carried off sheep and children in the night and ate them.

With a few hardy souls I made long journeys into the
mountains to see where they lived. We searched and searched but
found nothing except a few footprints and some scat.

Discouraged, I went back to the village. There, I found them
everywhere. Or, rather, they found me! The first time I lay down
to rest on the grass outside in the public park, I lay on one of their
dens. They were so much smaller than I had thought, being small
and black, with six legs and a segmented abdomen, and very active
in sunlight. The guard wolves had very unpleasant bites, although
it did not hurt too badly. I could not figure out how they could take
down a deer. Perhaps while the deer was resting, millions of them
would attack it and bite it.

When I got up, I stepped on them and must had killed
hundreds by accident. I wondered if I should gather up their little
black bodies and turn them into the forestry units for 20 Leva and a
cubic meter of wood each.

A lot of mythic nonsense has been written about these
wolves, but you only need to look around your feet to see them. True
they hunt in packs, and they were difficult to kill with a gun (an
experienced hunter with really little bullets could do it), but you can
kill them with your feet or fingers. They were almost impossible to
skin, which may be why I had not seen any coats made from their
skins.

I no longer had illusions about how romantic and noble they
were, these wolves. There was no adventure and sport in finding
them. It gave me no pleasure to demote this rare legend to being a
populous nuisance, but it was my duty as a scientist of the first order.
(apologies to my cousin Mark Twain, who had similar problems with
wildlife in western Europe)

What Peace Corps Advertisements Really Mean
By Rick Sunburns

1. "The Peace Corps would insure you until you reach American
   soil." If you trip and fall to the airport tarmac, you will not
   be covered, due to the fact that no injuries occurred in the air,
   only on the ground.
2. "The Privacy Act Release Form allows us to pass your name ..."

to credit agencies, accounting firms, the CIA, and the Aryan Nations Recruiting.

3. "You were always a volunteer, which was why you are called an RPCV" after you leave. We always expect you to keep volunteering for things for us.

4. "The PC Fellows program offer graduate school opportunities." Like a volunteer, as a Fellow, you would work long hours for little money for the credit of others, if they choose you or if the programs still exist.

5. "Noncompetitive eligibility is a mechanism by which RPCVs can be appointed to federal positions without competing." It was almost as good as just talking to an employer and having them slant the description to your skills, except that no federal agencies offer it.

6. "Toughest job you would ever love" This means the longest vacation you would ever have to leave.

7. The "COS Conference" means Continuation of Silliness.

8. The "DOS statement" means the Dissection of Song birds.

Jill: Here are the meanings of the words. Sorry, although I am a sesquipedalian, I prefer not to offer exegeses of my words. My feracious brain is used to dwelling in its idiolalia, but I have become too delitescent. Now, my logodaedaly is a distant memory. I was and always will be grateful for your tempean presence. Thank you.
Boris Badenuf (www.badenuf4u.ho)

Cultural Objects Or the Zoo

We tried to assemble the whole city brochure, but had to write new text for the city, so it fit on the page. Then tried to take more needed pictures, for example, each of the churches in the area as well as the entrance statue to Aprilci. We tried to arrange for a meeting for Friday in Lovech, using Kosta as a translator. While we were waiting for Kosta, Vulko came up and announced that he had to take his father back to Pleven for an eye check-up. So, I grabbed the computer and zip disk and we went with him. On the way, he stopped and picked up his son, so the five of us were in the Lada. At Lovech he dropped us off, but came in and grabbed some of the finished Craftsmen's brochures — to which all of my final changes had been made, surprisingly.

As we sit down to transfer the pictures and text for Cali's Aprilci brochure, I noticed they had a new computer and the old one — the one with the zip program loaded on it — was missing. Samir said yes it broke down. Then we struggled for an hour trying to load zip software, but could not (it was on the zip disk, which could not be recognized without the software on the machine — Bulgarians claim that they invented the computer and much software; if so, this might explain the snafus that occurred so often).

Samir and Desislava asked us if we would like to walk around. We said that we would, but then they put on their coats and came with us — apparently, they meant with them. So, we drove to the zoo on the hill, the second largest in Bulgaria. We were the only car in the parking lot, although there were four teenagers loitering around the entrance. The zoo looked abandoned; some of the cages were broken; everything was overgrown with grass, weeds and trees. But we walked to the bird cages and there were eagles and hawks. The insides of the cages were clean and the birds looked healthy. We were told there was not enough money for food.

As we walked around, many of the animals were missing, e.g., giraffe and elephant, and others, e.g., brown bear, lion and monkeys, were inside.

We walked to the wolf cage; the wolf was lying on an outcropping in the cage. He walked down and came to the fence. I put my fingers through and he rubbed against them, then continued the length of the cage rubbing on the wires. I looked in his eyes, but only saw resignation. I wondered if there was any wildness left; maybe there might be, if he were suddenly free. I thought about it, and rubbed his pelt again. What an odd feeling to touch a caged wolf. He was shorter and stockier than *Canis lupus albus* or *tarandus* (he was *C. l. lupus*, the European wolf), with a winter coat. Very brown in color, a little like Legend, my wolf-friend in Oregon. He walked back up and flopped down again. I thought " goodbye."

We visited the leopard, polar bear, red deer, and surni. There was one large American bison, some ducks, an otter, three fox, and many more deer. The gong announced the zoo would close at 5:30, so we walked to the exit and paid there. We were the only humans.

Then they drove us to a larger newer market, where we collected cereal and things. Finally, we went to the Chinese restaurant beside the stationery store (a chain called Office One). We had shrimp rice, fried fish, sweet and sour chicken, peanut salad, and water. At 7:30, we went outside and waited for Vulko, and they drove home in their new classy Renault. After half an hour Vulko drove up and we returned to Aprilci by 9:30.

The Life of Water

The water was off today. Water and electricity were off regularly. We went to the mayor's office, but he had just called saying that he was going to Troyan all day. We asked about other times or about speaking with the Vice-Mayor, but Svetla, the PC environmental program director, and Vulko seem pissed about the snub (hey, it's Bulgaria). We went to a local restaurant and talked about the crafts groups in the city and in other countries.

Svetla left at 3 p.m. for Sofia; Vulko showed me how to pay the telephone and electricity bills. Calpurnia and I bought a few groceries (bread, jam, cola, tea, salami, etc.). Mariya came over and showed us how to work the big heater in the living room. It seemed that I had had it on the daytime setting (heat release) all of the time. It needed to be on heat at night and release during the day, so it would not use electricity during the day when rates were higher; it was a huge thing weighing maybe 500 pounds (it took four guys with rollers to even move it), so it had an immense thermal mass, but it was also slow to heat up. We rested, cooked, and watch a movie.

All Monday morning we worked on park proposal stuff. Then I met with Vulko and used his internet to send email to the Park. Vulko also sent email and called the Park, but Iurka Bacheva, the director, was at Botev. Vulko got a call back that we could meet Wednesday afternoon. He agreed to pick us up at the cafe by the generating station if we called him.

About One, Vulko drove us to the water station above Vidima, Vets, and we walked up the mountain to hizha Pleven. The trail was very steep and eroded but with wooden guard rails the whole way. The trees were at the peak of color, with many dead leaves all over. We walked slowly with many observation breaks (it was of course why I was here). It takes almost three hours and we got there about Four. Rex and Lassie greeted us with loud aggressive barking. We rented a room and dropped off our baggage. Then walked out the ridge to a good observation point and watched for an hour and a half, but saw only birds. We saw many leaves fall from the beech trees. There were a few Elen tracks and many horse prints around a watering hole. Wild pigs had rooted in some places.

After the sunset we walked back to the hizha for tea. Then about 5:30 we asked for dinner, and were told there was no food. Not surprised, even though it was a restaurant, we brought out our peanut butter sandwiches, which Calpurnia had made earlier. We had apples and bananas, and we bought a small chocolate bar for dessert. Although the hizha had a nice bar and large dinning room, and was surrounded by cut wood, there was no fireplace; heat was provided by a large electric furnace pointed at us; the two Bulgarian custodians sat at the next table and ate tomatoes and eggs.

We retired early to our room, which was small and clean, with two single beds, a sink, wardrobe, and small electric heater. The heater made the room warm. We decided to sleep in one bed; Calpurnia took the sleeping bag and I slept partly outside with a sheet and blanket. It was not uncomfortable, and we were very close, which was nice.

We spent the next day observing wildlife.

After we walked back to the apartment, which took three hours, we worked on the research plans for the park. The water went off about 7 p.m. catching us off guard. We only had one bucket of water and one jug of drinking water. The water had never gone off this often, unlike the electricity, which went off every week for an hour or two.

The water came back on at Eight, so we did the laundry immediately, which was a major thing to do, for two people. We cleaned up the apartment and put things away. Vulko had invited us to have dinner with him that night. We shopped for tomatoes, bread and tea, and a few others things that we bought almost daily. That afternoon Vulko came over to tell us that we could not eat with him. His family was okay; we asked about the father and daughter. We wondered if it was a water problem.

I decided to make lasagna for us, since we had all the ingredients except cheese, which I went out and got. As I was half way through the water started to get low, so Calpurnia did the dishes as fast as I dirtied them and then started to fill bottle and jugs. Just as the lasagna went in the oven the water went off again. We ate lasagna and left the dishes in the sink. It was decent but had a too much spinach, unlike the last one, which was just right.

Water was irregular. It went out regularly, although apparently the outages were announced on cable television an hour before; then everyone called everyone else and they all filled up old coke bottles with water. I was not on the networks, so I had only been called once. Now, starting in August, the city was on a regime, twelve hours off and twelve on. But, every week they decided to switch to day or night, so during the switch we either had water for zero hours or for twenty-four. Finally, it rained for three days in a row and we went off the system. Perhaps so many tourists had left that there was less demand on the water. But, I heard that the pipes were so old that over half of the water was lost in transit.

Having found out more about our water, I heard that much of our water has traditionally been diverted to Sevlievo. Then, yesterday I heard that the former mayor sold the rest to another city, Veliko Turnovo. I asked if the city was still being paid for the water, but no one knew anything. Later that day the water went off.

I thought the hotels used it when the students came here to go to the diskos. Some of the other outages were related directly to tourist use on holidays, especially Easter and Christmas.

Some time later, we heard that Aprilci would go on a water regime. The water would come on at 8 a.m. but go off at 5 p.m. Then it would be back on at 8 a.m. In practice the water went off at 8:00 a.m. every day and stayed off for twelve hours. The hotel owners were furious. The mayor said that it was not his problem. Angelar could not help me get to the woods today, so I decided to work on the brochure and web site. The internet cafe was not working at all because they were trying to winterize the connections from Varna.

The Tragedy of Electricity

With the electricity still on, the next day became a computing day, while waiting to hear from Angelar or Georgiu. I sent email to Park about my schedule for next two weeks. Wrote it out in Bulgarian and English and mailed the back-up letter. I should not bother, since no one paid any attention to things that were further in the future than two days.

I realized that this journal made it seem that I basically ate, slept and wrote on the computer. Partly this was because I had a separate wildlife database, so all of my observations went onto to it. Partly it was because food was a large part of life here; many kinds were always missing, everything had to be made from scratch, every business arrangement or meeting had to be done over coffee or dinner, and it was always frustrating. Partly, it was because I forgot a lot of things that I now take for granted, such as sheep, goats, cattle, and horses being on the road every day, such as the water or electrics going off every day, and such as freezing in unheated concrete Turkish toilets. Maybe I should take a day every month and emphasize the real daily differences of living here? Naaa.

All the next morning I refined the web pages and sized about fifty photographs for the pages. After lunch the electricity went off again and the computer battery wound down, so I took a hike up the north slope. No wildlife to speak of, just a nice magpie who insulted me cleverly.

When I returned the electricity had also, so I plugged in the computer and finished enough pages to show the craftsmen. At 4:30 we went down and everyone was waiting for us in Vulko's office. They wanted to work on the legal paperwork for the NGO. The lawyer and the application would only cost 55 Leva. Then we talked about the money left from the SPA grant and when to finish those parts of the project.

Finally, I gave the demonstration of the web site. Svetla

seemed to like her page, but there were not enough photographs, so we agreed to take more tomorrow. Ivan did not want his, but said he had a web page that was not finished yet and wanted to know if I could put a link to it. Of course, I answered. I was surprised and pleased that he had gone ahead and set up one of his own.

Electricity went off regularly, usually during a thunderstorm. It stayed off for one to four hours. Sometimes, during sunny weather or during winter cold, it went off longer. The infrastructure was very old. Someday it all would need to be replaced. I heard that some American companies were bidding to build new plants, including a microproject on the river, below the Swiss generators.

Saturday we had an early lunch. Just as I was working on the computer all the lights and heat went off. We checked the other apartments and they had electricity. I checked our circuits and they were all working, so I called the landlord, and tried to explain in Bulgarian that some circuit in the building had gone off and needed repair. After half an hour, Vulko came over and I showed him what worked in our switch box. Then we went downstairs and looked in the master box. He turned off the power for the whole building, leading to a chorus of concern, but the problem was simple — the master fuse had blown and I had a spare, which we installed.

The afternoon was more computer work, including an article for the *Echo* on the ecology of pets. It was cloudy and cold, but not snowing. All the doors were closed off so that the heater was heating the living room only. Calpurnia took a nap while I typed away — pick, pick, maybe I could write a score better than Mooflon Rouge.

A month later, the electricity went off, with a loud boom from the hallway. I checked the other apartments and they had electricity. So, I went out and unscrewed the master box — our main wire had blown off and then sparked and blown the fuse. I called the landlord, who came a few hours later with an electrician from the hardware store. The electrician marched up and put his screw driver across the gap — boom, it flew into the wall and his hair was smoking. I turned off the switch for all the power. He said that was not necessary, but he reconnected the wire and went down to get a new fuse. When he was done it seemed to work. I was thrilled, and glad to be alive without a screw driver embedded in my sternum.

Torte Magazine

Famous Toilets Or Buy the Paper First

How to Build a Dream Bulgarian Bathroom: Build a cube of concrete with a central drain in the middle and the toilet drain in one corner (punch holes in the floor). Then plaster the walls and tile the floor and the lower walls (this was optional). Then punch holes in the concrete for bolts to hang the water heater, sink, and toilet tank. Then punch holes in the concrete to bring in electricity. Then punch more holes in the walls to bring in the pipes for water. Install the toilet and sink; above them install a shower head. Put in a mirror and two towel racks (optional, also). Wala! It is done.

I was relatively lucky at the moment, to have a flush toilet, even if it could not handle any paper; most houses, bus stations, public facilities, and hotels had Turkish toilets. These were basically holes in the floor into which you voided your bowels. The second generation kind had ceramic footprints to show you where to squat. The newest generation had electronic eyes that flushed automatically from a bowl mounted near the ceiling. Actually it was physiologically a better way to defecate, but it had other problems, such as soiled clothes, wet floors and missed efforts (of the hundreds of others before you). Some of the new ones had toilet paper provided, but very few. In the large stations there was a grandmother parked outside selling single pieces of toilet paper for 10 stutinki (5 cents). The best advice I ever got was always to carry small pieces of tissue everywhere (and I did).

The worst toilet I ever saw (or used) was in the bus station at Sevlievo. There was one small room, with walls black with waste (and three small stalls with no doors). Three of us were in line, waiting our turn. An elderly woman chased us out, then started spraying the place with a fire hose, dousing the walls and ceilings that were thick with unidentified man-made materials. When she was done, I was reluctant to go into the stall so I went into the pissatorium (cannot think of a better word here), which was a single large room with a drain channel along all four walls (also dark brown, but formerly white). I used it and left.

The buses had no toilets. Some of the long distance ones, for four to thirteen hour trips, had toilets, but they were locked. When you needed to go, you asked the bus driver to stop and then squatted or stood next to the bus. Once, I waited and waited until a small boy had to go, then I rushed outside also. Six or seven other people also rushed out, but they only needed to smoke.

Working in the park or wilderness reserves, things were quite easier. One simply adds one's "signs" to those of the other animals. Once, we stayed in a small village nearby, in an abandoned house (many villages were decreasing at about twenty percent per year). There was no water or electricity, but it still had beds and many wool blankets. When I used the outhouse I discovered that it was a small wooden building with a door and a small hole cut in the floor. It seemed to require a degree of precision that the human body could rarely achieve. When I looked closer (sorry, just curiosity), I noticed that there was no hole under the outhouse, just grass. Furthermore, the whole house was on wooden skids. There was no toilet paper. The waste drained slowly into the street.

In the Forests of Bulgaria

Many beech forests in the Park seemed to be regrown from a cut in the 1930s. There were a few areas of old-growth, but none of those trees seemed older than 150 years. From a distance, these areas looked very wild. However, hiking through them, one saw many trees with carved initials in them and many spots littered with old cans and food wrappers. It was a disconcerting contrast. This was the largest extent of beech forest in Europe. It was very popular with many people who liked to hike in the mountains. It had a wonderful ambience, though, and we were always happy to be in forest.

I was commenting on the state of the forests to Closimir, the city forester, one day in his city office, which seemed to be always kept at 90 degrees and very dry. Closimir invited us to visit his own forest, which he had been allowed to buy from a forest unit after it had been harvested. Alta was visiting us, so the three of us met with Closimir and Aleksander to drive up to his plot in the forestry unit. After a fifteen-minute drive, we hiked into a four-decare plot of 54 trees. Signs of the recent harvest were evident, mostly in sawn stumps and some branch litter. Closimir said that seeds were gathered from the trees in the fall here for planting elsewhere. Closimir said also that he would like to name a tree after each of us, a kind gesture. So, we each picked out a tree; Calpurnia, Alta, and Aleksander chose tall, straight trees. I chose a misshapen beech of about 50 years. Closimir asked why I had chosen that tree and I replied that it may have genes that the other trees did not, and it was a survivor. After inspecting the trees, we sat and had beers and soaked our feet in the stream. The discussion turned again to the openness of the canopy and plans for this plot of land.

A Forest Scene

Later, I started thinking about Andrei's forest, where he had invited me to help with a small harvest. The site was 40 decares on a slope (40-110 degrees) facing almost due east. The canopy closure was about 95-100 percent. Where the canopy was solid beech there was virtually no understory, only dead leaves and rocks. Where it was solid pines, the understory was dried needles and rocks. In the mixed part of the forest there was some regeneration of beech and a herbal layer, with raspberries, ferns, grasses, rose, wild ginger, and many mosses. Animals were abundant: especially spiders and ants, slugs, frogs, and butterflies. No large mammals were in evidence.

Based on evidence at the site, a mature beech forest seemed to have been clearcut about 51 years ago and replanted in Scots and black pines. After an interval of two years the beeches started to naturally regenerate. Growth was rapid, in some cases trees were growing at two rings per inch (about 1 per cm) for about the first 30 years, then the canopy closed in and growth slowed (15-20 rings per inch) for another 10-20 years. Then about six years ago there was another harvest that released all the remaining trees. This year was the latest harvest and trees had been marked in a thin-from-below pattern. I agreed that a small harvest would open up the forest and aid regeneration, but I also argued that the harvest should be small and very selective, that older trees should be encouraged, and that some trees be left shaded to encourage long-fiber growth, which created more valuable wood.

Carrying Logs on Foot in the Dark

It was a Friday at 8:00 a.m. Andrei picked me up in his red Lada and then we picked up the other four workers and went to his forest (40 decares) east of Vets. We stopped for supplies, then had coffee and banitsa by the river. Or rather Andrei ate all the banitsa and the guys drank all the coffee. At 8:30 we went into the forest. Three of us were wearing sandals. One was wearing rubber ankle boots to keep his feet dry I guessed. One was wearing shorts. Two were wearing t-shirts. I was wearing long sleeves and a vest, and Mitko was wearing a work jumper. Everyone else was in sawmill work clothes, basically trousers and short sleeves. We had four small axes and one Husqvarna chainsaw. The saw operator and I were wearing logging boots. There were no safety glasses, earplugs, helmets, gloves, or any safety equipment. No first aid kit, no spare chain. Just a can of gas and chain oil. Why so little? No money. Young Andrei, his age differentiated him from boss Andrei, was carrying two ropes. In fact, with a small pool of men's names to choose from, there was a lot of duplication, so an adjective was added before the name, such as "Black" for hair or "Young" for age).

After an hour of chaos, we sort of divided up into teams. Andrei was the chief, Mitko was the feller, I was the swamper, Young Andrei was the marker and helper. Ivan and Danyel (this was embarrassing, I could not remember their names for sure) were the haulers. Mitko hung up many trees, but the trees were thick — to drop them we had to saw other trees. After a tree was down Young Andrei marked the logs, which were all four-meter lengths, the longest that the sawmill dryer could handle, and Mitko cut them. I then swamped them and the two boys carried them downhill towards the stream or pulled them with the ropes.

Hauling Logs

I also took photographs and then cruised the property to look at the trees, making notes and measurements.

Lunch was an hour by the stream, with bread and water, and peanuts. Young Andrei and Mitko caught a trout with their hands. Back at work we dropped about twenty more trees on purpose and a few to release hangers. The trees had been marked by the Forestry Enterprise and the cut had to be below the maximum volume. Then a forestry inspector would come when the trees were down and stamp them. Afterwards they could be loaded and trucked to the mill. This should happen next week.

I got back at 5:30 to eat with the neighbors. Calpurnia said that she went over to lunch but no one was there. We knocked on the door and no one was there now. Probably just another Bulgarian language miscommunication, one of an indefinite series.

We worked in the morning, trying to get on to the internet, which sucked, and then took the bus to Troyan. On the street we saw Closimir and went to coffee (what was he doing there we never found out, although we suspected that he was having an affair). Then we all went to the local internet cafe there, but it was filled with kids playing games. We were told to come back in half an hour. Half an hour later we were told that there was no connection; she had even tried Veliko Turnovo with her card, but it was no good because of the rain. Closimir went back to work and we went shopping for envelopes and eggplant. Also found more granola. Then we bused back home.

At 1700 we went to the cafe and met with Aleksander, Zhan and Andrei. Andrei invited us to his sawmill. After tea, we went to the sawmill.

The sawmill was run by a huge 1918 steam generator. The individual planers and bandsaws were run by electricity (which could be generated by the steam engine, but I knew it was not). The factory was old and large. It had had two major enlargements, which Andrei did not receive under privatization, which meant that the city owned the two large rusty metal buildings surrounding his large white brick building; they were allowing them to fall to ruin, while asking Andrei to buy them for an exorbitant price. There were two very large planers, one a 16-inch and one a 30-inch. There were two large band saws. But the main saw was an old saw, not a head saw, but eight vertical vibrating saws that cut of six planks at a time. I had never seen any setup like this. I thought it must date from the 1930s.

Friday I started the day by drafting my article for the *Echo* on Bulgaria's declining population. I wonder if it made sense in 600 words (cut down from 3000). After that, I walked to the sawmill and got Andrei to help me buy the beer, my contribution to the sawmill guys; we needed his car to carry it. We bought two cases of "Spirka" for only 16.00 Leva (and a bottle of coke and vodka for Cali and me; no Stolichnaya, so I had to stay with the ultra-cheap brain-killing Savoy Club).

Met Calpurnia there and we sat for two hours feasting on French bread, imported from Sevlievo, ripe tomatoes, krastavitsi, and worst. Talked in Bulgarian and English, depending on who was teaching whom what. Toasted the dead, but not forgotten, Emil, by pouring part of our drinks on the ground and offering his memory and forgiveness to god (pronounced "Bok").

The next month, we took a hundred Leva from the bank, and called Andrei to help us with the beer. He was drunk and could not pick us up, so he had a friend meet us at Iva's market. I had promised to buy two cases of beer to pay for the window (the barter system), but the friend said vodka would be better, so we bought vodka, orange juice and coke.

At the party we found there was plenty of beer and vodka, but no kebabche. Andrei sent one of the boys, who also had had too much to drink, to walk out to get some; he returned with 2 pounds of peanuts, which we all ate with beer and screwdrivers. I had four drinks to catch up, but gave up when the guys started drinking straight. The conversation was in Bulgarian. Calpurnia showed them the maps, which they all wanted. I promised them all maps next time instead of the beer, saying it was safer. They agreed. Andrei switched to English and wanted to know what "pear" meant. As we were talking, a man in a new Citroen drove up and wanted to speak English — he vacationed in Florida every year, had a home in Lovech and a rest house in Aprilci (about 3000 square feet we heard). Then he left, and Andrei informed us that nothing this man did was legal, so we talked about crime and corruption.

Calpurnia and I went back to work on the computer and read our mail. I went shopping for tomatoes, cheese and cola.

It had been a busy spring. I spent all morning working on the internet, answering mail and trying to improve the web page. Andrei stopped by and asked us to come to another little celebration of the opening of his driers (for the wood sawed). I had been taking photographs of the mill since last June and took the camera along. We met at the mill; the employees were drinking, and Andrei arrived with about twenty Kebabche. We had beer (coke for me), kebabche and tomatoes for an hour. Then he showed us how the driers worked. He has installed old steam radiators (from an abandoned hotel, and I wondered if they were from the Agrotel) on one side and new plastic fans on the other. We went down into the guts of the building and the giant steam engine was working to provide the steam. The engine was fabulous and huge — it could heat the whole city I think. Much bigger than the ones I worked on many years ago. Sawdust was shoveled into the burner every twenty minutes; fortunately there was a lot of sawdust. The engine part was not working and the flywheels were not turning. Only the box was used to provide steam. The engine was built in 1918 (or 1908 we think). It was huge and as black as the walls around it. A few new relays were all that had been added. It started to drizzle, so we walked back. Calpurnia thought that parts of the mill, the telephone office, and other parts of Aprilci could be a working history site for tourists.

Park Business Or Telepathic Meetings
I left for Gabrovo and the Park at 8:20. Calpurnia decided to come along to avoid cabin fever in Aprilci. The bus left at 8:30 and arrived in to Sevlievo at 9:30, and we ran to the minibus, which was waiting at the station. Today, for the first time, it was not full — there were four vacant seats. In Gabrovo we immediately grabbed a donut (or whatever it was called, Keefla, maybe) and then took the bus to the Park office. Only Iurka the director was in the office — all the others were at the ranger-training course.

Iurka was working on the budget and refused to be interrupted, so Calpurnia left a map of Aprilci and I left three invitations to the Telecenter Opening. Then we took the bus back to the center of town. We shopped for envelopes, batteries, and various other necessities, but we had very little money since the PC HQ has not deposited the allowances yet. Then we called Dr. Tsacheva, about the meeting to discuss her grant for animals last year, and try to make it earlier than 2 p.m. There was no answer.

We ate in the new pizza restaurant downtown, Tempo, and it was excellent—a wood-fired oven—the best pizza in Bulgaria. We split a garlic Margarita pizza. Then we called Tsacheva again. After walking to the Animal Protection Society Office at 1:00, we found it closed. So, we had tea at the university hangout, which had a billiards table. We watched students play, then went back before 2:00 and waited an hour. No one showed up. We walked slowly away, but called one more time from a phone on the street, and walked to the bus station. We had heard that she had been attacked and beaten by mafia goons, because of her campaign to help dogs. We had no idea where she was or if she was hiding; she had agreed to meet us. Another mystery. Perhaps the meeting was to have been telepathic. We missed the 3:30 bus, which only had four passengers, but bought a ticket for the 4:00 bus.

Unfortunately this was a local bus that stopped in every town, so instead of taking only twenty-five minutes like the minibus, it took an hour. At Sevlievo we bought tickets to Aprilci, on the only direct bus of the day to Aprilci. We arrived at 6:30 and ate leftovers. It was October and the participants in the new wolf survey wanted to meet in Sofia, which meant we had to take the long bus there. The 5:30 a.m. bus to Sofia arrived at 10:45. I took a cab to the museum, which only cost 78 stutinki, while Calpurnia walked to PC HQ. Of course, I was there first, then Russinov came in and asked where Georgiu was. I could not say. Then at 11:05 Georgiu came in. One of Russinov's students came and then a colleague, a big bearded veterinarian who also studied and tracked wolves.

We moved to a cafe and talked about the details of the survey. How many cars, how many people, nights, groups, and so on. The survey was postponed until November. Georgiu wanted this only for ranger training. Russinov wanted more money for January and March. I agreed not to invite any volunteers or Balkani members to this survey. After two and a half hours we parted ways.

I met Calpurnia and we headed to PC HQ. She met with Pentcho and I met with Venelina. Venelina had been calling both Gabrovo and Troyan about the assessments (and the missing Tsacheva). After lunch, we went to the internet cafe. I found out that everyone from Balkani was working in the field, so I sent email that I would not go to the evening meeting, but would wait for Desislava's draft of the proposal.

We ate at the American Cafe called Stateside, which was okay, but not great. Then we decided to go to a movie, but which one?

We walked by three theaters before going to get tickets to AI, which was a nice sci fi (except for the dough boy aliens). Then home to the hostel, which had a large group of Aussies pre-partying.

A two-day trip to Sofia for a meeting. Breakfast at DD and then shopped at the Oasis. Back to HQ and talked to Venelina, who had a confirmation for another grant assessment for next Monday. Then some more shopping for food and to the bus, which left at One; and we got to Aprilci by 6:00 p.m. Ate food and read. The reading material was mostly leftover classical readings (Verne, Cicero, etc.) from the PC library or my scientific books and journals. Every once and a while I found poetry (Wordsworth) or science fiction (*Neuromancer*) for sale in English, but all books were expensive and books in English were rare.

The Park had invited us to a grand opening of a new trail in Kalofer, where they hoped to open a new office next year (I had originally asked to be stationed in Kalofer because the two rangers there had three new computers in the old office).

Took the 8:00 bus to Troyan to meet with Aleksander, the head of the Park office in Troyan. He was driving us to the Park meeting in Kalofer (pronounced kal-loaf-air). At nine we had tea and a croissant at the bus cafe. At 10 we waited for him. At 10:30 we called him and he sent someone to pick us up. The guy came on foot and we walked to the office, on the other side of town across the river. At the office, Kosta, the assistant director of the Park, was there, as was Rumiyana, the forester, and one of the rangers. We sat; we all looked at one another. Kosta said Aleksander would not be here until 12:30 and then we would all leave at 1:30. He suggested that we go to lunch. So, we went to the internet cafe for an hour and then had a pizza.

Back at the office, we waited for an hour and a half; everything was late. One Niva jeep left with Kosta and Rumiyana. Finally, we left in a huge Russian jeep that seated nine. We drove directly across the mountain to Karlovo and then Kalofer. Once there, the women went to a hotel and the men went to a campground. I shared a cabin with Aleksander. The cabins were not heated or insulated; there were six thin blankets and some sheets so we divided them up. Then we went back to town for rehearsal.

Calpurnia and I had no official duties so we talked to people in the audience, mostly from other towns, but sometimes from tourist groups or the Parks (also, the two other Parks, Rila and Pirin). After rehearsal we broke up into groups for coffee. Then, it was time for dinner at the Camelia restaurant. We sat in an unheated wing and all wore winter coats. The dinner lasted until midnight, with only a little rakia and vodka and a lot of tea and coke. Dinner was chicken with potato salad and cabbage salad, both of which were better than the chicken. Then the rangers and I drove back to the camp. They all gathered in an unheated basement to have rakia, while I went to bed and tried to sleep — it was freezing. I turned all night and finally ended up sleeping in a ball (the warm fetal position).

Up at 8:00, we drove to breakfast at the same restaurant and had a typical Bulgarian breakfast of salami, cheese and bread, with a hard-boiled egg. Then to coffee in the plaza to wait until the ceremony began at 10:00. We took photos of the ceremony, which began with a talk by Iurka, giving credit to the Swiss and American help, and mentioning us and the Peace Corps. Then the rangers were sworn in and each signed a commitment, which was presented to the new Minister of Environment and Water, a young lawyer about thirty years old. Then awards were given. The flag was raised, and the rest of the events were announced. We talked to Peter Hertz, the AED Contact, for a while about funding and tourism.

Calpurnia and I went to the Botev museum and looked at and photographed the crafts exhibits. Then we visited the house with all of the art of the school children, done to celebrate the park, with mostly water colors and conte crayon sketches, which were all very good. Then we remembered the cocktail hour at the Mayor's office. We talked with George Capt, head of the Swiss aid; we exchanged gossip of Aprilci's mayor, Gospodin Balakov. Then we ate very well indeed: Fake shrimp, deep-fried cheese balls, potato cakes, and stuffed tomatoes. We each got to cut our own piece of cake, which was shaped like the park. Then everybody raced off (I thought they were like schools of fish, in their sudden darting movements from place to place, that seemed so mysterious to us observers). We stayed for a little but then the helpers started eating. We talked to Mariana the wife of Aleksander Hertz. She was from the Netherlands, and knew Swahili but not Bulgarian.

Then we were driven by car to the opening of the City Park. There was a large picnic and we shared a kebabche and coke. I asked the Minister of the environment if I could visit her in Sofia to discuss wolf monitoring for the entire country; she suggested two weeks hence, surprised that I spoke Bulgarian, surprised that she understood it, or surprised by my effrontery in asking her. We photographed the park and the opening of the Park ceremony. It was a nice strip of land bordering the white river. We watched a demonstration of historical Bulgarian fighting skills (which looked oddly like Tai Chi), as well as horsemanship with three boys. We talked to the three biologists from Sofia who would work next month on the wolf survey. The new one, Grisha Genshev, was father of two of the horse riders. He also rode and whipped his enemies, that was, plastic coke bottles mounted on stakes. We visited the horses,

227

stroking them, and walked back to the cars.

Back at the city, we went back to a cafe until it was time for dinner, which was at Restaurant Rosa, which was actually closed; the dinner was catered by the same firm that had set up lunch. It started at Seven and went until midnight. We drank wine and coke. Dinner was a buffet, with deep-fried chicken gizzards, fish, and potatoes. Several salads, including potato and rice. Desert was cookies. Then they kept bringing out other things like kebabche and fruit. We sat alone at a table for the first hour then were joined by tourist operators from Samokov — very large people who ate a lot and spoke only Bulgarian. The people at the table behind us were speaking English and we found out that they were with USAID, a man and his wife and daughter, and Aleksander Hertz's daughter. So we talked with them a while. They all left early, but we were bound to wait for the rangers, so we went to a table with Nikolai and others from the Park, most of whom spoke only Bulgarian. We danced and the rangers started a long horo. Finally, we were driven to our respective places. I wore clothes and hooded jacket to bed and was much warmer.

Ranger's Horo

Up at 7:30, Aleksander said that we would leave at 8:30 a.m. rather than at noon. This was a welcome idea, since otherwise we could only take the 6 p.m. bus to Aprilci. But, we picked up Calpurnia at Nine in front of the restaurant where we were to have breakfast — it was closed, and there was no breakfast. Aleksander changed his mind and decided not to go through Kazanluk and Gabrovo but to retrace our first route. We drove to a cafe and had tea and a croissant. We stayed there half an hour. I tried to get my chit signed (required for Park reimbursement) but could not find anyone with an official stamp. Petya looked, then Aleksander looked, then we gave up looking. We drove out of town about Ten, then stopped for tea, and tripe soup (which we declined); we walked to an orchard and looked around at ripe apples. Then we drove slowly across the mountain in the Russian jeep. Arriving in Troyan, we let off the rangers. Aleksander offered to drive us to Aprilci and we agreed with relief; we talked about ham radio in Bulgaria all the way; he was an operator. We agreed that in ham was the salvation of the world.

In Aprilci, we invited him to the Telecenter, then the bazaar, then to lunch on kebabche at the Gameyski cafe. There Angelar and Dimiter showed up after half an hour. We went back to the apartment, then had to go to class at 3 p.m., but no one showed up, so we went home and loafed.

A few weeks later, it was time to plan the wolf survey, We left at 8:20, on the bus to Sevlievo, first. In Sevlievo, we immediately caught a minibus to Gabrovo, which got in about 10:15. Early, we looked around the town for an IBM computer battery; after four stores said it could only be gotten in Sofia, we stopped looking. Then we had to take the local bus to the end of town and the Park Office.

There, we had a small lunch in the cafe near the Park, and walked to the Park. There we were met by Georgiu. We talked with him a while, then with Nikolai. They said that the scientists from Sofia would not be there until 1:30, so we all went to lunch at the same cafe we just left. Georgiu sat with one of the women from the office. Nikolai, Calpurnia and I sit together. I had only bread and Sprite.

Back at the office, we were told that the scientists would not be there until 3 p.m., and they were coming to work on an educational project, although they could talk to us for a few minutes. Georgiu said that he would drive us to the bus station to make the 4 o'clock bus. So, we waited, speaking mostly to Nikolai, and reading more facts about the Park. I looked at maps of Severen Djendem. Then Georgiu said that they would not be here for another hour or more. We asked Nikolai to make a reservation for us at the Panorama Hotel, which he did.

They finally came after Four, but two talked to Iurka and the others. Georgiu, Calpurnia and I met with Dr. Russinov. He was wary about volunteering to work on the wolf monitoring. I asked for his help; he agreed to help with the outline, as well as work on a one-day survey, and on the results. We hammered out a schedule to exchange information, then to meet later.

After our meeting we were introduced to his two colleagues. Then we went to have dinner at the dessert cafe by the river. Finally about Eight, we walked to the hotel. We got there just as the hostess was closing. She gave us a room at the Bulgarian rates — we were the only guests in the hotel (this was the hotel run by high school students, whose school was right next door).

After a surprise hot shower, we went to sleep, serenaded by barking dogs (announcing their territorial imperatives). My bed was so uncomfortable I put it on the floor by Calpurnia's. The dogs barked all night.

We woke up to dogs. We left early by dogs and walked to

the bus station. Breakfast was a donut reheated. At the bus station I bought a car magazine—I wanted to read something, so I read about new Peugots. Because it was Saturday, there was a direct bus to Aprilci (the mountain resort center of olden days). The bus took only an hour and ten minutes to get there. At home, we cleaned. Then worked on our projects.

Tuesday morning, we worked on letters and applications. Vulko drove us to Gabrovo at noon to get the signatures from Iurka. After talking to Petya about the letters and projects, we waited for an hour for Iurka to finish with the arrangements for the public forums on the Park, which started later in March and went into April.

Iurka swirled into the room and started asking pointed questions about the projects. For instance, she asked Vulko for the map of Aprilci to include more of the park territory; she and Vulko argued about the area, but then she approved the letter supporting the map. Then I presented my letters starting with the Craftsmen and going on to the AOL computers and wolves. She signed both PCPP requests for the wolves and agreed to have the letters the next day.

Then we went to Vulko's main office in Gabrovo. He brought down an interpreter and we all had lunch, which we paid for. The interpreter read the English and translated it as we ate. We get money for our bills; we expected the telephone to be well over L300 and the electricity to be over L100. Then we drove back to Aprilci in the snow. It was a spring blizzard. The roads were white and all the trees covered with snow. The roads were all one-lane this back way and very beautiful. We accidentally chased a jackrabbit up the road—he was clocked going 36 km/hr.

Modernize While You Wait

On January first, I woke up before Seven and went on-line to download research protocols for wolf monitoring. This was very productive. I did not feel well, so I stuck to yogurt and fruit juice. There was four inches of snow on the ground and it was snowing enthusiastically. Later I made apple sauce, which was excellent with ginger and cinnamon.

We lazed around waiting for the kids to come with switches and beat us into giving them a One Lev note, a popular Bulgarian New Year's Day tradition. No one came, so we watched a movie on television. The stores were open but had no supplies. There was no bread, so we had sandwiches from frozen bread. Went back to bed all day to keep warm. More brownies, later, excellent this time with orange peel and olive oil, measured in the new glass measuring cup. We read then went to bed in the cold room.

Tuesday, the second, I worked again on the computer from 7 until 9. Calpurnia went out to buy bread but all that was left was small loaves of wheat bread and one mekitsa. I downloaded more wolf and research information, then we worked on grant information all afternoon. But, first had lunch at the small pizza place; the pizza was forgettable but the fries were good.

Day three of the new year, again on the computer by 7 and worked until 9. Made pancakes for breakfast. Then more grant work and wolf proposal work. Paid the rent and went to the post office to pick up a box, but the place was deserted for two hours, even after we had fries at the new cafe. Called Angelar about the wolf survey; no answer. Went for a hike in the snow to check out animal activity near Black Peak, a cold but unrewarding survey. That night was more work on the computer.

Today's first emergency, well, the year's first emergency: Calpurnia noticed that the Tourist Office was dark and cold. The electricity, telephone and internet had been turned off for nonpayment of bills (some were three months overdue). So, we met with Vulko for coffee, and he explained that he had enough, 260 Leva, to get things reconnected but that there may not be any Swiss money until March. The head of his group, Sylvia, who earned an impressively high 1300 Leva a month (for being a figurehead it seemed), was negotiating with the Swiss. Of course, the city had refused to support the Tourist Office since April 2000, which complicated matters (I had heard that the mayor barked out his own territorial imperatives).

We reworked our grants, so that we could channel another 200 Leva to him for support on ads and the web page. The coffee lasted two hours; Calpurnia said she would work at home, and Vulko said he would work at his home. We were still waiting to hear if the Supreme Court would remove the Mayor; we thought not, since the new President was a communist, like the Mayor.

Dimetar came over to tell me to be ready tomorrow morning at Six. We had tea and biscuits and talked about the Park.

After a long trip through the Park, I had a few days back in Aprilci, so I prepared information for the English class, on business forms. For class we met in the pizza-cop-fireman café (and I could not even remember the real name, possibly because there were never any signs). Closimir showed up for the first time in a month. The class went half an hour over to 7:30, but was very animated.

The next morning, I worked on the Balkani proposal and got bids from the web for various things including GPS and laptops. Desislava called and we set up a schedule for finishing the project and going on with the Park survey in Tusha. Worked on the HTML book for five hours. Worked out some dynamic code for the web pages so that Kosta's vase would glow from the inside.

Today, reworked web page for Ecoforestry, then went back to the Aprilci web, which had a surprising number of small errors. Found some good ideas in the new HTML book. Finished the Balkani application and mailed it out for comments.

At lunch I found Leaping Dragon Hiding Tiger or whatever the movie was called, so I rented it. It cost 3 Leva (or about $1.35). It was very good, although the video player still refused to show color.

The phone died in mid-call to Vulko; apparently, the 1928 lines could not handle rain. Most people bought cell phones, rather than a new digital set that had to use 70-year old lines. Watched Sleeping Tiger Snoring Dragon again and the color came back half way. Wonderful movie.

Sunday breakfast was an exciting combo of cereal and tea, with grapefruit, which was very old and the last of it. The Sunday Bazaar was larger than normal, but the past week had been warm and the snow had been melting (and refreezing). Worked on the page for Veshen and redid the photos for Kosta and Valeri. Prepared another lesson on business and writing resumes for the English class. Sava showed up for class tonight; said his babysitting times were at odds with many classes.

Monday, Tuesday, Wednesday, Thursday, now, I spent the afternoon preparing for the Craftsmen meeting. Finished the budget and a script to talk about the budget. I always needed more words to talk in that language. We met in the Center restaurant, the most smoke-filled restaurant in the world. It was crowded with card-players today, but we found a table for six. We went over the budget very closely and assigned responsibilities to finish the furniture, remodeling, and web page — Vulko's partner in Sevlievo would take it over and maintain it. My Bulgarian was fast, furious and erroneous, which amused Ivan and Kosta to no end. Since only Kosta knew any English, he rose to the occasion and translated some of my efforts. It was still hard to grasp subtle discussions. Anyway, we finished about 7:15 and went to the telecenter to talk with Trifon, who wanted to meet tomorrow.

Tea Magazine

Wolf is Man to Man

Tracking Wolves Or Ten Steps Behind

In Sofia, after the six-hour bus ride, Calpurnia met with various PC people, while I met with Venelina about my SPA. I showed her the new version and we turned every page. She made suggestions and I scribbled on my clean draft. There were always ways to improve I knew, but six trees had sacrificed their lives for unnecessary clarification.

Lunch was at McD's and then we went to the Culture Palace (NDK) to see the Tourist Show. Since we both worked for the Bureau in Aprilci, we gathered information to take back to Vulko. Unlike the Varna show and smaller shows, this was spread over three floors and had many international displays. I gathered information on Crete, Cyprus, and Malta. Typically, Bulgarian contacts often were reluctant to release any information or help. You must beg for flyers — this was quite the opposite of the foreign exhibits, who showered you with unwanted maps, folders, and brochures. It was quite a contrast. Afterwards, we walked to the Balkani Society meeting near the American Embassy, with the blocked off streets and fleet of new white gigantic GMCs. Petko was there with several of the people, so we started immediately, filling in the blanks of the wolf proposal. Then, Desislava came, and we filled out the Bulgarian cover sheets. Everyone signed and we were through by 10 p.m. We walked back to the hotel and went to sleep.

About 7:30 I got to the PC HQ to use the old Mac in the basement to make changes from yesterday. I finished before my meeting. At an early meeting with Iliana, the acting head of the environmental program, I asked her to print the final draft and she did, thankfully. Then, we went over every page and looked for problems. None were found. So, I gathered it all up and went back to Venelina, who accepted it and assigned me a number (#1) — I was the first to submit my proposal. She was in a good mood and signed my form for travel reimbursement. At last, after nine months of planning the proposal was official; now, if we could just get the money.

I took my reimbursement form to the cashier, Dimitor, who refused to reimburse me. He took me to the travel maven, Eliza, who said it was not reimbursable. I was prepared for this manure and whipped out the SPA Handbook, where it said that three trips would be reimbursed: one for planning, one to submit the project and one to defend it to the committee. So, she took it to David Leigh, who read it and said it was ambiguous, that it really meant that we were prepaid for it in December. I point out, to no avail, that the word prepayment never appeared anywhere and that reimbursement meant just that, receiving money after you had spent it on bus fare. David said no, but said he would write an article for the paper telling everyone that the trips were not reimbursed. Eliza gave me the overage, which was almost $50, which was enough to pay the hotel bill. I got signatures to show that I was working in Sofia, to ready myself for the next combat with the evil bean-counter. This was getting ridiculous. A civil servant, who made over $100,000 a year, refused to pay out $40 for travel to a volunteer, who got $2400 a year to pay for $3600 in expenses. Sometimes the PC HQ was the hardest part of being in Bulgaria. They were the highest hurdle in cultural misunderstandings.

For lunch I took Calpurnia to the 'Journalist Cafe,' a small old elegant cafe (with no signs or ads outside). It used to be the meeting place for foreign media and Communist officials. Decor was dark red with white table cloths. The waiters were all over 60 and superbly trained. They actually offered us dessert! Calpurnia and I had traditional fare, then she had Creme caramel for dessert. That afternoon, we were back at the Trade show, where we met Aleksander on his way to submit his SPA proposal (which was based on Calpurnia's).

We spent a couple hours at an internet cafe; I kept trying to arrange the volunteers for the wolf survey. I would take the bus to Pavel Banya to meet the others; Russinov's car was full. The Balkani had arranged for a staff member from the ministry to accompany us, who was also a member of Balkani. I had tried to get two PCVs to go. Calpurnia sent me an electronic Valentine's card and I one to her. We ate at McD's and went to another movie, Corelli's Mandolin, which was better than the book, in parts. The movie theater was filled with young couples, and all the girls had a single rose. Much sniffling was heard. It was Valentine's Day; I had become such an unromantic boor. Then we went shopping for Italian spices and cereals, at the Oasis (Aprilci offered no real stores, just micromarkets with bread and beer).

Back at the hotel, we packed. Calpurnia was going back to Aprilci, and I was going to the wolf survey near Tuzha. I took the back pack and my briefcase; she got the suitcase and purse.

I walked Calpurnia to the 8:20 bus to Aprilci. It was a direct bus, although it stopped in Troyan first. Then I went back to the internet cafe for a few hours and sent rapid emails trying to arrange to times. Finally, I would ride with Dr. Russinov. Paul could not make it, but John would take the bus to Pavel Banya. Georgiu and one ranger would drive from Gabrovo, while the section head and three rangers would drive from Tuzha to Pavel Banya. The hizha only had nine beds in one room, so we had not asked any women, either volunteers, rangers, or scientists.

At noon I walked to the Natural History Museum and waited in Dr. Russinov's office. Then I waited some more. No one was there. So, I waited outside. After an hour Russinov drove up with the veterinarian, Aspanuch, who had brought his wife, a historian. After an animated discussion it turned out that the other biologist, Grisha, could not make it, nor could Russinov's assistant. So, Aspanuch had invited his wife. Then they told Kosta at the Ministry that he would have to take a bus to Pavel Banya (he refused). I could never figure this out—was it a language problem or a cultural caste one?

We were an hour late starting, but after an hour of driving, we stopped to buy groceries. The store was closed so we had coffee nearby. As soon as we walked in the staff turned up the music loudly. We went to a table in back, but the vet's wife wanted the table the staff was using, so she ousted them. Then asked them to turn off the music, then complained about modern music (I thought I did not want to spend much time near this woman). Finally we went out, but the store was still closed (no note on the door either), so we went to a smaller micromarket and get cheeses and salamis. I bought peanuts, juice, and yogurt. Aspanuch got cookies. Then we started off, but after twenty minutes, the wife wanted beans for soup, so we stopped again. Then, Dimetar decided we needed carrots, so we stopped again, but he and Aspanuch bought pastries, also, saying we needed glucose to think.

Finally, on our way for fifteen whole minutes, the wife announced that she had no spices for the beans for soup, so we stopped again and she looked for bean spices. Now, finally on our way, she and Dimetar had an argument about Thracian settlements. They asked me and I said the Thracians were here long before the Bulgarians. So, we had an animated discussion, although I was never sure if we understood one another. Dimetar spoke some English, so we could clarify some things.

So we were over an hour late at Pavel Banya. John, Georgiu, and the rangers had been drinking coffee for an hour. The Minister was not there! So, we immediately had more coffee while Georgiu went to get gas. Then about Six, we drove for only about five miles to a small village called Skobelovo. It was next to Sachrane, where I was stationed in July 2000. In the village, we divided up for a few minutes. Because of the wife, she and Aspanuch would stay in the village at the parents of a ranger, who gave up their beds (and slept in their living room). John and I were asked if we wanted to stay there; I said no, but then Georgiu said that the hut we would be staying in only had six beds, not nine (that was true, I knew, the other three spaces were the foam seats in the dining room). So, we agreed. One of the rangers let us have his room, with a double bed. Then we all drove up in the two Lada Nivas (Russian jeeps) to the forestry enterprises house on forestry land. I asked about it and was told that Georgiu was friends with the head of the forestry unit (the same one who wanted me to kill wild pigs for nibbling on shoots in his forest, which precipitated my moving to the park).

There, we fixed dinner, of marinated cabbage, peanuts, kebabche, and kyufte, not to mention rakia and homemade red wine. The house had two bedrooms, each with three beds and a small wood stove. There was a kitchen with a wood stove and counter (no water but a sink). The dining room had one long table and a huge fireplace. There was no toilet or even outhouse. I was told to walk at least one hundred meters away, so I found a nice tree. As the night went on, the rangers walked considerably less than the one hundred meters and the place became mined with human droppings. We drank to midnight, then the vet drove us back to the house, where we had tea and coffee with our hosts and watched the Olympics on their television for an hour. The house was nice but had no bath or toilet. The outhouse by the garage was made of concrete, but the pit was only 8 inches deep. There were no lights, so the host gave me his cigarette lighter; unfortunately I burned my fingers holding the light to unzip—could have been worse I guess. Finally, we got to bed. John stayed on his side and I stayed on mine, fortunately.

The ranger woke us at Six (four hours of sleep was not enough I told them). We had tea and drove for the hour to get to the forestry house. The road, in the light of day, followed the river. It was made of gravel with some large rocks and boulders. There, we had leftover cheese and meats for breakfast (I had bread). Then, we drove straight up the mountain until the road ended.

As we neared the end of the road, I saw eight or nine dark shapes moving rapidly down the slope towards the road (I always looked as far ahead to see if we startled any wildlife with our roaring Russian jeeps). Wolves I thought, and shouted "*Chakai*" which means wait, having forgotten the word to look, "*Viditai.*" Since I was pointing the cars stopped, and we watched. It was a herd of wild swine, with six or seven young piglets. They were all black. They crossed ahead of us and we drove a hundred meters and then stopped. As we were looking at their footprints, we saw old wolf prints. We measured them and photographed them. A male, female, and two yearlings. The rangers followed them but I backtracked them, down a talus slope and into the beech forest where I lost them in the leaves (I thought I needed to learn better tracking skills). It was freezing, but not quite snowing; the trees were all covered with rime, which dropped on me as I walked.

Then I caught up with the rest. We followed the tracks along on old logging road. There were also the pig tracks, roe deer, red deer, and fox tracks, then a mountain hare track. Quite a highway. The old road became a path, which the vet and four people followed; Dimetar, Georgiu, John, a ranger and I followed the tracks into the woods, up hill. After a few hundred meters we lost the tracks, but then found them again (but they were now coming downhill and there were only two not four animals). So, we followed them through the leaves. There was snow under the trees, but it was intermittent. We found excrement from one of the cubs (half size). It indicated red meat in their diet, so we thought they had made a kill recently. Then we lost the tracks again, but kept walking up above the treeline.

There, we found another set of tracks; either another set of wolves (unlikely), or the parents had ditched the cubs for a romantic evening together. The tracks started out straight but soon indicated that the wolves were playing, running around each other, racing downhill or uphill then coming together. This went on for a few kilometers. I tracked the lower hill, and Dimetar the upper. The make had run large loops around the female, dipping his nose in the snow and prancing back. At once place on the slope above the tree the snow had more footprints together — perhaps the tie, although I could not see where the males prints pointed the opposite way. The male's prints made small digressions from hers as the moved across the slope in the snow. Finally the tracks went down into a forested glen, where the ranger, Curly, thought they had a den. He had seen another den over one mountain, at the foot of an Austrian pine, but did not know this area. He argued that we should follow. I argued that we should not; we knew there was a den there but we were not prepared to radio-collar anyone or photograph the den. So, we had a brief lunch of cheese and salami (I had bread and cheese) at a logging landing. Then tracked downhill into the woods. We startled a red deer, which ran, then a roe deer, which also ran.

After seven hours of tracking, we went down hill and were met by the river by the two jeeps; the other group had found only bear tracks and went to get the jeeps. Near dark, we headed back to the house. One of the rangers, nicknamed Spas, made pork and worst in the fireplace. We drank until midnight, then the four of us drove for an hour to the house, where we drank tea until dawn.

Mating Dance Scene

Today we slept until 7:30, since the rangers had to come here drive to us back. When they arrived at the house here, we all had tea and pried ourselves into the jeeps. This time we drove west and directly into the mountains. It was cold but clear. The road ended after an hour. We again divided into two groups. The vet took one group with his wife, and went around the slope, and Dimetar, Curly, John and I hiked directly up the mountain. Finally getting past tree line and into snow, we found old tracks, but the snow was hard and icy. Curly thought they were wolf, Dimetar thought jackal, and I thought fox. We each supported our arguments (although I was sure I was right, since I had found some perfect fox prints elsewhere in better snow). But, there was reasonable doubt. The wolf tracks could have been a small female, distorted by snow. Jackals rarely liked mountains, but the size was right. There seemed to be only one animal.

At the crest we saw two wild goats, with their dark winters coats. We watched them for an hour and rested. I found a flat rock to stretch out on. Took some photos, having remembered the camera. Then, we reached the peak and headed down the other side, angling towards the jeeps. In the distance we could see the other group, eating and goofing off.

Another two hours and we were back at the jeeps. After an hour of driving we meet at the Pavel Banya cut-off and played musical vehicles. The three Sofiaites took the station wagon and left. One ranger drove back to Tuzha and one waited for a ride. The five remaining piled into one jeep, with our packs (it only seated dour adults). We drove to Kazanluk and dropped off John at the train station and Curly at the center. Then Georgiu, Dimetar the park security guy, and I drove to Gabrovo, driving through Shipka pass, which had snow on the north side but not the south. They dropped me off at the bus station there.

At the apartment I was greeted by Seth's Bulgarian girlfriend, "Duski," who said they were leaving in an hour. So, I went have lunch, pizza, and shop for disks and books. Finally I went back and did a laundry and had potato salad and coke. Then the doorbell rang and it was Joe, who forgot his keys and could not get into his apartment in Dryavno. Since we shared the apartment, he wanted to stay. So, we talked for a few hours and watched more sports (I think it was still downhill skiing after six days). Then he went to the internet cafe and played games until 2 a.m. I could not since I was wearing my swimsuit and sweater and everything else was in the washer. So, I read.

I waited for Joe to get ready the next morning, before leaving and locking up, since I had the only keys. He went to a meeting at the YMCA and I went to the park. The bus came immediately, so the trip only took twenty minutes rather than fifty. The park office was in a renovated building at the edge of town. Like western towns like Tucson, Gabrovo was long and thin (due to the river valley rather than the roads). I immediately met with Nikolai, then Georgiu, and we went over the survey results and plans. Georgiu announced that the Ministry would give us 2000 Leva to continue the wolf monitoring, so we would go out again in March. I had written a three-sentence proposal in Bulgarian, which had been included with the Park budget, so I was pleased.

After the meeting I went to a new supermarket, which was larger than a market and had many kinds of olive oil, soaps, tuna, and other delights. I found sponges for the first time and a Danish pastry. I stopped for pizza then went to the apartment and finished my notes. At 3 p.m. I caught the bus to Sevlievo, where I worked in the internet cafe for an hour before catching to 5:30 bus to Aprilci. Calpurnia was waiting and we had tea with Aleksander. I unpacked. We went to teach class. Hours later, finally we caught up on romantic matters. I ran loops around her — should any of you desire to make love like wolves, you must have a firm surface . . .

Preparing Another Survey

On a trip to Sofia to have meetings for surveys, we arrived at One to check in to Hotel Maya, which was a pleasant surprise. A large room, with two twin beds (the Bulgarian standard) with night tables with lamps, a couch, benches around a coffee table, mini-refrigerator with a television on top, and a large wardrobe. On hooks by the door were two terry cloth bathrobes, and slippers below. The radiator was on and the room was warm. There was a separate bath in the hall next to the room and we had our own key — the bath was tiny but very warm (for about $16 a night, this was our new favorite).

We left and had a tri-monthly burger at McDs. At the PC HQ I went to talk to Albert, Calpurnia went to language to drop off forms. I called Georgiu about the Park survey. He said we were going on Friday; I responded that I was in Sofia and would like to travel with Dimetar. I called Dimetar and after four hours of phone tag, a soon-to-be Olympic sport, we spoke and he said we would leave at 12:30 on Monday. Christine came by HQ and was hungry so we went to Goody's (a British fast food chain for smokers). Then we returned to HQ and saw Alta who was also hungry so we went to a different McDs (there were at least three in Sofia, now).

Then we all piled in a taxi and went to Jamadvice for their travel tickets (Calpurnia and I had decided not to go to Budapest or Paris, but to stay in Bulgaria). Afterwards we went to Pizza Hut for yet another dinner. Then Calpurnia and I went to the Balkani meeting and met with the whole group about their wolf project.

Desislava introduced us to everyone. We sat together on one of the stuffed chairs. The meeting, which was very informal, started with reports on projects: the new dam protest, the country bird survey, and the educational projects for two sets of local schools. Krum described the Karakachan dog project, which provided these dogs for free to shepherds concerned about wolves attacking their sheep. Desislava talked about the past wolf survey and the plans for the new one in the Kraishde region. I talked about the wolf surveys in the Balkan park. We agreed to partner on the new surveys. I would invite Balkani personnel to the Park and they would invite Calpurnia and me to Kraishde, and perhaps a few rangers. I offered to write three grant proposals for surveys, traps, and telemetry equipment.

About Nine we walked back to the hotel (which was a small hotel with only four rooms!). Christine and Alta were already asleep so we had a coke and donut and went to sleep. Saturday was the SPA meeting. We came, we listened, we rubber-stamped. Then we ate and were merry.

Monday I waited for Russinov at his office and we drove to the southeastern part of the Park. We stayed at another forestry unit lodge and drank all night. Although I was up around Seven, the rangers had trouble stirring. It was snowing regularly and has been for some time. There seemed to be about seventeen inches of new snow. Finally, we had cheese and bread for breakfast and we piled into two 4WD jeeps (the Lada Nivas). We had intended to have three groups of three but Dimitar wanted to go talk to the hunters, so we regrouped into two groups of four). Dimetar, Angelar, Georgiu, and I went to investigate one set of the region, while Boleslav, Bulchru, Hikmet, and Dimetar (who was a policeman for twenty years and now headed the Park Security) went to another.

After driving for forty minutes uphill on forestry and park roads, we started stopping every time a track crossed the road. At the third stop we found a wolf print on the road, but the snow had started to fill it in. It must have been about an hour old. With Dimetar leading we left the car in the road and followed the trail up hill into the woods. Soon, three more sets of prints joined up (it was hard to tell because wolves were very efficient and walked in each others tracks). The trails followed roe deer throughout the forests separating and recombining regularly. At one point they had flushed a deer towards one of the young males, but he did not catch her. I had followed these tracks myself while the others stayed with the main group. The deer was leaping through the snow but the wolf did not get into a run, only a walk and then a lope, so they must have been relatively far apart. Near a field the trails converged again. After two hours we lost the group to low undergrowth.

Wolf tracking

After walking back to the jeep, we drove up to the end of the road. From there we hiked straight up the mountainside. Finally we reached a meadow, where a group of red deer (elk) had bedded for the night. The piss and excrement were encased in ice and snow. We tracked a few roe deer but saw no wolf prints.

After 3 p.m. we met up with the other group, who had seen only an old bear print. Then we returned to the lodge and had cheese and bread for lunch. It was still snowing, but very lightly. At the lodge, we enticed the Karakachan sheep dog to walk in the snow and we measured the footprint, which were demonstrably different from the wolves (much thinner in the pads even though the dog was very large, 200 pounds).

We all took naps until about 5:30, then Georgiu and I went over the night vision scope while Angelar got the pay together for the rangers. At 7:30 dinner started, with the salad and rakia first. By 9:30 we were served fried cheese, Chicken kabobs and kebabche. I sat with Dimetar Russinov so I could get a translation now and then; he spoke enthusiastic broken English, but the others spoke none. We discussed the findings and the planned for tomorrow. We had intended to drive to Tuzia to train the next group of rangers on the south side, but the snow was making good tracks rare, so he and Hikmet would return to Sofia Sunday morning; they invited me to travel with them. I talked to Angelar and then agreed. The party lumbered on again until after two but I left by 11:00 so I could get enough sleep. I seemed to have no desire to party every night.

Sunday, I was up early again and packed. Then I went over to the restaurant and played with the dog (a collie named 'wolf'). I cleaned off the cars. It was snowing lightly. Georgiu and Dimetar the policeman left, Then, I had tea with Dimetar and Hikmet, before we drove out. The roads were icy, but we made it to Aprilci in just over an hour. Dimetar invited me to join the Wilderness Fund, a group of biologists, by invitation only.

During the ride we discussed the kinds of excrements and

what they meant. I pointed out that I had not seen the "licorice" kind (which results from gorging on red meat of a deer), but only the "hairy" kind, which meant scavenging or eating small animals like mice, with bones and fur. I suggested that the wolves had not done that well. Dimetar had seen the licorice sort, but not often. We also discussed the average pack size and the average age of wolves shot by hunters and shepherds.

In Aprilci I picked up a few supplies and then went home, which was warm. Calpurnia was doing laundry and we went to the bazaar for the Sunday shopping. After a lunch of potatoes and kebabche, we relaxed before catching up on computer work.

A month later, the next survey. I took the early buses to Sevlievo and Gabrovo. Walked downtown and to the bus stop for the Park bus. Dimetar drove by and picked me up in a Park jeep, so I got there by 11. Met with Nikolai and Georgiu, about the photos and documents, then we left at noon.

First we drove by Georgiu's apartment, so he could change out of his silk shirt and into ranger garb. Then we drove to the edge of Gabrovo to a large meat magazine, where many kinds of unmarked meat were in plastic unmarked bags in the freezers. Georgiu and Dimetar chose about ten of them, which turned out to be chicken parts, pig's feet, pork ribs, kebabche, worst, and pork loin. Then, peanuts, wine, beer, twenty two loaves of bread, margarine, four blocks of yellow cheese, and big tub of mayonnaise.

Then we left, after an hour, and a drove over the mountain to Kazanluk, where we dropped off two repaired computers to that Park office. Then we drove to Pavel Banya, where Dr. Russinov (who had taken the train) and the other rangers from Karlovo, Pavel Banya, and Kalofer, were waiting in a small cafe. We had the obligatory tea, beer, and coffee, then Russinov decided to have lunch (it was 3:30), so I gratefully tagged along and had a shopska salad and coke; he had soup and bread.

Then, we loaded up into two jeeps, five people per, and drove up the mountain to the forestry hut. The Gabrovsko river was the boundary between the forestry units and the park, and the road meandered back and forth across it. This was where we had stayed in March for Survey II. We unloaded the jeeps. The hut no longer had water as the stream had dried up; it was off the grid and had no electricity, but the rangers had brought a generator that could be hooked up to the light bulb wires in the kitchen and dining room, whose benches acted as three beds. Each room had its own small wood stove. I mentioned to Russinov that there were still three hours of light, so he said good idea, but then he and Dimetar, the head of the district, had coffee and talked. So, I started walking up the road. I watched a roe deer cross the road, finding my camera as it disappeared. After half an hour, the jeep roared up and picked me up and we continued, stopping every 100 meters to look at tracks.

Then we turned the corner and there was a brown bear in the road. She ran up the hill five meters, and Dimetar floored the jeep then slammed the brakes. We got out as she stopped and looked back at us; her face was a much lighter brown than the body which was dark brown. A beautiful, young, healthy female. She sort of grunted at us, made a motion to charge, counted us, then turned and kept going up the hill and out of sight. I tracked her just to see the tracks, which were not very good in the forest floor duff. I remembered then that the camera was in my pocket.

We looked around and saw a mouse, then a hawk. Then drove up to where we had seen the wolf prints last month. I saw another mouse and two sets of red deer tracks. After another hour of looking and planning for the next day, we went back.

The rangers had finished preparing dinner and were eating the salad and drinking the rakia. It was before Eight. We sat and had salad and rakia. There were three salad plates and two bread plates, so we ate by taking out food with our forks. We shared the bottles by drinking straight from them, even the water. Then, one of the young rangers came in and started to grill strange pork pieces in the fireplace. Six at a time, putting the cooked ones in a pot. He served them all at once, and we ate and talked until 10:30. I went to bed early, as usual, but then Dimetar the security chief also retired – there were three rooms with three beds each and a tenth in the kitchen; Dimetar, Georgiu and I shared one room.

Up at seven, breakfast was leftovers, from the same plates at the table from the night before; the rangers lathered their bread with mayo, then added cheese and pieces of meat. We divided into two groups of five and piled into the jeeps, driven by Dimetar and Spas Russinov (no relation to Dr. Russinov, although there seems to be a family resemblance in the face). The drivers tried to pass each other on the dirt roads leading up the mountain. Ha, ha.

At the final fork, we went north and they went south. We had agreed to meet at a shepherd's lean-to for lunch. At the end of the road, we parked and hiked directly up the mountain. As usual, my body protested that I was trying to kill it and my heart pounded and lungs bellowed air. So, I stopped now and then to scan ahead with the binoculars. Suddenly I saw a furtive shape on the ridge, and whispered to Dimetar that it was a large mammal, hoping it was a wolf. As we all looked, three others followed and it was revealed as a small herd of roe deer. After a few minutes, they heard or saw us, and raced away. We kept going to the ridge, which emptied out above the treeline. We saw patches of snow and went over to look for tracks — there were tracks, but they were old and melted; they looked like roe deer and red deer. I kept going to the summit and I could actually see Aprilci in the distance. We had crossed from the south to the north!

We found some deer scat and kept looking for tracks. Then, we headed down a few ridges to an old pasture with the shepherds lean-to. Next to it, there were rows and rows of concrete pilings — there had been a shed for cows many years ago and nothing was left but the pilings. The other group came over a ridge and joined us. We looked at the map and planned out another pincher movement around a hill that might have a den on the side. Dividing into two groups, we went down hill and around the entire hill, maybe seven kilometers. Just before we joined up, we found a fresh carcass of a female two-year old wild swine; there were tooth marks on the bones, and only one hind foot remained on the spine, rib cage and legs. Just uphill was a pile of wolf scat filled with swine hair (odd that last night we also had pig to eat). I wondered if our feces smelled the same. So, I pissed discretely near the edge of the trail to let them know we were here, the nosy humans who stepped in their tracks and pried apart their scat to see what they ate.

Now, as a group we went directly up the next mountain. I had my second wind, so I arrived second only to Gavril, one of the youngsters. Dimetar the security chief, a competitive athletic guy, was third, but as we then walked along the ridge looking for tracks, he redeemed himself by setting the fastest pace. After an hour, it started to rain, and by the time we returned to the lean-to, it was blowing straight down. Despite my almost waterproof clothes I was soaked and shivering. Everyone raced to the lean-to. Under the lean-to, we broke out the cheese and bread. Dimetar had brought deer meat salami and two other kinds of salami. The down pour got worse, so we ate all the bread, then exchanged reports on wildlife signs. We started another fire and it filled up with smoke, but at least it was warm. Grisha Blagoev, who was supposed to meet us at the lean-to, had not shown up. This was the second time he had not shown up. I had not seen him since October (he and his sons also ran a historical show of Bulgarian hunting and horsemanship skills, so perhaps the song of show business had commanded his attention).

Poster Bag Tur

When the rain let up, we crossed a ridge and walked through a forestry unit (read clearcut), then downhill to a logging road. Only deer signs on this part of the ridge. Dimetar fetched the jeep and we met him at the bottom of a ridge. We drove back to the hut and took a break after 4:00 p.m. I took a nap, but when I woke up I was locked in the hut and could not get out to piss. I squeezed out a back door just as both jeeps came back; they only had gone for water fifty meters away. I walked over to the river, then walked along it away until I could get to the middle by hopping across boulders. There I meditated, having forgotten how restful was moving water. After an hour, I tossed twigs in the river and watched where the current takes them — in one place the current flattened them on the bottom. I took a few photographs, then looked for trout. I saw a few shadows and I knew they were there, so I left them alone.

I returned to the hut and the salads were almost ready. In a nice division of labor, the four young rangers did all the work — at last an advantage to being old, and I was the oldest. Russinov was in his forties. Dimetar the Security Expert asked how old I was and then asked me to guess his age; I thought he was in his forties, so I guessed 45. Wrong, he was 32 and I was embarrassed. Georgiu and the young Dimetar were in the early 30s also, and the rest of the rangers were barely 20. After an hour of eating salad, bread and the alcoholic beverages, Spass decided to try fishing, so we tossed another salad. After an hour he was back with four small trout, but the young Dimetar made him go out to clean them, so he drove down the road away from the hut. We fixed a third salad, and Dimitor and Gavril cooked the chicken, kebabche, worst, and potatoes. They finished, but Spass had not returned so we had more bread and beer. When Spass returned he started cooking the fish, then everything was on one plate for each.

So, we talked and ate until about 11, then Dimetar and I went to sleep. The young Dimetar and Dimetar Russinov left for Gabrovo so Russinov could catch the early train to Sofia. This was a surprise to me as I thought he would be here for the entire time. I could not sleep so I listened to the others talk for four more hours.

Security Dimetar and I were up around seven and went outside and talked. While he went into the woods (there was no outhouse), I went down to the river and washed. It was freezing (I remember that the Spartans lived much further south). Then we sat outside and talked while the rangers all slept late. It was drizzling. I walked down the road looking for signs and met young Dimetar, who was returning from Kazanluk — he said he saw wolf tracks downhill. Back at the hut, he and Security Dimetar took a jeep and went uphill. Georgiu and I ran downhill. After ten minutes, four tired rangers caught up with us. We walked about four kilometers without seeing anything but deer sign. Then, one wolf print—it was *over* the tracks of the jeep, so it was fresh. Then another wolf print on the other side of the road. Georgiu measured them and I wrote them down and photographed them. One average male wolf and one female or yearling. The two walked down the road, stopping when a roe deer has crossed, but then continuing down. After four kilometers, we lost the tracks, but kept going. Then we backtracked to the last track and looked for evidence of direction. We found a set of roe deer tracks going off the road. I thought the wolves had left the road before then, but found no tracks. There were no tracks up from the river or down to it. Everyone walked ahead of me so I amused myself by tracking them; hard to do on gravel, even as I could see them. I caught up to Gavril and Dimitor who were a botanist and ornithologist, so they took pleasure in identifying the birds and flowers, and I in learning them.

We got back to the hut around noon and had a brunch of cheese sandwiches with mayo, rakia, and water. Not to mention small bits of leftover meatage. I started to clean up but Georgiu said not to spoil the youngsters, so I went to pack. I was startled by gunshots. I went out and saw the rangers practicing by shooting out bricks from an old storage building across the road. One gun was very large caliber. I kept forgetting that everyone except me wore a gun for protection (from me, animals, poachers, politicians, or foresters, I did not ever find out). I took some more photos and spend thirty minutes in the river again, lying on a wet boulder.

Back at the hut, young Dimetar and Security Dimetar arrived and we threw everything in the jeeps and left. We all drove to Pavel Banya, where Kostov was waiting to take three of them to Karlovo. Young Dimetar and Dimitor took one jeep, and I rode with Security Dimetar and Georgiu. But, first we all went to the railroad station to have the trip reports stamped with the date. In Gabrovo we dropped off Georgiu and then drove to security Dimetar's house. He had bought it four years earlier and was still finishing it. There was a large wall around it and it sat on the hill above the city. The inside was quite nice, with all modern appliances (and antlers on every wall of the living room). I met his wife and daughter, who had ten years of English. So, we talked while Dimetar changed clothes. They gave me tea and whiskey. Dimetar brought out a knife made by a friend of his and gave it to me. We talked about hunting and killing, which he has stopped doing since he works for the Park now. They wanted to visit Aprilci to see a new dog; they had three now, including a Doberman and Rotweiler.

So, the four of us drove to Aprilci getting there before Five. We visited Tsonko to look at the fox terriers; he would pay next week and pick it up later. Fortunately, it only took me five minutes to find his house—he was my first landlord, when I lived in the house with no stove, bath, toilet, heater, or furniture. Calpurnia was home and surprised, but had just cleaned the living room. So, I invited them up and they had English tea. They were eager to return, so we said good-bye. I give Angerina a book in English.

We had a small dinner of left-over tortellini and then caught up on talking and problems (brochures and PC rules).

At home again, we had cereal for breakfast with yogurt. How nice not to have old cheese. Then the morning at the internet exchanging messages. The meeting for the Minister had been set for the Ninth. I filled out an application for the Fish and Wildlife Service.

The afternoon was spent transcribing notes and sizing photographs from the weekend. The mail came and I had another article in the *Echo*, "Capitalism, communism, and community."

Dinner was peanut butter sandwiches. After dinner more computer work, then a movie on BTV. These were real treats on this television, which lost sound, color and then picture every ten minutes or so.

It was time to clean the apartment for Paul and John, PC biologists from Blagoevgrad, Rila Park and Malko Turnovo, Strangja Park, respectively. Calpurnia had decided to stay and collect the pottery from Kosta and the lace from the Baba for the craftsmen display in the tourist office. They arrived at 9:30 from Gabrovo. We had a quick breakfast and then Vulko arrived to drive us to the foot of the ridge of Hizha Pleven. We loaded the station wagon up and drove up the one-lane road, meeting only one car, passed carefully.

From there we hiked the long way to the hizha, skirting the ridge and going close to the water hole. We found a large beech tree and spent a few minutes taking photographs of each other and this old tree, maybe 220 years old, the oldest so far. At the hizha, we checked in and paid. We were assigned room 19, so it was almost full. We dumped the packs and left for the peak. But, not before eating cheese sandwiches that we had brought with us, on the patio outside; the air was hot and clear.

Going up the hill, where I had been before and recorded goats, fox, and deer, we found virtually no signs of wild animals. Then we passed about twenty seven people coming down from the peak, so that explained the full hizha—the last time I was there in February it was deep snow and impassable to most humans.

The trip to the peak was uneventful, although it was baking hot and we had to drink from mountain streams every ten minutes, as well as soak our heads. The views were tremendous and the skies were clear. I kept telling them I may not make it with them to the promised land, but I would be there in spirit. But, then I kept going, pushing my legs like wooden pistons. We finally arrived after 5 p.m. At the top, a stone marten ran from us around the building (there were old radars and dorms at the peak, from the Army installation). As we walked around we startled the marten again, who ran around the building and hid. There were a few raptors floating around, maybe a buzzard and eagle. After resting for an hour and looking over the north and south valleys, we started down.

The trip down was harder on the legs but easier on the lungs. We got back just as the sun set. At the cafe, we ordered salads and chicken (I had potatoes instead), as well as tea, beers, and cokes. We had to order from the bar, pay, and then give the order to the cook, who cooked it and told the barmaid, who told us when to pick up the food from the kitchen. Alas the cook was lazy and the barmaid had to keep telling him to cook the food. So we finally ate and went back to the room to sleep.

Sunday morning. I had not been able to sleep well. My muscles were too tired, then I had nightmares about fleas and ticks. But, we were up at Seven and went down to eat our left-over cheese sandwiches. The barmaid was there and sold us a fresh Keefla (bread filled with marmalade).

We walked down the ridge to the water plant. There we went directly into Severn Djendem. A ranger came out and told us we could not enter the Park. I replied that I worked for the Park and my colleagues were ekolozi also. Then we walked on, leaving an unhappy ranger to rehearse his complaints.

The first road was level and kept-up. So, we talked about the other Parks. Strandja was the newest Park, formerly a military reservation—that made it most pristine, but also with the least infrastructure, such as hizhas or trails. After calculating exactly which ridge we should climb, we left the trail and climbed straight up. After an hour of hard climbing, we crossed an old road, and used it to climb higher, then straight up again, going past a small meadow, which I recognized, through more beech forest to the main meadow (almost every ridge has a natural meadow on top, where sheep used to graze—they still were natural, in the sense that they were created over thousands of years of human use and many species adapted to them, but now deer and wild pigs grazed there—the biodiversity that gradually built up was being gradually lost now that juniper shrubs and trees were starting to reclaim it, an unusual problem for preservationists). I got there first and looked around for the prune tree that the bear tore apart the year before. Not finding it, I cruised the meadow, finding a large semi-permanent pond, filled with wild pig tracks, a few frogs and many newer tadpoles. There were no bear or wolf signs.

After a rest there and inspection of the perimeter, as well as the spruce plantations to the west, we started down the next eastern ridge, which should have lead to the reservoir for the power station. After a few kilometers, the ridge turned straight down and we plunged through the dark cool forest looking for a trail. Many animals paths but no trails. Then we found an old wolf scat; the measurements were perfect, but it was old. Most organic material had leached out in the rains. Only hairs with a few small bones were left.

Wolf scat

Further down the slope, there was fresh bear scat, filled with seeds and rosehips. But, no other signs. Good habitat but probably no den in that area.

We found many kinds of orchids, which John had been studying. Then we were unable to find a path. The razor back ridge had been going down much longer than it went up! Finally we crossed a path and it was the path that led to the eastern branch of the Vidima river, so we followed the river back to the Vets station.

By now it was after 6 p.m. and we hurried to reach the last bus at Seven, but we missed it by ten minutes. So, we had to walk all the way, on sore legs and blisters, to Novo Celo and the apartment. Calpurnia had spaghetti ready, so after we took showers, we had food and drink and exchanged stories of the two days. Calpurnia had bought the lace tablecloth from the baba and the ceramics from Kosta, after some reverse haggling to pay higher prices, and she showed them to us.

We were up again at Seven. I made toast, coffee, cereal, and orange juice; Calpurnia cooked an omelet. So, we fed the guys, then Paul took the 8:00 bus to Troyan and John the 8:30 bus to Sevlievo and to Gabrovo and Malko Turnovo. We packed the ceramics and mailed them to Calpurnia's Mother; it cost 49 Leva at the cheating post office.

We cleaned up the apartment, took a load of books to the library, then spent a few hours at the internet getting caught up. Then a few hours making notes and finishing reports.

Back to River City

We slept late. The snow had slackened, but was still blowing. The
Bazaar was the smallest ever, only jeans, coats, and vegetables,
although a huge truck of cabbages was selling from the tailgate. We
bought a few apples.

Calpurnia had been working on a translation of the SWOT
analysis of the office into English and enlisted my help. We finally
finished about Four and then had to pack for Gabrovo again. Because
of the snow we and Vulko would take the 6:30 bus. It was cold so we
waited in the Gameyski cafe. The bus was only 5 minutes late; the
driver warned us that the roads were bad and we may miss the bus
from Sevlievo to Gabrovo. This bus was a 20-year old Kausbauer or
something, much more luxurious than the 50-year old Chavdars (but
was it immortal? Only time would tell).

The roads were one-lane in the best of times, but unplowed
were very nerve-racking. The bus slid along. We got to Sevlievo late;
the bus station was dark, but about seven people waited. The last
bus came in late and left about fifteen minutes late. When I bought
the tickets, the driver said he was not going all the way to Gabrovo,
but would meet a bus from Gabrovo in a small village half-way and
we would exchange passengers. Perhaps it was just the last bus's
way of minimizing dead-runs. Anyway at the village midway a cold
bus awaited us. The buses exchanged passengers and we went on,
thankfully.

We arrived in Gabrovo about 9:30 on a snowy night. Vulko
walked to the hotel. We walked to our new apartment (shared
anyway). The elevator worked and the halls were warm. What a
surprise. At the apartment, the outer grill was unlocked, so I could
not test the new key. But, the old key would not work in the door. In
frustration I knocked on the door and Joe answered — his key was in
the other side.

We did not expect to see him, but he did not want to go
back to Dryanovo in the snow, so he stayed the weekend and
did laundry. We asked if it would be a problem for us to stay. He
was apologetic. The phone was not hooked up anyway. He was
scheduled for Wednesday, Thursday and Friday nights, and we got
Sunday, Monday and Tuesday. As we were talking the water went
off. Gabrovo was still on a water regime. Off at ten p.m. and back on
at six in the morning. We sat and talked until midnight, comparing
experiences. The radiators had been turned on at last (which
meant that there had been at least five days in a row of freezing
temperatures), and the PC oil-filled radiators were also on. Then
Calpurnia and I made the bed in the bedroom and Joe made the bed
in the living room (which had the cable television).

The bedroom had two single beds with mismatched mattresses

and box springs pushed together. There was a large wardrobe and matching dresser. A small night table with a strange reading lamp was against the window. One mattress was stained with rust or blood. In the wardrobe were five blankets and four pillows. Despite the unappealing sight of the beds they were comfortable and the room was very warm. We slept relatively well.

Joe was up first, showered and caught the early bus to Dryanovo. We got ready and left at 8:00 to walk to the Stara Planina tourist office. I dropped Calpurnia off and walked on to the bus stop to catch the city bus to the Park office. As I was waiting there. I heard my name — Iurka and her driver were waiting at the curb for me and drove me to the office. The driver was full time and his only job was to drive Iurka around in the new Mitsubishi Land Cruiser bought with USAID money (all the other vehicles were Lada Niva 4WDs). We talked about the survey projects coming up.

At the Park I waited for Georgiu and waylaid him when he came in. We started to discuss the wolf survey, but my Bulgarian drove him crazy and he screamed for Petya, who knew some English. The three of us retired to the conference room and confirmed the arrangements for next Friday. Afterwards I talked to Angelar, Svetislav and some others, who were there for the monthly meeting. The new calendar and poster had arrived. They looked good, but the poster, gold print on black, did not have enough detail of the hiking routes to be very useful. Too bad, I kept asking for people to let me proof or comment on things, but no one ever asked. I supposed it would be reprinted later in another format — still, it looked good, and would look good, on walls as a decoration.

I caught the 10:30 bus and went back to the apartment and cleaned, mostly dusting and repairing the bathroom wall, which had a 14-inch hole by the toilet. Then, I walked to the Tourist office to meet Calpurnia for lunch. As I was waiting she dragged me in so I could listen to the morning session end. Then, we were both invited to lunch at the Architect's Club next door. The food was poor, as was the rakia. The building, however, was exquisite.

The afternoon session dragged on until Six. I was fragile from lunch and missed some of the excitement. I took notes and participated anyway. At dinner, after 7:30, we went to a Serbian restaurant, in an old building in the center of town. The food, and red wine, were excellent (traditional Bulgarian, not Serbian). We talked to Francois about the Swiss program. He and Vulko made many jokes about the Mayor of Aprilci, the honorable, or horrible, Gedeon Balakov. I suggested making the telephone company into a museum; Vulko thought we could have sight-seeing tours of the mayoral office, since he was never there. Calpurnia suggested putting a bed in the Tourist office and renting it out. An added attraction: people could see how a functioning tourist office in Bulgaria worked. Francois announced to Sylvia, the head of the regional office, that Aprilci's financial problems had been solved. Of course, we were on our second bottle of wine, which helped. Just before eleven, Calpurnia and I left. The others had no food or glasses left, but did not want to leave.

At the apartment, the water had been turned off. We turned on the heat and went to bed. We tried to sleep late, but I was up before seven. We packed and walked to the office, expecting to be late. It was Francois who was late. This part of the workshop was an exercise in making contracts and planning. We mostly listened, although made a few suggestions. The day was over at 1 p.m., although we milled around, trying to decide on rides. When we tried to leave, to have lunch at the pizza restaurant (my real reason for being in Gabrovo I said), Stelka offered us a ride to Aprilci with her and Vulko. We accepted gratefully, since it meant we avoided three hours of slow buses and a later arrival. The trip took less than an hour and we were dropped off in front of our apartment blok. The others were going to check out a hizha.

After dropping off our bags, we went to get groceries, which meant salami, coke, bread, cheese, and cookies. The heaters were turned on but it would be many hours before they put out heat, so we huddled in the living room and worked on wolf proposals (reading and criticizing them for the review next month). I made pizzettas for lunch/dinner. Calpurnia made mint tea. I worked on the computer, the next article for the *Echo*.

We started the next day by making a decent breakfast of yogurt, grapefruit, toast, and tea. Then worked on the computer, then to the internet cafe. Then to the Tourist Bureau to work on the business plan. The afternoon was spent on the PC market basket survey as well as expense report for the year. This survey was supposed to teach us to live within our budget, which we had no trouble doing, except for the office costs and costs for secondary and tertiary projects, except for my cola habit—and so on. So, I tried to explain to the PC that if they were going to arrange these projects for us they should help with financing if the host agencies could not—I expected nothing but a sea of deaf ears. When I got frustrated, I carried two boxes of books to the library. I asked them if they could get a car for the remaining four boxes; she said tomorrow sometime.

Then just before Five, we got ready for class; the class was still stuck on prepositions. We met in the Pepsi cafe and started. We were all drinking tea. Then many people came in and the music got louder, so we decided to move to the new cafe in the old vegetable store, the 'torte' cafe. We sat down and ordered tea. After half an hour she said she was closing. So, we moved to Iva's small cafe, with just two tables. At one of the tables were two guys from the sawmill. As we were discussing the finer points of English and then Bulgarian grammar, the waitress came over and corrected Aleksander about the use of the word "za." It turned out that she was a teacher (the other waitresses were doctors and engineers, but I guessed the teachers made as little as doctors here). The session ran late and then we scheduled the next one for Sunday.

PC Conferences or Forced Vacations

It was time for the annual Price Corpse conference for the new recruits. I left at 8:00 for the bus for Troyan. At Troyan the bus agent told me that I had to buy the ticket on the bus, because it was a private bus. At ten the bus came and because it was mid-day, the driver skipped all of the small villages. Nevertheless, it was almost full and I sat next to a tobacco-chewing baba in a black outfit. We got to Sofia and I got up at the stop by Lions' Bridge (which was a straight shot to the PC HQ), but the light was green and he did not stop. That meant an extra three blocks walk.

AT PC HQ I ran into Svetla and asked her help making my overheads for the lecture. We followed the directions on the new gigantic xerox, but everything jammed each time. Finally, we asked the secretary; she said ignore the directions and just do it normally. We did; it worked. I looked for books on Vasil Levski Street. Then decided to walk to the South Station. This was almost a mistake in the heat, but I walked through the largest park, whose name I forgot, and it was almost cool. After meandering around, the tram tracks met up with the road again. I recognized the bus station because it was hidden under a freeway overpass. Again I tried to buy my ticket inside, but I was told it was a private bus and I must buy it directly. Since I was two hours early (there was no 2:30 or 3:30 bus, only the 4:30), I walked around and drank coke.

Finally it was 4:30 and we left in the new minibus. The trip was supposed to be an hour, but in fact was two and a half hours. At Panagyurishte, everyone got off at the *aftogarata*, but I asked the driver to drop me off at the hotel; surprisingly he did. We drove by struggling, envious people. After I checked in, I met Christine in the lobby. She needed help checking out of her room and into the hotel. She asked for a room first, before we walked to pick up her luggage; the clerk asked if she wanted to stay with me. She said no. That seemed unusual for a clerk to ask that, but we went to the PC apartment for her things. The apartment had four single beds for the four girls, including Milli, Jody, and Sylvia, but Christine said that at least eight other people were staying there and they partied every night and she, who had been drinking and diskoing every night with Danyel in Pelovo, said she could not take it anymore.

I did not have much to do at the conference, except give a few lectures and leave. I took the 7:00 bus to Sofia. It went to the Princess bus station. I sat next to Tiffany, Ben's friend, who talked during the movie (the bus had a movie and coffee). I walked to PC HQ and talked to Sheila about reimbursements. I went shopping at Oasis and picked up chocolate and tuna, then shopping at the Minimall. Then to the bus. Again it was a direct bus so I got to Troyan by 3:30. I had coke and fries at the bus station cafe, then got to Aprilci by 6:00. An 11 hour trip each way; less than 100 miles as the crow would fly.

Calpurnia was waiting for me at the bus stop. We worked for a while then had tuna salad. Took turns reading aloud from a Bulgarian poetry book.

I gave up on the computer Office Manager and used Fetch to transfer files. But I had to rename all the (287) image files to take out dashes, which were not allowed by Yahoo. Then it three hours to load the files with Fetch. Finally the web page was up and had only a few errors. Then I met with Trifon, who informed me that the Mayor (the evil one) required him to set up a web page with a Bulgarian ending (bg) rather than the ending I had (net). I suggested that I use my site for the craftsmen and link to the new site. This made things more difficult. The site looked good, and I tried it from different computers. It was slower on older computers. Then we packed our bags for the In-service Training (IST) in Stara Zagora.

On an overcast and dark day, we caught the 8:20 bus to Sevlievo; we always had to go through Troyan or Sevlievo to get out of Aprilci, which was a dead end in the mountains. It was 15 minutes late. So, we were 15 minutes late into the city. As we entered the bus station I saw the van was pulling out, so I leapt across the ice and flagged down the driver, who happened to have two empty seats and pulled over. This saved us an hour of waiting and the local bus to Gabrovo. The trip took only twenty minutes instead of the usual hour (minivans were replacing many old buses for short runs that had fewer people—they also made more runs).

At Gabrovo we walked on ice to the apartment. Joe was still asleep so we left our bags and a message, then walked to look at magazines and eat pizza. Coming out of the Pizza Tempo, Calpurnia had a bad fall on the ice. Had not seen her cuss in a while. Helped her limp to the afternoon bus to Stara Zagora. We had never been to this city, which seemed to be one of the few not laid out lengthwise along a river. We consulted our old map and walked through snow and ice to the hotel, another classic edifice of socialist design. The rooms had been remodeled—the hole in the bathroom floor had been plugged and every thing seemed to have their own closed drains. We took baths, our first in months.

Alta was in her room, so we all went to eat at the Happy Bar, the Bulgarian food chain. We had the safe chicken, tomato salads and fries. That evening, we split the good Cuban rum, in Cuba Libres; perhaps later we would find Cuban cigars.

The conference began with thirty-three ekolog volunteers. After introductions and the welcoming talk, Calpurnia and I offered our hour and a half presentation of proposal writing. It was fairly good, although the repeat performance that afternoon was much better. I lectured for forty minutes on grants; then Cali worked through an exercise with the participants.

Angelar and all the other Bulgarian colleagues came, except for Vulko, who had a separate conference in Gabrovo. About Four we all put up our displays for the Gallery walk. As usual, Alta had no information from her counterpart (who also got in six hours late), so she made a poster by hand—I drew an Iris on it.

That night we took Angelar and Elizabeth (a new ekolog) out to dinner at a good restaurant called Krem. More chicken. After getting more coke for drinks and chocolate for addictions, we retired to our room. There was a knock on the door and the Peace Corps Director Albert Foster invited us to dinner at The Forum, the best restaurant in Bulgaria—a place he always had a steak at. Naturally, full as we were, we agreed, but he sat and talked for three hours— this was natural for Albert. We teased him that he always asked us when he knew we could not go. We talked about his career, which he confided in us would end later this year as our own PC career ended. Then we talked about the Ambassador and his wife, who would also be leaving this spring for a new country. Then, about Bulgarian politics, our projects, and our adopted daughters, Alta and Christine. Christine had just received news that she did not pass the State Department exam, so Albert had a history CD for her to give to her English classes. Albert decided to call her on his mobile phone, so we all talked to her to cheer her up. Then I embarrassed Alta and Calpurnia, by suggesting to Albert that he give as much attention to Alta, who was just as accomplished. Albert agreed. He agreed to write us all letters of recommendation. Then he left at 10:30 to find dinner.

After a good breakfast of toast, *palachinka* (pancakes with marmalade), pizza, eggs, and juices, we took a taxi to the bus station. Angelar headed to Gabrovo. The three of us were told the bus for Sofia left at ten, but I asked a bus driver who was loading and he said they were going to Sofia, so we boarded. Alta and Calpurnia sat together. Four of the other seats were broken, so I got one of the broken ones, but at least I was by myself. There was ice and snow on the highways and the bus swayed and rocked like a ship on unpleasant seas.

After three bumpy hours, we were in Sofia and took a cab to the hotel, the Maya. The cab had his meter set four times as fast as normal, so we got off early. He got out first and waved a baseball bat. I suggested he relax and we would pay the fare. The price was high (only $3.30 but high for us and more than the usual $0.75). The hotel was as nice as last time. This time however, we were put in the new section (the hotel was made from two large apartments where each room has become a hotel room and each bathroom has been divided into fourths, making a narrow crowded room, but with hot water and private entrance). The rooms had beds, couch, wardrobe, television, minifridge, as well as shoes and robes to wear (a double was $32 a night, which was very high for Bulgarian — in other cities, the same room was only about $11).

We had a snack in McDs, then Calpurnia and Alta shopped for clothes while I went for books and magazines. I found what I wanted but did not buy them, which was always dangerous, since they would be gone tomorrow. That evening, we ate in a Chinese restaurant, where the food was decent and plentiful — there were a surprising number of Chinese here, although we heard that they were virtually prisoners since they spoke no Bulgarian and were not paid much. After dinner we talked in one of the rooms.

Up at Seven and off to the 8 a.m. bus to Troyan, which was late. We did not care. Sat in the cafe and had tea, then caught the bus to Sofia, which was half an hour early. Got in to Sofia at 1 o'clock and went to the PC HQ for meetings with Iliana and Dimiter. Met Alta and Christine at the HQ and walked to Macedonia Square to catch the bus to Sandanski, which was an hour late. The other PCVs were a drunken mob, for the most part, but at least they seemed happy. Alas, the bus had to stop several times for toilets and got pulled over by traffic police once (for an unspecified offense, but we thought it was mooning cars from the window); the driver got the warning.

At the Hotel Sandanski, Christi and I blocked the exits while Calpurnia and Alta ran to be first to get rooms. It worked, ha, ha, ha. We got to relax while the long lines at check-in slowly unwound. Then it was dinner. We ate in the hotel restaurant, and had it to ourselves, except for Ron and Dan, two elderly volunteers who asked to eat with us (which meant they would eat every meal with us for the next three days — of course, that was okay; Dan was 60 now, the ex-police trooper, and Ron was 44 and an ex-prosecuting attorney from Atlanta — in fact, we three men were the three oldest volunteers in Bulgaria). Food was okay; it was traditional Bulgarian. To bed early to read.

The first of three days of meetings were designed to help us fill out the official paperwork of the PC. After the first session, I skipped out and went swimming in the Olympic-size, heated pool; got tired after 1200 meters. Rested and went to lunch, which was vegetarian (salad and cheese). After lunch, however, I attended all the sessions and filled out many pages of important forms.

Dinner was at a pizza restaurant, which was decent. We walked around the town, which, being five miles from Greece, was more Greek than Bulgarian. Got vodka, baileys, and coke for drinks. Went to rooms and the four of us drank and read more of the crucial paperwork.

The second day, ditto for entire day (swam 1400 meters), but dinner was at a nice Bulgarian restaurant and the food was excellent. I tried chicken filets baked on cheese and bread, with wine. Postprandial relaxation was more drinking and laughing over forms.

The third day, ditto (except 1600 meters swimming). Then, it was off to Sofia. Dr. Todor played with my new bandages (small cut on the spine, a hazard of falling), then we went shopping for pizza dough and cereal. Snow turned to rain and back. The bus at 1 o'clock was fast but we had to wait in Troyan until 5. At 6 :15 in Aprilci, we saw Vulko working and went in to help for an hour or two—he was rewriting the text of the brochure, which had not been finished or proofed. The floor of the office however, had been finished with wood—a surprise; he had spent all of the remodeling money on the floor while we were gone. The apartment was freezing, so we turned on the heater. Then waited under the covers for ten hours.

The Word According to Spellcheck Or *Fun with Words*

At the beginning, I had converted my worldly goods into a laptop and digital camera to take with me. It was a good choice. I was able to keep a notebook, as well as produce "professional" looking grant applications. Whenever I tried to run the spelling and grammar program, it had trouble with Bulgarian and American names, as well as many real words. This, along with the typical American propensity to abbreviate names or issue nicknames, lead to some real strange phrases during later conversations. The amusement factor was very high, so I would regularly run the spellcheck just to see how it had butchered the words I wanted to use.

For instance, my host family, Ilian and Rumiana Iliev, was shortly renamed "iliac and romaine olive." The arrogant little computer program also suggested "alive" for their last name. They lived in the delightful town of "Dentist" (Dupnitsa), in "Bullpen" (Bulgaria).

In this less foreign of foreign countries, we learned to toast before drinking "racial" (*rakia*, a deadly plum brandy, usually homemade), by saying "Nice driveway" (*Nazdravya*, for good health). Then we would all dance the "charge" (*chalga*, the rock and rap of the eastern blok) until we got tired and had to take a "paycheck" (*pochefka* or rest). Later in the evening, we ate "debauches" (*kebabches*, rolled beef-pork-cumin burgers) and "Persian cartons" (*persiani kartofi*, french fries). Then we would go to "lego" (*leglo* or bed) and spend the night "spying" (*spiya* or sleeping).

Places

Bulgaria: bullpen	Dupnitsa: dentist
Aprilci: acrylic	Novo cello [new village]: novel cello
Dryavno: drano	Pazardjik: pass logic, hazard hick
Plovdiv: plodder	Lugat: log out, lug out
Varna: vernal	Sevliev:(relieve, believe
Shumen: showmen	Iskur: slur, issuer
Burgas: beer gas	Veliko Turnovo: venice turnover
Tsarevo [king's town]: starved	Xisar: disarm
Vratsa: brats	Pelovo: pelvic
Pavel Banya [Paul's bath]: gravel banyan	
Sandanski (sandbank)	Chiflik: chiefly, chalk
Sachxrane: saccharin	Panegyurishte: panegyrist
Teteven: tighten	Hizha, hut: hoser
Stara Planina [old mountains]: stars planned	
Severen Djendem [forest region]: severe denuded	
Kazya Stena [park region]: casual stain	
Strangja [region]: strand you	Davinci [a bar]: deviance
Aftogara [bus station]: antiglare	Vodapod [waterfall]: voodoo
Chakalo [hunting blind]: cachalot, cacao	

People

Pentcho: poncho, pinch	Angelar: angler
Mariya: marina	Vulko: vulcan
Veshen: vessel	Venelina: vanillan
Iliana: liana Stelka: stalker	
Kaloti: coyote	Venelin: vineland
Iskra: oscar	Ralitsa: relics
Vanya: vandal	Penka: penal
Polya: polyp	Zora: Zorro
Rada: radar	Ivailyo: invalid
Boyko: bunko	Iliana: liana
Trifon: Triton	Purvanov: purveyor
Tsonyo: stony	Dr. Tsacheva: Dr. Trachea
Dimitrina: dalmation	Pesho: pesto
Bulchru: butcher	Boleslav: coleslaw

Mariya: marina   Yordanka: ordnance
Closimir: consumer   Vasily: vastly
Baba [grandmother]: babe   Dyado [grandfather]: dildo

Activities
Chalga [kind of music]: charge
Horo [kind of dance]: horror
Na gosti [visiting]: no gusto
Nazdravya [salute]: nice driveway
Pochifka [rest]: paycheck
Vruski [influence]: risky

Things / Foods
Chavdar [bus]: chador   Zankmet [vice-mayor]: shammed
Lev [money]: leg   Leva [more monies]: levy
Spionen [spy]: spinner   Rechnik [dictionary]: rethink
Rakia: rakish   Kepabche: debauche
Terator [soup]: tractor   Banitsa [roll]: banister
Bilko chai [tea]: biker chair Capriols [goats]: carpools
Sladko [sweet]: slacks   Kyufte [meat patty]: yurt
Tikva [melon]: diva   Plodovey [fruits]: phooey
Meso [meat]: mess   Zakuska [breakfast]: babushka
Shopska salata: shopper saliva
Pileshko shishchi: plucky oilskin
Portokolo sok [orange juice]: protocol sock
Lichna carta [passport]: lichen crate
Lada Niva [4-wheel drive jeep]: lava knives
Div svinkska [wild pigs]: diva stinks
Surni [deer]: submit

Words
Bulgarski [Bulgarian]: bulwarks   Samo [only]: salmon
Nishto [nothing]: ditto   Glava [head]: guava

Just so we don't get carried away and think that foreign names were funny, the computer can change American names into odd words as well. For instance,

   Calpurnia Donne: capturing done
   Alta Strittland: all stricter
   Christine Sailor: crispy sailor
   Andrew Panagakos: draw papa duck
   Joe Rehman: job remain
   Barbara Tainter: bar tainted
   Dan Partana: dam partner

Or, even worse, the computer, with some encouragement, could mix

up names as anagrams, for instance:
>   Bulgaria: airbag lu
>   Country of Bulgaria: young burial factor, or
>   buoyant cigar flour
>   Peace Corps: recap scope
>   Peace Corps volunteer: pervert canoe couples, or
>   conserve place troupe
>   Night wolves: woven lights, or vowel things

Someone stop me before I reworditate (reverberate?) everything!

A few days later, one of the volunteers told me that she had been looking up the meanings of Bulgarian proper names. Many of them meant "Harmony dawn" or "Bold killer." So, I started translating everyones' names into their meanings.

Local Television

At a festival, for some reason, I was sought out by a camera crew from Lovech, who wanted me to say who I was and where I lived. I could not escape, but I saw Dr. Karanova and asked her over to help me if I started to fail. After a few simple questions I was asked to comment on the causes and solutions of poverty in Bulgaria. I started several times, to say that Bulgaria was a rich country, or that other countries, even the United States, had a lot of poverty also, but then finally said the question was too complex to be answered at a festival. Then she asked a political question about the new party in power. I repeated my last answer, and they lost interest in me.

After a good long lunch, we went back and took photos until Five or so. The celebration continued until after 7:00. We walked around and listened to the music, which had lasted beyond the 5 o'clock ending. It was a nice evening, and so many people seemed to be enjoying the fair. I started writing an article on why Bulgaria was wealthy.

After laundry and cleaning we went on a hike to Ostrets, about an hour and 20 minutes walk. There we had tea and spotted the bus back to Aprilci. So, for 80 stutinki we took the bus. We were met in Aprilci by the head of the cable television station, whom we had met with Emil last Friday. She told us that the community meeting, on tourism, was starting immediately, so we went to the zala (wedding hall) to take part.

It was a long meeting, going from One until almost Five. Trifon was on the panel to talk, but left at the break to work. After the break, I tried to point out that Calpurnia and Vulko had been doing most of the things discussed. That the best thing for tourism in Aprilci might be a clean city with good bus and taxi connections.

Instead of a debate or thoughtful acknowledgment, Bulchru complemented me on my Bulgarian and then went on to talk about what they should spend the Swiss money on. That night I was on cable television, the token American expressing himself in halting Bulgarian on unpopular topics.

Worked on the articles for wolves for *Eko Planeta*. Then bought two breads, one for sandwiches and a thin one for falafels (plus there was no baking on Sunday, bazaar day). Class was at Five and the assistant at the cable television had decided to join us and speak English. Like many who do not speak regularly she was shy about speaking, but seemed to follow the conversation. Then she reminded me that I had agreed to be interviewed for the television. And I reminded her that I preferred seeing the questions first so I could prepare. She agreed and we worked on the questions together, finally coming up with eight multi-part questions that should cover everything. We wrote them in Bulgarian and I agreed to write the answers before the next class.

Up at 5:30, sliced grapefruit and bread. It rained last night, so everything was wet and warmer. Men were standing in front of the news vendor, talking about something. Four more people were waiting for the eight o'clock bus to Troyan. A few men were standing by the cars in the square. Tall girls and short boys were heading towards their school down the road, all dressed in black of course. Two women with babies were sitting in the bread store, kissing the babies. The line was only two people ahead of me, I was able to get bread and yogurt.

Worked on text for television interview. Then off to the internet, which was technically working but so slow that I turned it off after 15 minutes of a blank screen. Coffee with Aleksander and his friend from Portugal; he was a telecommunications engineer. He wanted to start taking the English classes.

After working all afternoon, we had class at Gameyski's restaurant because I wanted persiani kartofi with my coke. There were six of us including one guy from the sawmill and the woman, Venelina, from the television station. They went over our six pages of answers and corrected the grammar. They suggested I rewrite the questions and answers and we would have a trial interview in the studio on Saturday, with the real interview on Monday. I suggested we had class at the station, also.

I worked all day preparing for my interview. I wrote out many possible questions and my answers in detail. Then I worked on the web page design. Lunch was pleasant. I made my own pizza.

We had decided to hold English class in the Cable Television Station, which was in a house next to Kosta's and Petya's.

261

Aleksander, Andrei, Calpurnia, and I met Vanya there. The engineer, Evol, had everything ready. Then Vanya walked out to talk to someone. Andrei thought he would help me practice, so he asked questions and I answered and Evol filmed it. Calpurnia sat between me and Aleksander. Since the door was locked Vanya could not come back in. The interview practice took about 45 minutes. Evol unlocked the door and Vanya came in with her boss and two more engineers. We all watched the tape and were amused at my pronunciation of words. Aleksander, Vanya, and Andrei were telling me how to pronounce words. The boss brought out champagne, and we all drank. They were not celebrating the interview after all, but the fact that they got 16,000 dollars to set up an internet service for Aprilci; the money was from the Swiss. Last week, I had written to the Swiss to suggest that they not grant the money since Aprilci already had an internet cafe. Obviously, they did not change their minds.

At home I rewrote my answers and added a question. Dinner was potato salad.

After working for a few hours, the next day, I hiked to Vidima through the woods. Almost no wildlife beyond a few birds. Back for a short lunch of potato salad and a sandwich. The afternoon was spent on the final rewrite for the interview. Fear of embarrassment was a potent force for learning the fine points of a language. The evening continued with more writing.

The next morning I took the written interview to Vulko to make sure I was pronouncing the words correctly. Instead of just helping me do that, he spent over two hours refining my word endings and suggesting new words. I reluctantly made the changes since I had been learning the other for almost a week.

I rewrote one more time, and then it was time to go to the interview at 3 p.m. at the station. Only Vanya and Evol were there. We looked over the new questions and then began. The first three questions went well, but then I had to refer to the written sheets due to the complexity of the answers.

She asked me who we were and where we came from, as well as why we came to Bulgaria, and we gave true and politically-correct PC answers. She asked about our education and experience. I presented myself modestly as the next Goethe and Calpurnia as the next Curie.

We talked about our projects: *Kakva e vawata profesiq? Sega, Nie sme dobrovolci ot Korpus na Mira. Rabotim kato ekolozi. Predi dve godini, Marsela bewe in "ener rabote] po izgra" daneto na sistemi za prehistvane na vuzduxa i vodata. Minalata godina, Tq zapohna da paboti kato koncultant v Turistihesko Byuro v Aprilci. V momenta, Tq raboti po proekt za izrabotvaneto na karta, browuri, i internet. Raboti su]o, i v Nacionalen Park Centralen Balkan, kudeto razrabotva matematiheski modeli i pomaga pri nabldanieto na divi ivotni. . . .*

I made a few mispronunciations. Then Vanya asked a few things not on our list, but I was able to answer most of them (I thought). A long time was spent comparing Glendale Oregon to Aprilci, in terms of churches, costs, income, and services.

"How many churches?" asked Vanya.

I answered: "Just in Glendale, a town of three hundred, eight churches."

"Why so many? Does everybody go?"

"Not everybody goes, but there is no bazaar, no center; the library is sort of deserted, like here. Church is a major social event where everybody can meet. Churches sponsor picnics and baseball games. I used to go to church on Wednesday nights to practice singing with the choir."

"So, they are less religious than Bulgarians."

"No, I think it is a different outlet. Socially, I mean."

"You said gas was cheap. Is it really that cheap."

"Well, the government subsidizes it, so it is artificially low. It does not pay for the infrastructure or real costs. Of course, we pay dollars by the gallon, rather than Leva by the liter."

"So many Bulgarians want to go to America because of all the jobs. Do you think that is good?"

"It is always good to want to better yourself, but jobs in America are not that plentiful. Most of the professional jobs are taken by overqualified people. Most of the other jobs are service jobs that pay less."

"I had a friend in Chicago who was able to send money back here."

"I mean, the jobs pay more in America, but everything there is more expensive, from rents to food and electricity. I know many Bulgarians, married or single, who share apartments and cars to be able to send money back here."

"So, we should not go?"

"Go, when you can, but be sure not to be blinded by myths or expectations, especially those from American television programs."

Then, more time was spent describing our projects here in Aprilci. It was very delicate, because we had had many people asking us for help raising money for hotels and restaurants. We emphasized that we were ecologists and could only put people in contact with other people or help them to use the internet. I always wondered what people actually heard. The interview ended. Vulko, whose name means 'wolf,' said it went well. No champagne this time, but tea and orange juice.

I am Not a Spy Or *Spooked on the Loose*

On the street one day, I was talking to the town drunk, or rather the town drunk was telling me that I could live with him and help him with his English. Suddenly, he asked if I was a spy. I said no, just a volunteer. Then I asked what I could possibly be spying on here. He sneered and said I was almost too clever for him; if he told me then I would know what to spy on, and things would get worse.

A while later, I asked Aleksander if everyone thought we were spies. He said yes, most people probably did. I shrugged. I reminded him that our government had professional spies that were highly paid and relatively invisible. He shrugged.

We had prepared potato salad and cookies for the postponed picnic today. We went with Aleksander to the bazaar to buy bread and beer, more tomatoes and kebabche. Andrei did not show up so Aleksander called him; he was busy and could not come right away. So, we shopped for more meat and beer, knowing that the act of buying beer would reach Andrei's highly tuned senses. Almost immediately, Andrei roared up in his old Mazda. We packed the food, the he and Aleksander went to pick up a plastic table. Calpurnia and I walked towards the raspberry plantation, the site of the picnic, but we saw a knife display for the first time in the bazaar. It was a craftsman from Etura, near Gabrovo; I bought one good knife for about $6, but saw two others I'd like to buy later.

As we approached the field Andrei drove by. The first thing we did was to start a fire, which Aleksander did, although I fed it for an hour, having to hike into the forest to break branches. Andrei started cooking. Aleksander revealed to us that his nickname was Burt, but could not explain it, as he had always been called that.

As usual Andrei had more funny stories about what the people in Aprilci thought of us. We were definitely CIA spies. I asked what we could be spying on, other than the new raspberry fields. Andrei says that he asked his friend Tosko the same thing; Tosko's clever answer was that US spy satellites fed us information and we had to verify it on the ground. Then, he had asked Andrei, if we were successful in the US, why would we come to a poor country like Bulgaria. Therefore, we were either spies or complete failures wanting to get rich in Bulgaria at their expense. The logic seemed good to me. I tried to present the ideas of altruism or service, but they sounded a little hollow. Andrei had answered about our idealism in service of humanity. Of course, I really wanted to have a two-year vacation looking at wild animals, completely paid for by the PC. I supposed that idealism was as good an answer as any, so I kept my mouth shut.

The shishkabobs were ready so we ate them. Then we drank and talked for four hours about Bulgaria and America. The mayor for instance received $40,000 for a cable internet, but just put it in the bank; when the Swiss came and asked if the project had been started, he said, no, he could not start it or the city council would get rid of him. Oddly, Trifon had not provided service to the city anyway, so there seemed to be no hurry — it has been eight months since the project was granted. We packed up before dark and went back down hill.

At the class next week, only Andrei showed up. We had class in the pizza restaurant. It went well. After class, we saw Mariya cleaning up her store (next to her cafe) and went to talk with her. She asked us if we could give her the pizza recipe. We said yes, of course. Then I offered that Andrei and I would could cook the first samples, but she said no one would eat anything Andrei cooked. We laughed (Andrei's wife lived in Sofia, but Andrei lived here and rented a small room, because the sawmill was here). I asked if the cafe had an oven; she said no, but she would cook them in her house. Andrei said that was illegal because she had no permission to prepare food outside of the cafe or a factory without a license. I asked what they would do. He pointed to boxed pizzas from the Czech Republic, which I said I had tried and were awful. Mariya said they would reuse the boxes and tell everyone that was where they came from. I said what if they wanted to buy more — certainly they would not taste the same as the commercial ones, and we did not want to give the business away. Andrei thought that no one would go to the Czech factory, but he apologized for involving me in an illegal business. I said I was only a spy, I meant, observer, or advisor.

Electing Royals & Communists

We went out early. I get dressed in my calvary shirt, cowboy boots and Aussie hat. It was raining all morning. We waited an hour for the President, Petur Stoyanov, taking photos. First his guards came flying up the street in jeeps. They got out smartly and marched to their positions; this took another forty minutes. A group marched to the center of town; smaller groups took positions near the new statue and around city hall (I could smell burning envy from the mayor). Stoyanov came marching up the street, preceded by guards and then school students, After the cheering died down, he gave a short speech at the city hall garden, at the new bust of Maragonzov, a historian of the 1876 revolt, then moved slowly to the city square and the 1876 guns and sabers monument, where flowers were placed. I was standing next to him, taking pictures of the guards and crowds. We nodded to each other. I could not imagine doing that in America with our inauthentic President

Calpurnia was ill and went back to lie down. After an hour, when I went back to get her, we went to the square in time to see the President and a small entourage moving towards the Convent (monastery), so we followed. He went inside and gave another talk, about the courage of the nuns and the importance of keeping these traditions and churches. I remembered that seven nuns had been killed; in fact, their bare skulls were on display behind the church in a small building. He came out and addressed a small crowd, mostly rangers and park people. We followed and took more pictures. He walked past us. We greeted him and shook hands. His eyebrows elevated a millimeter at our accents. Then he was gone.

We were surrounded by Iurka and people from the Park, so we took their pictures for a few minutes, talking about the debates. Then they were gone. We talked to a nun for a few minutes, then drifted back to the center to look around. The dedication had taken five hours.

Sunday the Seventeenth, Election Day! We were in Pelovo to observe. People streamed into the high school to vote all day. It seemed that virtually the entire town was voting; we passed the mayor and the head of the school, on their way to voting. We had a breakfast and did a small laundry. Then went for a walk to buy food and flypaper. An early lunch was cheese sandwiches from the new toaster. At 13:00 we went to the bus but it was 30 minutes late so we went by car to Pleven. There we had dessert then went to the internet cafe which was slow and losh (bad). The direct bus to Aprilci left at 4:20 and got us back at 6:45. Dinner was chicken and rice. Then, we watched election results.

Back in Aprilci the next day, Calpurnia worked on Tourist Office while I rewrote the last grant. We met Andrei, who told us that Emil had been killed in a motorcycle accident on Sunday. His face was ripped off on a dumpster as he tried to pass two cars while driving his unlicensed motorcycle drunk. He left behind an elderly mother and handicapped brother. No classes at all. We heard that Simeon had won the election. Simeon would have been Tsar Simeon II after the war.

Who is Simeon Saxe-Coburg-Gotha? He was crowned king of Bulgaria in 1943 after the death of his father Boris, who was very popular. After most of the family was executed by Communists, Simeon fled to Egypt, America and then Spain. He had been educated at the Valley Forge Military Academy in Pennsylvania. He had been a businessman in Spain for the past forty years, although I had never heard exactly what his business was (tourism I thought).

It had been two days and we had not read or heard much about the election. More work in office and on grants. Then, much more news on the election. Simeon had plastered every city with posters, out-papering his opponents 5 to 1. Because no party would sponsor him, he had started his own party, referred to as the "yellow" party, which grew quite rapidly. Finally, there was a joint press conference with the heads of each party. Everyone looked grim and bitter, although maybe Simeon was just exhausted or leaking crocodile tears. The reporters asked questions. When they got to Simeon, last, most of the questions started with "Your majesty." In fact, everywhere Simeon was referred to as Simeon II. I wondered if this would cause formal difficulties when he became Prime Minister, and people tried to refer to him as "Your majesty Prime Minister Simeon II." Of course, Bulgarians were justifiably proud of this historic first, where a royal was elected to office.

Despite its anachronistic love for the monarchy and rosy-colored memories of the pre-World War II times, Bulgaria is a democratic Republic and had supported Simeon's party as an expression of the widely held desire to keep changing. The red party (the Communists who kept power and headed the government twice after 1990) last lead the country into an economic collapse in 1997. The blue party (the moderate right-center democrats) tried to get the country stable and prosperous, but they had been dogged with reports of wide-spread corruption.

It was the hope of the people that Simeon would bring immediate prosperity, which in fact was one of his campaign promises ("Prosperity within 800 days"). It was also reported that he would offer five-year interest-free loans to every citizen for the asking (I heard this from the regional blue party chief, but never read it in the Bulgarian). It was the hope of the politicians that the entry of Simeon into the race would mean more compromises instead of the see-sawing between two often unpopular parties (does this remind you of an election last November somewhere outside of Europe?). Things are still being sorted out.

In the new Parliament, Simeon's Party was one seat short of a majority in the National Assembly, which meant that he must form a coalition with one of the other parties in order to appoint ministers and run the country (this was referred to as the 30-day coalition limbo). Among the urgent topics to be considered were: continuing privatization, membership in the European Union and NATO, and ending corruption.

A few days later, the election was still the hot topic. I had to double-check the news in English on the internet; the last twenty minutes was very eventful. Got another $300 for the craftsmen, due to an error in the addition of the grant. Heard from the *Sofia Echo*; they agreed to have me continue to be a columnist — my column would be on ecological thought experiments. Then received

267

permission from Albert to print the column! Although I was forbidden to write about political topics (and for human beings everything, from sex to coca cola, was political)!

That night was our advanced English class, which we had at the Garden restaurant in the center (the main dining room had been closed until September, but it was pleasant and very large in the garden). The topics were the elections again. It turned out that Simeon was still one seat short in Parliament of a majority, so he would have to form a coalition somewhere with someone, probably the blue party.

Now, it was the time for the Presidential elections. It was also time to go to the English Class, which was in the Center Restaurant—also known as the Pepsi, because the Pepsi distributor has captured it, Because Pepsi labels were blue, it was favored by the blue democratic party, leaving coke to be claimed by the communist party. And, because I liked coke, I often found myself sitting with red party people, much to the chagrin of Andrei and others). Vanya and Vulko had promised to come, also. Andrei and Aleksander were there with Aleksander's friend Sava (short for Zhan), who wanted to start classes. Vulko showed up later, but left after half an hour. Sava started talking after an hour. The topic was the Presidential election. In fact we had all watched the debates on Monday night and joked about Blagoev attacking Stoyanov all the time. The moderators lost control. Stoyanov made the mistake of attacking back, thus appearing less presidential. Andrei thought most of the candidates were insane, even my favorite, Dr. Beron, who was head of an archeological museum. I pointed out that a scientist in America never would get to run. Andrei thought that proved Beron was insane. Class ended at 7:00. I had wisely rented two movies, Automatic and TC 2000, both chopsaki movies. Calpurnia drifted to sleep and I watched both the movies, perfecting my fighting skills.

Sunday the Eleventh of November and today was the presidential election, US veteran's day, and Alta's birthday. Calpurnia turned on the television to check out the commentary. I made a large American breakfast, with Bulgarian ingredients. First I fried salami, cut thinly, then I fried potatoes in the fat. Putting both in the oven, I started pancakes, from scratch naturally, with applesauce and chocolate bits. We had a little bit of maple syrup left, so we used that (the first jar came from the Ambassador's wife last year, the second was sent from Virginia in May). I made cinnamon tea and Calpurnia made coffee. We had fruit juice and grapefruit, which was now available (for a short time anyway) in Aprilci. After breakfast, more computer work. Then it was time to shop at the bazaar for more cabbage!

Better Times

Class was at Three today. Aleksander came early and Andrei was late. Aleksander told us about Bulgaria before the "changes." Every town had a movie theater that played only state-approved and Bulgarian or Russian films. But, in the mid-1980s, a few entrepreneurs set up video salons using VCRs and imported tapes. The first tape that was played in Gabrovo, where Aleksander was going to school, was "First Blood," which Aleksander called "Rambo Part One." It was a great hit as a film and provided the Bulgarians with an accurate picture of Americans at war they supposed (of course, they were still receiving the accurate pictures from Ally McBeal, Bay Watch, and that zip code soap opera).

After more computer work, and a dinner of leftovers, the television announced that the communist candidate was ahead of Aleksander Stoyanov, who was supported by the blues and the tsar. An interesting development, it seemed to show that there was a nostalgia for communist times already, especially on the part of older people and pensioners.

After Simeon agreed to back the current President Petur Stoyanov, a member of the blue party, for President, it looked like no one could expect to come close to the number of votes he would get. But, things started to go wrong. Just before the election for instance, the government canceled the Christmas bonuses for all employees. Then, in the debates, Aleksander waved some dirty letters of one of his rivals. Of course, the other candidates all attacked Stoyanov and the moderators were too overwhelmed to control the debate. During that debate, one of the candidates, Georgi Purvanov, was out of the country on business.

Some people I talked to thought that Purvanov, and several of the candidates were "retarded" or "insane," even my favorite, Dr. Beron, the head of an archeological museum. Purvanov was considered to be a threat to Bulgaria's aspirations to be a member of NATO — in fact, his running mate, a retired general who had been removed from his position by Aleksander Stoyanov, had voiced opposition to belonging to NATO.

But my friends, who were mostly blue (democratic) or yellow (Simeonesque), vastly underestimated the desire of voters to have rapid change. Of other Eastern block countries Bulgaria has seemed to be most bogged down in corruption and problems. So, the people were impatient for significant improvement. Oddly, though, voter turnout was below half for the election (41.5%), although it rose to over half for the run-off.

Surprisingly, Purvanov, who had been dismissed as a loser, won both the election and a run-off election. He was the third president since the transition from communism, and the first Socialist party candidate to be President of Bulgaria.

The last time Simeon was the leader, and the communists got power, he had to flee the country. Now, democracy had brought about a quite unpredictable circumstance. Although Bulgaria was a stable and improving country, the last two elections had made it seem capricious and confused (as a result of mixed signals, perhaps). With the popular drive to European Union accession and membership in NATO, and the intent to move to a capitalist economics, it was unlikely that history would repeat itself.

Another day another class today. We met in a different restaurant, by the Police Station (where the police and firemen eat). It was quieter. We explained verb tenses and Aleksander told us Bulgarian jokes. Sample: In the section of Hell where bad Bulgarians were kept, there were no guards. Satan knew that if one Bulgarian tried to escape the others would pull him back, so no one can get any advantage.

We talked about communist times, especially now that a communist was the new President. Aleksander suggested that the people expected Bulgaria to be rich in 1990, but it had not become rich, so they thought a Communist President would bring back the good old days. Andrei told us that there was a work camp nearby in Lovech for the bourgeois and intelligentsia; his father had been held there for a while. He told us where to look for the old camp, on the hill by the new Cross. We all became uneasy talking about this, although Calpurnia and I were interested in finding out more. We made up a list of topics for future classes. So, the class chose "advertising" for the next lesson.

A busy Saturday arrived. Shopped for cabbage and potatoes. Worked on computer. Since the class was going to be in the apartment, and the topic was pizza making and American cooking, I started the sauce. The snow continued all day and there was over 12 centimeters.

At 5:00 Aleksander and Andrei showed up with wine (the good Kahn Krum) and pudding (small German containers costing 95 stutinki each). So, I made the pizza by myself. Calpurnia had made coleslaw and an apple crisp for desert. During dinner the conversation kept returning to the new President, George Purvanoff, a communist with a new party. Andrei noted that the last time a tsar was in Bulgaria, he was ousted by the communists. Now we had a tsar as premier and a communist for president. What would happen?

They started to wind down about 8:30 and decided to leave. Calpurnia and I went to bed early, but watched the late movie for an hour on the b&w, in-out tv. The movie was bad, another immortal evil villain tormenting a buffed mortal hero (yawn). So, I read about forensic anthropology.

Mistaken Identity Or *the Tsar and I*

One evening long ago in Dupnitsa, Joe and I had arranged for our
host families to meet for the first time, Alta's. Calpurnia's, mine, and
Joe's, at the Club 13 near his house. It went well. I smoked and drank
gracefully.

Then I got coerced into going dancing. But the night club, the
hotel above the gardens, was full, so we sat, ate and talked instead.
Calpurnia was not well. Joe was very solicitous; I started to check on
her, but Joe volunteered to go instead, then was chased back. When
Calpurnia returned she sat with her host mother between us; when
we talked we had to lean across her back. I was told by a waiter
that I could be mistaken for the Czar. Perplexed by this comment, I
decided to try to find his picture the next day. Then I forgot about it.

Later, I would have another hint. After working on the computer for
an hour, even getting on the internet for another twenty minutes,
I left to hike into the park. Vulko offered me a bicycle, which I
accepted. I made record time getting there on wheels. In the village
of Vidima several schoolgirls followed me, laughing and pointing.
I thought they said that I was the Tsar on a bicycle. In the forest I
hid the bicycle and walked along the other trail past the hunting
hut; it went to another water catchment. I walked uphill and down
looking for trails and wolf signs. Found some interesting looking
scat but could not decide if it was wolf or fox – it looked slightly
too small. I lay down on a bed of leaves and watched a hollow for
movement. Many birds, no animals. On the way back, I noticed on
every bit of scat on the road, mostly cow or horse, there were two
black butterflies that lifted when I walked by and then returned after
I passed. Another day without a wolf sighting. I meant to look for
the Tsar's photo.

Going through a small town by bus, a major center for bus routes
on the way to Sofia, the bus stopped for a fifteen minute break.
Everyone got off and raced to the toilets or to the small magazines
for cigarettes or food (few did both oddly). Not having any money,
I sat and looked out the window at the gypsy children, who were
playing on the steps of the city hall, although they suddenly flocked
to the bus passengers asking for change. One of them noticed my
face in the window and came closer. Some of the other children
watched him, as he hesitantly came to the front of the bus and then
up the stairs. He came in a few steps and asked if I was Tsar Simeon
II. I replied no. Then he asked for five stutinki. I smiled and gave him
the five, the only coin I had. He raced from the bus before the driver
could see. Then the driver and passengers returned and we started
up without counting heads. The gypsy children followed the bus,

pointing at my window. I pushed my nose against it and waved, not very dignified for a Tsar.

The Tsar &
Pan — Twins?

In Gabrovo one day, weeks before the national election, I was walking to the Park Office. The street was fairly crowded. I stopped in front of a bookstore window — in fact, I saw the book "Tarzan of the Apes" in Bulgarian. As I turned around there was an elderly grandmother, dressed in black, looking at me.

She approached warily and grabbed my hand. Then she bowed and kissed it, saying "only you can save us!" (I think that was what she said).

I looked at all the people looking at us. I looked back down at her and said, in my best Bulgarian, "We need to have your help. We can save ourselves only if we all work together." Somehow, I visualized a giant poster, with me leading a phalanx of smiling workers into the progressive future.

Her forehead wrinkled and then she smiled. I realized then that she had mistaken me for the Tsar. I also realized that the Tsar's Bulgarian language skills, from so many decades in exile in Spain, were not that much better than mine, which doubtless further cemented my identity in her mind.

She backed away respectfully, and I continued walking west to the office, rapidly and self-consciously, but greeting everyone politely with my third-grade Bulgarian.

In Aprilci, I got Calpurnia to take my picture with the life-size poster of the Tsar by the monument. As I was standing there a few people stopped to see what we were doing. They were behind the poster and could not see the two faces side by side. I was expecting to have my hand kissed, at least, but the people here already knew me as an American spy, fund-raiser or crazy wolf-tracker. Afterwards, we went had tea. I noticed several people walk by the poster and look at it carefully.

Doing Good Against the Will of the People

After lunch I worked on the wolf model. Then it was time for class. We met in the Gameyski restaurant and had tea, but it was noisy and they said they would close early. Aleksander suggested we walk to the Dr. Tsorov Hotel, because he wanted to ask for our help. So, we walked there in the snow. The hotel had been rebuilt over an old home, which was no longer even visible. It had a nice stone dining room, with radiators heated by the fireplace.

After talking about the lessons for a while, then giving out the Christmas gifts, we had tea. The owner came over and told us his story. He had borrowed 60,000 Leva for two years at 20,000 Leva interest, and now had difficulty repaying the loan. He wanted to get a new loan or an American investor. We suggested that we, as ecologists, could not do much except help him with a web site or internet, but he said he had two web sites. We asked about his prices (and found that they were the highest in Aprilci). We also suggested that the problem may be getting tourists here, especially with the Cyrillic language, local buses, and no town infrastructure. But, he wanted to borrow money to add two rooms, a swimming pool, and a bar patio. He treated us to tea and we finished class.

Andrei offered to get a Christmas tree for us, but we said we did not want to kill a tree for a few days of green (the whole city was surrounded by pines). I went back to work on the computer, the wolf model, which was becoming more complex with more variables and more differentials.

The past ten days had been nonstop grant applications, especially Netherlands, AOL, SPA, Global Fund, and Winant. My ass hurt from sitting.

A week later, we were in Sofia to apply for two SPA grants in person. Calpurnia was sponsoring the Tourist Bureau and I the craftsmen NGO. After a donut at DDs, we walked to the Peace Corps office. I sat in on the first hour of the SPA committee (having been selected for the committee on the next term). After 10:00 a.m., I went with Calpurnia to meet with the people from the Balkani Wildlife Society at the Happy Bar and Grill. We had tea while we waited, then Desislava and Aleksander came. We exchanged information and offered to work with them. They gave us posters and stickers. We expected to go to a regular meeting later in the month on Wednesday. With luck, we would start a joint wolf survey this summer.

Then Alta joined us for lunch and the BWS folks decide to leave. Alta and Calpurnia had chicken Cordon-Bleu, while I had pileshche sheeschi (chicken shishkabobs) and fries. After a nice leisurely lunch, we went back to the Peace Corps. I talked to David Leigh and then waited for Kosta, as Calpurnia went to her interview, which ran over about 45 minutes.

Kosta and I went in and introduced ourselves to the committee. Venelina and the committee members introduced themselves: Filip, Judi, Hayden, Mina and an unknown blonde of indeterminate age. The first questions were simple clarifications, demonstrating to us that the committee had not read the proposal very well, then the bombs started appearing. Venelina said that they did not wish to fund a storefront. I had to ask for further details twice and get their rationalization. It seemed that the PC did not wish to get tangled with the laws for businesses in Bulgaria, so Kosta and I agreed to keep the storefront as a display only. Then there was a discussion on what a trade show was and why it was important for the craftsmen to attend went to them.

After the meeting, Kosta left and Calpurnia and I took Vulko down to the hotel to check in. But, first we stopped for drinks at a local cafe (two on every block remember). I had vodka and coke, Calpurnia had wine and Vulko had rakia or whiskey. On the way Vulko saw one of his students working in a dress shop and she joined us. We talked about the schools.

We went back to PC HQ and picked up Filip, Judi and Alta and went to a Chinese restaurant for dinner (another one; there were five within a two block area). We split lemon chicken, peanut chicken, and two salads. Not quite as good as the night before. Vulko, Judi and Filip went to the movie, "Castaway," then Alta, Calpurnia and I went back to the hotel to have a drink and talk.

Calpurnia and I invited Vulko to the internet cafe, but he had other plans, so we went. Then we picked up a few more groceries (and books from the Peace Corps library). Went back to the old mall and to the Oasis, where I got Harrison's Fully Choco granola (from England — with this, peanut butter, coke, tea and pizza, I could live in Bulgaria forever).

It was three months later, and now I was on the SPA committee, with Alta and Christine. We were getting ready to bus to Sofia for the presentations. First, however, I got a call from the TEFL (English) program; they begged that I accept another application for the Small Project Assistance (SPA) program (which funded volunteers projects, and showed them how to apply for grants), which they had left on their desks until after the deadline. I said I would try but he could always apply in the next round in November. They said no, this was his last chance, that he would leave in only six months, and we had a fatuous argument about whether he could apply later (of course, I was right, since he was not leaving until next July, and the mantle of arrogance fit perfectly on my broad shoulders). Then we packed and got ready for the trip to Sofia. Even getting to sleep before midnight.

Friday, the interview day for the candidates (always on a Friday, so we could work and travel on the rest of the weekend). We, the large committee, started at 8:30 and finished the new handbook requirements. I agreed to write a section on formatting and provide other suggestions to Jason. Then the interviews started. We were to only have seven, but it had blossomed to eleven, as people changed their minds and rushed to make appointments the night before. The new format was that one person asked questions for all of us and one person took notes. Each person had thirty minutes, with or without their colleagues, to answer questions and make their verbal presentation. Things went smoothly for the morning. Calpurnia brought us each a burger for lunch, which we ate in the dining room in the basement.

The afternoon ran into to problems with some of the presentations, especially Martin's, since it was late and missing things; one member of the committee recognized the text and compared it with his own application — an almost perfect example of plagiarism, even down to a fake bid with a fake letterhead. His application was waste-basketed.

Then we spent hours on Milli's project, which was essentially a duplicate of a project she had done the year before; after finally reading the first project application, we found even she had said it was identical, so she was denied. This had been a strange meeting; only four of eleven had been approved. Two of the disapproved should have been approved I suspected. Finally, about 8 p.m., we were finished. These two days had been state holidays. We had a salad for dinner. Then talked in one of the rooms.

Sane Days Or Coffee, Cigarettes and Vodka

Three months later, a whole day was spent on the remaining three wolf proposals. For Calpurnia it was a full day in the office. I tried to search the web for wolf grants. I actually got on for an hour before the crashes took their toll of sanity. Then I met with Angelar and Petko about the wolf survey schedule. Agreed to finish more grants, then finished writing up procedures for observations.

We worked on one wolf proposal and a few other things, then took the direct bus (Trans5) to Sofia for the next SPA meeting, arriving about 6:30. We checked into the youth hostel. Alta and Christine, and Martin, were already there. So we went out to eat at Murphy's Irish Bar. The next day everything was normal.

In Sofia, the afternoon was spent looking for bookstores. The large store next to the Lumiere cinema was disappointing. We did find some good books at unexpected stores. Then we went to the Balkani Wildlife Society for the Wednesday meeting. We talked to two young students for an hour, until Desislava was finished, then we talked to her for an hour about their and our projects. We agreed to work on two of their projects.

On the way back to the Hostel, we stopped in the new internet cafe for two hours. It was fast and cheap. At the Youth Hostel, we found that three guys had left their bags on other beds. We tried to go to sleep, but talked for an hour. The generator at the museum started across the street. Then the disco across other side of the street cranked up. About Three a.m., the guys staggered in and collapsed from a night of partying.

The next morning we learned from the hostess that they were Australians, touring eastern Europe, the new "Ugly Americans" (having taken the title from the Germans and Japanese). We were up early and left before anyone was awake. Had breakfast at Dunkin Donuts, which seemed to only attract Americans, and so was deserted except for us. Then we shopped for a few hours at the Oasis, getting the staples for the next few months, mostly pizza mixes, herbs, and tuna. Back at PC HQ, we picked out another seven books. At the bus, we got on, but start streaming sweat immediately. The buses were not air-conditioned. I bought a few cokes.

The bus trip was uneventful. In Troyan, we bought grapefruit and waited at the cafe. Then, took the bus to Aprilci. We unpacked and rested. Worked on biodiversity lecture.

Back in Aprilci, Vulko wanted to start the day by going to the cafe, which we did, going to Iva's cafe. There we saw Aleksander, or rather he saw us from his window in the Coop. He asked for help translating his letter to his Japanese pen pal Koko; I did. I said I wanted to see the library, which I had not seen since last September. So, Vulko accompanied us. It was open, which was a surprise. I asked for the hours and the two women said from Seven to Three weekdays, although I had gone twice the week about 10:00 and the building had been locked.

Vulko saw Rahil Koleva, head of the tourism school and they talked about the forum and a brochure. Calpurnia and I explored and each found a book to check out. The check out procedure was the same as renting a video — we wrote our name on a piece of paper with the name of the book. I asked how many books were checked out at any one time. The answer was zero.

The Telecenter Or *Gaming for Leva*

One local entrepreneur, Trifon, asked us to help him apply for American money for a computing center. He already owned a small 3-computer game center across the street from the Mayor's office and across from our apartment. His building had a disco in the basement and and a bank and wholesale soda outlet on the first floor. Most of the second floor was deserted offices. As it happened, we had just been told of a USAID initiative to put computer centers, called telecenters, in small mountain towns throughout Bulgaria. So, we spent many hours over coffee filling out the applications.

As it happened, the richest man in town, well, the village to the north, asked us to discuss an application with him. He sent a Mercedes for us and treated us to a light lunch in one of his restaurants. Then we visited the empty rooms where he wanted a Telecenter, and went back to his office at the cattle breeding station to discuss the mutual benefits of an agreement. As much as I like to be bribed. bought or coerced, I said that we had already completed an application and signed an agreement in Novo Celo. He was polite and suggested that he would have a better chance of success. We had to walk back to the village, as the car was not available.

We finished the paperwork for Trifon in the next several days and he carried it to Sofia by hand. He was certain that he would get the grant. For months, we watched Trifon and the masons build a concrete block wall to close in the wide hallway and expand the area for more computer desks. The work started slowly. Trifon decided to convert the janitor's closet across the hall into a toilet. He started tiling the walls first, a good sign. Then had to punch a hole in the concrete floor for the toilet drain; I never did see how it hooked up with the pipe.

I asked Trifon if they would convert the other janitor's storage area into an office for me. He agreed! That day the mason framed the door with metal bars and walled that in with a leftover sheet of wood and used another sheet for a sliding door. There was an electrical box in the area, so I would have electricity for a light and to charge the laptop, but there were no lights, windows, heater, furniture, or other amenities. I put a door on waste cans for a desk and stacked the junk along one wall.

Worked with Vulko at the Tourist Office on reorganizing his hard drive. Then after a normal lunch of peanut butter sandwiches, we took the bus to Troyan—Calpurnia to work on the internet and me to find the holy grail of cereals: Harrison's Fully Choco granola (it would be great even without the three kinds of chocolate pieces). Also, I went online for an hour and a half and got caught up.

Met Trifon in Troyan and he gave us a ride back home. He announced that he had received the grant. Then I went up and took photos of the remodeling of the now official Telecenter.

Thursday, worked in the Tourist Office, Translating map information into English and finishing grants for wolf research. Then, spent additional time with Trifon in the Telecenter. Internet was down while the walls were repaired and painted; waiting for the server table and hubs to arrive.

Friday, I met with Trifon and we went to Caprice cafe for coffee again. We talked about the possibility of a new factory in Vidima that would pay good wages. He had heard rumors and wanted me to find out if they were true. I said I would ask. Then we visited the diskotek, which had been being remodeled since May and was still torn apart. Apparently the bank loan had not been forthcoming (perhaps because the bank was on the floor above and they did not like chalga music). I wanted to get on the internet but now the room was crowded with kids playing Doom. Back home to work on my own laptop computer.

The following week, Calpurnia went to work and I went over to see if the internet center was working. It was, sort of — that was, I could look but not send email. Calpurnia came over and tried. All of our cards were now expended so that we could not use the internet in the apartment.

So, we started out to coffee with Vulko. I went to library with my letter. Calpurnia typed the German translation of the hiking routes. Talked to the Baba about having tea with her niece, who was visiting. Her niece spoke some English, so we agreed to meet at Noon at her apartment. Went to talk to Trifon and went on internet for a while. Trifon wanted to know if a new factory was coming to Aprilci; I said I would ask on the internet. Could not find anything, although the Vidima Co. was a subsidiary of American Standard. Other internet info was interesting. The AED had not yet bought the computers for the Telecenter and would only ship after 3-4 weeks — Trifon was surprised as he thought they would be arriving today — they would however arrange for a grand opening in September.

The next day, since I was already dirty from hiking early, I went over to the Telecenter to work with Trifon. Today we cleaned all of the windows and washed the floor. It took me several hours to scrap off all of the old notices and posters from the windows. In typical Bulgarian fashion, washing the floor consisted of taking a hose to the walls and floor and directing the water down the stairs. It made a nice waterfall on the stairs, then flowed out of the building down the front stairs, and onto the sidewalk and street. It looked really clean, except for the mess at the foot of the stairs. Then I checked email.

Thursday the 27th of August, it rained all night and all day, the first time since July. Vulko called at 9:00 and said he had a group of tourists in the office now. We went down and found out that the people were one Romanian, one PCV, and the rest from cities around Bulgaria. They were trying to make a tourist network to recommend each other's towns to tourists. We each gave a presentation on our projects, then broke into informal groups to talk about tourism and parks — the girl from Romania worked in the highest and newest Park in Romania. Then, suddenly they had to leave and drive for three hours to the next small town. With Vulko, we went to coffee, and he told us, offhand, that they had come in last night and slept in Aprilci. It did not seem to occur to anyone to tell us the previous night.

The Twins Fall

Tuesday, 11 September 2001, after starting the day at the cafe for an hour, we translated the final pieces for the map. At the cafe, people came and talked to us or Vulko — a good way to see people, since everyone was either drinking or serving coffee during their business meetings. After lunch we went to Troyan to meet with the mapmakers, who needed a final review. Vulko had hired a teacher to help, and we met her at the central plaza. We went over everything, checking all the train stations and catching another batch of errors or inconsistencies, but the map looked good.

About five we had tea and chocolates, then a secretary raced in and whispered to Mitko, who turned on the radio. He said excitedly in Bulgarian that the twins had collapsed (the towers were called "bliz-nazi" in Bulgarian, an odd word for twins). We listened to the radio describe two planes crashing into twin towers in NY — it seemed such an odd accident, as if the planes collided and then fell into the towers. Vulko suggested that we leave immediately.

We drove with Vulko back to Aprilci. We turned on the television but were interrupted by Bulgarian colleagues calling us and asking us if we were okay and what we thought of the terrorist acts. It was strange to see such destruction in NY, since all summer we had seem it in Macedonia, Serbia, Israel and Palestine. Calpurnia knew many people at the Pentagon and was upset. I noticed that Flight 11 was the one I took every two months to get from Boston to Oregon (through LA); how easy it was to be a victim these days, just be on the wrong flight at the wrong time.

I worried that next nuclear blasts would go off and the US would retaliate immediately and violently instead of referring the act to the international court. We were a stupid species, stupid in our devotion to abstract countries, stupid in our love for mobs and revenge, stupid in our personal decisions and vengeances (but then I was also a prime example). The television was dedicated to the terrorist acts, the first real invasion of American soil.

The next day, there was almost no mention of the tragedy on the local television. The Aprilci police came by and asked if we needed protection. We said, no thank you, we were okay. Trifon wondered if the Telecenter dedication in 2 days would be cancelled. We said no. We were sure everyone would come. We went to have coffee with Trifon at the Caprice cafe.

The next day, I went over to the Telecenter to work, where Trifon's father had finished painting the downstairs walls (after trying to put up new wallpaper, which was very lumpy). Trifon was putting up pictures, and I suggested that I make a series of photos showing the development of the Center. He liked the idea so I went back and spent two hours selecting, sizing, and printing two series of photos. Then we put them on the walls also. Iliana and the people from AED were there; they had brought a large American Flag, which we put on the ring outside with 3 Bulgarian Flags — so much for keeping a low profile after September 11th.

I told Iliana that the Ambassador was sick and could not travel to Aprilci (it was a social lie, to save face). I mentioned that the Peace Corps Director was also otherwise engaged and could not come, as promised (Social Lie number duh). Then I told her that I gave the invitations to Iurka and the park staff, but most of them were in a course and could not attend; she said she called Iurka. We exchanged information about other openings. No other Americans showed up; afraid of being in public I guessed.

The Grand Opening

Early on opening day, Calpurnia and I went over to the Telecenter to help with the last minute setup. The Tourism School had loaded three tables with delicious foods, including fried chicken fingers on toast points — a first for this town I thought. I took pictures, while Calpurnia, who was more socially adept, talked to the locals. Only a few of the AED people, Vulko, Calpurnia and I were dressed up; everyone else, including Trifon, was wearing *obiknoveno* (ordinary) garments. One of the mayor's pals, who started a new tourist bureau, walked around trying to sell their old, sad, poor maps for five Leva (they had no street names or details like ours had); what bad taste we thought.

At 10:00 a.m. the Opening began with words from Rahil, the head of the Tourism school. We were thanked by name for participating in the project since last November (it had been a lot of work, from paperwork to painting and sweeping, not to mention meetings and having to keep inspiring the young owner who kept threatening to emigrate to America and become a computer programmer). I took thirty photographs of the speeches and crowds. Trifon received many gifts from AED, including a clock and a box full of $2500 worth of internet coupons, which he was to give out over the next three months to humanitarian groups, such as doctors or teachers. The mayor spoke about 30 words, the minimum to avoid any kind of commitment, yet seem grateful for the project; he was a die-hard communist and resented the success of anyone getting Swiss or American help.

We overheard interesting comments about our English class. After the formal opening, everyone streamed upstairs and started to play with the computers or watch. We all broke up and worked the crowd, offering to help or explain. I talked with a few of Trifon's (mostly silent) partners and with some of the people from out of town. Calpurnia was buttonholed with the mayor and Nora (from AED); then I was grabbed, also. It seemed the mayor had asked Nora for help in teaching English to the municipality (which I assumed meant to only the city employees). We reminded him that we had taught English in the school for a year, and were still teaching an advanced conversational course to some interested people, including two of the city employees. I said that we did not have as much time now, but would be willing to help them get a real teacher, and maybe we would consider teaching another class. Calpurnia suggested that Closimir could teach them. The mayor's little reptilian eyes do not seem to open or close, but at least he was polite for the first time in thirteen months (of missed meetings).

Calpurnia and I availed ourselves of the food, which was very good, with syrene stuffed tomatoes, cookies, cucumbers, chicken fingers, and some ham things that we did not touch. The food had been prepared by the hotel-restaurant high school where we taught. We talked some more with Nora and Rahil, then shot another 25 photos.

New computers

Ciaran

Angelar came while I was working in the Tourist Office. I took him over to my new computer office (which was still filled with tools, cables, plaster, paint and computer parts). I showed him the web page. Then we went over the details of the survey. I understood that I would stay at Hizha Pleven from Wednesday to Saturday and then return through Severn Djendem. He showed me the trails on the map. So, I would start with Botev and survey the south slopes. The other rangers would be north and east. He had given up trying to have a ranger partner with me, since I was too slow and liked to work alone.

More computer work in the afternoon. Trifon asked me to meet him at 10, to manage the club, while he and his sister, who ran the internet club with him, went to meet the mayor about their rent and whether he wanted the city offices to be provided with internet.

After working on the web page for a few hours — so many photos, so much text — I walked over to the internet. There Trifon asked his sister to stay and for me to come with him to meet the mayor. The mayor of course was in Lovech. Trifon stalked in and out of the office three times while I waited in the hall. Then we met with the *Zamestnik* (vice) mayor in the mayor's office. Trifon talked about the web page and asked him to give me information about Aprilci. The zamkmet thanked me for all I was doing for Aprilci, yaddada yaddadata. I told him that I would put up the site in December. This was an odd meeting since the mayor was backing the new internet project funded by the Swiss and had betrayed his agreement with Trifon to reduce his rent so the city would get free internet.

Afterwards I tried talking with Trifon, but he was depressed about having to pay rent that was higher than anyone else renting a city building. So, I went back to work in the apartment, which was warmer. Calpurnia came up for lunch and we had leftover potato salad, with extra red peppers.

Then Dimitor called from the central square; they were here early for a site inspection (every site gets inspected once a year for professional and medical reasons). He had six cases of books for the library, which he, the driver, and I lugged up the stairs. Then we met about my job, which was strange since I was assigned to one city (Stokite) and met in another (Gabrovo), while working in the third without an office (Aprilci), thus resulting in higher telephone, travel, and print/copy expenses. Over tea and brownies we talked about Calpurnia's job, also, as well as teaching English, working with Balkani, the library, the internet center, and so on. I showed him the web site.

He and I went over to see the office, still cold and cluttered, then met with Trifon for a while. Fortunately, all the computers were in use by several kids each; unfortunately, all were playing games, and Dimitor knew that that should not happen on USAID computers. Finally, we went to the Tourist Office and talked with Vulko. Dimitor's attention was occupied by trying to make reservations for friends of his to stay in Aprilci, but we talked about tourist projects. He got to see the map and some of the brochures. He left around Three and we went back to work until Five.

Networking for the Village

I met with Trifon about software for the internet club; he wanted to have graphic and formatting programs. I suggested a few for web page creation, which we needed to finish for Aprilci. He informed me that city hall had relented and would let him install internet access, but they would not lower his rent. I again suggested that he charge them an amount just over his rent (but three times what others were paying).

I started working at Six a.m. because it was quiet, but also because the first person logged on grabbed the entire bandwidth, which made for a problem later on. I had finally put posters on the walls of my office, and Trifon had removed the old television set, stove, and tools. It was clean, but very cold, with no stove or heater, so I dressed like I was going to the mountains. The web pages were written in HTML, CGI, and a little Java to spice it up. Then, I prepared for class. Today it was abbreviations and acronyms; the business lessons had been finished, and the web page terms, also.

Off to the internet office at Six again. Decided to not to shop at the bazaar but Calpurnia wanted tomatoes, so we went after all. More vendors showed up now that the snow has almost all melted. Many were getting aggressive now, pushing things at shoppers and following them around bawling lowers prices at each step. For lunch we bought some kebabche and fried potatoes. Good lunch, spicy but greasy; so vowed never to eat it again. Later, we went for a long walk to Zla Reka (evil river). Stopped in the new restaurant there and had tea. Walked back. Entertainment in Aprilci was so inexpensive.

At the office at Six, I was locked out until 8:30 — suspected the mayor wanted revenge for some imagined slight. Then, did more computer work at home to finish the web site and prepare to turn it over to the Bulgarian crew. Vulko had recommended the guy who maintained the Tourist Association Site. Work, work, work.

I got up at Seven and went to my office next to the internet club. Then waited for Vulko at 9, but he called to say his father was ill and he must take him to the hospital first (I thought he said cataracts of the eyes). We left late, and went to the hospital first and dropped him off.

Early to the office the next day, but the building was locked again. I went back and fixed toast and tea, then found it open at Eight. Maybe it was a new schedule. I sent email to the volunteers about the wolf project. Then back at the home office, Georgiu called and said the wolf survey would be next week. So, back to the internet office to send new emails.

Then I prepared the (almost finished) brochure and put it all to a zip disk. Vulko picked us up around noon and we drove to Troyan to drop off Rahil, the head of the Tourist School. Then, on to Lovech. There, Vulko met with another Tourist Office and we waited. Then we found the ad agency, with only one stop for directions. We presented them with the brochure files.

The next day, internet had problems, so there was no mail. Talked to Trifon about a computer for the library; he was selling his old computers, but said he could not take less than 600 Leva for the least. I said that I had 200 leftover from a grant and I could add 200 of my own money; I asked if he could donate L200. The silence. How eloquent. The discussion faded away.

More work with Vulko about the craftsmen. We signed the agreement for new furniture and paid out 880 Leva to produce the displays.

Met with Trifon about the Aprilci web page all morning. He had not yet had the mayor sign the order to permit use of aprilci.bg but I suggested that we link the pages, so ours would be in English and German and his would be in Bulgarian — the problem was that the German translator knew no English, so we had to translate into Bulgarian first. Interviewed Veshen about his art for the Craftsmen and Artists Association. Took photos of his art. Made changes to the whole web site. Especially the colors for vlinks and alinks, which I learned must now be put in style sheets.

Spent all morning making small changes to the Aprilci web page, especially my Bulgarian titles. Met with Veshen to proof the photos. For lunch, Calpurnia and I collaborated on a soybean casserole, but it was not cooked so we put it back in the oven, which only heated the back part, so the food had to be rotated. How will I pass all this specific knowledge to the next tenant?

Aprilci was dreary and cold. Even my office was so cold I had to wear my winter coat. Was still searching for wolf information and funding, as well as for the occasional job opening. Started to post my resume to the "Monster board" but the system went down, so I had coffee with Trifon. He was the only Bulgarian I know who got up after fifteen minutes and had to go back to work, but then there were a lot of kids in the Telecenter, so who knew what they would do if he were gone for an hour or two.

Modeling Wolves

The next week, I bicycled into the Park to look for tracks and signs. I found a new trail that wound west towards Vets, but did not have time to take it then. Back by 3 p.m. It only took an hour to bike back from the Park to Aprilci—it was all downhill.

At the apartment, took a shower and read for a while, before starting to fill out the latest forms for grants or equipment for schools or the park. Television news reported new terrorism in Africa. America was out of the news, now, or old news. Someone's tragedy was always someone else's news, I supposed.

The last day of summer I thought. Worked on a model for wolves in Bulgaria. I could not get the equation quite right—should have paid more attention in calculus, but that was 35 years ago anyway. So, I made a model using the spreadsheet program and put a different equation on each line. That worked surprising well, so I expanded the model for different conditions and scenarios. All the scenarios had wolves being extirpated by 2006 or earlier if hunting was kept up. Only the one with one out of four wolves having an average of eight pups allowed the population to increase with hunting. I thought that that was unlikely, alas. With the low rate (one out of six having three pups), the wolves would be gone by 2003, mostly due to hunting. In fact, without hunting, that rate could slowly increase the population at half a percent per year.

On Monday, Calpurnia went with Vulko to pick up the finished map. I worked on the computer. She came back with 2000 unfolded maps—the company had no folding machine, so they must be folded by hand. I folded one, and she folded ten. Vulko sold three right away for five Leva each. We had never discussed selling them, much less a price, but he was using the same price as the Remark Tourist map that came out last spring (with just an outline map of Aprilci, and with no streets or names). Time for a vodka.

The following Monday I worked on ecology articles. Also for *Sofia Echo*, one on hunting and one on the UN. But, Brendan asked for one on terrorism and NATO. Called Albert for PC permission, but he said I could not write on political issues. Called Nikolai about projects for the park. Not much to write about when one was only writing about writing.

Nikolai called and said the appointment with Georgiu Stanchev and Dr. Russinov was at 10:00 on Wednesday. I reminded him that even with the 5:30 bus I could not get to the museum until after 11:00, so he changed the meeting to 10:30 and said they would be there when I get there. Why not 11 or 11:30 I said, but he was asking about directions. I gave up.

Of course, there was the English Class. Despite the fact that we had seen Svetla and then Closimir, on the street, neither of them came so it was just the four of us, as usual. I noticed a trend: If we started with Bulgarian questions, then the class became a Bulgarian class for us. If we started with Aleksander's correspondence or Andrei's vocabulary list it became an English class for them. Sometimes, it was both. We all lit cigarettes, in self-defense.

On Friday, I sized photos for Calpurnia to send. Wrapped packages of dolls to various friends in America. Took all morning to wrap and address packages, then mail them at the Post office. The post office was so slow, like they could not work while being watched. The head was there but thankfully did not wait on us (he usually tried to cheat us by making us pay special rates). Instead the doctor's mother waited on us. She made us go to the package window and took the four packages. Then she moved back to the stamp window to look up rates, but since they were posted on the wall by the other window, she had to walk back. Then she went back again to get the stamps. Then she had trouble weighing them because Calpurnia's was just over a kilo and she could not figure out how much to charge. Finally she just asked if we could come back in an hour, which we did. Everything was finished by then and she presented the bills to us, about 25 Leva for four boxes.

After finishing my article on wolves in Bulgaria, I sent copies to Albert and the editor of the magazine (by logging on at home, a rarity when it worked — the telephone lines were so old and bad).

The next Wednesday, I met with Angelar and went over my schedule for the next six weeks. He seemed confused by having that much planned ahead. He suggested I go out with Boleslav next week, but I said that I had to finish the web page for the craftsmen, which was true since I could not find a Bulgarian volunteer to do it. The rest of the day was spent expanding the interview to every unforeseen question on wolves or terrorism.

Christine called and said someone was ringing her doorbell and she was panicking. Calpurnia remembered that tonight was Halloween, and then Christine remembered that she had told everyone in her classes at school about this American holiday the last of October. She shouted through the door and one of her students answered. We stayed on the phone while she gave them chocolate (her own candy bars no doubt). I was glad we had not mentioned it to anyone here. Another bizarre frustrating month ended.

The first day of November. I spent the entire day writing out Bulgarian questions and answers. While I was at it I made up word lists for animals, plants and geological and geographical terms. But, being Tuesday, we had a class from Five to Seven, in the Center restaurant. We had decided to start with real lessons, rather as the center point, and tonight was pronouns, which they were having trouble with. But, after we described the English use, they described the Bulgarian use. It was an interesting contrast because it explained many of our mistakes in both languages.

Breakfast today was even bigger, with fried potatoes and hard salami. The web page unfortunately blew up with the new photos, which were too large to be reduced. So, I gave up for a few hours and walked north of Aprilci up into the hills. There was a small settlement there with four houses. The only wildlife were crows and chickadees. Not even any deer prints.

Lunch was the wonderful hot potato salad, with a Danish roll for desert. We had now purchased all the good desserts in town, so it was back to peanuts and crackers.

After lunch the librarian came by with the car and we loaded the donated books from America; I followed it over on foot and took pictures of them being cataloged. Then I mailed the PC materials. I saw Kosta and Petya and invited them to look at the web page. So, we made changes to their page. Afterwards I copied parts of the wolf book and studied it a bit. Dinner was the renowned shopska salata, soup, and sandwiches. The evening was preparation for tomorrow morning, when Angelar would whisk me away to the mountains to look for wolves.

Wolf print

Angelar called at Seven to tell me that the survey was canceled because of snow — the roads from Sofia were too icy for the scientists to travel. It was reset for next Friday. I reminded him that I was in Sofia next Friday for the SPA meeting and would have to leave from Sofia with the scientists.

After a leisurely breakfast of tea and mekitsas (with sugar and cinnamon), I cleaned up my desk and then went to the internet cafe to send email to the various parts of the survey. My office was freezing, then the battery on the computer ran out. The internet club was empty so I used one of their computers. Vulko had been doing the Tourist Office budget and roped Calpurnia into translating; the hardest words were American words that had Bulgarian endings, such as donora (donors) or detaili (details). It looked like it would snow here soon.

Then I read mail and worked on articles. I should be working on the wolf article, but instead I worked on my newspaper editorial on economics in Bulgaria. Dinner was pizzettas and cola, with a few cookies for dessert. I went back to reading, thus closed out the weekend.

Monday, I worked all day on application for Balkani Wildlife. Fleshed out a research proposal and request for GPS and laptop computer. Piddled around on the web page, while waiting for the artists to make up their minds.

Tuesday, worked all day on SPA, reviewing nine applications, including three repeats. Wrote up recommendations. Got almost everything printed (before the printer ran out of ink again) and put it in folders for Sofia. This quarterly punishment I applied for because Filip said it would look good on my resume, to be on a granting committee (at least my expenses were paid).

I wrote letters and suggestions to the SPA Committee, including the first five issues of "Ask Miss Spa," a way to resolve rumors and misinformation about the program. I also tried to suggest ways that we could start being more objective, e.g., if Noser did not get a grant, than neither should the Chipmunk, Belle or Goofy (all nicknames in code of course).

Before noon I checked on Calpurnia, and she and Vulko wanted to have coffee so we went to the new Vegetable Cafe (where the old vegetable store was — it turned out that both this and the new bridge store were owned by the same person, who wanted to diversify and capture the early morning coffee crowd). We talked about grammar then Calpurnia and I bought bread for lunch.

Just after lunch, we were visited by the PC doctor, who had us fill out questionnaires. Every year they made a village visit to see if we were still alive. This was it, and we were. He left after an hour to drive to Sevlievo to see Deborah; then he had about seven more volunteers to see in the following three days. The sun had not shined lately, but the snow had stopped. Afternoon was computer work. Sad. More letters on expenses, more violence in the news. What would Gandhi do?

Slept late, then worked on the model for a few hours. Went for a walk, and noticed that *all* of the stores were open, and a lot of people were also walking around, although there was nowhere else to go. It was still snowing. For dinner, Calpurnia cooked chicken and potatoes, in a pan, with virtually all of our seasonings on it, especially rosemary. The chicken, weighing over a pound, had been bought frozen in the market, the day before. I made a cornbread stuffed pumpkin. The snow stopped about 3 p.m. In the evening we listened to music.

Better Times

The next day was a national holiday, so more of the shops were closed than were yesterday. After a few hours of work another proposal, which was almost finished, now, I went on a long walk above the city; many dogs, no wolves. The day was quite sunny but cold.

I made a pizza for lunch (mostly to avoid leftovers). Then worked on Bulgarian grammar for a few hours before class. The class met at the Gameyski restaurant, which was noisy and smoky. I suggested we move to the new cafe, which used to be a vegetable store. We did, but after an hour a noisy group came in there. It was the *same* people from the restaurant. I suggested they were rude and loud, but Andrei said they were his friends — they just drank too much and talked too loud. When they started smoking we decided to quit the class, after two and a half hours (because everyone had vacation for the next month, they wanted more classes, instead of less, so we were doomed).

After a walk around Aprilci — since we were the only Americans not in Paris this week, we felt we had to let our community know that we were here, working on their web pages and grants — I made a pizza late, but it was almost good. I could not get the dough right, and I had to use kashkaval instead of mozzarella, etc., etc., etc.

The weekly mail came, so we had an English *Newsweek*, a Bulgarian *Eco Planeta*, and a *Sofia Echo*. My friends in Oregon had sent a *Mad* magazine and a tape of Saturday Night Live. The rest of the evening was spent reading and watching.

Monday, all day was spent finding and revising the bids for the project. Then making Calpurnia's changes to the text, and printing out the whole works. Called Venelina about the Wednesday meeting. Called Desislava about the Wednesday night meeting, and Vraya about the Thursday morning meeting. Put everything to disk. Called Georgiu about the wolf survey this Friday, but he was not there. Packed survey clothes to take to Sofia.

While Calpurnia walked to the bazaar, I worked in my office (the windowless, heatless, furnitureless office in the Telecenter that I rented for ten Leva a month — a good deal despite the shortcomings). I had to wrap up the wolf survey results and ship them to Dimetar. Then finished the 2001 observation log and sent it to Georgiu. So I worked until noon.

Calpurnia returned with kebabche, so we had leftover mashed potatoes with them. Afternoon was more computer work and a walk. For dinner I made a pizza to celebrate not being eaten by wolves and bears. Then more computer work. The *Echo* published another ecological thought experiment article, so I worked on new ones.

Ciaran

Kebabche girls

I met with Vulko to go over the final changes to the brochure. Dr. Karanova came over and helped with the translation to Bulgarian. I asked Vulko to make the final approval, when the final draft came. He agreed reluctantly. Vulko canceled his trip to Sofia and we worked all day on the brochure, rewriting and retranslating the text. I was amazed that he was so dedicated about this. That afternoon we rushed to Troyan to check the translation. Then back to Aprilci, where he and Calpurnia filled out the forms for a new volunteer (describing the projects), while I taught the English class.

Vulko drove us to Pleven and dropped off his father for an eye operation. But, the operation was canceled so we picked him up again and went to Lovech to work on the brochure. At last I got to proof the entire brochure and alas found many errors, which they were willing to fix. We finally left and wound our way back.

It snowed all night but did not stick; it started again about Six and stuck; it was like being in a cloud. Made homemade donuts and tea. Then worked on articles and correspondence. Searched internet for job information for an hour. After the usual jaunt to the bazaar, made potato salad and kebabche for lunch. After doing another laundry, it was too cold to hang them outside, so we hung them inside by the heater. The day's work was to make final changes to the text for the Craftsmen brochure, then start the one for the Tourist Office. So, I made a dummy. I had taken over 2500 photos now in less than a year. Many were worthless, a few were memorable.

Worked on the brochure for the Tourist Bureau. Told Vulko I wanted to rent a bike so I could take pictures of the entrance and churches. He said he would drive, but we only went to one church. His camera was better, so I let him take the pictures. I preferred using mine to set up the model for the brochure, then he could take the final pictures for printing. This worked out well on the last brochure. Assembled text for the brochure. Translated all English text into German, using the German Assistant program. Needed to have Bulchru or Mariya check it before print. Started a wash, then worked on my notes, wildlife reports, photographs, and anything else that required me to sit in from of a computer tapping and listening to B. B. King. Worked on photos for the Aprilci brochure.

Desislava said the Balkani grant money was in the bank, so we could order the receiver and computer for the wolf project. Went on walk by the hospital and by the old factories. Again, nothing but birds, although horses cows and sheep were in evidence everywhere. Packed for the trip to see the Minister and work for Balkani on the wolf trapping program. Wrote up notes for meeting with the Minister, Mr. Boshinov.

The next day, Meril and Milli called and said they were going to Sofia at 10, so we skipped the bus and waited. They were late but Meril drove at 190 km/hr so it took less than two hours to get to the center, even with a stop for gas. As a result, we were in town fifteen minutes early, but they dropped us off by the university, so we had to walk for twenty minutes, with full backpacks and a small bag. We checked into the "expensive hotel" Maya, which costs $30 a night for a double room with bath down the hall.

We made the rounds at the Peace Corps, meeting with Georgiu Pashov about a volunteer for Aprilci, then with Dimitar about our final work and meetings, then with Venelina about the SPA and PCPP grants. Finally, we went to the Irish Harp for potato wedges, a chicken sandwich, and a drink. That evening we called Petko and Desislava at Balkani and confirmed the meeting. It rained wildly.

Supporting Players for the Erotic Adventures of C

Some of the volunteers had ambitions to find mates or spouses in the pool of available Bulgarian women and men. Carrol was not one of them; he always said how perfect his mate, now in England, was.

For some reason, alas, he was always getting beaten up or robbed in secret gay bars (Gayness was not tolerated very well in Bulgaria, and American gays seemed slow to learn that they could not be proud of their persuasion and still be safe.)

The last thing we heard was that he had asked the State Department to bar his friend, Ivan, from getting to the US. It seemed that Ivan had used Carrol ruthlessly as a source of income and gifts. He had also used Carrol's plush Sofia apartment—not all volunteers lived on the level of the common people—as a center for prostitution. Carrol had found out by accident while trolling for new talent himself, as he was directed to his own apartment for a good time. After a high-profile and high-decibel confrontation, Carrol had thrown his friend's toys, clothes, and gifts onto the street.

Then, after—[Censured by the Peace Corps Secret Standards Division. Readers do not need to be told the details of oral, genital, and anal possibilities of physical expression, nor the trouble that often accompanies it—recensored by President G. Walnut Shrub and the Red States Moral Majority Whip Task Force]

Trapped in Mountain Snow

Tsonyo was right on time at 6:30 in an extremely old Lada. We drove to Vidima and met Boleslav at the cafe, where we all had tea and croissants (and since every letter in Bulgarian was pronounced, it was pronounced krow-e-sants). Everyone complained about the weather which was snowing lightly and which was supposed to continue until Friday. We left then for the base at the water plant. Once there, they said, "good observations" and headed up the ridge. I went directly to the hizha. The trail was covered in snow and leaves, so footing was precarious. It took just under an hour, and I was sweating despite the snow; I was really getting weary of lugging backpacks everywhere.

Finally, I reached the hizha. No one was there, so I had tea, then checked in to the room for three days. It was the same room, number 7, that I always got. I suspected that most of the rooms were empty and unused (and they kept them locked so I could not peek). There was a small electric heater, which I turned off before it burnt down the building. I left immediately for the mountain, but it was so cold, with a northerly wind, that I turned back and put on all the long underwear and an extra wool cap. As I went up the woods, I could see many stories in tracks. For instance, a wild swine has crossed the trail about a mile up, and a fox followed it for a while before veering back on the trail. A hundred meters further, a roe deer crossed and the fox followed her also for a while. The fox certainly kept to the trail otherwise.

Suddenly I was out of the forest, but in a cloud of blowing snow. The path wound through many rock crags, then split a field. It wandered horizontally along the slope west for several kilometers. I came to a first frozen stream below a waterfall. I started to cross it but the ice was slippery; I tried to cross on snow but there was ice underneath. I looked down the mountain and saw nothing but grey rock and snow. I was able to find small rough areas where ice had not covered the tips.

I *fell* on the other side, but was able to catch a boulder, before going over the edge. I pulled myself up, carefully, slowly, and started again. The trail felt good, except for the pain of course. Had I fallen a meter earlier, I would have slid and bounced to the bottom of the mountain. I passed three more frozen streams and waterfalls, without mishap. Then the trail turned south and straight up the mountain. The wind was at my back, which helped going uphill. My lungs were starting to feel frozen. Visibility was worse now.

Then I was on the level and then going downhill, then uphill. I could not see the mountain. I knew it was to my left, from seeing it on a clear day. There were some trail poles but they were leading down again, and I knew it had to be wrong, so I turned west and started up what I thought was the mountain base, but now the wind was cutting through my two caps, one with a face mask, which was now solid ice from my breath, slobber and mucus. I huddled behind a post and repositioned the caps. My watch said it was almost 1:00. If I went to the top, then I would need shelter for the night. If there was none I was screwed, so I turned back and followed my rapidly-filling footprints. I virtually ran down the slope slipping and sliding to get out of the wind. I lost the prints, but found the trail — well, a trail. But, I crossed the streams carefully. After an hour or so I was below the wind and the snow was falling off. Then I was below the clouds and could see Aprilci and the ridges. I took a few pictures, but the camera was frozen, so I was not sure if I would get anything.

On the horizontal trail again, I stopped behind a rock and had a few peanuts. My lungs and throat hurt. I considered that I was getting too old to do this kind of thing. But, I lay back and looked at the curtains of clouds blowing over.

I saw wolf prints that were now covering my tracks —

I had been followed. But, I did not see how I could have passed the wolf. The prints were relatively small and could have been a female or yearling. She seemed certain I was stupid enough to die and leave her my body for food. I was stupid enough, of course, to climb mountains in a blizzard to finish a survey, just relatively lucky today.

Now I was also able to see the scenery, which was spectacular. I walked out to a huge outcropping and lay down on the snowy grasses and watched clouds. The sun was actually shining on Aprilci only, so I took another photo. I walked back on the real trail, noticing that I had been two meters above it on the way out. Then in the outcroppings, I rested again. It was after three and I had to be careful to return in the light, although I did remember the flashlight this time. In the woods I rested one more time on a large fallen tree, Beech of course. Looking back with the binoculars, I thought I saw movement in the trees, wondering if it was the wolf — perhaps she thought I was wounded and about to volunteer to become carrion. Good odds, I felt, but not today, as it was all downhill from here.

I reached the hizha after four and immediately had water, tea, and coke. No one was there; only the three employees painting the kitchen. The hot water machine was broken so they put a pot on the wood stove, which heated the large dining room. From that room, I could see part of my trail under the clouds. The mountain was still hidden. At 5:00 p.m. I went to room 7 and crawled into the sleeping bag with long underwear on.

Despite my intention to leave by 7:00, I was still asleep. But, I went downstairs for tea and croissant and was out the door by 8:00. The sky was clear and the sun was peeking over the ridge. As I repeated the first leg of the trip, through the woods, I notice that the wolf had followed me back towards the hizha yesterday. It was sunny, but with a cold breeze. Through the crags and into the field, I decided to change my direction to go west first. I saw that there was a trail going straight up the closest mountain, so I decide to take it, and then cross over to the ridge trail to Mount Botev.

After an hour of going straight up, through rock slides and in snow, I realized it was a bad decision. Unfortunately, going down looked far more dangerous than continuing up. So, I continued up. At the first sub-peak, there was a cable stretching all the way up, fastened every two meters or so with iron posts. This made it easier to climb, but my hands started freezing to the posts.

I had to stop, rest standing.

Hiking down

As I got higher, the wind increased and the snow started blowing. I could never see the peak, only the nearest sub-peak. I accidentally surprised a mouse back into a hole. Then I noticed that there were a lot of mouse tracks into holes. No wolf prints, so only hawks and eagles would be threats. It was hard to breathe; my heart was racing, so I slowed down to a crawl. Sometimes the rocks were so steep I had to leave the cable and work my way around; other times I could pull myself up with the cable, then detach the frozen gloves.

Finally I was at the peak. To the west was another peak, Ambaritsa I thought, so I walked in that direction for a while, scanning the area with binoculars. Then I turned back and looked at Botev, which was slightly higher. The walking was easy now. The wind was in gusts. When it stopped I lay down on the snow and had a few peanuts. I can see the Sredna Gora mountain range, which paralleled the Stara Planina (Old Mountains). That range was dark, while these were coated with snow. At the top here there was about seven centimeters of snow left from blowing. The trail was well-marked. Soon, I come upon prints of a hare. Shortly afterwards the prints of two foxes following. The foxes veered off after the hare but returned and seemed to be headed for Botev. I stopped and took photos in all directions. Before I got to Botev, the trail dipped a few hundred meters into a pass. I could see the trail posts leading to the south; then I found some footprints from yesterday, my own, from the boot pattern. Botev had been in clouds, but these blew off as I watched. The wind had picked up. I saw chamois prints in the pass.

I decided to climb Botev again. Again the wind was at my back but it was cold and I was getting tired. It was afternoon, maybe one o'clock (my watch seemed to have frozen). I started the final ascent. What I thought was an easy trail from a distance was only an eroded gully. Since it had less snow, I climbed the gully, stopping three or four or five times to curl up and rest partially out of the wind. Finally, I was on the peak.

I thought I saw a tan chamois on the next ridge over but there was too much blowing snow and I could not locate it with the binoculars. I looked around the peak, then walked around it. There were five buildings next to the two radio towers, which looked exactly like ICBM missiles (doubtless on purpose, since it was a military installation for over forty years). I saw no signs of activity. The buildings were closed, even the one that looked like a dorm or hizha. I walked around, but the wind and blowing snow were bitter. It was difficult to see and my tracks were already obliterated. I stumbled into the wind. Suddenly I realized that my right hand was frozen to my cap and the fingers could not be moved. I tore the hand off from the cap and rammed it in my pocket. Gradually, as I tried to race down the slope, the fingers thawed, little one first. Again I was racing to get out of the blowing snow.

Back in the pass, I took the route from yesterday. There was no wind in the pass, so I walked slowly. I saw movement on the slope under the peak. Through the binoculars I located a female chamois (black instead of tan). She saw me and started to run up the slope. I watched for a while then walked briskly down slope. When I was lower than she, she stopped, doubtless calculating that I could never catch her from below. Shortly I came to a table rock in the sun and stretched out. I watched her through the glasses. She grazed for a while, then I lost her. She had been rolling in the snow and got up. Then grazed some more on the grasses. I had a few peanuts, then took some snow off the grasses by me and swallowed it for moisture. I made whistling noises, but she possibly could not see me on the rock or hear the noises (the wind was from the north again, so it would not reach her).

After a good rest, I walked down the trail and through the cuts through the ridges. On the horizontal trail I could see that the wolf had followed my trip back yesterday, also. Every so often was fresh scat. I found one more set of chamois prints that went directly up the slope. Could not identify sex. There were also mouse prints on the trail, fresh, and one continued for almost two hundred meters, quite a long way for a mouse. At one of the waterfalls, I lost my balance on the ice and pulled a tendon. I didn't fall, but now it was uncomfortable to walk or climb. Back through the crags and into the forest, the trees were rimed with snow and ice and all were white. In the forest it was calmer. I rested one last time on the downed beech, cleaning snow off my jeans and boots. The sun was setting.

I limped the last slope down to the hizha. It was about 4:30 so I called Calpurnia to see what was up (it was our anniversary); no answer. I went back to the bar and had cold water and a coke. I hung my coat and sweater, and as many clothes as I could modestly remove, in front of the stove. Then Dimitor and three rangers from Troyan came in the door. Rex, the giant German Shepherd rescue dog was inside and Mike, who was Dimitor's rescue dog, barked at each other through the glass windows. Dimitor said Boleslav was waiting for me at the water plant. I paid for one night and went up to pack.

Then Dimitor slogged down with me, so I could not figure out if he was babysitting the rangers or babysitting me. My leg got worse on the way down, until I was hobbling like an old man at the base. Boleslav was not there so we played with the dog and compared observations. He had seen only tracks, as had the other rangers, before they holed up before Noon yesterday. Then Boleslav came driving up with another ranger I did not recognize and all of us got in the small 4WD Lada. Boleslav had seen two chamois and was quite happy. I related my sightings.

Dimitor & Mike

He dropped me off at the apartment, after the others, so it was 6:30. I told him I could not work tomorrow because I would not be able to walk, which was true; but, I also wanted to save what was left of my body for the wolf survey. No Calpurnia, but I looked again and saw her working in the office. We talked to Vulko and then went out for a real Bulgarian anniversary dinner, soup, fries, and kebabche (what else *was* there?). Going back to the apartment, the vegetable vendor stopped us and asked for help with her heater. It was a Japanese heat pump with instructions in English. So, we read the instructions and turned it on heat — it had been on cool all summer, but the place was freezing now. We suggested she leave it on over night. She gave us three grapefruit.

Lost Beautiful Night

The following Friday, I did more computer work all morning. Lunch was peanut butter sandwiches and cola, how American. I went to the bus at 1:00 but found it was not there until 2:30, so came back and worked on the introduction to a proposal.

At 2:30 I caught the bus to Vidima and then started to walk to Mandrata, where the night blind was. Made notes and photos on the way. I was in the snow now, but it was rotten and made walking hard. The higher I climbed the deeper the snow got. I have been trying to express in writing how long these hikes took. I supposed if I added ellipses to each sentence, it would be more expressive but more awkward, like this: As I was walking . . . . I had to dodge old snow caps over branches . . . . the walking was tough . . . . it was getting colder . . . . I shivered . . . .

Then, I saw my first wolf print of the day. It could not have been too old. I followed it until in branched off down the hill; I stayed on the trail. . . . . An hour later, near dusk I saw someone hiking with a dog, ahead of me. I hailed them; they paused. I waved my arms, but they both moved quickly uphill. Perplexed by this behavior, I did not hurry to catch up, just walked normally towards where they left the trail. There, where I saw them I found fresh bear tracks leading uphill (these were brown bears, like American Grizzlies), one small set, one large. I searched my memory, wondering if it could had been a bear I rudely waved and shouted greetings at. Probably a female with her cub, not a dog following her. I was glad I did not run towards them, but also glad I did not run away from them. I measured the large print, and found that it was about the length of my size eleven foot, with hiking boots, but wider. I took many photos of the prints, since they were so clear. I sang praises to the bear clan the entire time.

As I kept walking up the trail, which had a switchback that took it on a line to intercept the bears, I entered a cloud, then the dark pine forest. I was getting nervous, and then found a wolf track coming towards me — that meant he had turned off the trail when he heard me coming. I hoped the bear did too. Maybe they were both waiting to eat me; maybe they would fight it out to see who got to eat me, the tasty, potato-filled clod. The road lengthened relatively far ahead of me, extended by anxiety and the unknown darkness.

Then I finally came out of the forest and found a small hut, roofless but with old concrete walls. One corner had little snow in it. I thought it might be fortifiable, but freezing, so I decided to press on for the night blind. In the snow, I lost the trail but keep going up. My feet sank into snow and I fell into the eroded holes several times. I mentally figured out how far back the roofless hut was. Then

297

through one last long woods and I was on the ridge. It was all white and I could not find the trail under the smooth snow, but I could see the trees towards the blind. I walked out of the cloud. It was a half moon. The mountains were in higher clouds, the valleys in lower clouds. Only this ridge was free of clouds. It was quite beautiful and I was quite relieved. Now I could see death coming if it was reaching for me! I stood for a while and regarded the moon. I turned around and looked back at the woods.

As I walked along there was another wolf track that I seemed to be backtracking. Perhaps the same one as below. I measured the tracks and photographed them. I looked again at the moonlit landscape.

What I Saw

I stopped. glad to be there; drank it in.

It was perfectly quiet and peaceful. It was beautiful.

I howled several times, although the formal howling survey had been completed for a while. I walked slowly towards the game trail and the waterhole. I lost the wolf tracks for a while, but found them circling the waterhole. There were also wild pig tracks closer to the waterhole.

I went up the hill to the night blind. My legs were wobbly. I kicked open the wooden door and made myself at home, eating a few peanuts (the universal food) and drinking some water. The trip had taken almost six hours. I sat up for an hour and observed but no one was moving. I took a nap but had muscle cramps, so did some more observing. The moon was so bright I could use regular binoculars. The owl came. Back to lie down, more cramps. These were lower leg muscles that I had to pound with a board until they stopped spasming. So, I just observed until about 1 a.m. No movement at all; no visitors, no hunters, no prey, just silence. Then putting the sleeping bag on the floor and wrapping my pants for a pillow, I slept a little. I heard footsteps in the snow outside, and leapt up, but it was a Karakachan horse left loose for the winter. I suspected the others were over towards the cheese building across the ridge.

Up at six, I cleaned and repaired the one glass window. Packed the pack, and left. It was before dawn but bright, so I started back down.

On the way I measured the footprints again, and found new ones either crossing my trail or following it. The last was a bear that had followed my prints for several hundred meters before turning down slope, perhaps when he heard me coming just now. The snow was frozen and easier to walk on.

I walked all the way to Aprilci. The whole trip back took 5 hours. My legs were sore so I had a shower with everything on, snow, mud, rocks, and clothing. At the computer I downloaded the camera, and admired the many good photos, notes and measurements.

Humor does not Translate — Bulgarian Stories

Sitting with Petar and Andrei in class, the next afternoon, we asked them to tell a joke. Petar started with a joke about the Titanic: Two Bulgarians had tickets to sail on the Titanic. Waiting, they decided to have a few drinks at a bar nearby. They got drunk and missed the boat. Petar and Andrei started laughing heartily, but stopped when they noticed we were looking at them with a quizzical expression. We were still waiting for the punchline. Petar tried to explain why it was funny. I thought we missed the juxtaposition that causes laughter. Andrei offered another joke: A Bulgarian opened a restaurant in a foreign country, but no Bulgarians ate there, even though they were desperate for home food — because they did not want him to be more successful than they were. Again our expressions returned while they were laughing. Again they tried to explain the humor.

Andrei suggested that we tell a joke. Calpurnia could not remember any so I told two, but they did not laugh; actually, neither did Calpurnia. Here was one of the jokes: A businessman decided to take off the afternoon and see what he could find for amusement. This was New York and a lot was going on. He walked past a few offices and businesses, but didn't want to shop or talk. Then he saw a sign for a humorist's convention. Perfect. He went into the theater and stood in the back. A man had just come on stage. He looked at the audience, looked at his feet, and then said "143." The audience roared with laughter. While they were still sputtering, the man walked offstage and another went to the podium. He immediately said loudly, "91!" Again, the audience roared with laughter. After a few more numbers, the businessman thought, "hell, I could do that." So, he went to the stage, looked at the audience, and said, "200." The silence was deafening. Not a single twitter. So, he slunk off the stage and went to the back of the auditorium. Speaking to himself, he asked, "What happened? Nobody laughed." A man standing nearby sighed, and said to him, "You told it wrong."

At 6:30 we went to Aleksander's house for dinner (his mother actually cooked it). Andrei was there. We ate in a small room with a large bookcase and fireplace. Aleksander had a small boombox for playing his country music. On the side table there were six bottles of beer, three bottles of wine, and one bottle of rakia. On the table were deviled eggs in white sauce, a salad with lettuce and cucumbers, and a plate of peanuts. We started by drinking a toast with rakia, then poured wine. Andrei took the bottle of rakia and the rest of us split the wine. After an hour and a half, bread came. Then the main course, which was persianeed rabbit, a pepper stuffed with beans and cabbage stuffed with beans. His mother had killed the rabbit that morning. This was a very traditional Bulgarian meal.

We ate and talked for four hours. Aleksander and Andrei regaled us with tales of the Mayor and his behavior, such as being drunk at City Council meetings, or the Vice mayor and his behavior, such as being drunk, driving, fleeing the police, crashing into a house near the Polyclinic, getting beaten by the police, and then screaming, "I am the Vice Mayor," or maybe "Mayor of Vice" until the police apologized and let him go home (only in Bulgaria?).

Andrei told us some traditional Bulgarian stories. Here was the best: A stork and his three sons were flying across the Atlantic. It was stormy and the young storks were not as strong as the father. The eldest son asked if he could rest on his father's back, because otherwise he could not make it, and he promised to care for his father when he was old; the father answered that he knew the son would not care for him and he must fly on his own. After a while the eldest son fell into the sea. Then, the second son asked if he could rest on his father for a while, making the same promise to care for him when he was old, but again the father did not trust him and would not carry him. The second son fell into the sea. After more hours the youngest son, said he was tired and must rest, but he told his father that he would not care for him when he was old, but he would care for his young when he had them. The father thought and let the youngest son rest on him. Before they reached land the father failed and fell into the sea, but the youngest made it to land.

This day in Sophia was dedicated to reviewing all of the SPA projects, compiling the questions and making preliminary findings. We were locked in the room all day. Some projects were woefully incomplete; others were partially incomplete. The ones that were complete most likely would get funded.

Dinner was at the new Bulgarian Perfect restaurant by the new tram station. We had salads and split a Bulgarian pizza, which usually had corn or ham or both. Went back to our rooms and watch CNN, which was dreary reporting on violence. Calpurnia and I talked about another of Andrei's stories from class about aging and wisdom; this one was about a society who decided that the elderly were redundant so they made them all go live together in a ghetto. After a few years there was a poor harvest and all the young people ate the seed crop as well. Then they scoured everywhere to get seeds to plant in spring, but couldn't find any. Finally, one man went to his old father and asked how they could find seeds. The father said he knew, but would they reconsider letting them live at home. The young man asked where; the father said, find ant hills and look for seeds in the bottom of them. So, the people were saved for another year, but the elderly did not receive any respect.

The English class was only review now. At first we arranged for the party next week, to say goodbye to our friends here; we listed twenty five people to invite to the Center restaurant; then we tried to talk down the price with the owner; he did not budge, so we changed the shopska salad to a zelen salad (the same thing but without green peppers), thus keeping the tab to under five Leva per person. Then, mostly we talked about Bulgarian customs and myths.

We were getting quite a collection of Bulgarian sayings: (1) Friendship is friendship, but cheese is cheese (someone has to buy the food); (2) He is missing his first seven years (as an insult to describe someone rude and without manners); and (3) The husband is honey until noon.

We also had a few new jokes: (1) Where was the place of the son-in-law? Between the window and the ficus (to keep the plant warm in winter). (2) A husband wanted to kill his wife; he told his friend that he was going to beat her, but the friend said to use poisonous mushrooms. A week later the friend asked if the wife was dead; the husband said yes. The friend asked how. The husband said he had to beat her to because she wouldn't eat the mushrooms.

Then Andrei told us about his other wife. We said what? Yes, this was his spiritual wife; he like many Bulgarians married young and then later found someone closer to his spirit. So, we asked what about the Australian widow that he was searching for? He said his first wife had given permission for him to marry there, as long as she got to immigrate there later. Thus ended the class.

Pan & Aleksander

Signs of Wildness

Lost in the Forest Lost in the Mountains

At 8:00 I left for Troyan and there caught the 9:45 bus to Chiflik. The buses were on time. In Chiflik I took the city bus to the large public pool, the basin, at the edge of town. From the Chiflik basin I walked south towards the Hizha Xaideshka Pesha. After passing an unnamed and abandoned hizha (which I felt compelled to explore since it might have been the one I wanted), I entered the Kozya Stena reserve. It took two hours to reach the hizha, which was at the end of the road and hidden under the beech and pine trees. There I walked up the private drive and through the two buildings until I saw a sign that pointed to the reserve path.

I followed the sign for the east trail along the edge of the reserve. But, after several hundred yards the trail disappeared in the stream. By following the map I figured that I would go uphill and parallel the stream. The rise must have been ninety degrees and it took me an hour to reach the ridge after many rest stops to catch my breath. I followed an old landslide but used the trees and shrubs for handholds. I must have been out of shape.

From the ridge it got easier for a few hundred yards, but then the ridge went straight up the mountain. Each time I thought I was near the top another new ridge started. Then it started to rain; I was not wearing raingear, but a shirt and vest. I got wet. After the fifth sequence of rough climbing I was on a small grassy knoll (maybe half a football field). I lay down on a hummock of grass in the drizzle. It was so comfortable. With my heavy backpack under my head, I started to doze off thinking that I might die if I had to climb for another hour. This seemed to be a good place to die; the rain cooled me and the breeze was light. There were sounds only of birds. I was at peace. I watched the clouds put on the masks of animals and plants, felt the rain, thought dying here might not be so bad. I dozed a little. Judging by the wetness of my coat, I had rested for twenty minutes. Then I thought if I could not make it by sundown I would have to find a place to stay dry and to sleep. The first five steps were slightly downhill, then I was climbing again.

On the next ridge I had to climb a sheer rock face. It was easier than the landslide or grass, but I realized that I could not turn back because the handholds were so difficult; also, my pack unbalanced me. I started to fall again but grabbed an old pine limb (with splinters); the force of my grip tore off my sports watch and broke it—the second one since February. I saw some very good caves, just the right size for bears. I peeked into one but saw no evidence of habitation; besides, how would the bear get there? The top of the ridge became a bare stone needle, so I had to climb along the side, grateful for the few small pines. I swung from pine to pine like Tarzan, also grateful for my careful attention to E. R. Burrough's novels. I thought each ridge was the peak because I could see light behind the pines, but I was fooled each time.

After two more huge ridges I finally reached the top, which was a permanent mountain meadow. It was the highest peak around so I could see the valley and other peaks. There was no evidence of a path or hizha. I started to walk along the sides but the grasses and junipers were so high, and it was still raining, that I was soaked to the waist, and getting soaked above the waist. Only my hat kept my shoulders dry. I walked down a little to look for shelter. It was after Four and I had been climbing for over six hours. I kept picking my way down the south side. Then I saw a break in the peaks and looked for a rock overhang. After a short rest, I scanned the slopes. In the near distance I saw what looked like a path, so I climbed down a trough between the junipers. Then, I saw the three small painted bars that marked paths in the park (each path had a different color combination). I turned east, knowing that the hizha had to be there but knowing also that if I was wrong I would have to walk to the next hizha twenty miles further on the trail. The trail was fairly comfortable although it followed the ridges. After forty five minutes I turned a corner and there was the hizha, on the skyline just below a peak.

I met two girls on the front walk and introduced myself and asked in flawless Bulgarian where Dimitur might be. They looked confused and asked in their languages if I spoke French or English. I replied in English and they were happy, because they were two volunteers for the trail restoration project. One was from Belgium, the other was from England. Inside I met Dimitur again. They were working on introductions, so I had a glass of water and waited. I sat with my back to the fire and could feel the clothes drying.

After their introductions, I was asked to introduce myself and talk about my projects, which I did. A few had questions about the wolf populations but Aleksander, freshly returned from Romania, had the most.

After dinner, which was rice, mushrooms and mayonnaise (nothing not white foods I guessed), Dimitur, Petko and I talked about wolves in the park. The count of 375 had been killed in the year 2000, according to the hunters and foresters. I agreed to work on a survey quite similar to my own but in the Rhodope Mountains. I went to bed early; the mattress was comfortable but the pillow was filled with fungus and dead rats.

After a breakfast of Musli, milk, and oats (nothing not white), we all went out to paint reserve signs. We finished about 12:30 but it took two hours to walk back to the hizha for lunch. Lunch was cold spaghetti and kashkaval cheese and mayonnaise (the off-white diet was being eaten now).

After lunch I went for a walk with the botanist from Sofia, Kalina, who was working on her Magisters degree in the park — she wanted to work for the park. She identified many plants that I did not recognize; the ones I did, I learned the Bulgarian names for.

I helped to wash and cut more mushrooms for dinner. Dimitur had picked about twenty pounds of oyster mushrooms from the forest floor while everyone was painting. I kept the mushrooms under water until the pale worms emerged then pulled them off; Dimitur said why bother, they were extra good protein, so I just washed them. After dinner, we all played cards and made conversations. Not much near dark, we were all asleep. The next day we went west on the trails and painted the old faded signs on rocks. That night I realized that everything we ate was white. Subtle, but bleached.

After a brief breakfast of oats and tea, I started down the mountain. The first part was through the beech forest, then the trail dived directly downhill, with some pines. I heard a fox bark as I passed a hollow. I barked back; after I walked a hundred meters, he barked again. Then nothing but birds. It took only an hour to get to Hizha Haydushka Pesen. The forest was the beautiful beech, solid beech, of the smallest reserve, Kazya Stena. I hiked for another hour downhill on the road to get to the bus at the Chiflik basin. At the bus stop I had a coke and waited for forty minutes. Then the bus arrived, turned around and departed to Troyan, and Aprilci.

At 1:00, I was at the apartment. Calpurnia was there and gave me some bread. Then we went shopping for her 51st birthday, getting only a small blouse, ice cream, and a rental movie. The evening was very relaxed. July 4th (her birthday) was not celebrated here. I made pizza with pineapple and salami, then recounted my mild white adventures.

I had planned a few days at the night blind, looking for wolves. These summer days and nights were perfect for observation and walking. I asked Calpurnia to come with me and alternate work and sleep. We got up early, but went over to the internet cafe to work for a few hours. We had asked Vulko if he would drive us as far as the base of the mountain, but he left town for a meeting. I asked Trifon if he would but he disappeared before he answered. I called Andrei to tell him we would be late for his post-dryer party; I hinted that we would like to be picked up or dropped off, but he was busy. So, finally we called a taxi to drive us through Zla Reka and Vidima, to Vets, up to the base of the mountain. He was fast but it cost eight

Leva for the thirty minute drive (which we had walked last spring in three hours).

We started hiking just before 1 o'clock, reaching the first stop, Hizha Pleven, on the first ridge. Over a coke, we asked the proprietor to point out the trail to Mandrata. He did, and said follow the yellow poles, and it should take only two hours to get there. Knowing it got dark at 6:20, we set a good pace. After half an hour we lost the poles. How, I did not know. I scouted in every direction but saw nothing but rock and boulders, no signs. I looked at the relief map and thought we should cut directly into the beech forest over the ridge.

We did and climbed straight downhill. After an hour I admitted this might be a mistake, as there was no trail. Then I suggested that we head south to where the trail should be. After another hour, still no trail. But we had crossed a stream and were heading up the next ridge. There we found we were lost. So, now, I looked at the map, again, and saw where we might have missed the trail. Rather than back track for hours, we kept going straight up to the next ridge. From there, after another hour, we could see a familiar ridge with binoculars. At this point we went due south up the ridge to try to intersect the trail, which should have been heading towards us. After a while we found a wildlife trail and followed it. Then, we found some horse manure on it so we know someone had been there within a year. The trail led through the deep beech woods and up past another ridge. Finally near the top of the fourth ridge, we saw the roof of a springhouse that I recognized. We climbed up and got water. The sun had set but it was still giving reflected light enough. The trail led to Mandrata, the old cheese factory and then to the night blind overlooking a game trail and a watering hole.

Finally, we were there. We rearranged the old single metal springed bed and put pieces of wood on it, then a table cloth and a sleeping bag, in the last of the light.

We took turns all night watching the water hole with the new night scope (made in Russia, sold in Wal-marts everywhere). At first it kept getting darker and darker. No animals. Then the moon came up. Then the owls started hooing and making other sounds. Then another night bird started. Over the night, an elk came by and bellowed (it was their mating season), then a wild pig grunted close by. I thought there was an entire herd over the hill. A ground squirrel ran up to the cabin, illuminated by the night scope, which I finally get focused and working. Calpurnia had been dozing. About Five I got in the sleeping bag to keep warm and fell asleep until 6:30 — just when the deer seemed to have arrived.

In the light I walked down to the watering hole and counted footprints, about ten surni (roe deer), one red deer (elk), two wild swine, and about nine horses (which I had seen the evening before on their way to a quieter pasture for the night).

We spent an hour cleaning the cabin and fitting the table cloth over the old windows. I suspect we removed forty pounds of dirt and old leaves. Then we hung up the candles and matches and left. We tried to find the real trail and did immediately — it had been around us the entire time but it skirted the ridges at some distance. So we walked back and it only took two hours. At the Hizha we had another coke and went down the trail to the water plant. On the way, we meet Angelar, Boleslav, and Milko, repairing the fence along the trail (which has to be a ninety degree slope). We exchanged stories and went down to the water plant. After a twenty-minute wait the cab returned and carried us back to Aprilci.

Black peak

I took a long walk towards Black Peak. Saw no signs of anything but birds. But, at least the sun came out for an hour. Later, I walked back and worked on the internet for a few hours, sending out applications for funds and answering various Peace Corps people about the old grants. As I was leaving with bread for lunch, a funeral went by: Led by the priest in black, with his black homburg in his hand, a green Russian jeep followed. Hanging out the back, literally, was an uncovered coffin, with flowers around the deceased. The widow, comforted by four friends, walked behind, crying softly. All in black. Then more friends walked by in twos and fours, talking quietly. They walked through town and then up the hill to the cemetery.

Along the sidewalks the rest of us continued to buy bread and vegetables. I lost sight of them, but, since I visited the cemetery regularly, I knew that they would park outside the gates and six men would lift the box into the ground. Then dirt, then the flowers, then the church bells. No other music; I thought the New Orleans style would have been more fun, but this was a different culture, with different approaches.

Invisible Wolves Or *Chasing Shadows*

It was late March and we took the 5:30 bus to Sofia. At 10:30 we walked to Jo's apartment and talked to her for an hour. Then we went to lunch at an old Communist hangout, the restaurant without a name, where the western press used to meet the state leaders incognito. After lunch we hurried to the PC office and then the internet cafe. At 17:30 we walked to the address of the Balkani Wildlife Society. The meeting was late but interesting. I gave a brief presentation of projects and observations. We decided to work on a joint project, a wolf survey in Western Bulgaria.

The next day, I met with Venelina and then Svetla, about projects. At 3:00 I took the trolley to the west bus station — my first since July 2000. It was crammed with people and I had trouble spotting the station, but I got the right stop. I flagged down the bus to Pernik as I thought it was leaving; it was empty, and we had a spirited conversation about where I wanted to go, until the driver stopped at Sector 1, where I should had gone anyway. I apologized sheepishly and he got an ice cream cone for himself as the bus filled up.

At Pernik, I finally found a phone card and a phone that worked, and called Desislava. It was after Five and she drove to the train station to pick me up. We shopped for vegetables and fruits for the weekend. I paid for most since I suspected the others would cover the rest of the food and transport.

At her apartment, I read the society report on wolves for 2001, and made changes and suggestions. Then I read a few magazines on wolves and watch a lynx video. Jivko came and introduced himself. Then Danyel, then Hristo, her husband, then her mother-in-law and two-year-old son. Then suddenly, we were ready. We all crowded into a Daihatsu jeep and drove out to the edge of the city to visit the Karakachan sheep dogs, who were noisy in the dark; noisy and threatening — only the puppies were friendly. Then we drove to the village of Sadovik, where Hristo's family had an old unlived-in farmhouse. Jivko did not stay. So, Danyel and I each get a room upstairs and the family stayed downstairs. Dinner was about ten and was soup and salad, with cheese-filled, grilled worst. I had the salad. Bed by midnight. The sleeping bag was hot.

Breakfast was toast with organic blackberry jam and water. Only Desislava, Danyel and I would be doing the survey. We drove north for an hour to a small village on a dead end road. We parked in a field near a building, another unlived-in place, that the society was renting for the telemetry project. In most of these villages in western Bulgaria, half the houses were abandoned as people moved to the cities for jobs. We walked uphill.

307

Ciaran

The forest had all been cut about thirty years ago and replanted in pine. The pine made ribbons around the mountains, which were rock and open at the top, with grass and shrublands below. There were many old roads and trails. It had rained so that there were many prints. Foxes had left their scat on rocks and old bottles so that we would know who they were. Wolves had left theirs along the roads and at intersections, smelly messages of presence also. Dogs, jackals, and other mammals had left prints and dung around. Surprisingly it was a good area for mammals. I had become expert at sighting scat (and the "scatman" nickname was born).

We made a giant circle until we saw all the possible trap sites. The road continued quite a way, surprisingly since it seemed only to be used for harvest; there were not any real evidences of herding here. Along the way, we ate rosehips and wild cranberries. They had beechnuts, but I was afraid of allergies. We collected scat, running out of bags and using kleenex wrappers and napkins. Then we walked back to the jeep and drove back to the house. We had bread and apples, then started dinner, which was not ready until after Nine. The scat would be taken to Sofia to the lab, to see who ate whom. We talked until after dark. Our schedule really did revolve around the sun.

The next day, after yogurt and toast, we drove due west towards the Yugoslav border, and a range of hills. This area had not been investigated before. There were quite a lot fewer tracks and scat. The walk was long, but every time we found scat, we found blackberries (I suggested the connection was real— everyone, including us humans, ate the berries and then shit three meters away). So, we cut large branches of berries and ate them like popsicles as we walked. Then we went directly up the highest local peak (about 1400 meters). There we had our first and only rest break of the two days, eating peanuts and cookies and looking at Yugoslavia and Bulgaria in the distances.

We walked back to the village, and stopped in a cafe for tea. The owner said he saw a wolf that morning about Eight, just the time we were going the other direction out of town. The wolf was following us! He had been so frightened he went to a gypsy baba and had a spell cast for him. We raced out and found a few tracks on top of ours. We measured and photographed the tracks. We had been outsmarted; and we were truly bummed. Then we walked back to the house and had a snack of soup and melons.

That afternoon, they dropped Danyel and me off at the bus station and we took the bus to Sofia, then the tram north; he got off but I rode to the end and checked into the youth hostel. Called Calpurnia and had a burger. At the hostel the news was on so I watched it before going to bed; everyone was silent. After I was almost asleep a discussion started about how bad America's response would be. I slept instead.

Monday morning, I stopped at the Oasis for teas and cans of tuna, then went to the PC HQ to meet Svetla and Boiko. Gathered up some books and vitamins; bought a few souvenirs, got a burger — it was first day of school and every kid in the universe was having a burger — and got to the bus an hour early. I had a couple cokes and started reading Faust, which I had started after Troyan, in the bus cafe. Calpurnia was waiting for me in Aprilci, so we had the new tuna for dinner. Never thought of tuna fish as a rare delicacy, but there it was. Then, we read all the mail and newspapers.

Speaking for Wolves

We were in Sofia to meet with Desislava and present our proposals to the Ministry of the Environment. After a quick tea, we went back to PC HQ to talk with Tsvere and Eliza about our paperwork. Then talked to Dimitar who had decided to cancel his attendance at the meeting. We walked to the Sheraton and met Desislava. We sat for more tea at the Perfect cafe, a new cafe near the underground church, and discussed our strategy, which dovetailed quite well. Desislava was smart and motivated, and knew virtually all the work being done in Bulgaria.

Before 11:00 a.m. we arrived at the Ministry. We were admitted and told the guards that we had an appointment. They checked our credentials and asked us to wait at the base of the stairs. The Minister, in charge of nature preserves, Mr. Boshinov, glided down the long spiral staircase to meet us and we walked upstairs to a large meeting room. He was an elderly, kind, and slightly confused man with a doctorate in forest engineering. He was confused as to why we were there, since he told us that they had had an inventory of wolves since 1997 and good knowledge of them before that.

I talked first, praising Bulgaria's efforts and nature, and suggesting that the country was poised to become the first nation to create a complete biological inventory of its resources, as well as a science-based monitoring of wolves. He immediately said there was no money, but repeated that they knew how many wolves lived in the country. I suggested that the knowledge was hearsay and described the procedures used by the forestry units to count wolves (e.g., by asking their friends to guess — the higher the number, the easier it was to kill more).

He asked what we were doing.

I described our work in the park, and Desislava described what Balkani had been doing. We described the scientific methods we used for surveys. He politely asked us to send him reports that they might consider, and we agreed to do so. We went around again about what kind of research and monitoring were needed, linking it to both the Ministry and Park obligations to monitor wildlife and to the European Union requirement to do so. He smiled a lot, but his body language suggested that he could not do anything, even if he thought it would be a good idea. We exchanged pleasantries about the weather and city. We thanked him for his time about ten minutes before the meeting had to conclude.

Afterwards, we stopped for tea again at the Central market, an old market, like the one in Providence, Rhode Island, that had been refurbished and had many small permanent vendors of foods and goods. We agreed that we had to try the meeting, and that we would send reports, but suspected that nothing at all would come of it. We talked about having a big Balkan-wide wolf meeting in December. Desislava called Krum and arranged for us to meet at the Balkani office at 5:00 to go to work on the field trip. This would be Calpurnia's first trip west.

We had a quick sandwich at the Harp and spent the rest of the afternoon at PC HQ, going through forms and paperwork. At 4:30, we walked to the Balkani office — it started to rain. We crossed the major boulevards, dodging cars that were running red lights through pedestrian crossings; truly, Sofia was a city for cars, which drove everywhere, ignoring signals, and parked on sidewalks, forcing people to walk in the streets. Must be worse than even Florida or France.

At the office, we met with the guys who were working on the Dam Protest. Saw a book on birds of Vitosha Park, then left with Desislava, Krum, and Kamen. We stopped at the yard where the Karakachan dogs were kept and bred. The pups were even larger now. One of the dogs had given birth to three new pups, that we watched but did not touch. Philip, Hristo and Jivko's father had been making traps for stone martens, so we inspected the traps, playing with them and talking to him about other of his projects (he also made traditional Bulgarian masks for celebrations).

At Pernik, Desislava left us at the market and we bought groceries, including cheeses, three loaves of bread, peanuts, pasta, tomatoes, cereal, yogurt, spices, salami, and tea. Of course, dog food, which was two dozen chicken heads. We drove to Breznik and got a few more things, such as eggs and more bread. Finally, about eight we arrived at the house in Sadovik. The dog Arul was waiting and happy. Calpurnia cooked omelettes and I made a few cheese sandwiches. After eating, we played with the dog, then with our new GPS devices and walky talkies. We talked for a few hours about the project and went to sleep.

Breakfast was cereal and bread. We drove near Arul mountain (after which the dog was named) and divided into two teams. Kamen decided Calpurnia and I were too old and slow, so he went alone. Calpurnia and I went with Krum, who drove to another town two ridges away. After hiking uphill for three hours, we met on a ridge; Kamen was there before us loafing in the sunny grass. We ate our cheese sandwiches and went over the maps. There did no seem to be any wolf signs in this area. We saw hawks, buzzards, frogs, then signs from roe deer and fox.

We split up again and went around the ridges. We got lost, although the GPS told us where we needed to go. Not finding a trail we crossed a rock ridge and talus slope, finally following a stream to a trail. We had seen the village two ridges away, but once in the forest, got lost again and off the trail. I took a few photographs and made notes about the signs we did notice. No wolves, though.

Krum Boils Traps

We arrived back at the jeep; Kamen was waiting. So, we drove back to the village of Sadovik. There we prepared the traps by boiling them with willow shoots; these were the traps made in Bulgaria from the Romanian model of a trap sold in Texas, thus saving a few thousand dollars. The clothes, stakes, chains, and bags were also boiled. I started making sauce and pasta.

Again, we ate before 10:00 — this must be a new trend. The dinner was okay but the Bulgarian pasta, instead of being individual rotilli, formed a glutinous mass that had to be cut into cubes, a new food or art form, perhaps. I also made dinner for Arul, who was not happy that he had not accompanied us on this trip. But, he was a good dog and played after dinner. It started to rain again. We went over the maps again. Krum and Kamen had received an anonymous love letter from one of the girls in the village and went to the bar to check it out. Calpurnia and I went to sleep in the same sleeping bag.

Saturday, breakfast was leftovers and cereal. We made sandwiches for lunch. Then we drove to Paramunska Mountain, which was a new area where Desislava had heard that a wolf print was sighted the week before. As one group, we walked out of another small village (with maybe twenty people living there), carrying our binoculars conspicuously — we had told all the villagers that we were a bird-watching society. We saw more deer and fox signs, as well as squirrel and hare prints. We went from rocky barrens to new forest to old beech forest. This was a forestry unit, so there were many trails and some wood seemed to be harvested by the coppice method. It looked like only posts or rails had been cut.

We walked to the end of the trail and then cut through the forest to find another trail back. The forest was very sweet and easy to walk through. Then we found our way back. The GPS units had already stopped working due to weak batteries. The guys used the walky-talkies, although they only seemed to work for in-sight situations; they were supposed to have a chip that allows real distance operation.

After two, we were back to the vehicle, and we drove to Breznik for soup and salad. This was the first time we had ever eaten out during this project, so we were surprised, but the guys wanted to have their favorite soup. Then we drove to Pernik and dropped off the jeep at a parking lot near an abandoned factory. This was necessary because this car had been kidnapped twice already for ransom (and it was paid twice!); the jeep was actually registered as a handicapped vehicle since it was given to the society by a handicapped person (to save the society on taxes).

Then we walked to a bus stop and waited for a bus to Sofia. We took the bus, which let us off at the western bus station. Then we had a take a tram to the center. Kamen went with us, since he had to catch another bus to his apartment. It started raining and we got soaked. We went back to the Maya Hotel and checked in. I thought we were again the only people in this hotel, so we had our choice of rooms. Then we went shopping for spices and cereal (for ourselves). And again to the Harp for a sandwich (this was either a rut or a good habit, but at least we do not risk bad food or noisy, dirty or uncomfortable rooms like the youth hostel or Hotel Niki). I read and Calpurnia slept.

We were up early to pack on Sunday morning. We walked to catch the 8:20 bus to Aprilci—the only direct bus to Aprilci from about anywhere. The bus wound around the country and we arrived just after 1:00 p.m. We dropped off the bags and bought yogurt and vegetables. Of course we met many people and explained where we had been over numerous teas. I made a pizza and salad for lunch, which we repeated for dinner also. Then we unpacked, did a laundry, and rested. Then, we downloaded the photos and worked on our computers, roughing out a report for the Ministry, as well as several articles for Swedish and American conferences.

Strangja & Strangja

After a month of missed communications and misunderstandings, I made arrangements to start a wolf survey in the far east, in the Strangja Park, a former military reservation, now a state park. Calpurnia had decided to work half time on my projects. We prepared for the trip, but had to prepare for class, first. Only Aleksander showed up for class, with the Canadian girl, since he was teaching her Bulgarian. I called Desislava and Petko to cement the times for a western wolf survey, but they were getting ready to leave immediately for Sofia. They said that they would only be there for a few days and then leave Friday for the Easter Holiday. They could not pick us up in Pernik or Breznev. So, we arranged to meet them on the Ninth in Sofia to meet with the Minister.

I had forgotten that it was the Easter holiday, but we decided to start that Friday anyway. So, we took the afternoon bus to Gabrovo, which was on the way east to Strangja. Stayed at the communal apartment (which was Mary's old apartment, but with all of Filip and Kim's appliances in it—they had all left in June 2001). Walked around the town. Had a pizza at Tempo. Then went to a movie at the new theater. Sent email to Betty Lou and John in Strangja asking them for help in the Park (for my wolf survey there). Spent quiet evening at apartment—the first that either Joe or Seth had not crashed there at the same time. Planned the trip to Strangja.

The next morning we found that buses to Burgas were not running due to the six-day holiday, except for one at 17:10. So, we took the bus to Kazanluk. From Kazanluk, we could get a train to Burgas, but only after 2.5 hours, so we read at a cafe, after buying a coke and coffee.

The train got into Burgas by 14:30, when we had a quick lunch and caught another bus to Nessebur, on the coast. Finding that there were no more buses leaving south for the villages near the park that day, we walked all the way into town, past two reject hotels and found the Hotel St. Stefan, where we looked first, then decided to stay the night. An internet cafe was nearby; having no replies from anyone, I sent more email. We took showers and found a restaurant. We were the only customers and the food had been thawed. We ate it, but were not thrilled. We walked around the city, which was built over Thracian, Greek, and Roman ruins, and took photographs.

Since we had no email from our contacts the next day either, we decided to stay a day. We walked over the city the entire day. Lunch was fast sea food at the local docks, cold, greasy, but cheap and fresh. We walked onto the shore part of town and looked around, then back. We walked down to the shore. The beach was mostly rock and shell.

We decided to eat dinner in our hotel, since theirs was the

best menu we had seen all day. There was a lot of construction, for hotels, magazines, houses, and restaurants. Many places were empty or closed up. It was clearly not the summer season (we knew, since prices were half the published prices). Our room, the best we had ever had in Bulgaria, was about $24). Salads were shopska and potato. I had salmon in parchment with rice pilaf and roasted potatoes. Calpurnia had Mackerel shishkabob, also with rice and potatoes. The food, at last, was excellent. We walked after dinner.

As we were relaxing in the room about midnight, we heard a priest in the street. He was standing in front of the St. Stefan church, across the street, reciting mass to about 50 people with candles. We watched from the darkened room. It was of course Easter here and this was good Friday for the Bulgarian Orthodox Church (a break-away from the Greek Orthodox Church). Still no answers by email or phone from any colleagues on the wolf survey. We debated whether to continue alone or wait for the contacts to answer us; no doubt everyone was on vacation.

After another day of loafing, we took the 10 a.m. bus down to Burgas and met Alta for lunch. She had been finishing her project on ecotourism and was pleased for a break; she was also been getting ready to visit her family in America for a few weeks. We met at McDonald's but were too tired to walk anywhere else and settled for the McFood, which if not minimally healthy was a known quantity and quality. She walked us to the bus to Tsarevo. We got on immediately but had to wait twenty minutes until the bus filled. There were not many buses during the holidays. We decided to go to Tsarevo first because it was larger than Malko Turnovo. Both were in the Strangja Park. The bus there hugged the coast, and we saw evidence of many holiday hotels, most not working. The coast was beautiful; I could not feel bad, since it was more wild without people. This area had been a military reservation until 1989, so it was the least developed area in the country.

At Malko Turnovo, a crowd of people was waiting to go back to Burgas, but this was the last bus and the driver had to argue with people that they could not go until the next day, which was also a holiday (St. Georgi Day, which this year followed Easter weekend and Labor day, which was May 1st). We walked around the town but it was a small town and did not seem to have much in the way of restaurants or hotels, although there were at least eight cafes. Finally, after walking to the sea, we huffed up hill and found one of the hotels in the old Tourist Guide. It was being remodeled, but he offered us an apartment for 60 Leva or a room for 40 Leva. We took the room and then walked around. Then we walked to the Park on the point; it had no beach but the rocks were interesting and we could sit in the sun. It had been sunny for the past two days, a welcome change from the mountains, where it had rained or snowed since November.

We ate in the local pizza restaurant, DaVinci, and had pizza and salad. It was warm and the crust was decent. We walked some more and returned and tried to plan the trip to Malko Turnovo. We found that the bus was not going there at all on Sunday — the hotel owner had called the bus master for us. So, we tried to plan a way back to Gabrovo or Sevlievo, but could not figure how to get back to Aprilci. The fastest way, through Sofia, was also the longest, but at least the buses to the capital would run on Sunday, we were told. So, we went to an internet café and looked for answers. There were none, so we decided to take a bus to Sofia the next day. An uncommon project and a surprise vacation.

Monday, we walked to the bus. We had reservations but only six other people showed up. Usually these buses were full or had standing room only. The trip was uneventful and five hours later we were in Aprilci, fixing spaghetti and washing clothes, and working on the laptop computers.

Thought Experiments — Why Bulgaria is Wealthy

I was surprised when the *Sofia Echo* agreed to let me publish a monthly column on thought experiments. I sketched out a few based on questions that people had asked me or on facts about Bulgaria herself, such as the declining population, as a result of people leaving the country and the remaining people having fewer children. The first one was very interesting, but after the first, my column was moved into another editorial page; the only constant then was my title for each one, beginning "Ecological Thought Experiments."

Thought experiments were easy to frame and understand, really. Einstein and Infield, in their book *The Evolution of Physics*, suggest that knowledge of laws of nature can be gained through the contemplation of idealized experiments created by thought, Gedanke-Experiment. For example, to address the equality of inertial and gravitational masses (that was, how the problem of general relativity was connected with gravitation), Einstein imagined an elevator at the top of an incredibly high building, and then imagined what research would be done in this local moving environment. Such experiments might seem "fantastic" he said, but they might help us understand what we were trying to understand.

Although ecology was orders of magnitude more complex than physical systems, perhaps we could imagine and use such experiments to help us understand what was happening with our complex environment in Bulgaria, which was composed of many interlocking ecological systems. Thought experiments could let us examine things and change them without really modifying or destroying the unique systems under study, whether political, economic, social, or ecological. The kind of thought experiments that we could develop might include:

• How is wealth measured? Many Bulgarians had two or three or four homes, from their efforts, from inheritance, and from privatization. In these homes, they had electronics and furniture; around the homes, gardens, cars, sheep, forests, and wild nature. Most were educated and healthy. How could they complain about being poor? Very few had enough money. Perhaps money was not the best measure of wealth.

• What would happen if we let the number of people decrease? Bulgaria has a small and declining population; instead of treating this as a problem, we could consider it an advantage. With ecological planning, Bulgaria could become the first balanced nation on earth, by linking its population to its carrying capacity and wild environment.

• What should we do with things out of place, trash, for instance? This is a major problem for any country with ambitions to be a tourist destination. There seemed to be no consciousness about cleaning up common or public places, perhaps due to the influence of old communist rules.

• Why could not Bulgarians live longer? The key to health may be in eating less and participating in healthy forms of play, rather than in replacing organs and fixing things that let us continue our original dangerous behavior. Smoking, for example, was a major health problem in Bulgaria. Cigarettes are cheap.

• Could we imagine the country without trees? Let us imagine that forestry and conservation both had failed, and that Bulgaria had no forests and was without trees in general. Both state practices and privatization may have unforeseen consequences. Of course, Greece was still a popular tourist destination, without its original forests.

• Could we create a wilderness Inventory? Few if any countries had one of these. Bulgaria could be the first green country. Bulgaria has a beautiful environment. Due to its unique history it is blessed with what many other countries are trying to restore.

• What should be done with domestic animals? A large problem that cities are trying to solve by killing all the stray dogs in a city. An education campaign would solve this problem fairly quickly. Dogs and cats are perfect companion animals for people (as our ancestors recognized when they domesticated wolves), especially in cities, where living can seem impersonal. But, they must be cared for by us and their reproduction must be limited.

• Could Bulgaria survive without an army and navy?

Imagining giving over all military power, except for local police or national guard, to the United Nations. Wars are being fought over resources and territory, as well as for religious and personal reasons, without an international referee with power or respect.

• How far can we go replacing natural services with industrial ones? Some economists and ecologists had already started to calculate the true costs of natural services (once considered "free goods").

Of course, many other experiments were possible, dealing with: Computers and the education of the young and old; the number and condition of roads; hunting styles and limits; capitalism, communism, and community; and, the future of the country.

One expectation that modern life had raised in people was that "there was no right answer." The best response to a problem or a question might be a hypothesis, that is, a thought experiment. Thought experiments could let us examine things and change them without really modifying or destroying the unique systems under study. In practice, this meant thinking first about all the possible connections, before actually making changes. Through an experiment, we could create explanations and discover answers in a dialog with others. That might be the best way to solve our modern problems.

Famous Irish Bars of Sofia

In Sofia, I was in the SPA meeting all day. We reviewed our rules and made up sets of questions for the formal review. This committee reviewed all of the applications made in this quarter of the year; this time there were nine applications. Unfortunately this took until after 7 p.m. Then the four of us went to the new Irish bar, Flanagan's Irish Harp, two blocks from the hotel. This was a quiet bar with many wall-mounted televisions and a multi-level floor. We ordered three different kinds of potatoes. Alta had chicken, Calpurnia had Captain's pie, I had Caesar salad, and Christine had a special sandwich. There were only two other sets of customers, so we were able to talk easily. Back in the room, we talked for a few hours and watched BBC, which was a rare treat.

The next day, before the bus left, Alta and Calpurnia went window shopping again, for a dress for Alta for the next training in March, which was also a party for close of service. I raced to book stores and collected a science fiction, Count Zero, an HTML book, a Macintosh magazine, and several used books from the PC library. Alta bought her dress.

That afternoon, I walked to the movie theater to see a movie

317

with Jet Li, called The One. It was mildly amusing, although the acrobatics were enjoyable. We all met and went back to a new Irish restaurant.

Three months later, for the next SPA meeting, we took the 8 a.m. bus to Troyan; the Chavdar was working well this morning and rattled less than normal. In Troyan, we waited in the cafe with tea and coffee. At 9:30 the Sofia bus pulled in and we were first on. So we sat quietly for half an hour watching people load up the bus. Most people had baba bags (apparently, they were used for groceries as well as long distance travel so the police would not know when you were going on long trips within Bulgaria).

In Sofia, we walked to the hotel, then had a sandwich and went to the Peace Corps, which was nice and quiet also. We decided to go to a movie in one of the few theaters that had been renovated. The movie was Rush Hour 2, which was amusing. We were the only people in the theater at 3 p.m. For dinner we went to Flanagan's Irish bar—there were now at least five Irish bars in Sofia; none served Guinness, but all had potatoes and the Bulgarian interpretation of Irish food (more like British food actually). We had potato wedges and a real Caesar salad.

In the evening we walked back to the Hotel Maya. I worked on the SPA grant and Calpurnia watched Olympic sports, in which they showed every heat of every race (on 24-hour sports channel). This hotel was made of two apartments, which had been converted to rooms. Each apartment has four rooms, each room had two single beds, a sofa, refrigerator, chairs and a table (with a large cable television). The bathroom had been divided into four mini bathrooms, where the shower was over the sink and the sink was over the toilet. They had been replumbed, so although it was very small and awkward, it was very warm. All this for only $25 a night. It was better than the youth hostel or Hotel Niki, where one bath was shared by eight rooms.

Today at the SPA meeting, as usual, we had to argue about standards and whether they should be enforced. Talking about spelling caused great consternation and Venelina left the room, after saying that Bulgarians did not know how to spell in English. Still, even with the stress, we finished before 4 p.m. Albert, the PC Head, congratulated us, and said that he had reserved the room until 10 p.m. Fortunately there were only eight applications.

We went back to the Irish Harp for a good dinner. This time, we had chicken sandwiches. Too tired to see a movie, we walked around, bought some books and magazines, then went back. Sounded boring, but the rest was welcome.

Working near Strangja over a holiday, we decided it was time to return. We reached the bus station at 7:30 to find we had missed a direct bus to Sofia. So, we took the 8:00 to Burgas, getting there at 8:58 and catching the earlier bus, which was waiting until 9:00. The bus to Plovdiv was also there, but would have entailed three bus rides and a taxi to get to Aprilci by midnight, maybe.

So, we took the bus to Sofia. The prices had been increased by half for the holiday, but by then we had no choice. The driver said we would be there before 1:00, in time to make the 1300 bus to Troyan. But, then the trip took over five hours. At the Sofia bus station, we found one bus to Lovech, but no others. Rather than risk being stuck there, we walked into town and got a room at the Maya. It had no bath in the room, but we were familiar with it. It was raining heavily now and we got soaked looking for food. Most places were closed for Easter. The Irish Harp however was open, although we became the only customers. I had Caesar salad and potatoes; Calpurnia had a club sandwich. Afterwards we walked to a movie theater, which was packed, but we watch Ocean's Eleven and wondered if Bulgaria would ever have as much electricity as Las Vegas. The city here was almost deserted; many streetlights and signs had been turned off. Afterwards we walked back and fell asleep early. Fireworks woke us up around midnight. The hostess later told us there was a concert at the Cultural Center.

In Sofia a last time for SPA business, we experienced another Doughnut moment — at least they were making double chocolate donuts again, although they tasted like dirt. The Mango strawberry tea was good. Back to PC HQ we met with Venelina about the projects. Petko called from the suburbs and we met at the Perfect restaurant underground by the Serdica station. We sat and talked for an hour about the project on wolf telemetry. All that neat equipment but no wolves caught yet. He was going to Italy for a month to work on more data for his PhD dissertation.

We had lunch in the Arabian vegetarian restaurant, Baalbeks; we had falafels and humus, with coca cola, the universal solvent. Back at HQ we met with Venelina again to get her final comments on the projects. Calpurnia meanwhile had agreed to pay her telephone bill from Pazardjik from November 2000, which had just been sent to the PC. I suggested paying a few dollars by check (which the city could not cash apparently), but she gave the cash to Iliana to mail to the City. I could not see how she was legally bound to pay a bill they could not show existed, with not one single documented note or call, but this was Bulgaria.

Finally we raced down the street to another new theater and watch Lord of the Rings, hoping, nay praying that the movie was better than the book (I gave up on page one, but Calpurnia had gotten to page three). It was mildly interesting but slow, very slow, and three hours long. It had the usual killing of five hundred monsters per person per minute, followed by inane conversations about magic. What a terrible sacrifice just to listen to the English language being spoken!

We found a new Irish bar, The Shamrock, but they were heavy on sham and on rock, with flashing disco lights, so we left after a rum and coke, fleeing to the security of the known Harp, where I had a Caesar salad and Calpurnia a burger. The Shamrock was much larger and noisier; it did not have the good drinking and talking ambiance, so we crossed it off our list of favored places. Then back to the room to read the new newsweaks.

Legend of the Wolf Family Band

In a hurry one time, we just put "Wolf family" on the bulletin board for events, to cover all four of us. It was quicker than writing four names. It added mystery to a simple list. I wondered if it could ever backfire on us.

At one Ceremony, Albert Foster made a joke that the Wolf Family Rock Band would perform afterwards. Christine made strangling motions, but the bandleader thought we were serious and asked me, as the obvious patriarch, what we would sing — I said Roy Orbison and Elvis Presley, but the other band members made threatening noises and motions. Albert kept making the joke over and over at the awards and at every announcement. Christine turned the most delicate shades of red, each one deeper than the last.

On Saturday, all four of us, the Wolf family, of course, took a taxi to the bus station. The taxi cost only 86 stutinki, or about 40 cents. An honest cab driver! We gave him 1.50. Alta and Christine's bus was full so they had to wait for the 8:30, but that was also full, so they bought tickets for the 9:00. Ours came a little late but we got on first. By the time we hit the last station in Sofia, there was no standing room. This was a private bus, but it was a local — it would stop at every village, and did. I read a sci-fi book, Calpurnia a Newsweek. After four hours and forty minutes (and about eighty miles) we were in Aprilci.

We unpacked and make lunch, which was homemade pizza. We read. I took a nap, then worked on computer. Dinner was soup and bread. Then we cranked out more reports and letters to the SPA candidates. Then, I started writing down some lyrics, so I would not be limited to Elvis or Roy, if we ever sang publicly. Finally, I turned up the stereo and sang along with 40-50 good songs, until Cali had to quiet me.

Wolves Versus Technology Or *Sophisticated Empty Traps*

I woke at 3:30 after a dream involving the justifiable deaths of many ugly lawyers and judges. Tried to get on-line, but authentification failed, along with the line and whatever. Tried eight times, then went back to sleep. The doorbell rang at 5:00 but no one was there. At 8:00 I tried again to get on another five times, but nothing worked. After a pleasant breakfast of tea and bread and yogurt, I worked on the wolf proposals. I had trouble with the radio-telemetry one because I had no definite costs.

Wednesday, I worked at the internet sending messages. Started to flesh out the telemetry proposal. Watched television at noon. Bought Bulgarian papers. Checked internet news. More Bulgarian friends called and asked if we were okay or if we needed anything; they were also very kind and reassuring.

I had submitted one grant application to the Peace Corps, but had to prepare a last minute defense on radio-collaring wolves, especially a Safety Plan. Worked on email correspondence.

At noon, with Aleksander, we went to the school to discuss having a volunteer there, to teach English. He spoke very loudly and clearly in Bulgarian so we would understand, then said he hoped a new volunteer would speak better Bulgarian. We suggested they would, also speaking clearly in Bulgarian, if they were younger, but pointed out that they would be teaching English. He asked for a volunteer with two years experience; we told him that most of us left after two years and that those who stayed, stayed for specific projects and were rarely reassigned. He said he needed someone who spoke better Bulgarian; we agreed, but he did not seem to notice that we had been speaking Bulgarian for thirty minutes. He filled in the form and gave it to Aleksander who brought it to me at about 4:00.

Lunch was a sandwich, then afternoon was even more computer work; the memories of walking through forests was starting to fade, sigh. That evening, we packed for Sofia.

In Sofia, as a board member, I helped with most of the presentations. For my own, I had to step aside and not vote, of course. This day was the actual interview and defense. Some people were woefully unprepared and others had brought three counterparts (I had two counterparts, collars, electronics, posters, and photo albums — Desislava had decided not to bring the puppy and trap). So, our presentation ran overtime. Petko and Desislava answered most of the questions. I provided the technical information on equipment. It went well. They found one mistake and asked for one letter promising office support (but the application had been signed by Desislava, the Director, who would have to write the letter anyway, but rules seemed to be rules).

Several days later, we went back to Sofia, on the 8 o'clock bus to Troyan and Sofia. I called Desislava, who asked me to call back at 3:30. I had a chicken sandwich and went to the PC HQ to meet with the Environmental Program people. I called her back and she said she had to go immediately to the Minister of Agriculture to pick up the wolf taxation numbers for 2002 — I asked for a copy — and then go to Pernik to be with her family; she invited me to come along and sleep on the floor, but I told her that I could work in Sofia and take the bus to Sadovik on Tuesday. She agreed, with relief I thought, as the entire family included four generations in one apartment. So, I checked into the Maya and went to sleep.

Early, I worked in the PC office all morning on the interminable paperwork, then had a burger. After Noon, took the tram for 40 Stutinki to the west bus station. Waited an hour for the bus to Pernik. At Pernik it was raining and I had to wait another hour for the bus to Sadovik. I bought the ticket and asked for the correct sector and the clerk said right in front. The bus wandered through Breznik and another fifteen villages before getting to Sadovik. One of the last three passengers left on the bus, I walked up the hill to the other side of the village. At the house I was greeted by Arul and another Karakachan guard dog, who bark wildly, until I presented my hands to be smelled. The new dog was one of the puppies that I first saw in September, a young female called Shara. Desislava was there with a Belgian called Roland, who had been volunteering for the past five years; he was also a photographer. Petko and Kamen were back from ten days camping in the far west; their trap line had caught only a small boar so they had pulled the traps today. We talked about the problems, equipment, and strategies. Desislava would check the traps tomorrow and Petko and I would scout new territories. So, we drank and talked until about 10 p.m.

We woke at 5:30 Wednesday morning, earlier than usual. Desislava and Kamin left for the trapline. Petko and I made breakfast, toasted cheese sandwiches, and egg omelettes. When they came back, Petko and I left, walking to the village of Izbor and the high ridge beyond. We walked over the ridge, Mogilla Hill, into the forestry unit, and to Rekalska Mogilla, the hill next to the river. We found weasel, ermine, and marten scat. Then fox prints and scat. We saw a wild cat ducking in front of a bush. The cat was healthy-looking and cautious. We checked the tracks for a few minutes and recorded and photographed them for the records. Petko identified the birds, including *Meriops apiaster* and *Monticola saxatilis*. I could not remember the common names. I could never remember both Latin and common names it seemed. Must be dementia; the timing was right.

We ended up on a small paved road leading to a forest unit.

The wretch tending the forestry garden told us that his boss was in the woods and would shoot us without warning. Petko reminded him that that was illegal, and we left with bad feelings. The foresters here were either ignorant gits or engaged in illegal operations (or both), so we carefully retraced our steps. Petko was pissed and went over all the laws in Bulgaria relating to guns. I was more worried about being shot for an Elen or wolf, but Petko said that trespassers had to be warned in numerous ways before any shooting, and furthermore, the person with the fewest weapons was presumed innocent, e.g., if we had a revolver and someone else had a rifle, regardless of who attacked first, we would be innocent; he had a phone and I had a folding knife. The law would protect us for sure.

We walked around the ridge without incident. It started to rain. Finally, we came to a road but veered off it and over another ridge to Sadovik, returning in time for a late lunch at 3:00. That afternoon, we discussed the strategy for the next few days. Desislava left for Pernik. The house ran out of water, so we had to go to the well to get buckets and fill old plastic bottles. I was wet and freezing, so I changed clothes, crawled into the sleeping bag and read an hour.

I started to make dinner, although I was not interested in cooking or eating. I cooked macaroni with a nice tomato sauce, with onion, mushroom, and some meatballs. We talked until about Nine, then Petko and Kamen went to the local pub for a few drinks and to see if any of the girls had a crush on one of them. I told them they were both handsome, but get away from me. I fell asleep soon.

Petko, Kamen and I get up at 5:30 and drove to Lyalitsa and checked traps. Kamen dropped us off and drove to Paramoon. We walked straight up the ridge and found an old trail. I was breathing like a blast furnace, wondering if I was too old or out of shape. Then we walked into the mountains; I could not see where the traps were. It started to rain. I finally noticed a spot of dead grass and Petko said that in fact each dead spot covered a trap; fish fertilizer had been sprayed on the trees. The mist played with us around the peaks. It was a beautiful place that shepherds no longer used. There were no tracks or signs of wolf presence. There was fox scat, and many birds, but no other mammals. All of the traps were undisturbed. So, we walked back and waited on the road for Kamen.

Petko sets a trap

Kamen called on the new walky-talky and said that his traps were also empty, so we waited until he walked to the jeep and drove back. We drove back to the house and had a late breakfast, of bread and eggs, with some left-over spaghetti and salami.

Kamen left to Sofia to work on his exams at the university; he was studying to be a lawyer, the growth profession of the decade in Bulgaria, but at least it he would be an environmental lawyer. We worked on checking out the GPS units and walky-talkies; then checked the maps for new areas with rumored wolf presence, possibilities for resetting traps.

After a lunch of butter sandwiches (for a change), Petko and I took the dogs and went out to the western part of town, up into the hills, to look for wolf signs. This was an area frequently used by shepherds for sheep and cattle. We saw plenty of evidence of domestic animals, and weasels, but little else. The dogs went wild running back and forth, destroying most of the uninteresting tracks. I tracked the dogs for fun, and determined they were not wolves by the shape and size of their paws. My deduction was confirmed with a surprise slobbery kiss from Arul.

Back at the house, had sandwiches for dinner and talked. Petko walked to the pub for beer. I read to sleep. There were two pubs. He favored the one with the prettiest bar girl. When I went with him, I got shots of straight vodka, which cost about $0.05, and looked at the men playing cards. After I said no, I was not the Tsar, they had not talked to me much. Alas, I did not know how to play cards or have fun.

Up at 5:30, we were preparing to check the traps, when Desislava called and told Petko that they had to finish the paperwork for the Pirin Park plan, so we should pull the traps. Before we could leave, she called back and asked us to wait for her. After an hour and a half, Petko went back into his sleeping bag and I played with the dogs. Then Desislava showed up with her three year-old son. We all drove in the jeep to Lyalitsa, where Petko and I pulled the first set of traps. Then we drove to Paramoon, where Desislava and I went to pull the next set. But, on the way, I spotted a few wolf prints, new wolf prints, made since the last rain the night before. We carefully tracked the prints, but lost them in the forest a few hundred meters from the traps.

Desislava went first and motioned me to stay, but I pretended not to understand. We checked all the traps along a path up the ridge into the deep woods — this was where wolf prints were found a month ago by a forester, who had called Balkani. All of the traps were empty, but we decided not to pull them. So, we walked back.

Desislava and Hanko drove back to Pernik. Petko and I made

a lunch of cheese sandwiches, then drove to Celo Sigurci, where we followed the trail we took last April Twelfth, when I found two wolves trails leading over the ridge there. This time however, we walked for four hours and found no traces, although the badgers, fox, and martens were all home (but out of sight). We walked back to the jeep and drove to Paramoon, where we hiked out to the set of traps we checked that morning and renewed the fish scent.

These wolves were impossible. Four thousand years of dodging human missiles had taught them to work at night and to trust no one. It seemed that we could not get closer than the sight of a green shadow or vanishing tail tip.

We got back to the house about Seven and had cheese sandwiches, which I actually liked and rarely get tired of. Petko forced me at knifepoint to go to the pub. We sat with the old geezers from the village, playing cards for toothpicks (although a few were toothless and several more sported steel or silver teeth). We talked with a few, mostly politics. I had vodka and Petko a few beers. No girls attacked Petko. We actually got home early.

Up at 5:30 again, and we went out directly to check the last string of traps, nine in a row uphill from the village of Paramoon on Paramoon mountain. We expected to catch a wolf, since there was evidence yesterday and we had renewed the scents. But, there was nothing. We walked back slowly, reviewing the trap placement and any possible oversights. Perhaps if we had 10,000 traps.

Back at the house by 10:00, we had a late breakfast of tea and toast. I washed my clothes in a bucket—it had been raining for the past ten days and everything was muddy. The sun came out and things looked like they might dry. Petko went for a walk with the dogs.

When he came back, I fixed cheese sandwiches for lunch. After lunch we hiked west of Sadovik again, through the hills that had been grazed for thousands of years. These hills had not grown back forests although there were a few trees that could serve as shelter for wolves. We thought the sheep might be tempting, especially since the populations of red deer had been falling and now the roe deer numbers were falling. The fault seemed to be that poachers hunting at night with jeeps, spotlights, and automatic weapons had reduced the numbers. But, there did not seem to be any wolf signs in the area. We were depressed and returned before 5:00 p.m.

As I was fixing cheese sandwiches, Petko went berserk and threatened to cut me: "Pan, you bastard, can't you fix something else!"

And, I replied, "Petko, you bastard, I'm too tired to cook. What do you want?"

325

"Pan you bastard I am sick of bread."

"Petko, you bastard, you cook!" Of course, "bastard" was not a term of respect or endearment in Bulgaria; it was the worst thing you could say to someone.

Of course, he wanted something different. He found an old chicken leg in the freezer. I found some rice that I bought in April. There were three cooked potatoes from Monday. The rice was put in water at the bottom of a pan; the chicken was cut up and added, then the potato slices were layered on top. The mess was doused with olive oil and spices and cooked for an hour. Petko made a tomato salad, also, with syrene cheese. He served dinner and it was quite decent. His mood improved. We went over the eighteen maps of the region (scaled at 1:15,000) and discussed strategy. Then we went for another trip to the pub. This time he had vodka and I smoked, blowing smoke rings and french-inhaling until I was dizzy. After another vodka I walked back in the dark. Petko stayed and talked with some of the villagers — people we saw working in the fields as we were driving to trap areas. He told them that we were just amateur bird-watchers.

Today was the last day for the traps, for a week anyway. I insisted that we take all the blowguns, anesthetic, collars with us in my backpack, just in case. We drove to Paramoon and walked up the mountain halfway before I remembered that I forgot the blowpipe. Then we saw a roe deer, female, walking away from us. A hundred meters later another roe deer. The raven spotted us and alerted the entire forest. We hoped the raven was there to tease a trapped wolf. The first trap was empty, then they all were.

"Bastard traps," said Petko.

So, we each said "shit" and took alternate traps. I sprang mine, then wrapped the chain around it and dropped it into an orange bag. We walked them all back down and get into the jeep. Another "shit" and we were gone. It was a beautiful sunny morning, no rain or fog.

Back at the house we cleaned and packed. By eleven, we were in Pernik meeting with Desislava and trying to figure out what was so problematic. We finally concluded that wolf numbers had in fact dropped for the past two years. I suggested other areas around Smolyan, but that was too far to commute, and over five years time had been invested in the Kraishde region.

Petko and Desislava decided to set out some of the traps in five days. We went over the budget. Then Petko and I walked to the bus stop with our heavy packs. We saw the bus in the distance and sprinted the last half mile, making it easily, although I was breathing like a walrus. The bus went to Sofia. Petko got off at the city limit and I took the tramvai to the center.

I called Calpurnia and suggested that she take the late bus to Sofia; she agreed. So, I checked into the Maya hotel, then had a sandwich and saw a movie, Kiss of the Dragon. After a much-needed shower and a rest I walked to the bus station and waited. There were only two buses there, instead of the usual forty. But, after seven, they started arriving from Pleven, Kazanluk, and Gabrovo. The one from Troyan was twenty minutes late and Calpurnia looked frazzled when she got off—the bus had picked up twenty school kids from the monastery and they had rioted with food.

We walk back into town, then went to the Irish Harp for a chicken sandwich. Back at the room, we talked and went to sleep.

We took the 8 a.m. bus to Troyan and then Sofia, with a full back pack and sleeping bag. Stayed and read on a bench until the bus. The Chavdar buses were a major source of cultural entertainment. I noticed that the bus drivers accepted packages, boxes, and food for people, then delivered them at various stops on the way. Most people who rode the buses went from small village to small village. Few of us went all the way to Troyan or Sofia.

In Sofia I went to the PC HQ and got Sheila to give me a new bandage for my back; she said it was healing well, then cut off the scab so it could heal deeper first. After a quick burger, I called Petko and arranged to meet him at the PC office at 3:30. I assumed that he would pick me up in a car, but he arrived on foot and we walked to the new underground tram, where we went to the far west outskirts and his parents' apartment. They lived on the top floor, so I chatted dutifully with his mother and sister, explaining why I was here; they were watching a Spanish soap opera (the rage here for over two years now), so when conversation lagged, we all watched a beautiful woman scream at a handsome man passionately.

Petko finished packing his back pack, then called Julia, who agreed to drive us to Pernik, but we had to travel back into Sofia to meet her, so we took the underground exactly back to the center and then a tram to NDK (Endaka), the cultural center. She was waiting under a bridge with her van; Tervel, a forester, was with her. So, we motored out to Pernik, but stopped at a garage to pick up a new truck, which has been donated by the International Bear Foundation and Bridgette Bardot, but had to have a new rear axle installed. Four of us lifted the old axle into the truck. Then, we drove to the farm, where the Karakachan dogs were raised, to drop off the old axle, which would be stored for parts. The new axle, which cost about $400, was not new but was used, so the parts may be handy later on.

The three puppies that I saw when they were a few weeks old last September now weighed about 300 pounds and looked like small horses; they also barked fiercely, but when we went inside they whimpered and slobbered over us. Then one of them escaped while we were carrying the axle. Four of us chased him (after putting the axle down naturally), but he ran down the road to a field where boys were playing soccer. We surrounded him at a distance and herded him towards the farm gate but he discovered a culvert under the road and dived in before we could stop him. For the next hour, we alternately tried to lure him out or sat around and talked. Finally, he backed out and we herded him back, where the other dogs mobbed him to smell the whole story.

Then, we were off to Cidar's and Desislava's apartment (actually his parents lived there), a penthouse on the 16th floor. As usual, we had tea and talked, then played musical cars. Desislava introduced me to two new volunteers, Sheila, a woman from Germany, and Bluff, from Bulgaria. Petko, Tervel, Sheila and I drove to Sadovik. Desislava and the others would follow on Saturday.

By the time, we got to Sadovik it was past ten. It was raining. A dog barked threateningly—it was the two-year old Karakachan named Arul. I tried to make friends but he rammed his nose into my balls and snorted and sniffed. Now we were intimate friends, again, although I did not return the favor. Petko decided that we should have rice. I cut bread. Tervel made soup. By midnight, we had finished and went to bed. Petko slept by the wood fire; the rest of us went upstairs, which has three single beds in one room and a double bed in another.

It was raining. We made breakfast of yogurt, cereal and leftovers, then forged out with our rain gear. As we were driving to a new set of villages to investigate for wolf presence, Desislava called and asked us to help round up some Karakachan horses, which had been left out to pasture for eleven years—seriously, the guy just turned them out and now, three generations later, he wanted to round them up. If we helped, we could have a few. But, we heard that they had now divided into three separate herds, led by two males and one female.

At the assigned location, we found no evidence of horses. Petko asked a few shepherds, while I walked through the river looking for prints or scat—there was nothing. After a few more calls, we gave up and went on to the first village, Kovachentsi I thought.

Tervel dropped off the three of us then drove to the rendezvous village, which was two hills away; he would make a circle on foot then meet us at about 3 p.m. We walked up through the village, talking to the shepherds and farmers. This area had been inhabited for many thousands of years. Petko told me that twenty years ago there were hundreds of thousands of sheep and cattle, but now both the human and animal populations were dwindling. Those left were self-sufficient, but actually could not sell animal products, such as milk and meat, because they could not meet the European Union standards. One shepherd usually gathered sheep and goats from three to twenty families and then took them into the hills for the day, returning each to the proper owner before dusk. The fields for potatoes and other crops were being planted now; they were usually on the edges of the villages, although each house had a small garden beside it. Many people, mostly women, were out working these fields, planting the spring crops. We saw very few young people (of course, they could have been hiding the girls from Petko).

Then we were out of the village and the fields and into a small scrub forest. We heard then saw a cuckoo. Then a raven, then a harrier. I found the first scat of the day, from a fox, so naturally I measured and photographed it (it might be the only thing I found after all). Then we came across roe deer prints leading up the hill from the river. Then shortly after the prints of a wolf who seemed to be following (but not chasing) the deer – the prints were 10 by 7.5 cm, so it could be a small male or large female (although at this time the females should be well pregnant).

The rain was making it hard to track because it was washing the prints away as we followed, but we followed the wolf for a kilometer or so uphill. The wolf was following the road. I took a few photos in the rain, surprised that the camera still worked (I was soaked to the skin now). On the other side of the road I found a stone marten track (just one). Petko and I discussed why he would be out in a clearing and not in the trees. Petko said that unlike Pine martens, stone martens had adapted to open areas and hunted mice.

Finally we descended into a village, but asked and found out it was the wrong village! The shepherd said we must cross another ridge. Then Petko asked each shepherd we passed and each gave a slightly different instruction. Finally, we reached the correct village, but it was deserted. I smelled smoke, so Petko shouted. His shout was answered but it took us a while to find the house. It turned out that we had taken a wrong turn and should had gone over another ridge. We walked along a paved road which we were told led to the village. At a major intersection, relatively speaking since most of these roads were single lane and the paving had worn through to gravel, we saw a jeep drive by and shouted. It was Tervel, who figured we were lost and got a shepherd to help him. The shepherd got out, and we all talked for a while in the pouring rain. Then he went back to his sheep and we drove back.

But, Desislava called and told us where to meet the horse owner, so we drove to another village. The horse owner, said his neighbor, had just left for Sofia, so we went back. Petko decided to take a shortcut through a field but we got stuck and the engine died.

Fortunately, it started after several minutes of cranking and we could get unstuck. At the house, Desislava called and said the owner was driving back to the village and could we meet him? I said we could not, but got outvoted. I suggested that I would start a fire and cook dinner on it. The others said they should be back in an hour or two. I said that they would not find him, and I would plan dinner for three hours. They left.

I started a fire in the stove, which was in the living room but was a real old fashioned cook stove with an oven, four burners and a warmer next to the firebox. After it was started I washed in the cold spring and changed to dry clothes. I cut up tomatoes, peppers and onion, but only found salt and pepper for spices (four shakers of pepper and two of salt, a culinary disaster). There was no pasta, only spaghetti and macaroni, so I cooked macaroni. I found some meat, so cooked meatballs also (for the first time since 1973 I thought, since becoming a vegetarian, I never cooked meat, although I ate it in restaurants or with the family). I timed dinner for three hours, but they did not appear. I started a mystery book that I got from the PC HQ. Five hours later, they returned, not having met the horse owner, but having gotten stuck in the mud again. I reheated dinner while they used the spring to clean up. We finished the red wine. They liked the heavily peppered dinner. They fell asleep before they could get to the bar.

Saturday, it was still raining, but very lightly. Petko and Sheila dropped off me and Tervel at another village; we were going to walk to the village of Vereda, where they would park and make their own circle. We started up the river valley. Tervel, the forester, had looked at the map and then given it back to Petko. I asked if he knew where we were going (I thought I did, since I could translate it into hills and valleys)? He said yes, he was good at maps. Immediately on going up from the river, I found a wolf track; it looked like two wolves, moving single file, one large one small, maybe a yearling. The rain had washed away almost everything but these tracks, so we thought that they were made after dawn. Some tracks were very good. We followed for over three kilometers, losing them sometimes on rock, grass, or gravel, but always finding them again.

Then we found a strange digging and a badger print. The badger had been looking for beetles or ants maybe. The badger had also left scat in one of the diggings; the scat had beetle carapaces. We backtracked the badger since he was heading down hill, perhaps after the wolves passed uphill. Then there were a few stone marten tracks, with five toes. As we were going down a hill, we heard a shout — it was Petko and Sheila, who had just found the wolf tracks, also, but they were where we were five minutes before. Petko had taken some measurements, but his seemed larger by a centimeter than mine. We compared notes; he was measuring from the claw tip and rounding up, where I rounded down from the tip of the pad. So much for exact science.

The four of us continued. The rain stopped; the sun peeked out, so we stopped and had lunch, a cheese sandwich and apple each. We were sitting amid many caterpillars, same color but different sizes. We noticed bees, flies, spiders, and beetles were also out now. Three different kinds of flowers but none of us knew the Latin names — all mammalogists. We discovered an old car pushed over a hill, the first such I had seen here, and told them in America it seemed everyone in the country did that. Here I was told they repaired them forever.

Then we walked over two more ridges and found the correct village the first time, but we were at the wrong end of it and had to walk up hill a few miles. At the jeep, we tied the dog, Arul, and went for a beer (I had coke, although I heard that Bulgarian beer was as good as any, from local hops).

Back to the house by seven, it was still light. We washed, then washed potatoes and rice for dinner. We had more soup; mushroom this time. We ate and talked until midnight. Petko talked, that was, and the rest of us acted as orchestra to the solo.

Dead wolf = 50 Leva + firewood

Another breakfast of yogurt and leftovers. We drove to Svetlya and met Desislava. We decided to divide up into three groups now and all meet in Vereda, where we met yesterday. Now we were checking the east ridges rather than the west ridges. The trails here were all grassy, so not many tracks. Desislava, Tervel and I dropped off Sheila and Petko, then dropped off the car. We planned to make three large loops around the village. After a while Tervel circled south and Desislava and I continued up hill. There were a few summer houses near the top, but closed up for winter and spring. We saw another cuckoo and a woodpecker (what I thought was a sapsucker). No prints of any kind for a long time, then fox, then marten. The fox had been eating rosehips for every meal, so the scat ranged from yellow to pure red. Some was displayed on rocks. The marten had left scat on rocks for us to find, also, but it looked like he had been eating

331

meat, mice perhaps, but no bones. Then we found several wolf scats, which we collected and recorded on the new forms. Several prints, but the rain had been unkind. We got lost in a thorn forest, which was painful. Then we came out at a rock outcropping. I voted to go straight down to the river. Desislava agreed, but I found in hindsight that we would have had an easier time going up the ridge and then down through a meadow. For all its noise the river was only two feet wide.

From there, we found a trail between two villages. Lined with sheep prints and manure. We saw a few cattle, but no sheep at all. After an hour it led directly to the jeep, where Tervel was waiting, eating his cheese sandwich. So we had a picnic. Then drove to a rendezvous with the others. They were not there, so we drove to another village where a man had killed a wolf in the last year. We asked to see the skin, but his answer eluded me. We gave him a brochure and drove back. Still no Petko, so we napped in the new sun. The phones were not working for the second day, perhaps the rain had ruined a tower somewhere. Finally they came up the hill, led by the dog, Arul. We compared notes, looked for a cafe but none were open, so we drove back to the house in Sadovik. Desislava drove to Pernik. We cleaned up, finished the leftovers, and followed. To get to the train, we had to have coffee again and play musical cars. Cidar was going to Sofia, but had to wait for his brother. We talked and waited. Desislava and Sheila went to do errands. Finally, Jivko came and he, Cidar, Tervel, Petko, and I drove to Sofia. We were dropped off at the south bus station.

Petko got on one train, Tervel and I got another and went to the center. From there I went to the Maya Hotel and got a room for about $18. Then called Calpurnia. Then had a chicken sandwich at Flanagans. Everyone was playing darts, so I watched while I ate. I went back to the room and watched television for a while, choosing between French, Russian, Italian, Spanish, English, and Bulgarian programs. The room looked across the boulevard at the statue of liberty and wisdom (she had an owl and a book), as well as on the Sheraton, Tsum department store, and new underground tram entrance— everything was lit up all night, but the room was quiet.

On the way to PC HQ, Monday morning, it rained tremendously and I was soaked immediately. Sheila changed the bandage and we talked about wolves. She said Bulgaria would have another earthquake this Saturday. There was a small one a few weeks ago that dropped a few houses, but that was all. I met Gabriel by accident and he wanted to do something, so I took him shopping (he was the defense attorney in Atlanta, now teaching English). We went to the health food store then the Oasis. I got cereal and tortellini and he got cereal and German bread.

Then I went to the bus and sat and read until it left. I was the first so I sat behind the driver (not the first which was blocked off but the next, on the shady side of the bus). The sun had come out. The bus station was completely full of buses and people. Then I decided to walk through the bazaar next to the bus station. It had grown since they closed the bazaar next to the train station. The usual things were on sale: watches, running suits, running shoes, candy, and batteries. I went back to the bus without buying anything.

After a mere six hours of busing, I was back in Aprilci with Calpurnia, who was waiting at the bus with a bottle of coke and a loaf of bread — ah, the woman knew what I liked! We had a pizza on bread and a shopska salad. Then caught up on events.

Pizza & Honors

A few days, it was time to celebrate with the people from the Central Balkan National Park. We took the 8:30 bus to Gabrovo. But missed the 9:30 van from Sevlievo — that meant that we had to take the state bus at 10, which traveled to every village between towns. We arrived in Gabrovo after 11 and walked to the apartment with the bags. Joe was there, so we talked for a while before calling Nikolai to ask where we would meet for lunch.

Nikolai said to come to the Park, which we did by taking the number Four bus out to the edge of town. There we met with him and then Georgiu about the Global Fund grant — mostly how to spend the last of the money so the project could be finished. Nikolai said lunch was not until Two. Georgiu got phone calls so we left to have a coke at the local cafe. Then we met with Georgiu again until Two. Just at Two Iurka asked for our advice for the new brochure for the Park, with a child's painting on the front. I dared to suggest that the painting was not dramatic enough as a mountain scene so she plugged in another painting with snow. That improved the contrast but then the title colors seemed too bland.

Finally Krasimir rescued us and we drove to the Tempo restaurant, but then had to wait another half hour for Iurka and the others, so we drank coke or beer. People straggled in slowly and we finally ordered after 3 o'clock. Everyone, except for Iurka and Krasimir, had pizza. Iurka had a chicken dish, as did Krasimir. We ordered extra beers and cokes. We also took many photos of the group together, a first.

The Park gave me a carving of a brown bear, and brochures for Calpurnia. Lunch broke up about 4:30, just enough time, as Calpurnia noted, for everyone to go back and leave work early. We resisted a ride back and walked around town, ending up at the new movie theater. All the movies were bad, except for a French movie,

"Crimson River," about the devil. Imagine French with Bulgarian subtitles. Neither of us had had French for over thirty years and so had to read the Bulgarian to understand the movie!

As we walked out the skies opened and it poured rain. We ran from tree to tree, then decided on a salad at a little shop. As we turned in, Dimetar Nikolev drove by in the jeep and offered us a ride. He had not told about the luncheon since it was his day off. He drove us to the apartment. We lied, socially, since he was a nice guy and wanted to take us drinking, that we had a nagosti in Joe's apartment. So, he called his wife and daughter so that we could talk to them on the phone. Then we went upstairs, dried off, and went to bed — after seeing the soccer highlights first.

Alphabet Day

Another year had gone buy and it was time to visit our host families in Dupnitsa for the last time. The first two hours in Sofia — all roads lead through Sofia — we went around to the various offices to get signatures on our closing file, showing that we had returned the distiller, books, and dictionaries. We applied for reimbursement for our travel but were told to wait. Because, we no longer had any Bulgarian money we cashed in our last $100 USD to last for the week.

Then, we had our closing interview with Albert Foster, who signed and gave us our Description of Service — the most important document for me since it would allow me to claim noncompetitive eligibility with government agencies, such as the Park Service. Albert asked a set series of questions, and we summarized the strengths and weaknesses of the PC program and staff. As I was working on my paperwork, I overheard Doug tell Albert that he had accomplished all of his objectives as a volunteer — he had been to London, Paris, Rome, Budapest, and Copenhagen. Sigh.

When Christine was finished with her interview, we went to McDs for a sandwich, then to the internet to check email. It was a good new cafe, with very fast machines and connections. Christine headed north to her bus and Calpurnia and I headed south on the tram to the west station. There the bus to Dupnitsa was waiting, so we boarded immediately. This was a public bus that stopped every 30 meters for people, but we managed to get there before Five. As we walked through town with our baggage, we talked about being there 2 years ago. We stopped at a cafe and had a coke, then walked on to the Ilievi house. Henrim the grandson was waiting at the window and Ilian, the grandfather, was waiting by the gate.

After we were settled in the room, my old room from the summer of 2000, we went talk to Luboslav, Inga, and Henrim, in their living room; things did not seem to have changed much, although Henrim had a new bicycle. We took photographs, gave out presents from America, mostly t-shirts, and talked to them about their, and our, work. Ilian came in and invited us all to dinner.

Upstairs, we started dinner with the usual Rakia, beer, wine, and whiskey (Calpurnia and I kept to Rakia, in moderation, finally having learned how to nurse a half-full glass for four hours). We talked about affairs in Bulgaria, such as the new taxes on everything, e.g. cigarettes had gone up about 60 percent in one week, the Pope's visit, which started the next day, and the other families. Dinner was salads, rice and shopska, then lasagna, which I had taught her to make in 2000 (good, but she had trouble with the sauce, and insisted on putting meat in, usually some kind of worst or salami). We all talked to 10 p.m. and then went to bed.

After a long breakfast, Calpurnia and I went shopping for groceries, mostly things that we know they would not buy. So, we got a bottle of whisky, two pounds of strawberries, four grapefruit, peanuts, corn, and some other things. Lunch was early, but it was huge, with salads, chicken, coated red peppers, mushrooms, fried cheese, and melbas for desert. We had to go for walks to kick-start the stomach muscles; then we talked some more.

Late in the afternoon, Petya, from Calpurnia's host family called and asked if we could visit her early, so we walked over there. Then she called Zlatka, who brought over her new baby, Shakleen (after Jacqueline). We talked, played with the baby and took more photographs, and drank gin. Then, we walked back to the Ilievis for dinner of omelet and new potatoes.

After a long breakfast with the Ilievis, including apple strudel, we dragged our bags over to Petya's house. Then I went shopping for gin, cigarettes, chocolate pastries, and groceries for Petya. We had an early lunch of chicken and potatoes, with tarator soup (cold yogurt), then walked through the center of Dupnitsa, which was celebrating alphabet day (Cyril and Methodius, the brother monks who invented this alphabet, the most important day for schools and culture). Everyone was out walking, so we greeted everyone. This was one of those nice Bulgarian customs, walking and greeting, and then stopping for tea and coffee. We walked to a cafe high above the city in the public gardens, which had been repaired nicely over the past two years.

After the hours of social things, we rested for an hour. Then we all took a taxi to Zlatka's new house, with her new baby and husband, Anaes Stoyanov, called Yani for short. The entire family, three generations, lived in one large house. The grandparents in the basement, the parents on the first floor, Zlatka and Yani on the second and Yani's brother on the third. Each floor had two bedrooms, living, dining room, and a bathroom. As we walked in Yani was loafing around in a running suit drinking beer — my God, what if women were right and men were just worthless sperm-bearers! The baby was out with Yani's mother, making the rounds of the neighborhood. We had rakia and coke, and talked. The baby returned, so we took photos, until it was time to feed her (in Bulgarian, she was an "it" linguistically until she was two years old). After her grandmother feed her I held her and she burped all over me, so I had to wash my shirt in the remodeled bathroom.

Then it was 7:30, time for dinner, so Yani drove us to the pizza restaurant, so we could meet the Ilievis there — we had offered to treat everyone to dinner rather than try to cook for so many families. It was hard to convince them since none of them ever ate out; it was simply too expensive (for us as well). The Napoli restaurant was on three levels; we ate on the second, which was cooler, next to an old dead tree. The food was decent, although it did not seem very Italian. Everyone had pizza or calzone, then beer and coke. Ilievis walked back one direction, uphill, and we went downhill. They all wanted to see us off in July and had decided to take the bus to the Sofia airport to do that. We tried to discourage it since we were afraid they would try to give us more presents and since it would be a tearful parting.

Back at Petya's apartment, which had a kitchen, living room and an added-on bath, we talked and watched television. A Bulgarian movie, "Letter to America," was playing. Seemed to be quite well done, so we thought we would try to find a copy to buy. Most movies here were American or Russian, although some channels had Spanish or German, which were all either dubbed or subtitled in Bulgarian.

We slept late and had a small breakfast, then it was time for the hegira back to Aprilci. We caught the Sofia bus at 8:50. After 10, we caught the tram to the center of Sofia. From there, we went to PC HQ to pick up our mail, then to the internet cafe for email. Except for Rake Penington, a volunteer, and one guard, we had the building to ourselves. I called Desislava and Petko about the next wolf survey, which should start the next day on Sunday, but I could not reach them, so I left messages and sent email. I decided to go back with Calpurnia. So, we had a sandwich, then hiked to the central bus station.

We got aboard the Aprilci bus early and read our books. Then it left at One, almost full. It was a private bus so it stopped only once every 24 kilometers, so it was faster. After a mere three hours, we were in Troyan, but had to wait until Six for the only bus. We walked around and took photos, then ate at the Chinese restaurant above the river. Rice and chicken. We noticed that the fountain was working for the second time in two years, so we took photos of it. Then it was time to take the bus to Aprilci, arriving at seven. Calpurnia unpacked and I went out to buy vegetables.

At 5:00, I cooked tamale casserole and peach cobbler for Desislava, Kosta and Petya. They were really late so I called them; Petya said that Kosta was on his way back from Varna and would call later, maybe another night. We called Desislava, and she apologized for forgetting, but she could not come tonight either. So we ate at 6:00. Then, at 7:00 Kosta called and said they could come over at 7:30, so we did the dishes and set up again.

They came with wine and candy and we had a good time until 10:30, switching back and forth to English occasionally. What did we talk about? Their history together as artists. My work in Alaska, Norway and Siberia. Calpurnia's work on submarines, which was supposed to be a secret from Bulgarians (they did have one sub in their Black Sea fleet I had heard).

Aleksander called and said that I could ride to Gabrovo with him tomorrow. I said happily, and then I called Joe, who had Mary's old apartment in Gabrovo, but only worked there two days a week, and asked if I could stay at the apartment for two days. He agreed and I would meet him for lunch tomorrow.

Aleksander wanted to leave early, at 8:00 and was waiting for me as I walked to the square. We walked to get his father's car (he was 32 and lived at home; had three jobs, including account; and wrote to five girls on the web, including two in Japan—I knew because I helped him draft his replies to emails and letters in English, the universal language of business and internet romance) and we drove to Gabrovo. Although it took over two hours by bus, we arrived in less than an hour and drove to the family house of one his friends.

Their house was on the hill, and inside was a maze; we entered through the garage and went up through three levels of stairs. She and her father were waiting upstairs, but had to come down and unlock the garage door for us. We sat in the kitchen, which seemed to be the only heated room, and had tea, while they caught up. Although Aleksander went to school there four years ago, he has not been back in over two years. She kept putting wood in the stove as she talked. After an hour and a half, I suggested that I would walk downtown, and asked if I should meet him here in the afternoon. He said no, he has to go to the apartment of his other friend. He asked to leave his car here, because the windshield was cracked and he might get arrested for driving in Gabrovo.

So we walked downhill to the center of town. Across the river and only a block from the bazaar (large towns like Gabrovo had permanent bazaars), we approached a large concrete block. The door was locked. Aleksander looked for a phone. But, then a man walked up behind us and shouted up at one of the windows. From the fourth floor a woman opened her window and tossed a velvet bag to him. It contained a key, and he opened the block door. Aleksander asked if we could come in — it seemed that we were visiting the same person he was (although he did not seem to recognize the woman). We rode up in a very small self-operated elevator, that missed each floor by about 10 inches (or almost 4 centimeters).

All three of us waited at the apartment door and were let in. Aleksander's friend, Polya (her first name was Polina), invited us into the living room, where her grandmother hurried with tea and coffee. The entire living room furniture was done in red shag, with a wall to wall wardrobe on one wall and silk flowers under the window. Polya had a little Pekingese that barked very nervously. After tea for an hour, I suggested that I must leave for my meeting with Joe. Polya gave me her number and said to call when I was finished and we would had some more tea. I said that I should return by 3:30, after going out to the Park office.

Joe and I had a quick lunch at Pizza tempo, the only wood-fired pizza restaurant in Bulgaria (it seemed). Then I told him I had to go to the Park office to pick up some reporting forms.

At the bus stop, after half an hour I got tired of waiting and started to walk. As I walked I started to look in the stores. At the old GUM-like store, which was now an arcade of small open shops, like a bazaar, I saw another Adidas watch, four actually. I looked at them and then bought the one that weighed the most. I was sure that they were all counterfeit, but the heavy one, which said made in Germany seemed to be the best counterfeit. This was my fourth one. The first two were lost in the woods in climbing accidents, and the third ran down. I paid 10 Leva, which was roughly what a battery would have cost. Then I walked on.

In another shop, I saw a workman tool, with two saws on it. Since I needed one I looked at all of them and took the second most expensive, for 16 Leva. I was still less than a third the way to the Park. I looked for and found a battery for the camera; the clerk spoke English and lived in NY for a year so we talked for a while in English. Then I decided to stop for another coke. The restaurant was a sladkarnitsa, or Sweets Shop, so I ordered a small piece of mousse cake. It was almost three so I gave up trying to reach the Park and started back to the apartment. From the corner I called up and they came down to meet me. I suggested that we went had a pizza at

Tempo, but they had just been there and brought back the leftovers for me, so we went upstairs and had left-over pizza with tea. They were still getting caught up. They had gone to school together. She has worked as a receptionist at a hotel in Dubai, and showed us pictures of a party a week ago. She had to go back early and was leaving again in four days. Aleksander thought that the people in Dubai placed a lot of importance on having white people wait on them.

They asked if I wanted to drive to a museum, but I suggested that they talk together and that we go to a cafe. So, we went to a new one behind city hall. It was next to a new duplex movie theater showing the Mummy and Pearl Harbor. I could not convince them to see a movie, so we had tea in the bar for an hour. Aleksander thought it was time to leave, so we dropped her off at the apartment. But, her mother was back and wanted to talk to Aleksander, so we had more tea and cookies, this time, in the kitchen with her brother and the grandmother. I was sure that Aleksander had been trying to sell them insurance (another of his jobs). Finally, we left about 8 o'clock, and crawled back to Aprilci. Aleksander was a very cautious driver, and we were wearing seat belts for the first time in Bulgaria. The new law had been passed and the police threatened to enforce it.

In Aprilci later, it was Aleksander's birthday. At 7:30 we went to Aleksander's party at his parents house. We were the first to arrive and the next couple did not arrive until 9:00. We talked with Aleksander, giving him the wine and brownies. We ate a salt salad, which was basically a potato salad layered and cut like a quiche cold. We also had rakia and wine. That was a mistake, since I could not remember anything else that was said or done.

In Sandanski

At the final P'lice Car conference with the Park, the conference went smoothly. Margaret Killmer, the Ambassador's wife, called in sick, Albert announced in his opening talk for the day, which was about garbage and trash. Then we had two hours to visit each other's displays and discuss them. The afternoon was dedicated to fund-raising with USAID, UNDP, Japan, and other groups.

Dinner began at seven and had live music — well, partially alive, since a couple played piano and guitar to accompany taped music; they also sang a strange assortment of English and Bulgarian hits. We sat with Sonia, Bob, Amber and their counterparts, including Angelar and Katiya. The talk was mostly in Bulgarian but we switched to English now and then.

As usual, Calpurnia and I started dancing. Everyone clapped

but no one else joined us. We thought about that and hatched
a plan. Calpurnia planned to ask Dimitar (the new head of the
Environmental Program and a most excellent dancer) to dance and
I would ask Nadya, a vivacious teacher and great dancer, to dance.
We expected that they would then dance with each other. Calpurnia
started, then I asked Nadya and we performed a fast tango to the
floor. After a fast swing (Nadya was excellent and lead me around
like a tyro; Dimitar was excellent and lead Calpurnia like a doll).
Then we switched. After dessert the band played a horo, which
Dimitar and Nadya started and Calpurnia and I joined. We got Alta
and Angelar to join, then there were about twenty of us.

After dinner, Alta, Calpurnia and I went to a bar under the
hotel for drinks. It was a nice California kind of place, done in pastels
and Art deco of all things.

Ditto squared for the next day, although we had group photos
at the end. I swam almost 1600 meters (feeling good now) in the
Olympic pool, which miraculously was filled full with water. Then
made it back to hear the last part of the last presentation.

As Calpurnia and the kids got ready for the "prom" (the
closing party), I drank and relaxed, after putting on my black silk
suit. I took photos of the girls in their evening dresses. They all
looked fabulous (but then I was a very proud faux father after all).
We trooped down to the restaurant for the ceremony. Of course, we
sat with Ron and Dan. We ordered a bottle of wine, which I paid for,
but then the restaurant gave us three bottles for free. The ceremony
consisted of many speeches, by staff, US officials, and Bulgarian
officials, as well as awards for attendance and committees (just like
the military).

Then it was time to dance, so as usual Calpurnia and I
started, then the young volunteers finally got up. Calpurnia danced
with Dan and I grab Ilyana. Then Venelina asked me to dance, and
Calpurnia took a picture. Then Dimitar asked Alta to dance and I
asked Christine. Then Calpurnia and I danced again, and Venelina
and I again. I danced with Ilyana and Theodora, then had a fast
dance with Nadya, who was so good, I almost was good. Cali and
I had a slow dance to end the evening (I seem to be getting to be a
popular dancer — must be the gyrations of hips and legs, thanks to
years of Elvis).

Around midnight it wrapped up and we all went to bed
(separately, I mean; well, not completely separately, just not all of us
in one bed).

Getting & Giving Presents

We were up early to do a laundry and clean up. Then, we went out to the forest to look for tracks (the south ridge overlooking Aprilci). There were not as many as I thought, so I went in the woods from the field and there were more, mostly roe deer, with one dog (or wolf — the snow was too deep and light to take good impressions — and one fox. I followed them for a few hours and hiked back for lunch.

After lunch, we decided to take the bus to Troyan to buy cereal and juice for the weekend, and maybe to find a few presents for the people here. We found a German cereal, good Bulgarian Juice, Austrian Mexican corn chips, Belgian marshmallows, and Irish cream liquor — in all a successful trip. Then at the bazaar I bought five pair of leather gloves for the "boys" in the sawmill (five pair came to about $4.20). We bought an English book for Aleksander, the most enthusiastic student. The bus back to Aprilci was crowded with workers and shoppers.

Unlike last Christmas, which had no advertising and no gifts for sale, this year had many thousands of toys, many of which were war toys, guns, daggers, even Bruce Lee Nunchuks and throwing stars. Of course, there were also toy cell phones in gleaming chrome and blue plastic, as well as cars and dolls.

Dinner was tuna salad on bread, with Irish cream liquor. Worked on the computer, read books. Ho hum.

Later in May we were invited to a birthday party for Vulko's daughter Alekka. Although we were half an hour late, we were the first to arrive. We sat to vodka and wine. We gave Alekka our gifts: a small dog doll, a card, and a chocolate bar. She played with the dog, thanked us, and gave us a piece of the chocolate. After fifteen minutes, a woman came over with a bag just like ours, and gave Alekka a small Paula doll (somewhat like Barbie but with black hair) and corduroy pants. There were no children at the party. Alekka had to take her nap, so we all sat and drank, and talked about the new things happening in town. Five minutes later Alekka was back and wanted her cake, so we ate cake, which was a burnt sugar caramel cake. We drank some more. Vulko brought out the red wine from the grapes around our porch, which was very fragrant, but somewhat weak (my kind of wine).

About four, we went back to the apartment for dinner, toast. Then we printed out the lessons for the English class and went to the Center Restaurant. No one was there. We waited for an hour, just reading our Bulgarian verbs. Then Andrei came with a long story about the disaster at work — the windows for the market being remodeled were too large and he had to chew out the workers; every time he went away he said something went wrong. Then Aleksander arrived from Troyan; he had been filling 200 bottles with wine for the Coop. Then Tosko arrived. He was with his three-year old daughter. So, we continued the lesson, on verbs, then went over Aleksander's homework, which only had four mistakes, usually too many verbs!

At home, after an hour I became depressed and decided to add some observations of life here; it was a foreign country and things were not the same here. It was frustrating at times. Less so, when I acted Bulgarian and just relaxed.

Becoming Bulgarian Or *Joy in Waiting*

Too many Bulgarians kept too much too close to their vests. No one told anyone else anything. Then, when they did compete it was directly and ruthlessly. This was not unexpected with the mini markets, since they all seemed to be successful. Our favorite vegetable market had been transformed to another cafe — there were now four cafes in a row on the main square.

A bad example of competition was the mayor and his cronies starting a new tourist center down the street from the regional center, which was supported by the Swiss and USAID. They rented an empty office and fixed it up, but had not been able to open it; we suspected that was because they spent all their money on a brochure and map to come out before ours; but it was not a real map and did not have very many ads, but it was out first for people to see, and it was in four colors.

Then the mayor started pushing for a new internet to compete with Trifon's; they wanted to get money from the Swiss to offer internet through the cable company. We expected to act as catalysts, but thought naively that the effect would be positive and serendipitous. Instead, people secretively stole ideas in direct competition instead of trying new ideas or partnership approaches for different needs.

Adjusting for the Bulgarian psyche: Bulgarians have been oppressed for over 600 years, first by the Turks, then by the Russians (or at least by communist rule), so they did not wish to stick up above the rest or to be proactive and start something that might fail (Bulgarian joke: Why were there no guards in the Bulgarian section of hell? Because if someone tried to leave the others would pull him back). The workers in the Park often put off work as long as possible. While this may appear as laziness, it made good sense. In Communist times, the bosses often changed their minds or the five-year plans before a project was ended. Hence, some of our projects, like the river-cleanup, were only decided and done at the last minute.

When I asked Andrei about why everyone waited before finishing, or beginning, projects, he said: "They are waiting until it has to been done, but also everyone is waiting for things to get better, for better times, to get richer."

Bulgarians, with few exceptions, were kind and hospitable; they shared without reservation. They were excited to be learning capitalism. The giant old GUM sort of department store in every town was now filled with small independent merchants.

In thinking about these things, I tended to overlook the real everyday frustrations and rewards. We essentially lived in a town of 1100 people (every one of whom knew what we said and did within an hour, what we wore, what we bought, or what we said), with very limited opportunities to buy more than basic supplies or to do more than drink tea and talk. Although we were ecologists, people expected us to help them build restaurants and cafes, find money for schools and the city, help start interest groups, and teach everyone English. I had joined the PC to force myself to do things that I never wanted to do: Be sociable, help people, learn a new language, become ascetic, or teach people how to monitor wolves. Whenever I had the opportunity to do something new, I did it, just because I the old dead me would not. Of course I missed that old me, the selfish dreamer, interested only in his own grand dreams.

As Andrei, Trifon and others have told me, I should not have expected to have an agenda and pursue it here, especially if it involved Bulgarians doing things on a schedule according to a plan. So, I was content to work on my own designed projects (wolf ecology) and spend the rest of the time talking, listening, arguing, reading, or writing. Thus, I had been told that, by relaxing, I was becoming very Bulgarian (similar to being a taoist perhaps).

Just Desserts Or *Honorary Citizens*

I did not get to bed until after midnight, so I slept late, to 8:40 or so. Breakfast was bread (sans cheese) and tea. Calpurnia and I dressed in the ski pants and walked south again to Vidima. The trip was through deep snow, but the waterproof clothing helped. We followed an assortment of deer, fox, and hares, as well as one unidentified set of prints that looked like it was made by a miniature deer (only sank in the snow an inch). Going downhill was much easier. We walked through town, then went home and tried to make Mexican food. We had all the pieces, even Mexican spices from Sofia. I refried pinto beans with spices. We put the beans on corn chips (from Troyan), then added tomatoes and cow cheese (we proposed a new motto for Bulgaria: "one country, one people, one cheese!"). Not bad.

Calpurnia napped, while I went exploring for new culinary adventures. I stopped to talk to the potter, Kosta, then to one of the students, Aleksander, who worked for the local Coop as an accountant. I talked to the news guy and bought a paper. I bought a bottle of champagne (the second best, for about 98 cents), coke, cow's butter, and grapefruit, which had appeared again after a brief absence. I found a few real coconuts and whole pineapples, which had appeared for the first time, but decided not to buy them.

After dinner of bread and cheese, we had a few cookies and then worked on our separate projects. Tonight I tried to finish an article for the Sofia newspaper, on the ecology of small animals, namely pets.

After a sleepless night, I started to work on the computer. These kinds of nights were strange and stressful. First I could not sleep since my heart was pounding or my brain was working overtime. Then my legs started to itch, then when I scratched I started to get uncontrollable cramps (although the last bad one was in February); the muscles started to spasm and all I could do was pound them with my fists and try to meditate before I tore myself apart.

I went over to the internet for two hours; today it was working really well; surprising since it had been raining for two days. But, I pulled off all the job matches for ecologist, then answered the email. Moira had written to tell me that Legend, my wolf, was dying of lung cancer (what a human disease, but then he had many human characteristics). I remembered running with him in the mornings; when he stopped to smell things I would sprint for all I was worth to reach an imaginary finish line, but soon he would lope past me and turn his head and look at me condescendingly as he went by. He must had known I was racing him. I walked around and ate chocolate for a while, thinking about him. I would miss having his nose on my neck while I was driving. Or sneaking a piece of meat to him after midnight. I was not allergic to his fur, as I was to dog fur.

After a sandwich for lunch, I worked on the files some more, then packed some papers. Computer work. Tried to finish the Wolf Survey 2 for the Park. That entailed making maps of the territory and placing photographs on pages to show the extents of the project.

Thursday, I mailed another box to Oregon and one to Virginia. We had noticed that the boxes that were medium-sized or smaller, and that weighed less than three kilograms do not need any paperwork as to contents or value, so they were faster and more efficient to mail.

After a night of troubled sleep, I drank milk for breakfast and Cali had tea. We made the mistake of starting to box things to send, and then spent two hours wrapping the boxes with white paper to meet the strict post office requirements. I mailed four dolls and a knife to Craig and Linda, then books to my parents and dolls to her parents. The books cost $28, which was high, but the other two boxes cost less than $10 total. I was amazed by how long each transaction took. This was obviously not NY or Boston, but each one seemed to take about seven minutes, regardless if it was just a stamp or paying the telephone bill or solving the problem of world hunger. There were three windows and two clerks, but the director, the one who cheated us every week, seemed to work all three windows, sometimes simultaneously for a single transaction. When I gave him the boxes, he weighed one, then went to another window to give out stamps. Then he came back but had to look for the cancel stamp, then for the receipt. Because the first two boxes were not heavy he only had to fill out a receipt in duplicate, but for the books, he had to fill out a customs declaration, which I filled out but he signed. Finally we were finished, then I paid the phone bill which was a little less this month but still almost $25.

I finished the Balkani SPA. Desislava faxed the last receipts, which were unreadable, but I made up a cover sheet for them and included them with the form. Also prepared maps and photopages for the grant completion.

Saturday, Calpurnia and I were up early and cleaned the kitchen. For breakfast, I fixed kyfte and lemonade, coffee and tea, but only Calpurnia and I had anything. After moping around trying to recover, Alta and Christine got ready and we took the 10 o'clock bus to Pleven, where we shopped for a flea collar for Chris's new cat and then had an early lunch at an Italian restaurant. Calpurnia and I had an unsatisfactory pizza.

Then we walked around and looked for music and books until it was time for the bus to leave. Our left at 2:00, Christine's at 1:00 and Alta's at 3:00. Our bus got to Troyan in record time so we decided to take a taxi to Aprilci instead of waiting three hours. It cost only thirteen Leva for the twenty six kilometers. We immediately did a wash and then rested. I read a book and Calpurnia the borrowed *Glamour* magazine.

Sunday, we were up early, I had milk. Calpurnia had tea, so I had tea also, the good Lemon-ginger tea from England. We cooked potatoes, then went to the bazaar to get souvenirs. We each bought three knives for gifts.

I decided to make the CDs of photographs for the Park, Balkani, friends in Dupnitsa and for the kids. This meant that I had to make three separate zip disks of photos (using the same disk but carrying it downstairs each time to Vulko's machine). Finally I was ready to

345

make the CDs using Vulko's PC. The Japanese CDs worked perfectly, but I only had three; then three of four of the Bulgarian CDs did not work—the error message said that there was not enough room. I tested it by reducing the photos to only fifty megabytes and they still would not fit. They were bad.

The next day, we went to the city council meeting at 2:00. We had been told we would receive an award. We filed in with the Council in their new meeting room. Then, we found we were first on the agenda. They gave us a plastic diploma; the Chair read the words, which thanked us for financial and other help for the city, education, tourism, parks, and communications. I asked to say a few words, and did, about what we did for Aprilci and to thank them for their hospitality, lying through my teeth that the city did anything but hinder or ignore us, refusing to meet with us and calling us spies. But, I lied admirably, and the moment of political temptation passed, slower than a fart but somewhat cleaner. Here was what I said, the English version anyway: "We would like to thank you all for being here today. We would like to thank you for your hospitality and for help with the Bulgarian language for the past two years.

"You had thanked us, with this award, for working on behalf of Aprilci. But, all we did was learn about Bulgaria and her people. You had thanked us for getting money for projects to help people and businesses. But, all we did was make friends and work on projects with them. You had thanked us for connecting Aprilci to the world. But, all we did most of the time was talk about what our lives were like in America and listen to what your lives have been like in Bulgaria, while consuming good rakia and wine.

"We want to thank you for hosting us, for making us a part of your community, for forming friendships with us, and for helping us learn about life here (especially how to make and drink rakia and wine). We had learned a lot about Bulgaria, the nature, the wildlife, and the people.

"In the years ahead, we will tell people in America about Bulgaria, what your lives were like, what your ambitions were, and what you want to communicate with them.

"In the years ahead, you will tell people in Bulgaria about what our lives had been like, about what friends we had made, and about what projects we had all worked on.

"And, thus, all the goals of the Peace Corps have been fulfilled: to learn about you, to let you know about us, and to work together to improve some things.

"And, thus, the goals of Bulgaria were also addressed: To make things better for people, to encourage her unique cultural traditions, and to protect the unique and wild nature, while letting people understand it and participate in it.

"Thank you for your hospitality. We want to continue our friendships and conversations. We want to return to visit you again as friends. Thank you."

We left early as they started arguing about the new internet center which they got funded through the Swiss to compete with the Telecenter that we got funded through USAID. Afterwards we got a few groceries.

At the apartment, I wrote up my notes, downloaded the photos, and rewrote my speech in English. Calpurnia did a laundry and made a salad for dinner. Just as we were eating Andrei and Aleksander, both members of the City Council, and we suspect the instigators of our new honor, came to the door and told us of the compromise on the Council. The new internet would not work in Novo Celo, to compete with Trifon, but would rather offer service to the outlying villages such as Ostrets and Vidima. We suspected the real reason was technical, that the cable company could not get the transmitters to work right. We had tea with Aleksander and Andrei. After a light dinner, more computer work, light packing, and preparation for mailing more souvenirs.

We prepared forms and reports for Dimitor, who was coming to Aprilci for his meeting with Vulko, about a volunteer serving here. He was early, and he and Vulko talked before I got there. Since Vulko spoke no English, we spoke Bulgarian. Calpurnia arrived and we offered praise for Vulko and suggestions for the town. The meeting broke up suddenly, when Dimitar announced that he had already met with Iurka, the head of the Park, earlier that morning, and he had to rush back to Sofia. We asked him to return our small heater and the water distiller to the PC. He agreed, but first we inspected my office in the building across the street (the unheated, unfurnished place where I had internet access on my Ibook) and then Calpurnia's office in the Tourist center, which had a new floor and new furniture, paid for by the two SPA grants for the craftsmen and tourism. Then we loaded the jeep and he left. Dinner was soup and bread.

Aprilci City Hall

Spring Cleaning

Today was cleaning day. Where the water distiller sat was new mold on the walls. The dust from ground and pulverized sheep manure and dirt had coated the entire apartment, even the spider webs.

Finally, I answered email and work on notes. Then we took a bus to Skandalo, with the camera. Looked for wildlife signs and took photos of the entrance to Aprilci and the river. It took over two hours to walk back to the town.

Sunday was a paperwork day to make sure all the PC forms were finished. Because we bought no food at the weekly bazaar, we ate at the Gameyski restaurant, and had shopska salata, persiani kartofi and kebabche. Vulko came and ate with us, then Andrei showed up also. It started raining like hell, so we moved under the new umbrellas on the new balcony.

After lunch, we walked to the Vidima ridge and looked for animal signs. Again, there was hardly anything, except for sheep and cows. Even the birds seemed to have gone further from the human habitations. Skipped dinner, then packed, checked computer messages, and went to bed.

The next day, we took the eight o'clock bus to Troyan, then the ten o'clock bus to Sofia. At Sofia, we carried the baggage to the small hotel Maya, and hurried to the Medical Office for our final physicals — the Peace Corps paid our way for three days in Sofia for these tests. Of course, we did not need to hurry as Sheila read us some things and gave us more forms to fill out. Finally we had the physicals themselves. The blood tests were taken and the TB test was given. My blood pressure was higher but I had gained back ten pounds, despite walking 70 miles every week into the forest in search of the elusive wolves. I was assured that everything was normal. Because of my long-broken tooth, I was given a voucher to get it fixed in America.

We waited for Christine to finish and all went to the Irish Harp (not a paid endorsement) for potatoes and chicken. That evening, we all shopped for the groceries that could only be purchased in a large city, such as German cereal and Italian spices. Calpurnia had been given pills for an infection, which had resulted in stomach cramps and nausea, so we went back early; she slept while I read an old novel from the PC library.

All morning I helped Calpurnia with her language, then we went to the PC HQ and had our final language exams. We each scored as medium-medium, which I think was generous. Strangely, Calpurnia was told that she scored higher than the last time because she used English words to complete full thoughts and sentences, while I was told that I scored lower than the last time for using English words complete sentences. Different testers, different standards.

After a snack, we all took a taxi to Jamadvice Travel, where Christine bought her tickets to Philadelphia, and Calpurnia and I made reservations to Washington. When we found that the tickets were only $536, we charged them to Calpurnia's credit card and kept the cash for souvenirs.

After dinner again at the Happy's Bar, we went to the movie theater, but did not want to wait for an hour to see a movie. Back to the hotel to read.

Waltzing with Wolves in London

We took the 5:30 a.m. bus to Sofia for the last time. Had the final part of the physical at PC HQ. Took a cab to airport, which had been rebuilt with blue glass and new smooth concrete. Where we met Petya and her daughter, Zlatka, who was my godfather after all. We checked in almost right away with the huge suitcases and dufflebag. Had drinks in the lounge. Then went to the plane.

Flew to Zurich. Shopped for a hotel at the SAS desk. Decided to try McDonalds Golden Arch Hotel close to the airport. Took the courtesy van to the hotel, which was a four-story modern Euro place. Checked in at 176 Swiss Francs (about $120; yipes, we were out of Bulgaria).

The room was small but with serpentine walls and golden arches over two twin motor-driven, hospital beds. There was a pole in the corner that held a large web television and a desk with keyboard (the keyboard detached and could be used from the bed). The shower was separate and glass, facing the bedroom, so when Calpurnia took a shower immediately, I could see her bathing. There was a separate toilet room and vanity.

The door card also was used to turn on the lights and things. We went downstairs and ate at the McDs restaurant, but were surprised by the very high prices, about $14 for two Mac "menus" with fries and drink. A large television appeared to be showing excerpts from the Kama Sutra; four children were playing a newspaper game in front of it, apparently too sophisticated to look at the different sexual positions being illustrated. I was not that sophisticated and observed with interest, as a professional biologist of course.

A good sleep on firm mattresses, then we ate breakfast downstairs, that was, Calpurnia ate, as it was too expensive for both of us to eat. Then, after goofing off for an hour, we went to the airport and shopped for souvenirs for parents, ending up with two boxes of chocolate because everything else was too expensive. The flight left just after noon and the plane was very comfortable.

Ordinary lift off, but after a few hours the plane dipped suddenly, that is, the plane went from 0 degrees to ninety degrees in a few seconds, heading straight down. The pilot announced quickly that the fuel pump between tanks was broken and required immediate repair. We were going to land in Venice.

We landed without incident, but waited on plane for hours, before being transferred to some sort of lounge. The airlines rebooked a few, but then, after dark, we were bused to a Holiday Inn kilometers from the airport. The staff hurried to serve us a dinner in a deserted lounge with warm spaghetti, cool bread and a lot of cold wine. The pasta was notable for having virtually no sauce, except for a red stain on the plate. We had seen nothing of Venice.

We went to our room which was unidentifiably pleasant and could have been in Illinois. Woke up and had a brief breakfast at the hotel. The airline then postponed the take-off, and we were told to amuse ourselves until 1:00 in the afternoon.

We immediately took a bus downtown and got lost among the canals and small shops. We put off buying any gifts until we could see more. But, suddenly it was noon and we were lost, really lost. Finally, after half an hour of running and asking for directions, we found the bridge to the mainland. We walked to a taxi stand, but there were no taxis. We called the hotel from a pay phone and were told the group had left for the airport an hour earlier, as the plane had been finished early.

As we were waiting a Bulgarian couple came up and asked to share the cab back to the hotel. They had moved to London years earlier and were returning from a family visit back home. We got back to the hotel, where all four of us were shoved on a bus and sped to ther airport, where we waited in line for another two hours—only half as long as the people who got there in the late morning. We never did get souvenirs, alas.

We got to London late. Got a porter in the airport to direct us to the correct train. At Victoria station, got another porter to take us up to get a cab. Then the cab took us to the hotel, passing many almost identical hotels on the way, all made from private 4 story homes. The room was small, in fact, we had to walk over the bed to reach the bathroom; the suitcases had to be stacked on the dresser.

The next morning, we called Alan and Phil at the Anglian Wolf Society in Wooten to set up a visit to their headquarters. They had agreed to fund the Balkani Wolf Project and could give us the funding the next day. They offered to pick us up the following day.

So, we spent the day wandering around inner London, riding two-decker buses and racing through every museum we could. This was the fourth of July and we found a bar down the street from the hotel that offered a free steak to anyone with an American passport.

The next morning, they were right on time in a giant black car that looked like a cab. We drove out to their headquarters and had lunch. Then, we went to meet their two Balkan wolves. The wolves were kept in the country near a farm and surrounded by a 6-meter-high fence with razor wire across the top, possibly to protect the wolves from curious humans. The wolves greeted us with paws to the chest, as a challenge to sort out the weaker humans, and we responded by pushing them gently down, like the good alpha animals we were. After a discussion about their history and diets, we all decided to take them for their daily walk around the farm, or rather to chain them to us and let them go where they wanted.

They were young scrawny wolves, a male and female, with thin fur, but very energetic. It rained during the walk and we all had to shake when we got back to the enclosure. We met with the staff and discussed their program. We made sure that they would send the grant money directly to Sofia, rather than have us send it later from the US. We also talked about their cofounder Runar Naess in Oslo. We explained that we were scheduled to leave the next day for Oslo to visit my professor, Arne Naess (no relation), and go hiking. We made an appointment with Runar in the morning. After the meeting, they drove us to the train to get back to London.

The next day, we left early for the airport. After two years of busing or bicycling, it seemed that we were trying to make up for lost time in flying. The flight to Oslo was relatively fast. I did not recognize the airport from my graduate student days 30 years earlier. Everything was new.

I did recognize the park where we met Runar, since it was behind the *Stoting* (legislative building) and down the hill from the Palace. After a working lunch on what his Alpha Group was doing, we took a bus out to the university to meet Arne and his wife, Kit-Fai. I keep thinking of Arne as 60 and me as almost 30, but we are 30 years older, now.

Naturally, we all walked up to the ski lift above Oslo and around the park. It was the first time I had ever seen it without snow! After arguing about Gandhi and Spinoza and throwing pine cones at each other, we went back to their house for dinner. Dinner was very relaxing with cod, noodles and a little wine.

Then we took the tram back to the hotel by the airport. Time passed so quickly these last few days. But, all I could think about was how quickly we got used to hot showers and fast vehicles again.

Entering America Or *Heat Stroke*

After ten hours of eating and reading, the dinner was beef stroganov, we arrived in Washington DC about 3:30 and went through customs first, since we were PC volunteers, possibly the only form of recognition that we would get for the next three years. At the airport we checked in to the flight to Sarasota. Then we called her family and mine. As we walked by the food area, we were captured by a California Pizza Kitchen and a Ben and Jerry's ice cream. We ate to bursting.

We found that a plane to Charlotte left in an hour and took that instead; this gave us two hours in Charlotte instead of less than one. We walked around and gawked at the consumer displays. We got to Sarasota a few minutes early. We were met by my parents and had our first ride in their gigantic Mercury Zipcode.

We sat out in the back yard and talked a bit, and drank and smoked, told a few stories, true ones, of course, then everyone retired for the night. The next day, we drove to the new 500,000 square-foot grocery store, and the cultural shock was immediate, as was sticker shock, traffic shock and heat stroke. It was good to be back, for the moment.

I made reservations to get to Oregon to work on a stream restoration project. Moira called and let me know that Legend had died a day earlier. I had been too slow, but I had to go to finish the project. I laid a mouse on his grave.

After a few months, we decided to send some gifts back to Bulgaria, but we wanted to send only things made in America. That was a problem. Everything in America seemed to be made in China. We were able to find some things, such as belts, belt buckles, t-shirts, Native American cigarettes, books, and small children's toys. So every ranger or colleague got a belt buckle from us, and every child got a Simpsons doll. And, everyone got postcards and photographs.

The Sofia Central Bus Station 2002

About the Author

Conor Ciaran began his professional career as an astrophysicist, where he learned to climb mountains and survive blizzards, so he is used to long periods of cold and silence. This has prepared him for other endeavors that require speculation and invention. After numerous budget reductions in Chile, Mexico, Hawaii, California, and Arizona, he retrained as a wildlife biologist at the University of Oregon. He worked on wolf projects in Alaska and Idaho, where he learned to climb trees and swing from vines. This has prepared him to cope with high doses of frustration and failure in other fields. Since a series of fatal accidents, which required numerous parts of his body and skull to be rebuilt with titanium and duct tape, he has devoted his time to writing fiction. This has prepared him to face indifference and nonproductive expenses. You can reach him, if you want, at: tarzan@apeman.us

In 2000

Colophon

Type:	Palatino
Software:	Indesign, Acrobat
Computer:	Mac G5
Photographs:	Precious Wolf
Design:	Rian Garcia Calusa, Cortez, FL
Cover Photo:	Lyalitsa factory
Back Photo:	Ostretska River through Aprilci

Petko at the new ban saw at the mill